THE COMPLETE WORKS

OF

WALTER SAVAGE LANDOR

———

VOLUME XIV

GIOVANNA I, QUEEN OF NAPLES, WITH HER CHILD.

SANCIA, QUEEN DOWAGER OF NAPLES, WIDOW OF ROBERT THE WISE,
IN NUN'S GARB.

MARIA DI DURAZZO, GIOVANNA'S HALF-SISTER, WITH A CHILD,
GIOVANNA'S NEPHEW.

From Alinari's photograph of fresco, thought to be by Roberto di
Odorisio, in the Church of Santa Maria del Incoronata, Naples.

[Poems II.

THE
COMPLETE WORKS
OF
WALTER SAVAGE
LANDOR

VOLUME XIV
POEMS

EDITED BY
STEPHEN WHEELER

II

BARNES & NOBLE, Inc.
New York
METHUEN & CO. Ltd
London

This edition, published in 1969

by Barnes & Noble, Inc., New York
and Methuen & Co., Ltd. London

is reproduced from the edition
published by Chapman & Hall, Ltd.
between 1927 and 1936

138684

Manufactured in the United States of America

CONTENTS OF VOLUME II

Section 2. DRAMAS AND DRAMATIC SCENES (*Continued*)

v

CONTENTS OF VOLUME II

Section 3. HELLENICS

CONTENTS OF VOLUME II

DRAMAS AND DRAMATIC SCENES

GIOVANNA OF NAPLES

[Published in 1839 when, with *Andrea of Hungary*, it formed one volume. Both dramas with *Fra Rupert* added were reprinted *1846, 1876* under a general heading. See vol. i, p. 279, vol. ii, p. 44, and notes at end of each volume.]

MALE CHARACTERS.

LEWIS, *King of Hungary.*
LUIGI, *Prince of Taranto.*
ACCIAJOLI, *Seneschal of Naples.*
UGO DEL BALZO.
SPINELLO, *General of Naples.*
RIENZI, *Tribune of Rome.*

FRA RUPERT.
BOCCACCIO.
PETRARCA.
PSEIN, *a Hungarian Captain.*
POPE'S NUNCIO.
PRIOR OF THE CELESTINES.

FEMALE CHARACTERS.

WIFE OF RIENZI.
FILIPPA OF CATANIA.
SANCIA, *her Grandaughter.*

PRINCESS MARIA.
FIAMMETTA.

MALE *in first heading om. 1846.*   heading FEMALE CHARACTERS *om. 1846.*
Grandaughter 1839, *Granddaughter* 1846.

GIOVANNA OF NAPLES

ACT I.

SCENE I. GARDEN OF CAPO-DI-MONTE.

BOCCACCIO *and* FIAMMETTA.

Boccaccio. Adieu the starlit gardens of Aversa,
The groves of Capo-Monte!
Fiammetta.   Why adieu?
Boccaccio. One night will throw its gloom upon them long.
Fiammetta. It will indeed: but love can dwell in gloom,
And not repine in it.
Boccaccio.   The generous man,
Who might have much impeded ours, gave way
To better impulses. My face is flusht
To think of his hard doom, and find myself
Happy where he was happy, and so lately!
Fiammetta. I too have sighs, nor for thee only, now.   10
Giovanni, had an angel told it me
The other day, I should have disbelieved.
We all are now alike. Even queen Sancia,

7 better] bitter *mispr. 1846, 1876.*   11 Giovanni] Giovanna *1846 (mispr.).*

Sancia, so calm in sorrow, said, *Death comes*
To some with flames across his angry brow,
To others holds green palm and aureole crown,
Dreadless as is the shadow of a leaf . .
But, while she said it, prest my hand and wept,
Then prayed of Heaven its peace for poor Andrea.
   Boccaccio. We may think too as wisely as the queen   20
When we attain her age; of other flames
And other palms and other crowns just now.
Like every growth, thoughts also have their seasons;
We will not pluck unripe ones; they might hurt us.
That lady then was with you?
   Fiammetta.   She herself
Led me up hither by the sleeve. Giovanna
Is there below, secure, in Castel-Nuovo.
Look you! what crowds are gathering round about it.
   Boccaccio. I see them, and implore you, my Fiammetta,
To tarry here, protected by queen Sancia.   30
   Fiammetta. And will you tarry near me?
   Boccaccio.   While the queen
Your sister is quite safe.
   Fiammetta.   What! thinkest thou
She ever can be otherwise than safe?
I will run down to her.
   Boccaccio.   There is no danger
At present; if there should be, my weak aid
Shall not be wanting. He whom she laments
I too lament: this bond unites me with her;
And I will keep her in my sight, and follow
(As lighter birds follow the powerfuller,)
Where'er the tempest drives her . . not to save,   40

---

14 Sancia . . . comes] *1846 substitutes twelve lines:*

      Whose sadness is scarce sadness, so resign'd
      Is she to Heaven, at this balustrade
      Lean'd and lookt over, hearing some one sing.
      "Impatient is the singer there," said she,
      "To run thro' his delight, to fill the conch
      Of song up to the brim, and wise were he
      Thought he not, O my child, as think he might,
      How every gust of music, every air,
      Breathing its freshness over youthful breasts,
      Is a faint prelude to the choirs above,
      And how Death stands in the dark space between,
      To some with invitations free and meek,
and continues in roman type.

    15 across his] athwart an *1846.*   17 *leaf* . .] leaf . ." *1846.*

But break the fall, or warn her from below.
   Fiammetta. Generously spoken, my own sweet Giovanni!
Do so, and I can spare you; but remember
Others may want a warning too, may want
Some one to break a fall, some one to save . . .
Giovanni! O Giovanni! to save what?
For what is left but love? . . save that, Giovanni!
   Boccaccio. Were any infelicity near you,
Crowns and their realms might perish: but your sister
Is part of you: had she but lookt into   50
Your cradle, and no more; had one kind word,
And only one, fallen from her upon you,
My life should be the price for it.
   Fiammetta.   Your life!
We have but one, we two. But until she
Is safe again, and happier, you shall keep it.
Go, go then; follow her; but soon return.
While you are absent from me, shapeless fears
Must throng upon and keep awake my sorrow.
   Boccaccio. To grieve for what is past, is idle grief,
Idler to grieve for what may never be.   60
Courage! when both most wish it, we shall meet.

      42, 46 *bis*, 47 Giovanni] Giovanna *mispr. 1846, 1876.*

[ACT. I.] SCENE II. CASTEL-NUOVO.

GIOVANNA *and* DEL BALZO.

   Giovanna. Ugo del Balzo! thou art just and firm.
Seek we the murderers out, and bring them forth
Before their God and fellow men, if God
Or fellow men have they. Spare none who did
This cruel deed. The partner of my throne,
Companion of my days . . until that day . .
Avenge! In striking low the guilty head
Show mercy to my people. Take from me
And execute with promptness this commission.
O what a chasm in life hath one day made,   10
Thus giving way with such astounding crash
Under my feet, when all seem'd equable,
All hopeful, not a form of fear in sight.
   Del Balzo. Lady! if all could see the pangs within
Which rend your bosom, every voice would pause

      3, 4 fellow men] fellow-men *1846.*

From railing and reproach.

Giovanna.　　　　　　Reproach who will,
Rail who delight in railing. Could my arm
Protect the innocent?

Del Balzo.　　　　　But strange reports
(With this commission in my hand I speak it)
Murmur throughout the city. Kindred, ay,　　　　　20
Close kindred are accused.

Giovanna.　　　　　　Such accusations
Have burst upon my ear: they wrong my cousin.
A man more loyal than the brave Taranto
Nor court nor field e'er saw: but even he
Shall not escape if treachery be found
Within the shadow of that lofty mien.

Del Balzo. No, by the sword of the arch-angel! no ..
Altho' his sister smiles this hour upon
Her first-born of my dear and only brother
The duke of Andria. Thou must weep, Francesco!　　　　30
And she, and I; for such dishonour taints
The whole house through, obscuring past and future.
Was he not in Aversa?

Giovanna.　　　　　　He was there.

Del Balzo. And were no orders given that he keep on
His mask all evening?

Giovanna.　　　　　　Yes, I gave those orders.

Del Balzo. The queen's commission reaches not the queen.

Giovanna. Imperfect then is that commission, Ugo!

Del Balzo. Freedom of speech is limited.

Giovanna.　　　　　　　　By what?

Del Balzo. The throne.

Giovanna.　　　　　For once, then, push the throne more back,
And let thy words and actions have their scope.　　　　40

Del Balzo. Why was Aversa chosen for the revels?

　　　　　　　　[The QUEEN *hesitates, and sighs deeply.*
One answer comes from all. Because the town
Is Norman, the inhabitants are Norman,
Sworn enemies to an Hungarian prince;
The very name sounds hostilely; the walls
Built in aversion to the pride of Capua.

Giovanna. I could give other answer, which such hearts
Would little understand. My happiest days
Were spent there .. O that there my last had closed!

　　　　　27 arch-angel] archangel *1846.*

4

GIOVANNA OF NAPLES

Was it not in Aversa we first met? 50
There my Andrea, while our friends stood round
At our betrothment, fain would show me first
A horse they led for him from Hungary.
The hands we join'd were little hands indeed!
And the two rings we interchanged would ill
Let pass the bossy chain of his light hair
Entwisted with my darker, nor without
His teeth was then drawn thro' it. Those were days
When none saw quarrels on his side or mine,
Yet were there worse than there were latterly, 60
Or than since childhood ever. We have lived
From those days forth without distrust and strife.
All might have seen but now will not know that.
    Del Balzo. Lady! the court and people too remember
That none more courteous, none more beautiful,
Lives than the prince Luigi . . they acknowledge
That prince Andrea's qualities fell short . .
    Giovanna. Del Balzo! cease! he was your prince but now . .
His virtues were domestic . . few saw those.
    Del Balzo. Few, I confess it; not so few the other's; 70
His assiduities, his love.
    Giovanna.   Do these
Remember too, whate'er advantages
The prince Luigi of Taranto had,
I gave my hand where they who rear'd me will'd,
That no contention in our family
Might reach my people? Ugo! tell me now
To whom show'd I my love? To them or him?
    Del Balzo. Lady! 'twas nobly done. Yet he was seen
To walk among the maskers on that night,
Was ordered to keep on his mask, was known 80
To watch Andrea in the balcony,
To rush away, to fight below the place
Where the inhuman deed was perpetrated,
And then to fly.
    Giovanna.   O! If Taranto could
Be guilty! . . but impossible! My sister
Saw him pursue three masks: and his own page
Found him in fight with one, where two were slain.
    Del Balzo. Would any court receive such testimony?
    Giovanna. Examine then more closely. I am lost,

64 too] do 1846.

Not in conjectures, for my mind flies off   90
From all conjecture, but in vague, in wild
Tumultuous thoughts, all broken, crost, and crazed.
Go, lose no moment. There are other things   [DEL BALZO *goes.*
I could have said .. what were they? . there are things ..
Maria .. why not here! .. She knows there are ..
O! were the guilty so perplext as I am,
No guilt were undiscover'd in the world!   97

[ACT I.] SCENE III.

FILIPPA, SANCIA TERLIZZI, DEL BALZO.

Sancia Terlizzi. Gentle and gracious and compassionate,
Companion and not queen to those about her,
Giovanna delegates her fullest powers
To stern Del Balzo; and already force
Enters the palace gates.
    Filippa.   Let them be closed
Against all force. Send for the seneschal.
    Sancia Terlizzi. Acciajoli has departed for Aversa,
There to make inquest.
    Filippa.   Who dares strike the door?
    Del Balzo, entering. The laws.
    Filippa.   Count Ugo! is the queen extinct?
    Del Balzo. The prince is. Therefor lead with due respect   10
These ladies, and the rest, away.   [*To an Officer.*
    Filippa.   What means
This violence?
    Del Balzo, to the Officer. Let none, I pray, be used.   [*To* FILIPPA.
Behold the queen's commission! In that chamber
Where close examinations must ensue,
In clear untroubled order let your words
Leave us no future violence to be feared.
    Filippa, returning the paper. The queen hath acted as she always acts,
Discreetly; bravely: it becomes her race
And station: what becomes a faithful subject
Let us do now.   [*The* QUEEN *enters.*
    Sancia Terlizzi. Turn: lo, the queen herself!   20
    Del Balzo. Lady! there is one chamber in the realm,
And only one, and that but for one day,
You may not enter.
    Giovanna.   Which is that, Del Balzo?

10 Therefor] Therefore *1846.*   16 feared] fear'd *1846.*   20 *Terlizzi*] *Terlizzo*
1839 (mispr.). Terlizzi *1846*

Del Balzo. Where the judge sits against the criminal.
Giovanna. Criminal! none are here.
Del Balzo.   If all my wishes
Avail'd me, there were none.
Giovanna.   Sure, sure, the palace
Is sacred.
Del Balzo. Sacred deeds make every place
Sacred, unholy ones make all unholy.
Giovanna. But these are our best friends.
Filippa.   My royal mistress!
The name of friendship and the name of justice   30
Should stand apart. Permit me to retire. . .   [*To* DEL BALZO.
Whither, sir, you must dictate.
Del Balzo.   Lead them on.   [*The* QUEEN *throws*
     her arms round FILIPPA, *who gently removes them and goes.*
Lady! would you protect the culpable?
Giovanna. Ugo del Balzo! would you wrong the queen?
Del Balzo. I recognise the lofty race of Robert,
And my arm strengthens and my heart dilates.
Giovanna. Perform your duty, sir, and all your duty;
Win praise, win glory . . mine can be but tears.   [*Goes.*

[ACT I.] SCENE IV.

FRA RUPERT, DEL BALZO.

Fra Rupert. Confessionals are close; and closer stil
The heart that holds one treasure.
Del Balzo.   Father Rupert!
What brought thee hither at this busy hour?
Fra Rupert. My duty: I must not delay my duty.
Del Balzo. What is it?
Fra Rupert.   I would fain absolve from sin
(Far as the Church allows) the worst of sinners.
Del Balzo. In few plain words, who sent for thee?
Fra Rupert.   In fewer,
I scorn thy question.
Del Balzo.   Father! thou must wait.
The prince's death involves some powerful ones,
Whose guilt or innocence shall presently   10
Be ascertained.
Fra Rupert.   What! and shall man hear first
The guilty soul confess its secret sin?

1 stil] still *1846.*

7

Shall not the angels carry up the tale
Before the people catch it?
   Del Balzo.   They, no doubt,
Already have done this.
   Fra Rupert.   Not half, not half.
   Del Balzo. Father! it seems thou knowest more about it
Than I or any else. Why reddenest thou?
   Fra Rupert. Dost think, Del Balzo, any word escapes
The sanctuary of consciences? the throne
Of grace and mercy on our earth below?   20
The purifier, the confessional?
So then! some powerful ones are apprehended
For what they did! O merciful Del Balzo!
Be sparing of a woman's blood, Del Balzo!
And age hath claims upon our pity too;
And so hath youth, alas! and early ties
Suddenly broken shock far round about.
Beside; who knows? . . thou canst not certainly . .
If any can . . they may be innocent,
Each of the three, one more, one less, perhaps: 30
Innocent should be all whose guilt lacks proof.
O my poor child Andrea, pardon me!
Thou wouldst not have sought blood for blood, Andrea!
Thou didst love all these women! most of all
Her . . but there's justice, even on earth, Andrea!   *[Goes.*
   Del Balzo. 'Tis so! that stern proud bosom bursts with grief.

[ACT I.] SCENE V.

   Maria. Ah why, Del Balzo, have you let come in
The filthy monk, Fra Rupert? He has frightened
Sancia Terlizzi almost into fainting.
And tell me by what right hath he or any
Ordered her up into her room, and taken
Her mother down below, into those chambers
Which we have always been forbid to enter?
   Del Balzo. Perhaps to ask some questions; for the queen
Ought to be satisfied.
   Maria.   Then let me go
And ask her: she would tell me in a moment   10
What they will never get from her.
   Del Balzo.   Perhaps,
O princess! you may have mistaken.
   Maria.   No:

8

GIOVANNA OF NAPLES

I never was mistaken in Filippa.
Rudeness can neither move nor discompose her:
A word, a look, of kindness, instantly
Opens her heart and brings her cheek upon you.
  Del Balzo. The countess has more glorious qualities
Than noble birth has given any else.
Whether her heart has all that tenderness . . .
  Maria. Is my heart tender?
  Del Balzo.   Be it not too tender,   20
Or it may suffer much, and speedily,
And undeservedly. The queen your sister,
Gentle as you, hath fortitude.
  Maria.   Giovanna
Is tenderer than I am; she sheds tears
Oftener than I do, tho' she hides them better.
  Del Balzo. I saw their traces: but more royally
Never shone courage upon grief supprest.
  Maria. The lovely platane in the garden-walk
Catches the sun upon her buds half-open,
And looks the brightest where unbarkt and scathed.   30
O find them out who have afflicted her
With that most cruel blow.
  Del Balzo.   'Tis what she bade me,
And what I am now hastening to perform.   [*Goes.*

GIOVANNA enters.

  Maria. Courage, Giovanna! courage, my sweet sister!
Del Balzo will find out those wicked men.
O! I forgot to tell him what assistance
Fra Rupert might afford him. Every crime
Is known to him. But certainly Fra Rupert,
Who loved Andrea so, will never cease
Until he find the slayer of his friend.   40
Ah my poor sister! if you had but heard
The praises of Del Balzo, you would soon
Resume your courage and subdue your tears.
  Giovanna. Before Del Balzo, sister, I disdain
To show them or to speak of them. Be mine
Hid from all eyes! God only knows their source,
Their truth or falsehood. In the light of day
Some lose their bitterness, run smoothly on,
And catch compassion, leisurely, serenely:

27 supprest] opprest *1876 mispr.*   30 scathed] unscathed *1876 mispr.*

Never will mine run thus: my sorrows lie   50
In my own breast; my fame rests upon others,
Who throw it from them now the blast has nipt it.
'Tis ever so. Applauses win applauses,
Crowds gather about crowds, the solitary
Are shunned as lepers and in haste past by.
   Maria. But we will not be solitary; we
Are not so easy to pass by in haste;
We are not very leper-looking.
   Giovanna.   Cease,
Maria! nothing on this earth so wounds
The stricken bosom as such sportiveness,   60
Or weighs worn spirits down like levity.
Give me your hand . . Reproof is not reproach.
I might have done the same . . how recently!
   Maria. Hark! what is all that outcry?
   Giovanna.   'Tis for him
Whom we have lost.
   Maria.   But angry voices mixt
With sorrowful?
   Giovanna.   To him both due alike.

[ACT I.] SCENE VI.

*[In 1846, 1876 edd. this scene forms the concluding part of Act I, Scene V which there
extends to 216 lines.]*

SPINELLO *enters.*

Spinello. Hungarian troops throng every street and lane,
Driving before them the infirm, the aged,
The children, of both sexes.
   Giovanna.   Shelter them.
   Spinello. Such is the hope of those base enemies,
That, unprovided for defence, the castle
May fall into their hands: and very quickly,
Unless we drive them back, our scanty stores
Leave us exhausted.
   Giovanna.   Dost thou fear, Spinello?
   Spinello. I do: but if my sovran bids me bare
This breast of armure and assail her foes,   10
Soon shall she see what fears there lie within.
   Giovanna. Let me too have my fears, nor worse than thine,
Loyal and brave Spinello! Dare I ask
Of God my daily bread nor give it those

              10 armure] armour *1846.*

Whose daily prayers have earned it for us all?
I dare not. Throw wide open every gate
And stand between the last of my poor people
And those who drive them in.
   Spinello.   We then are lost.
   Giovanna. Not from God's sight, nor theirs who look to God.
   Maria. O sister! may that smile of yours be parent   20
Of many. It sinks back, and dies upon
The lovely couch it rose from. (DEL BALZO *enters.*) I will go:
Del Balzo looks, I think, more stern than ever.
   Giovanna. Del Balzo, I perceive thou knowest all,
And pitiest my condition.   [DEL BALZO *amazed.*
   Spinello.   Standest thou,
Lookest thou, thus, before thy sovran, sir?
   Giovanna. Be friends, be friends, and spare me one affront.
Wiser it were, and worthier, to devise
How tumults may be quell'd than how increast.
On your discretion lies your country's weal.   [*Goes.* 30
   Spinello. Ugo del Balzo! thou art strong in war,
Strong in alliances, in virtue strong,
But darest thou, before the queen, before
The lowest of the loyal, thus impute
With brow of scorn and figure fixt aslant,
Atrocious crimes to purity angelic?
   Del Balzo. Heard'st thou her words and askest thou this question?
Spinello! nor in virtue nor in courage
(Our best alliances) have I pretence
To stand before thee. Chancellor thou art,   40
And, by the nature of thy office, should'st
Have undertaken my most awful duty:
Why didst thou not?
   Spinello.   Because the queen herself
Will'd otherwise; because her chancellor,
She thought, might vindicate some near unduly.
   Del Balzo. She thought so? what! of thee?
   Spinello.   Thus it appears.
But on this subject never word escaped
Her lips to me: her own pure spirit frankly
Suggested it: her delicacy shunn'd
All explanation, lacking no excuse.   50
Thou askest if I heard her at thy entrance:
I heard her, like thyself. The words before

41 should'st] shouldst 1846.

Thou didst not hear; I did. Her last appeal
Was for the wretched driven within the castle,
And doom'd to pine or force us to surrender.
For them she call'd upon thee, never else,
To pity her condition.
    Del Balzo.   Pardon me!
I have much wrong'd her. Yet, among the questioned
Were strange confessions. One alone spake scornfully
Amid her tortures.
    Spinello.   Is the torture, then,   60
The tongue of Truth?
    Del Balzo.   For once, I fear, 'tis not.
    Spinello. It was Giovanna's resolute design
To issue her first edict thro' the land
Abolishing this horrid artifice,
Whereby the harden'd only can escape.
"The cruel best bear cruelty," said she,
"And those who often have committed it
May once go thro' it."
    Del Balzo.   And would'st thou, Spinello!
Thus lay aside the just restraints of law,
Abolishing what wise and holy men   70
Raised for the safeguard of society?
    Spinello. The holy and the wise have done such things
As the unwise and the unholy shrink at.
    Del Balzo. It might be thought a hardship in a country
Where laws want ingenuity; where scales,
Bandage, and sword, alone betoken Justice.
Ill-furbisht ineffective armury,
With nothing but cross-shooting shafts of words!
    Spinello. Since every deed like torture must afflict
A youthful breast, so mild, so sensitive,   80
Trust it to me, and we will then devise
How the event may best be laid before her.
    Del Balzo. A clue was given by unwilling hands,
Wherewith we entered the dark narrow chambers
Of this strange mystery. Filippa first,
Interrogated if she knew the murderer,
Denied it: then, if she suspected any;
"I do," was her reply. Whom? She was silent.
Where should suspicion now (tell me, Spinello!)
Wander or fix? I askt her if the queen   90

77 armury] armoury 1846.

Was privy to the deed. Then swell'd her scorn.
Again I askt her, and I show'd the rack.
"Throw me upon it: I will answer thence."
Said with calm voice Filippa. She was rackt.
Screams from all round fill'd the whole vault. "See, children!
How those who fear their God and love their prince
Can bear this childish cruelty," said she.
Altho' no other voice escaped, the men
Trembled, the women wail'd aloud. "To-morrow,"
Said I, "Filippa! thou must answer Justice.   100
Release her." Stil the smile was on her face:
She was releast: Death had come down and saved her.
   Spinello. Faithfullest friend of the unhappy! plead
For us whose duty was to plead for thee!
Thou art among the Blessed! On, Del Balzo!
   Del Balzo. Sancia, her daughter's child . .
   Spinello.   The playful Sancia?
Whose fifteenth birthday we both kept together . .
Was it the sixth or seventh of last March? . .
Terlizzi's bride two months ago?
   Del Balzo.   The same.
   Spinello. And the same fate?
   Del Balzo.   She never had seen Death: 110
She thought her cries could drive him off again,
Thought her soft lips might have relaxt the rigid,
And her warm tears . . .
   Spinello.   Del Balzo! wert thou there?
Or tearest thou such dreamery from some book,
If any book contain such?
   Del Balzo.   I was there;
And what I saw I ordered to be done.
Justice would have it; Justice smote my heart,
Justice sustained it too.
   Spinello.   Her husband would
Rather have died than hear one shriek from Sancia.
   Del Balzo. So all men would: for never form so lovely   120
Lighted the air around it.
   Spinello.   Let us go
And bear her home.
   Del Balzo.   To me the way lies open;
But much I fear, Spinello, the Hungarians
Possess all avenue to thy escape.

             101 Stil] Still *1846*.

Spinello. Escape is not the word for me, my friend.
I had forgotten the Hungarians
(It seems) the queen, myself, captivity . .
I may not hence: relate then if more horrors
Succeeded.
    Del Balzo. When Terlizzi saw Filippa
Lie stiff before him, and that gentle bride   130
Chafing her limbs, and shrinking with loud yells
Whenever her soft hand felt some swoln sinew,
In hopes to finish here and save all else,
He cried aloud, "Filippa was the murderess."
At this she darted at him such a glance
As the mad only dart, and fell down dead.
"'Tis false! 'tis false!" cried he. "Speak, Sancia, speak!
Or hear me say 'tis false." They dragg'd away
The wavering youth, and fixt him. There he lies,
With what result of such inconstancy   140
I know not, but am going to inquire . .
If we detect the murderers, all these pains
Are well inflicted.
    Spinello.   But if not?
    Del Balzo.   The Laws
Have done their duty and struck fear thro' all.
    Spinello. Alas! that duty seems their only one.
    Del Balzo. Among the first 'tis surely. I must go
And gather up fresh evidence. Farewell,
Spinello!
    Spinello. May good angels guide your steps!
Farewell! That Heaven should give the merciless
So much of power, the merciful so little!   150

132 swoln] swol'n 1846.

ACT II.

SCENE I. CASTEL-NUOVO.

GIOVANNA *and* MARIA.

    Maria. I do not like these windows. Who can see
What passes under? Never were contrived
Cleverer ones for looking at the sky,
Or hearing our Hungarians to advantage.
I cannot think their songs are pastorals;

5 cannot] can not 1846.

GIOVANNA OF NAPLES

They may be; if they are, they are ill-set.
Will nothing do, Giovanna? Raise your eyes;
Embrace your sister.
    Giovanna.   So, you too, Maria!
Have turgid eyes, and feign the face of joy.
Never will joy be more with us . . with you   10
It may be . . O God grant it! but me! me,
Whom good men doubt, what pleasure can approach?
    Maria. If good men all were young men, we might shudder
At silly doubts, like other silly things
Not quite so cold to shudder at.
    Giovanna.   Again,
Maria! I am now quite changed; I am
Your sister as I was, but O remember
I am (how lately!) my Andrea's widow.
    Maria. I wish our little Sancia would come hither
With her Terlizzi . . those inseparables!   20
We scarcely could get twenty words from them
All the day long; we caught them after dinner,
And lost them suddenly as evening closed.
    Giovanna. Send for her. But perhaps she is with Filippa . .
    Maria. Learning sedateness in the matron life.
    Giovanna. Or may-be with the queen whose name she bears,
And who divides her love, not equally
With us, but almost equally.
    Maria.   If so,
No need to seek her; for the queen went forth
To San Lorenzo at the dawn of day,   30
And there upon the pavement she implores
Peace for the dead, protection for the living.
    Giovanna. O may her prayers be heard!
    Maria.   If piety
Avails the living or the dead, they will.
    Giovanna. How, how much calmer than thy sweetest smile
Has that thought made me! Evermore speak so,
And life will almost be as welcome to me
As death itself.
    Maria.   When sunshine glistens round,
And friends, as young as we are, sit beside us,
We smile at Death . . one rather grim indeed   40
And whimsical, but not disposed to hurt us . .
And give and take fresh courage. But, sweet sister!
The days are many when he is unwelcome,

And you will think so too another time.
'Tis chiefly in cold places, with old folks,
His features seem prodigiously amiss.
But Life looks always pleasant, sometimes more
And sometimes less so, but looks always pleasant,
And, when we cherish him, repays us well.
Sicily says it is the worst of sin   50
To cast aside what God hath given us,
And snatch at what he may hereafter give
In its due season . . scourges, and such comfits,
Cupboarded for Old-age. Youth has her games;
We are invited, and should ill refuse.
On all these subjects our sweet Sicily
Discourses with the wisdom of a man.
You are not listening: what avails our wisdom?
   Giovanna. To keep afloat that buoyant little bark
Which swells endanger. O may never storm   60
O'ertake it! never worm unseen eat thro'!
   Maria. I wish we were away from these thick walls,
And these high windows, and these church-like ceilings,
Without a cherub to look down on us,
Or play a prank up there, with psalter-book,
Or bishop's head, or fiddle, or festoon.
   Giovanna. Be satisfied awhile: the nobler rooms
Are less secure against the violence
Of those Hungarians.
   Maria.   I saw one who bowed
Graceful as an Italian. "Send away   70
The men below," said I, "then bow again,
And we will try which bows most gracefully."
   Giovanna. My giddy, giddy sister!
   Maria.   May my head
Be ever so, if crowns must steady it!
   Giovanna. He might have thought . .
   Maria.   Not he; he never thinks.
He bowed and shook his head. His name is Psein.
Often hath he been here on guard before:
You must remember him.
   Giovanna.   No, not by name.
   Maria. Effeminate and vain we fancied him,
Because he always had a flower in hand,   80
Or with his fingers combed his forehead hair.
   Giovanna. No little merit in that sullen race.

16

Maria. If he has merit I will bring it out.

Giovanna. Resign that idle notion. Power is lost
By showing it too freely. When I want
His services, I order them. We part.
Too large a portion of the hour already
Has been among the living. Now I go
To other duties for the residue
Of this sad day.

Maria.　　　　Unwelcome is Maria　　　　　　　90
Where sorrow is?

Giovanna.　　　Her sorrow is unwelcome;
Let me subdue my own; then come and join me.
Thou knowest where the desolate find one
Who never leaves them desolate.　　　　　　　*[Goes.*

Maria.　　　　　　　　'Tis hard
To linger here alone.

Officer.　　　The Seneschal
Of Naples, Acciajoli.

[ACT II.] SCENE II.

ACCIAJOLI *and* MARIA.

Acciajoli.　　　　　　　　By command
Of our most gracious queen, O royal lady!
I come for yours.

Maria.　　　That is, to bear me company.

Acciajoli. Such only as the humblest bear the highest.

Maria. Seneschal! you excel the best in phrases.
You might let others be before you there,
Content to shine in policy and war.

Acciajoli. I have been placed where others would have shone.

Maria. Come, do not beat me now in modesty.
Had I done anything, I might not boast,　　　　10
Nor should I think I was improving it
By telling an untruth and looking down.
I do not like our lodgement, nor much wish
To see an arrow quivering in that wainscote:
The floors are well enough; I would not see them
Paved with smooth pebbles from Hungarian slings.
Cannot you send those soldiers to their quarters?

Acciajoli. In vain have I attempted it.

Maria.　　　　　　　Send Psein
To me.

5 excel] excell *1846, 1876.*　　　17 Cannot] Can not *1846.*

Acciajoli. He, like the rest, is an insurgent.
Civilest of barbarians, yet may Psein   20
(With horror I must utter it) refuse.
    Maria. Fear of refusal has lost many a prize.   [ACCIAJOLI *goes.*
I hope the Seneschal will go himself,
Not send another. How I wisht to ask it!
But, at my years, to hint an act of delicacy
Is too indelicate. He has seen courts,
Turn'd over their loose leaves (each more than half
Illumination, dulness the remainder),
And knows them from the cover to the core.

[ACT II.] SCENE III.

    Psein, conducted by ACCIAJOLI, *who retires.* The queen commands my
      presence here.
    Maria.   The queen
Desired your presence; I alone command it.
Eyes have seen *you*, commander Psein!
    Psein.   Impossible!
    Maria. Yes, eyes have seen you, general Psein! they have,
And seen that they can trust you.
    Psein.   By my troth
To all that 's lovely!
    Maria.   Ah, sad man! swear not . .
Unless you swear my words.
    Psein.   To hear and swear
And treasure them within this breast, is one.
    Maria (PSEIN *repeating*). "I swear to love and honour and obey" . .
Ha! not the hand . . it comes not quite so soon.   10
    Psein. I have but little practice in the form;
Pardon me, gracious lady!
    Maria.   Earn your pardon
By your obedience. Now repeat again.
"Whatever perils may obstruct her path,
I give safe conduct to my royal mistress,
Giovanna, queen of Naples." (*He starts.*) Have you taken
Me for my sister all this while? I told you
It was not she commanded you, 'twas I.
    Psein. Oaths are sad things! I trot to church so seldom
They would not let me out of mine for little   20
(Not they!) like any good old customer.

    15 safe conduct] safe-conduct *1846.*

18

Maria. And so! you would deceive me, general?

Psein, aside. I am appointed: that sounds well: but general!
She said the same before: it must be true.

Maria. Tell me at once, nor hesitate. Another
May reap the harvest while you whet the sickle.

Psein. But I have sworn to let none pass, before
The will of my superiors be announced.

Maria. Behold them here! their shadow fills this palace,
And in my voice, sir, is their will announced.   30

Psein. I swore.

Maria.   I heard you.

Psein.   But before.

Maria.   Before
Disloyalty, now loyalty. Are brave
And gallant men to ponder in the choice?

Psein. Devoted as I am to you, O lady!
It cannot be.

Maria.   Is that the phrase of Psein?
We love the marvellous; we love the man
Who shows how things which cannot be can be.
Give me this glove again upon the water,
And queen Giovanna shall reward you for it.

Psein. Upon the water or upon the fire,   40
The whirlpool or volcano . . By bad luck
(What fools men are! they always make their own!)
The troops are in revolt. Pride brightens zeal
But not invention. How shall we contrive
To manage them at present?

Maria.   Tell the troops
We will have no revolts. Sure, with your powers
Of person and persuasion, not a man
Would hesitate to execute his duty.

Psein. We are but three . .

Maria.   We are but two: yet, Psein!
When two are resolute they are enough.   50
Now I am resolute, and so are you,
And if those soldiers dare to disobey
It is rank mutiny and halbert-matter.
Await the Seneschal: he now returns.   [*Goes.*

Psein. She knows the laws of war as well as I,
And looks a young Minerva, tho' of Naples.

35, 37 cannot] can not *1846*.

DRAMAS AND DRAMATIC SCENES

[ACT II.] SCENE IV.

ACCIAJOLI *and* PSEIN.

Acciajoli. Sorrow and consternation are around.

Psein. Men could not have cried louder had they lost
Policinello, who begets them fun,
While princes but beget them blows and taxes.
When will they see things straightly, and give these
Their proper station?

Acciajoli.　　　　　　Have you not *your* king?

Psein. O! quite another matter! We have ours,
True; but his taxes are for us; and then
The blows . . we give and take them, as may happen.

Acciajoli. We too may do the same, another day.　　　10

　　　　　　　　　　　[PSEIN *expresses contempt.*

So! you imagine that your arms suffice
To keep this kingdom down! War is a game
Not of skill only, not of hazard only,
No, nor of both united.

Psein.　　　　　　What the ball
Is stuft with, I know not, nor ever lookt;
I only know it is the very game
I like to play at.

Acciajoli.　　Many are the chances.

Psein. Without the chances I would throw it up.
Play me at Naples only five to one,
I take the odds.

Acciajoli.　　All are not Neapolitans.　　　20

Psein. Then strike off three.

Acciajoli.　　　　　　Some Normans.

Psein.　　　　　　　　Then my sword
Must be well whetted and my horse well fed,
And my poor memory well poked for prayers.
And, hark ye! I should like one combatant
As well as twenty, of that ugly breed.
Lord Seneschal, be ready at your post.

Acciajoli. I trust I shall be.

Psein.　　　　　At what hour?

Acciajoli.　　　　　　　　Not yet.

Psein. Ay, but the queen must fix it.

Acciajoli.　　　　　　　She inclines
To peace.

Psein. I know it; but for flight ere peace.

Acciajoli. Flight is not in the movements of our queen.   30
Psein. Departure then.
Acciajoli.   Sir! should she will departure,
Breasts are not wanting to repell the charge
Of traitor or intruder.
   Psein.   Here is one,
Lord Seneschal! as ready to defend her
As any mail'd with iron or claspt with gold.
Doubtest thou? Doubt no longer.   *[Shows the glove.*
   Acciajoli.   Whose is that?
   Psein. The names we venerate we rarely speak;
And love beats veneration out and out.
I will restore it at the vessel's side,
And ask it back again when she is safe   40
And the less happy lady whom you serve.
It then behoves me to retrace my steps
And rally my few countrymen for safety.

[ACT II.] SCENE V.

A HERALD *enters.* PSEIN *goes.*

Acciajoli. Whence come you, sir?
   Herald.   From Gaeta.
   Acciajoli.   What duty?
   Herald. To see the queen.
   Acciajoli.   The queen you cannot see:
Her consort died too lately.
   Herald.   Therefor I
Must see the queen.
   Acciajoli.   If you bring ought that throws
Light upon that dark treason, speak at once.
   Herald. The light must fall from Rome. Colà Rienzi,
Tribune of Rome, and arbiter of justice
To Europe, tarrying on the extremest verge
Of our dominions, to inspect the castles,
Heard the report, brought with velocity   10
Incredible, which man gave man along
The land, and ship gave ship along the coast.
   Acciajoli. Then 'twas prepared: and those who sprad the news
Perpetrated the deed.
   Herald.   Such promptitude

2 cannot] can not *1846.*   6 Colà] Cola *1846.*   13 sprad] spread *1846.*

Could not escape the Tribune. He demands
The presence of Giovanna queen of Naples,
To plead her cause before him.
    Acciajoli.   Is Rienzi
A king? above a king?
    Herald.   Knowest thou not
Rienzi is the tribune of the people?
    Acciajoli. Sir! we have yet to learn by what authority   20
He regulates the destiny of princes.
    Herald. The wisest men have greatly more to learn
Than ever they have learnt: there will be children
Who in their childhood shall know more than we do.
Lord Seneschal! I am but citizen
In my own city, nor among the first,
But I am herald here, and, being herald,
Let no man dare to question me. The king
Of Hungary is cited to appear,
Since in his name are accusations made   30
By some at Naples, which your queen must answer.
    Acciajoli. Her dignity and wisdom will decide.
I am well pleas'd that those around the castle
Threw no obstruction in your way.
    Herald.   The soldiers
Resisted my approach; but instantly
Two holy friars sprad out their arms in front,
And they disparted like the Red-sea waves,
And grounded arms before me.
    Acciajoli.   Then no hinderance
To our most gracious queen, should she comply?
    Herald. None; for Rienzi's name is spell against it.   40
    Giovanna, enters. O! is there one to hear me patiently?
Let me fly to him!
    Acciajoli.   Hath our sovran heard
The order of Rienzi?
    Giovanna.   Call it not
An order, lest my people be incenst.
    Hearld. Lady! if plainly hath been understood
The subject of my mission, the few words
Containing it may be unredd by me.
Therefor I place them duly in the hands
Of the lord seneschal. With brief delay
Your presence were desirable.

          36 sprad] spread *1846*.   47 unredd] unread *1846*

GIOVANNA OF NAPLES

Giovanna.   What time   50
Return you, sir?
   Herald.   This evening.
   Giovanna.   And by sea?
   Herald. In the same bark which brought me.
   Giovanna.   If some ship
More spacious be now lying at the mole,
I will embark in that; if not, in yours,
And we will sail together. You have power
Which I have not in Naples; and the troops,
And those who seem to guide them, hear your words.
   Herald. Lady! not mine; but there are some they hear.
   Giovanna. Entreat them to let pass the wretched ones
Who fancied I could succour them within,   60
Whom famine must soon seize. Until they pass
I cannot. Dear is Fame to me; but far
Be Fame that stalks to us o'er hurried graves.
Lord Seneschal! see Rome's ambassador
Be duly honored: then, whatever else
Is needful for departure, be prepared.

       62 cannot] can not *1846*.   65 honored] honoured *1846*.

ACT III.

SCENE I. ROME. CAPITOL.

Rienzi *and the* Pope's Nuncio.

Nuncio. With infinite affliction, potent Tribune!
The Holiness of our Lord the Sovran Pontif
Learns that Andrea, prince of Hungary,
Hath, in the palace of Aversa, been
Traiterously slain. Moreover, potent Tribune!
The Holiness of our Lord the Sovran Pontif
Hears sundry accusations: and, until
The guilt or innocence of those accused
Be manifested, in such wise as He,
The Holiness of our Lord the Sovran Pontif,   10
Shall deem sufficient, he requires that troops
March from his faithful city, and possess
Otranto and Taranto, Brindisi
And Benevento, Capua and Bari,

       2 Pontif] Pontiff *1846 and so throughout the scene.*   5 Traiterously] Traitorously
1846.   6 *comma wrongly inserted after* Pontiff *in 1876.*

Most loving cities, and most orthodox.
And some few towns and villages beside,
Yearning for peace in his paternal breast,
He would especially protect from tumult.
Laying his blessing on your head thro' me
The humblest of his servitors, thus speaks   20
The Holiness of our Lord the Sovran Pontif.
    Rienzi (seated). Lord Cardinal! no truer stay than me
Hath, on Italian or Provenzal ground,
The Holiness of our Lord the Sovran Pontif.
The cares that I have taken off his hands
The wisdom of his Holiness alone
Can measure and appreciate. As for troops,
That wisdom, seeing them so far remote,
Perhaps may judge somewhat less accurately.
The service of his Holiness requires   30
All these against his barons. Now, until
I hear the pleas of Hungary and Naples,
My balance is suspended. Those few cities,
Those towns and villages, awhile must yearn
For foren troops among them; but meantime
Having the blessing of his Holiness,
May wait contentedly for any greater
His Holiness shall opportunely grant.
Kissing the foot of his Beatitude,
Such, my lord Cardinal, is the reply   40
From his most faithful Colà di Rienzi,
Unworthy tribune of his loyal city.
    Nuncio. We may discuss anew this weighty question
On which his Holinesses heart is moved.
    Rienzi. If allocution be permitted me
To his most worthy Nuncio, let me say
The generous bosom would enfold about it
The friend, the neighbour, the whole human race,
And scarcely then rest satisfied. With all
These precious coverings round it, poisonous tongues   50
Can penetrate. We lowly men alone
Are safe, and hardly we. Who would believe it?
People have heretofore been mad enough
To feign ambition (of all deadly sins
Surely the deadliest) in our lord the pope's

37 any greater] *so in 1846*, [*type dropped 1839*].   41 Colà] Cola *1846*.   44 Holinesses] Holiness's *1846*.

24

GIOVANNA OF NAPLES

Protecting predecessors! Their paternal
Solicitude these factious thus denounced.
Ineffable the pleasure I foretaste
In swearing to his Holiness what calm
Reluctance you exhibited; the same 60
His Holiness himself might have exprest,
In bending to the wishes of those cities
So orthodox and loving; and how fully
You manifested, by your faint appeal,
You sigh as deeply to decline, as they
Sigh in their fears and fondness to attain. [NUNCIO *going.*
Help my lord cardinal . . this weather brings
Stiffness of joints, rheums, shooting pains . . Way there!

[ACT III.] SCENE II. CAPITOL.

RIENZI, ACCIAJOLI, PETRARCA, *and* BOCCACCIO.

Boccaccio. If there was ever upon throne one mind
More pure than other, one more merciful,
One better stored with wisdom, of its own
And carried from without, 'tis hers, the queen's.
Exert, my dear Francesco, all that eloquence
Which kings and senates often have obeyed
And nations have applauded.
Petrarca. My Boccaccio!
Thou knowest Rome, thou knowest Avignon:
Altho' so brief a time the slave of power,
Rienzi is no longer what he was, 10
Popes are what they have ever been. They all
Have families for dukedoms to obey.
Boccaccio. O! had each holy father twenty wives
And each wife twenty children! then twere hard
To cut out dukedoms for so many mouths,
And the well-fur'd tiara could not hatch
So many golden goose-eggs under it.
Petrarca. We must unite our efforts.
Boccaccio. Mine could add
Little to yours: I am not eloquent.
Petrarca. Thou never hast received from any court 20
Favour or place; I, presents and preferments.
Boccaccio. I am but little known: for dear to me
As fame is, odious is celebrity.

14 children!] *incorrectly* children? *1846.* 16 well-fur'd] well-furred *1846.*

25

Petrarca. I see not why it should be.

Boccaccio.   If no eyes
In the same head are quite alike, ours may
Match pretty well, yet somewhat differ too.

Petrarca. Should days like yours waste far from men and friends?

Boccaccio. Leave me one flame; then may my breast dilate
To hold, at last, two (or almost two) friends:
One would content me: but we must, forsooth,   30
Speculate on more riches than we want.
Moreover, O Francesco! I should shrink
From scurril advocate, cross questioning
Whom knew I in the palace? whence my knowledge?
How long? where first? whence introduced? for what?
Since, in all law-courts I have ever entered,
The least effrontery, the least dishonesty,
Has lain among the prosecuted thieves.

Petrarca. We cannot now much longer hesitate;
He hath his eye upon us.

Boccaccio.   Not on me;   40
He knows me not.

Petrarca.   On me it may be then,
Altho some years, no few, have intervened
Since we last met.

Boccaccio.   But frequent correspondence
Retains the features, nay, brings back the voice;
The very shoe creaks when the letter opens.

Petrarca. Rienzi was among those friends who sooner
Forget than are forgotten.

Boccaccio.   They who rise
Lose sight of things below, while they who fall
Grasp at and call for anything to help.

Petrarca. I own I cease to place reliance on him.   50
Virtue and Power take the same road at first,
But they soon separate, and they meet no more.

Usher. The Tribune, ser Francesco! claims your presence.

Rienzi. Petrarca! pride of Italy! most welcome!

Petrarca. Tribune of Rome! I bend before the fasces.

Rienzi. No graver business in this capitol,
Or in the forum underneath its walls,
Or in the temples that once rose between,
Engaged the thoughts of Rome. No captive queen
Comes hither, none comes tributary, none   60

33 cross questioning] cross-questioning *1846.*   39 cannot] can not *1846.*

GIOVANNA OF NAPLES

Courting dominion or contesting crown.
Thou knowest who submits her cause before
The majesty that reigns within this court.
  Petrarca. Her, and her father, and his father, knew I,
Nor three more worthy of my love and honor
(Tho born to royalty) adorn our earth.
Del Balzo hath supplied the facts: all doubts
On every side of them hath Acciajoli
Cleared up.
  Rienzi. But some will spring where others fall,
When intellect is strongly exercised.   70
  Petrarca. The sources of our intellect lie deep
Within the heart; what rises to the brain
Is spray and efflorescence; they dry up.
  Rienzi. However, we must ponder. So then truly,
Petrarca! thou dost think her innocent?
  Petrarca. Thou knowest she is innocent, Rienzi!
Write then thy knowledge higher than my belief:
The proofs lie there before thee.
  Rienzi.   But these papers
Are ranged against them.
  Petrarca.   Weigh the characters
Of those who sign them.
  Rienzi.   Here the names are wanting.   80
  Petrarca. Remove the balance then, for none is needed.
Against Del Balzo, upright, stern, severe,
What evidence can struggle?
  Rienzi.   From Del Balzo
The queen herself demands investigation
Into the crime, and bids him spare not one
Partaker.
  Petrarca. Worthy of her race! Now ask
If I believe her guiltless.
  Rienzi.   May we prove it!
  Acciajoli. She shall herself, if needful. Should more answers
Be wanted from me, I am here before
That high tribunal where the greatest power   90
And wisdom are united; where the judge
Gives judgment in the presence of such men
As Rome hath rarely seen in ancient days,
Never in later. What they hear, the world
Will hear thro future ages, and rejoice

69 Cleared] Clear'd *1846.*

27

That he was born in this, to raise an arm
Protecting such courageous innocence.
 Rienzi. Lord Seneschal of Naples, Acciajoli!
We have examined, as thou knowest, all
The documents before us, and regret   100
That death withholds from like examination
(Whether as witnesses or criminals)
Some inmates of your court, the most familiar
With queen Giovanna.
 Acciajoli.   Did she then desire
Their death? as hidden enemies accuse her
Of one more awful. I presume the names
Of the young Sancia, count Terlizzi's bride,
And hers who educated that pure mind
By pointing out Giovanna, two years older,
Filippa of Catana.
 Rienzi.   They are gone   110
Beyond our reach.
 Acciajoli.   Sent off, no doubt, by one
Who loved them most, who most loved her! sent off
After their tortures, whether into Scotland
Or Norway or Laponia, the same hand
Who wrote those unsign'd papers, may set forth.
 Rienzi. I cannot know their characters.
 Acciajoli.   I know them
Loyal and wise and virtuous.
 Rienzi.   But Filippa
Guided, 'tis said, the counsels of king Robert.
 Acciajoli. And were those counsels evil? If they were,
How happens it that both in life and death   120
The good king Robert was his appellation?
 Rienzi. How many kings are thrust among the stars
Who had become the whipping-post much better?
 Acciajoli. Was Robert one?
 Rienzi.   We must confess that Robert
Struck down men's envy under admiration.
 Acciajoli. If then Filippa guided him, what harm?
 Rienzi. She might have feared that youth would less obey
Her prudent counsels than experience did.
 Acciajoli. Well might she: hence for many a year her cares
Have been devoted to our queen's instruction,   130
Together with queen Sancia, not without:

127 feared] fear'd 1846, 1876.

28

GIOVANNA OF NAPLES

And neither of these ladies (I now speak
As president) have meddled with our councils.
    Rienzi. When women of low origin are guides
To potentates of either sex, 'tis ill.
    Acciajoli. I might have thought so; but Filippa showed
That female wisdom much resembles male;
Gentler, not weaker; leading, not controlling.
Again! O Tribune! touching low estate.
More vigorously than off the downier cradle   140
From humble crib springs up the lofty mind.
    Rienzi. Strong arguments, and cogent facts, are these!
                            [To an Usher.
Conduct the queen of Naples into court.
    Acciajoli. That, by your leave, must be my office, sir!
            139 Tribune] tribune *1846.*

[ACT III.] SCENE III.

RIENZI, ACCIAJOLI, GIOVANNA, *and* PRIOR *of the* CELESTINES.

    Rienzi. Giovanna, queen of Naples! we have left you
A pause and space for sorrow to subside;
Since, innocent or guilty, them who lose
So suddenly the partner of their hours,
Grief seizes on, in that dark interval.
Pause too and space were needful, to explore
On every side such proofs as may acquit
Of all connivance at the dreadful crime
A queen so wise, and held so virtuous,
So just, so merciful. It cannot be   10
(We hope) that she who would have swept away
Play-things of royal courts and monkish cells,
The instruments of torture, that a queen
Who in her childhood visited the sick,
Nor made a luxury or pomp of doing it,
Who placed her little hand, as we have heard,
In that where fever burnt, nor feared contagion,
Should slay her husabnd.
    Acciajoli.   Faintness overpowers her,
Not guilt. The racks you spoke of, O Rienzi!
You have applied, and worse than those you spoke of.   20
    Rienzi. Gladly I see true friends about her.
    Acciajoli.   Say
          10 cannot] can not *1846.*

29

About her not; say in her breast she finds
The only friend she wants . . her innocence.
    Rienzi. People of Rome! your silence, your attention,
Become you. With like gravity our fathers
Beheld the mighty and adjudged their due.
Sovran of Naples, Piedemont, and Provence,
Among known potentates what other holds
Such wide dominions as this lady here,
Excepting that strong ilander whose sword   30
Has cut France thro', and lies o'er Normandy,
Anjou, Maine, Poictou, Brittany, Touraine,
And farthest Gascony; whose hilt keeps down
The Grampians, and whose point the Pyrenees.
Listen! she throws aside her veil, that all
May hear her voice, and mark her fearless mien.
    Giovanna. I say not, O Rienzi! I was born
A queen; nor say I none but God alone
Hath right to judge me. Every man whom God
Endows with judgement arbitrates my cause.   40
For of that crime am I accused which none
Shall hide from God or man. All are involved
In guilt who aid, or screen, or spare, the guilty.
Speak, voice of Rome! absolve me or condemn,
As proof, or, proof being absent, probability,
Points on the scroll of this dark tragedy.
Speak, and spare not: fear nought but mighty minds,
Nor those but moving in God's shadow, truth.
    Rienzi. Well hast thou done, O queen! and wisely chosen
Judge and defenders. Thro these states shall none   50
Invade thy realm. I find no crime in thee.
Hasten to Naples! for against its throne
Ring powerful arms and menace thy return.
                  [ACCIAJOLI *leads the Queen out.*
    Prior of the CELESTINES. Thou findest in that wily queen no crime.
So be it! and 'tis well. But, tribune, know,
Ill chosen are the praises thou bestowest
On her immunity from harm, in touching
The fevered and infected. She was led
Into such places by unholy hands.
I come not an accuser: I would say   60
Merely, that Queen Giovanna was anointed

30 ilander] islander *1846.*   34 Pyrenees.] Pyrenees? *1846.*   40 judgement] judgment *1846.*   48 but . . . in] , unless where lies *1846.*   58 fevered] fever'd *1846.*

30

By the most potent sorceress, Filippa
The Catanese.
 Rienzi. Anointed Queen?
 Prior.   Her palms
Anointed, so that evil could not touch them.
Filippa, with some blacker spirits, helpt
To cure the sick, or comfort them unduly.
 Rienzi. Among the multitude of sorceresses
I find but very few such sorceries,
And, if the Church permitted, would forgive them.
 Prior. In mercy we, in mercy, should demur.   *70*
 Rienzi. How weak is human wisdom! what a stay
Is such stout wicker-work about the fold!
 Prior. Whether in realms of ignorance, in realms
By our pure light and our sure faith unblest,
Or where the full effulgence bursts from Rome,
No soul, not one upon this varied earth,
Is unbeliever in the power of sorcery:
How certain then its truth, the universal
Tongue of mankind, from east to west, proclaims.
 Rienzi. With reverential and submissive awe,   *80*
People of Rome! leave we to holy Church
What comes not now before us, nor shall come,
While matters which our judgements can decide
Are questioned, while crown'd heads are bowed before us.

84 questioned] question'd *1846.*

ACT IV.

SCENE I. RIENZI'S OWN APARTMENT IN THE CAPITOL.

RIENZI, FRIAR ANSELMO, *and poor* NEAPOLITANS.

 Rienzi. Who creeps there yonder with his fingers folded?
Hither; what wantest thou? who art thou, man?
 Anselmo. The humblest of the humble, your Anselmo.
 Rienzi. Mine?
 Anselmo. In all duty.
 Rienzi.   Whence art thou?
 Anselmo.   From Naples.
 Rienzi. What askest thou?
 Anselmo.   In the most holy names
Of Saint Euphemia and Saint Cunigund!
And in behalf of these poor creatures ask I
Justice and mercy.

DRAMAS AND DRAMATIC SCENES

Rienzi.   On what count?
Anselmo.   On life.
Rienzi. Who threatens it in Rome?
Anselmo.   In Rome none dare,   10
Under the guardianship of your tribunal.
But Naples is abandoned to her fate
By those who ruled her. Those, alas! who ruled her
Heaven has abandoned. Crimes, outrageous crimes,
Have swept them from their people. We alone
In poverty are left for the protection
Of the more starving populace. O hear,
Merciful Tribune! hear their cries for bread!   [*All cry out.*
   Anselmo, to them. Ye should not have cried now, ye fools! and choak ye!
Rienzi. That worthy yonder, looks well satisfied.
All of him, but his shoulder, seems at ease.   20
   Anselmo. Tommaso! art thou satisfied?
   Tommaso.   Not I.
A fish upon my bread, at least on Friday,
Had done my body and my soul some good,
And quickened one and t'other at thanksgiving.
Anchovies are rare cooks for garlic, master!   [*To* RIENZI.
   Anselmo. I sigh for such delusion.
   Rienzi.   So do I.
How came they hither?
   Anselmo.   By a miracle.
   Rienzi. My honest friends! what can we do for you
At Rome?
   Anselmo. Speak. Does the devil gripe your tongues?
   Mob. We crave our daily bread from holy hands,   30
And from none other.
   Rienzi.   Then your daily bread
Ye will eat hot, and delicately small.
Frate Anselmo, what means this?
   Anselmo.   It means,
O tribune! that the lady, late our queen,
Hath set aside broad lands and blooming gardens
For hospitals; which, with unrighteous zeal,
She builds with every church. There *Saint Antonio*
Beyond the gate of Capua! there *Saint Martin*
On *Mount Sant-Eremo!* there *Saint Maria*
Incoronata! All their hospitals!   40
No one hath monastery! no one nuns!

     24 quickened] quicken'd *1846.*   39 *Sant-Eremo*] *Saint-Eremo* 1846.

GIOVANNA OF NAPLES

Rienzi. Hard, hard upon you! But what means were yours
To bring so many supplicants so long
A journey with you?
   Anselmo.   'Twas a miracle.
   Rienzi. Miracles never are of great duration.
Hurry then back! Hurry ye while it lasts!
I would not spoil it with occult supplies,
I reverence holy men too much for that,
And leave them to the only power above them.
Possibly quails and manna may not cross you   50
If you procrastinate. But, setting out
To-morrow, by whichever gate seems luckiest,
And questioning your honest mules discreetly,
I boldly answer for it, ye shall find
By their mild winking (should they hold their tongues)
The coin of our lord Clement on the back
Of one or other, in some well-thonged scrip.
   Anselmo, aside. Atheist!
   Tommaso.   Ah no, father! Atheists
Never lift up their eyes as you and he do.   *[Going together.*
I know one in a twinkling. For example,   60
Cosimo Cappa was one. He denied
A miracle his mother might have seen
Not twelve miles from his very door, when she
Was heavy with him; and the saint who workt it,
To make him one, cost thirteen thousand ducats.
There was an atheist for you! that same Cappa . .
I saw him burnt . . a fine fresh lusty man.
I warrant I remember it: I won
A heap of chesnuts on that day at morra.
A sad poor place this Rome! look where you will,   70
No drying paste here dangles from the windows
Across the sunny street, to make it cheerful;
And much I doubt if, after all its fame,
The nasty yellow river breeds anchovies.

[ACT IV.] SCENE II. RIENZI'S OWN APARTMENT IN THE CAPITOL.

RIENZI *and his* WIFE.

Rienzi. I have been sore perplext, and stil am so.
   Wife. Yet falsehood drops from truth, as quicksilver
From gold, and ministers to purify it.

1 stil] still 1846.

Rienzi. The favour of the people is uncertain.
Wife. Gravely thou givest this intelligence.
Thus there are people in a northern ile
Who tell each other that the weather changes;
And, when the sun shines, say the day looks bright;
And, when it shines not, there are clouds above.
   Rienzi. Some little fief, some dukedom, we'll suppose,   10
Might shelter us against a sudden storm.
   Wife. Not só: we should be crusht between two rocks,
The people and the barons. Both would hate thee,
Both call thee traitor, and both call thee truly.
   Rienzi. When we stand high, the shaft comes slowly up;
We see the feather, not the point; and that
Loses what venom it might have below.
   Wife. I thought the queen of Naples occupied
Thy mind entirely.
   Rienzi.   From the queen of Naples
My hopes originate. The pope is willing   20
To grant me an investiture when I
Have given up to him, by my decree,
Some of her cities.
   Wife.   Then it is untrue
Thou hast acquitted her of crime.
   Rienzi.   I did;
But may condemn her yet: the king of Hungary
Is yet unheard: there are strong doubts: who knows
But stronger may arise! My mind misgives.
Tell me thou thinkest her in fault. One word
Would satisfy me.
   Wife.   *Not* in fault, thou meanest.
   Rienzi. In fault, in fault, I say.
   Wife.   No, not in fault,   30
Much less so foully criminal.
   Rienzi.   O could I
Absolve her!
   Wife.   If her guilt be manifest,
Absolve her not; deliver her to death.
   Rienzi. From what the pope and king of Hungary
Adduce .. at present not quite openly ..
I must condemn her.
   Wife.   Dost thou deem her guilty?
   Rienzi. O God! I wish she were! I must condemn her!
   Wife. Husband! art thou gone mad?

Rienzi.   None are much else
Who mount so high, none can stand firm, none look
Without a fear of falling: and, to fall! . .   40
No, no, 'tis not, 'tis not the worst disgrace.
  Wife. What hast thou done? Have thine eyes seen corruption?
  Rienzi. Thinkest thou gold could move Rienzi? gold
(Working incessantly demoniac miracles)
Could chain down Justice, or turn blood to water?
  Wife. Who scorns the ingot may not scorn the mine.
Gold may not move thee, yet what brings gold may.
Ambition is but Avarice in mail,
Blinder, and often weaker. Is there strength,
Cola! or speed, in the oblique and wry?   50
Of blood turn'd into water talkest thou?
Take heed thou turn not water into blood
And show the pure impure. If thou do this,
Eternal is the stain upon thy hand;
Freedom thro' thee will be the proud man's scoff,
The wise man's problem; even the slave himself
Will rather bear the scourge than trust the snare.
Thou hast brought large materials, large and solid,
To build thy glory on: if equity
Be not the base, lay not one stone above.   60
Thou hast won influence over potent minds,
Relax it not. Truth is a tower of strength,
No Babel one . . it may be rais'd to heaven
And will not anger God.
  Rienzi.   Who doubts my justice?
  Wife. Thyself. Who prosecutes the criminal?
Thyself. Who racks the criminal? Thyself.
Unhappy man! how maim'd art thou! what limb
Proportionate! what feature undisfigured!
Go, bathe in porphyry . . thy leprosy
Will never quit thee: thou hast eaten fruit   70
That brings all sins, and leaves but death behind.
  Rienzi. But hear me.
  Wife.   I have heard thee, and such words
As one who loves thee never should have heard.
  Rienzi. I must provide against baronial power
By every aid, external and internal,

48 Avarice] avarice *1846.*
61 won] won the *1846* (*mispr.*).

For, since my elevation, many friends
Have fallen from me.
  Wife.   Throw not off the rest.
What! is it then enough to stand before
The little crags and sweep the lizards down
From their warm basking-place with idle wand,   80
While under them the drowsy panther lies
Twitching his paw in his dark lair, and waits
Secure of springing when thy back is turned?
Popular power can stand but with the people:
Let them trust none a palm above themselves,
For sympathy in high degrees is frozen.
  Rienzi. Such are my sentiments.
  Wife.   Thy sentiments!
They were thy passion. Are they sentiments?
Go! there's the distaff in the other room.
  Rienzi. Thou blamed'st not what seemed ambition in me. 90
  Wife. Because it gave thee power to bless thy country.
Stood tribunitial ever without right?
Sat ever papal without perfidy?
O tribune! tribune! whom weak woman teaches!
If thou deceivest men, go, next enslave them;
Else is no safety. Would'st thou that?
  Rienzi.   To make
Any new road, some plants there must be crusht,
And not the higher only, here and there.
Whoever purposes great good, must do
Some partial evil.
  Wife.   Thou hast done great good   100
Without that evil yet. Power in its prime
Is beautiful, but sickened by excess
Collapses into loathsomeness; and scorn
Shrivels to dust its fierce decrepitude.
  Rienzi. Am I deficient then in manly deeds,
Or in persuasion?
  Wife.   Of all manly deeds
Oftentimes the most honest are the bravest,
And no persuasion so persuades as truth.
  Rienzi. Peace! peace! confound me not.
  Wife.   The brave, the wise,
The just, are never, even by foes, confounded.   110
Promise me but one thing. If in thy soul
Thou thinkest this young woman free from blame,

36

Thou wilt absolve her, openly, with honour,
Whatever Hungary, whatever Avignon,
May whisper or may threaten.
    Rienzi.   If my power
Will bear it; if the sentence will not shake
This scarlet off my shoulder.
    Wife.   Cola! Cola!   117

[ACT IV.] SCENE III. TRIBUNAL IN THE CAPITOL.

RIENZI, CITIZENS, &c.

Citizen. There is a banner at the gates.
    Rienzi.   A banner!
Who dares hoist banner at the gates of Rome?
    Citizen. A royal crown surmounts it.
    Rienzi.   Down with it!
    Citizen. A king, 'tis said, bears it himself in hand.
    Rienzi. Trample it in the dust, and drag him hither.
What are those shouts? Look forth.
    Usher, having lookt out.   The people cry
Around four knights who bear a sable flag:
One's helm is fashioned like a kingly crown.
    Rienzi. Strike off his head who let the accursed symbol
Of royalty come within Roman gate: 10
See this be done: then bind the bold offenders.
                    [LEWIS *of* HUNGARY *enters.*
Who art thou?
    Lewis.   King of Hungary.
    Rienzi.   What brings thee?
    Lewis. Tribune! thou knowest well what brings me hither.
Fraternal love, insulted honour, bring me.
Thinkest thou I complain of empty forms
Violated to chafe me? thinkest thou
Tis that I waited in the port of Triest
For invitation to my brother's wedding,
Nor invitation came, nor embassy?
Now creaks the motive. Silly maskerade   20
Usurpt the place of tilt and tournament;
No knight attended from without, save one,
Our cousin of Taranto: why he came,
Before all earth the dire event discloses.

6 *lookt*] *looked* 1846.   8 fashioned] fashion'd *1846.*   17 Triest] Trieste *1846.*
20 maskerade] masquerade *1846.*

Rienzi. Lewis of Hungary! it suits not us
To regulate the laws of chivalry
Or forms of embassies. We know there may be
Less folly in the lightest festival
Than in the sternest and severest war.
Patiently have we heard, as patiently   30
Hear thou, in turn, the accused as the accuser;
Else neither aid nor counsel hope from me.
  Lewis. I ask no aid of thee, I want no counsel,
I claim but justice: justice I will have,
I will have vengeance for my brother's death.
  Rienzi. My brother too was murdered. Was my grief
Less deep than thine? If greater my endurance,
See what my patience brought me! all these friends
Around, and thee, a prince, a king, before me.
Hear reason, as becomes a christian knight.   40
  Lewis. Ye always say to those who suffer wrong,
Hear reason! Is not that another wrong?
He who throws fuel on a fiery furnace
Cries, *Wait my signal for it! blaze not yet!*
Issue one edict more; proclame, O tribune,
Heat never shall be fire, nor fire be flame.
  Rienzi. King Lewis! I do issue such an edict
(Absurd as thou mayest deem it) in this place.
Hell hath its thunders, loud and fierce as Heaven's,
Heaven is more great and glorious in its calm: 50
In this clear region is the abode of Justice.
  Lewis. Was it well, tribune, to have heard the cause,
Nay and to have decided it, before
Both sides were here? The murderess hath departed,
And may have won her city from the grasp
Of my brave people, who avenge their prince,
The mild Andrea. Justice I will have,
I will have vengeance.
  Rienzi.   Every man may ask
If what I do is well: and angry tones,
Tho' unbecoming, are not unforgiven   60
Where virtuous grief bursts forth. But, king of Hungary,
We now will change awhile interrogations.
I ask thee was it well to bring with thee
Into our states a banner that blows up
The people into fury? and a people

40 christian] Christian *1846.*

Not subject to thy scepter or thy will?
We knew not of thy coming. When thy friends
In Naples urged us to decide the cause,
'Twas in thy name, as guardian to thy brother,
Bringing against the queen such accusations,   70
And so supported, that we ordered her
To come before us and defend herself.
She did it, nor delayed. The cardinal
Bishop of Orvieto and the Cardinal
Del Sangro on their part, on hers Del Balzo
And Acciajoli, have examined all
The papers, heard the witnesses, and signed
Their sentence under each. These we suggest
To the approval of thy chancery.
    Lewis. Chanceries were not made for murderesses.   80
    Rienzi. I am not learned like the race of kings,
Yet doth my memory hold the scanty lore
It caught betimes, and there I find it written,
Not in Hungarian nor in Roman speech,
Vengeance is mine. We execute the laws
Against the disobedient, not against
Those who submit to our award. The queen
Of Naples hath submitted. She is free,
Unless new proof and stronger be adduced
To warrant her recall into my presence.   90
    Lewis. Recall'd she shall be then, and proof adduced.
    Rienzi. We have detected falsehood in its stead.
    Lewis. I will have justice, come it whence it may.
    Rienzi. Cecco Mancino! read the law against
Those who accuse maliciously or lightly.
    Mancino reads. "Who shall accuse another, nor make good
His accusation, shall incur such fine,
Or such infliction of the scourge, as that
False accusation righteously deserves."
    Rienzi. Fine cannot satisfy the wrongs that royalty   100
Receives from royalty.
    Lewis.   Wouldst thou inflict
The scourge on kings?
    Rienzi.   The lictor would, not I.
    Lewis. What insult may we not expect ere long!
And yet we fare not worst from demagogues.
Those who have risen from the people's fist

             66 scepter] sceptre *1846.*

Perch first upon their shoulders, then upon
Their heads, and then devour their addled brain.
 Rienzi. We have seen such of old.
 Lewis.   Hast thou seen one
True to his feeder where power whistled shriller,
Shaking the tassels and the fur before him?   110
 Rienzi. History now grows rather dim with me,
And memory less vivacious than it was:
No time for hawks, no tendency to hounds!
 Lewis. Cold sneers are your calm judgments! Here at Rome
To raise false hopes under false promises
Is wisdom! and on such do we relie!
 Rienzi. Wisdom with us is not hereditary,
Nor brought us from the woods in ermine-skins,
Nor pinned upon our tuckers ere we chew,
Nor offered with the whistle on bent knee,   120
But, King of Hungary! we can and do
In some reward it and in all revere;
We have no right to scoff at it, thou hast.
Cecco Mancino!
 Mancino. Tribune most august!
 Rienzi, turning his back, and pointing to the eagles over his tribunal.
Furl me that flag. Now place it underneath
The eagles there. When the king goes, restore it.
         [*Walks down from the tribunal.*

    116 relie] rely *1846.*

ACT V.

SCENE I. PALACE ON THE SHORE NEAR NAPLES.

GIOVANNA, ACCIAJOLI, DEL BALZO, LUIGI OF TARANTO, KNIGHTS.

 Acciajoli. My queen! behold in us your native land
And lawful realm again!
 Giovanna.   But other sounds
Than greeted me in earlier days I hear,
And other sights I see; no friends among them
Who guided me in childhood, warn'd in youth,
And were scathed off me when that thunderbolt
Fell down between us. Are they lost so soon!
So suddenly! Why could they not have come? (*To* DEL BALZO.
Where is Filippa? where Terlizzi? where
Maternal Sancia?

    1 in us] us in *1846.*

40

GIOVANNA OF NAPLES

Del Balzo.   Such her piety,   10
Nor stranger nor insurgent hath presumed
To throw impediment before her steps.
For friends alike and enemies her prayers
Are daily heard among the helpless crowd,
But loudest for Giovanna; at which name,
Alone she bends upon the marble floor
That saintly brow, and stirs the dust with sighs.

    Giovanna, to ACCIAJOLI. Arms only keep her from me. Whose are
      yonder?

    Acciajoli. I recognise Calabrian; Tarantine.

    Giovanna. Ah me! suspicion then must never cease!   20
Never, without Luigi, Tarantine
Arms glitter in the field. Even without him
(Which cannot be) his troops in my defence
Would move again those odious thoughts, among
My easy people, guileless and misled.

    Del Balzo. His duty and his fealty enforce
What loyalty and honour would persuade.
Taranto is a fief: Taranto's prince
Must lead his army where his suzerein
Commands, or where, without commanding, needs.   30

    Acciajoli. He cannot see your city in your absence
A prey to lawless fury, worse than war.

    Del Balzo. Ay, and war too: for those who came as pilgrims
And penitents, to kiss the holy frock
Of father Rupert, spring up into soldiers;
And thus are hundreds added to the guards
Which that most powerful friar placed around
Him whom we mourn for. Three strong companies
(Once only eight score each) are form'd within
The conquered city. Canopies of state   40
Covered with sable cloth parade the streets,
And crucifixes shed abundant blood
Daily from freshened wounds; and virgins' eyes
Pour torrents over faces drawn with grief.
What saint stands unforgotten? what uncall'd?
Unincenst? Many have come forth and walkt
Among the friars, many shouted loud
For vengeance. Even Luigi's camp stood wavering.
Only when first appeared your ship afar,

15 name,] name. *mispr.* 1839.   23, 31 cannot] can not *1846, 1876.*   26 fealty]
fëalty *1846.*

And over the white sail the sable flag,   50
Flapping the arms of Anjou, Naples, Hungary,
'Twas only then the rising mutiny
Paus'd, and subsided; only then Luigi,
Pointing at that trine pennant, turn'd their rage
Into its course.
    Acciajoli.   Perhaps the boat I see
Crossing the harbour, may bring some intelligence;
Perhaps he may, himself . .
    Giovanna.   No! not before . . .
No! not at present . . . Must I be ungrateful?
Never! . . ah, must I seem so?   59

[ACT V.] SCENE II.

    An old Knight.   From the prince
Commanding us, O lady! I am here
To lay his homage at his liege's feet.
He bids me say, how, at the first approach
Of that auspicious vessel, which brought hither
Before her city's port its lawful queen,
His troops demanded battle. In one hour
He places in your royal hands the keys
Of your own capital, or falls before it.
    Giovanna. God grant he fall not! O return! return!   10
Tell him there are enow . . without, within . .
And, were there not enow . . persuade, implore . .
Show how Taranto wants him; his own country,
His happy people . . they must pine without him!
O miserable me! O most ungrateful!
Tell him I cannot see him . . I am ill . .
The sea disturbs me . . my head turns, aches, splits . .
I cannot see him . . say it, sir! repeat it.
    Knight. May-be, to-morrow . . .
    Giovanna.   Worse, to-morrow! worse!
Sail back again . . say everything . . thanks, blessings.   20
    Knight. Too late! Those thundering shouts are our assault . .
It was unfair without me; it was hard . .
Those are less loud.
    Giovanna.   Luigi is repulst!
Perhaps is slain! slain if repulst . . he said it.
Yes; those faint shouts . . .

           16, 18 cannot] can not *1846.*

Knight.   Lady, they are less loud
Because the walls are between him and us.
    Giovanna, falls on her knees. O! every saint in heaven be glorified!
Which, which hath saved him? [*Rises.*] Yet, O sir! if walls
Are between him and us, then he is where
His foes are! That is not what you intend?   30
What is it? Cries again!
    Knight.   Not one were heard
Had our prince dropt. The fiercest enemy
Had shrunk appall'd from such majestic beauty
Falling from heaven upon the earth beneath;
And his own people with closed teeth had fought,
Not for their lives, but for his death: no such
Loud acclamation, lady! had been heard,
But louder woe and wailing from the vanquisht.
    Giovanna, aside. Praises to thee, O Virgin! who concealedst
So kindly all my fondness, half my fears!   40
    Acciajoli. The dust is rising nearer. Who rides hither
In that black scarf? with something in his hand
Where the sword should be. 'Tis a sword, I see,
In form at least. The dust hangs dense thereon,
Adhesive, dark.
    Del Balzo.   Seneschal! it was brighter
This morning, I would swear for it.
    Acciajoli.   He throws
The bridle on the mane. He comes.
    Del Balzo.   He enters . .
We shall hear all.

[ACT V.] SCENE III.

    Luigi of Taranto, throwing up his vizor. Pardon this last disguise!
There was no time to take my vizor off,
Scarcely to throw my sword down in the hall.
My royal cousin! let a worthier hand
Conduct you to the city you have won,
The city of your fathers.
    Giovanna.   O Luigi!
None worthier, none more loyal, none more brave.
Cousin! by that dear name I do adjure you!
Let others . . these my friends and ministers . .
Conduct me to the city you have won,   10
The city of your fathers, as of mine.
Let none who carried arms against the worst

43

Of my own people (for the very worst
Have only been misguided) come into it
With me, or after. Well thou governest
Thy vassals, O Luigi! Be thy dukedom
Increast in all the wealth my gratitude
Can add thereto, in chases, castles, towns;
But hasten, hasten thither! There are duties
(Alas! thou knowest like ourselves what duties)   20
I must perform. Should ever happier days
Shine on this land, my people will remember,
With me, they shine upon it from Taranto.

THE END.

FRA RUPERT

THE LAST PART OF A TRILOGY.

THE FIRST BEING

ANDREA OF HUNGARY,

THE SECOND BEING

GIOVANNA OF NAPLES.

BY WALTER SAVAGE LANDOR.

[Published 1840; reprinted 1846. See notes at end of volume.]

MALE CHARACTERS.

URBAN, *Pope.*	HERALD.
BUTELLO, *his nephew.*	PAGE.
CHARLES OF DURAZZO.	MONK.
OTHO, *husband of Giovanna.*	CHANCELLOR.
FRA RUPERT.	HIGH STEWARD.
MAXIMIN.	LORD CHAMBERLAIN.
STEPHEN [STOURDZA], *a shepherd.*	COUNSELLORS, SECRETARIES, OFFICERS, SOLDIERS.

FEMALE CHARACTERS.

GIOVANNA, *Queen.*	AGNES OF DURAZZO.
MARGARITA, *her niece, wife of Charles.*	AGATHA, *sister of Maximin.*

ACT I.

SCENE I. VATICAN.

URBAN. DURAZZO.

Urban. Charles of Durazzo! I have found thee worthy
To wear not only ducal coronet,

Title. Fra Rupert, *rest om. 1846.*   *Characters.* CHARLES] CHARLES II., *1846.*

44

But in that potent, in that faithful hand,
To wield the royal sceptre.
    Durazzo.   Holy father!
I am half-ready to accept the charge,
When it befalls me, studying your content.
    Urban. So be it. The crown of Naples is now vacant.
    Durazzo. Good heavens! is then my mother (let me call her
Ever my mother, by whose bounteousness
My fortunes grew, my youth was educated)   10
Giovanna! is she dead?
    Urban.   To virtuous deeds,
Like those, she long hath been so.
    Durazzo.   His Beatitude,
The predecessor of your Holiness,
Who through her hands received his resting-place
At Avignon, when Italy rebell'd,
Absolved her from that heavy accusation
Her enemy the Hungarian brought against her.
    Urban. I would not make Infallibility
Fallible, nor cross-question the absolved,
I merely would remove that stumbling-block   20
The kingdom from her.
    Durazzo.   Let another then
Aid such attempt.
    Urban.   Another shall.
    Durazzo.   Another
Nearer in blood is none.
    Urban.   Ere long, Durazzo,
I may look round and find one, if not nearer
In blood, yet fitter to perform the duties
Imposed on him by me.
    Durazzo.   None, holy father!
Is fitter.
    Urban. Easy then are the conditions.
I would not place Butello, my own nephew,
Altho' deserving, and altho' besought
By many of the Neapolitans,   30
By many of the noble and the powerful
In every city of that realm, not him,
Durazzo! would I place, against thy interests,
So high. But haply from thy gratitude
Accept I might in his behalf a dukedom

           9 Ever] Even *1846*.

Or petty principality, dependent
Upon our See, or (may-be) independent;
For there are some who fain would have things so.
We must content the nations of the earth,
Whom we watch over, and who look to us   40
For peace and quiet in the world we rule.
Why art thou beating time so with thy foot
At every word I speak? why look so stern
And jerk thy head and rest thy hand on hip?
Thou art determin'd on it, art not thou?
   Durazzo. I cannot, will not, move her from her seat,
So help me, God!
   Urban.   Impious young man! reflect!
I give thee time; I give thee all tomorrow.   48

46 cannot] can not 1846.

[ACT I.] SCENE II. A STREET IN NAPLES.

MAXIMIN. AGATHA.

   Agatha, to herself. 'Twas he! 'twas father Rupert.
   Maximin, overhearing.   Well! what then?
What wouldst thou with him? thou must wait his leisure:
I have some business first with father Rupert.
   Agatha, gazing anxiously. Can it be? can it be?
   Maximin.   Have not men sins
As well as women? have not we our shrivers,
Our scourers, soderers, calkers, and equippers?
   Agatha, embracing him. Forbear! O, for the love of God, forbear!
Heed him not, Maximin! or he will cast
Thy soul into perdition; he has mine.
   Maximin. And who art thou, good woman?
   Agatha.   That fair name   10
Is mostly given with small courtesy,
As something tost at us indifferently
Or scornfully by higher ones. Thy sister
Was what thou callest her; and Rupert knows it.
   Maximin. My sister? how! I had but Agatha.
Agatha!
   Agatha. Maximin! we have not met
Since that foul day whose damps fell not on thee,
But fill'd our father's house while thou wert absent.
Thou, brother! brother! couldst not save my peace,
Let me save thine. He used to call me daughter,   20
And he may call thee son.

FRA RUPERT

Maximin. The very word!
He began fathering early: seven years old
At most was father Rupert. Holy names
Are covered ways . .
    Agatha. . . To most unholy deeds.
    Maximin. I see it; say no more: my sword is reddening
With blood that runs not yet, but soon shall run.
    Agatha. Talk not thus loud, nor thus, nor here.
    Maximin. Cross then
Over the way to that old sycamore;
The lads have left off playing at pallone.
I found out long ago his frauds, his treasons,   30
His murders; and he meditates a worse.
Agatha! let me look into thine eyes,
Try to be glad to see me: lift them up,
Nay, do not drop them, they are gems to me,
And make me very rich with only looking.
Thou must have been most fair, my Agatha!
And yet I am thy brother! Who would think it?
    Agatha. Nor time nor toil deforms man's countenance,
Crime only does it: 'tis not thus with ours.
Kissing the seven nails burnt in below   40
Thy little breast, before they well had healed,
I thought thee stil more beautiful with them.
    Maximin. Those precious signs might have done better for me.
    Agatha. Only the honest are the prosperous.
    Maximin. A little too on that side hath slipt off.
    Agatha. Recover it.
    Maximin. How can I?
    Agatha. Save the innocent.
    Maximin. But whom?
    Agatha. Giovanna.
    Maximin. Is the queen in danger?
    Agatha. Knowest thou not?
    Maximin. Hide we away our knowledge;
It may do harm by daylight. I stand sentry
In many places at one time, and wink,   50
But am not drowsy. Trust me, she is safe.
And thou art then our Agatha! 'Twould do
Our mother good, were she alive, to find thee;
For her last words were "Agatha, where art thou?"

42 stil] still 1846.

Agatha. Oh! when our parents sorrow for our crimes,
Then is the sin complete.
Maximin.   She sorrows not,
And 'tis high time that thou should'st give it over.
Agatha. Alas! our marrow, sinews, veins, dry up,
But not our tears; they start with infancy,
Run on through life, and swell against the grave.   60
Maximin. I must now see Fra Rupert. Come thou after.
He shall admit thee. Pelt him with reproaches,
Then will I . .
Agatha.   Brother! not for these came I,
But to avert one crime from his o'erladen
Devoted head. He hath returned . .
Maximin.   . . to join
Giovanna with Andrea? On with me:
We may forbid the bans the second time,
Urging perhaps a few impediments.
He hath been in some convent o'er the hill,
Doing sad penance on Calabrian rye,   70
How then couldst thou have heard about him? how
Find he was here in Naples?
Agatha.   There he should
And may have been: of late he was in Buda.
Maximin. You met in Buda then?
Agatha.   Not met.
Maximin.   How know
His visit else, if he was there indeed?
Agatha. While thou and Stephen Stourdza tended sheep
Together, I was in our mother's sight,
And mostly in her chamber; for ill-health
Kept her from work. Often did Father Rupert
Pray by her, often hear her long confession,   80
Long, because little could be thought of for it.
Now what a comfort would it be to you,
If this poor child redd better, said the friar,
To listen while she redd how blessed saints
Have suffered, and how glorious their reward.
My mother claspt her hands, and *What a comfort!*
Echoed from her sick bosom.
                              "Hath she been

<hr/>

83, 84 redd] read *1846.*

Confirm'd?" he askt. " *Yea, God be prais'd,"* sigh'd she.
"We may begin then to infuse some salt
Into this leaven" said the friar, well-pleas'd.   90
" *The work is righteous: we will find spare hours."*
She wept for joy.
    Maximin.   Weep then (if weep at all)
Like her.
    Agatha. Religious tracts soon tost aside,
Florentine stories and Sicilian songs
Were buz'd into my ears. The songs much pleas'd me,
The stories (these he cull'd out from the book,
He told me, as the whole was not for maids)
Pleas'd me much less; for woman's faults were there.
    Maximin. He might have left out half the pages, stil
The book had been a bible in its bulk   100
If all were there.
    Agatha.   To me this well applies,
Not to my sex.
    Maximin.   Thou art the best in it.
Those who think ill of woman, hold the tongue
Thro' shame, or ignorance of what to say,
Or rifle the old ragbag for some shard
Spotted and stale. On, prythee, with thy story.
    Agatha. He taught me that soft speech, the only one
For love; he taught me to repeat the words
Most tender in it; to observe his lips
Pronouncing them; and his eyes scorcht my cheek   110
Into deep scarlet. With his low rich voice
He sang the sadness of the laurel'd brow,
The tears that trickle on the rocks around
Valchiusa. *"None but holy men can love*
As thou, Petrarca!" sighed he at the close.
Graver the work he brought me next. We redd
The story of Francesca.
    Maximin.   What is that?
    Agatha. Piteous, most piteous, for most guilty, passion.
Two lovers are condemn'd to one unrest
For ages. I now first knew poetry,   120
I had known song and sonnet long before:
I sail'd no more amid the barren iles,
Each one small self; the mighty continent

95 buz'd] buzz'd *1846.*   99 stil] still *1846.*   116 redd] read *1846.*   117 Francesca]
sc. da Rimini: *see* Dante, *Inferno* V. [W.]   122 iles] isles *1846.*

Rose and expanded; I was on its shores.
Fast fell the drops upon the page: he chided:
"*And is it punishment to be whirl'd on*
With our beloved thro' eternity?"
"*Oh! they were too unhappy, too unhappy!*"
Sobb'd I aloud: "*Who could have written this?*"
"*Tenderest of tender maids!*" cried he, and claspt me   130
To his hot breast. Fear seiz'd me, faintness, shame.
Be calm, my brother!
    Maximin.   Tell then other tale,
And skip far on.
    Agatha.   The queen Elizabeth
Heard of me at the nunnery where I served;
And the good abbess, not much loving one
Who spoke two languages and redd at night,
Persuaded her that, being quick and needy,
'Twould be by far more charitable in her
To take me rather than some richer girl,
To read by her, and lace her sandals on.   140
I serv'd her several years, to her content.
One evening after dusk, her closet-door
Being to me at every hour unclosed,
I was just entering, when some voice like his,
Whispering, but deep, struck me: a glance sufficed:
'Twas he. They neither saw me. Now occurr'd
That lately had Elizabeth said more
And worse against Giovanna. "She might be
Guiltless, but should not hold the throne of Naples
From the sweet child her daughter: there were some   150
Who had strong arms, and might again do better
In cowl than fiercer spirits could in casque."
Sleepless was I that night, afraid to meet
The wretched man, afraid to join the queen.
Early she rose, as usual; earlier I.
My sunken eyes and paleness were remarkt,
And, whence? was askt me.
               "Those who have their brothers
At Naples" I replied "most gracious lady,
May well be sleepless; for rebellion shakes
A throne unsteady ever."
                First she paus'd,   160
Then said, with greater blandness than before,

"Indeed they may. But between two usurpers
What choice? Your brother may improve his fortune
By loyalty, and teaching it. You wish
To join him, I see clearly, for his good;
It may be yours: it may be ours: go then,
Aid him with prudent counsel: the supply
Shall not be wanting, secrecy must not."
She urged my parting: the same hour we parted.   169

168 not."] *so in 1846: quotation marks wrongly om. 1840.*

[ACT I.] SCENE III. RUPERT'S CELL.

RUPERT. MAXIMIN.

Rupert. Thou hast delaid some little, Maximin.
Maximin. Frate! I met a woman in the street,
And she might well delay me: guess now why.
Rupert. Who in the world can guess the why of women?
Maximin. She said she knew us both in Hungary.
Rupert. I now suspect the person: she is crazed.
Maximin. Well may she be, deprived of such a friend.
Rupert. No friend was ever mine in that false sex.
I am impatient, Maximin.
Maximin.   Impatient!
And so am I.

          MAXIMIN *throws open the door, and* AGATHA *enters.*
          Knowst thou this woman, Frate?   10
Rupert. Art thou crazed too? I know her? Not at all.
Maximin. And hast thou never known her? never toucht her?
I only mean in giving her thy blessing.
Rupert. A drunken sailor in a desert ile
Would not approach her.
Maximin, indignant.   Not my sister?
Agatha.   Scorner!
Insulter!
          (*Aside.*) He may have forgotten. Can he?
He did not see me, would not look at me.
Maximin. My sword shall write her name upon thy midrif.
Prepare!
Agatha. Hold! hold! Spare him yet, Maximin!
How could I .. and the man who ..
Maximin.   Speak it out,   20
Worthless one!

10 Knowst] Knowest *1846.*   14 ile] isle *1846.*

E 2

51

Agatha.   I am worthless. Let him live!
Oh let him live!
Maximin.   Thou lovest thy betrayer.
Agatha. The once beloved are unestranged by falsehood;
They cannot wholly leave us, tho' they leave us
And never look behind.
Maximin.   Wild! wild as hawk!
Rupert, on his knees. Vision of light, of love, of purity!
Dost thou revisit on the verge of earth
A soul so lost, to rescue it? Enough,
Agatha! Do not ask him for my life;
No, bid him slay me; bid him quench the days   30
That have in equal darkness set and risen
Since proud superiors banisht faithful love.
I am grown old; few years were left me, few
And sorrowful: my reason comes and goes:
I am almost as capable of crimes
As virtues.
Maximin. By my troth, a hundred-fold
More capable.
Rupert.   Both ('tis Heaven's will) are over.
Here let me end my hours: they should have all
Been thine; he knows it; let him take them for thee;
And close thou here mine eyes where none behold,   40
Forgiving me . . no, not forgiving me,
But praying, thou pure soul! for Heaven's forgiveness.
Maximin. I will not strike thee on the ground: rise up,
Then, when thou risest . .
Agatha.   Come away, my brother!
Rupert. Never, so help me saints! will I rise up:
I will breathe out my latest breath before her.
Maximin. It sickens a stout man to tread on toads.   (*Goes*)
Rupert, rising slowly, and passing a dagger through his fingers. And
    the stout man might slip too, peradventure.

24 cannot] can not 1846.   33 were] are 1846.

[ACT I.] SCENE IV. PALACE NEAR NAPLES.

DURAZZO. MARGARITA.

Durazzo. The Pope is not averse to make me king.
Margarita. Do we not rule already?
Durazzo.   Rule indeed!
Yes, one small dukedom. Any shepherd-dog
Might make his voice heard farther off than mine.

FRA RUPERT

Margarita. Yet, my sweet Carlo, oftentimes I've heard you,
When people brought before you their complaints,
Swear at them for disturbing your repose,
Keeping you from your hounds, your bird, your ride
At evening, with my palfrey biting yours
Playfully (like two Christians) at the gate.   10
Durazzo. I love to see my bird soar in the air,
My hound burst from his puzzlement, and cite
His peers around him to arraign the boar.
Margarita. I think such semblances of high estate
Are better than the thing itself, more pleasant,
More wholesome.
Durazzo.   And thinks too my Margarita
Of the gray palfrey? like a summer dawn
His dapper sides, his red and open nostrils;
And his fair rider like the sun just rising
Above it, making hill and vale look gay.   20
Margarita. She would be only what Durazzo thinks her.
Durazzo. Queenly he thinks her: queen he swears to make her.
Margarita. I am contented; and should be, without
Even our rule: it brings us but few cares,
Yet some it brings us: why add more to them?
Durazzo. I never heard you talk so seriously.
Not long ago I little heeded state,
Authority, low voice, bent knee, kist hand:
The Pope has proved to me that, sure as any
Of the seven sacraments, the only way   30
To rise above temptation, is to seize
All that can tempt.
Margarita.   There must be truth then in it.
But what will some men think when you deprive
Our aunt of her inheritance?
Durazzo.   Men think!
Do not men always think what they should not?
Margarita. We hear so from the pulpit: it must be.
But we should never take what is another's.
Durazzo. Then you would never take another's child
To feed or clothe it.
Margarita.   That is not my meaning.
I am quite sure my aunt has loved me dearly   40
All her life long, and loves me stil; she often

41 stil] still *1846.*

53

(Kissing me) said, *How like thou art Maria!*
You know, Durazzo, how she loved my mother.
   Durazzo. And she loved me no less: and we love her
And honor her.
   Margarita.   May we not then obey her?
   Durazzo. The Pope, who teaches best, says otherwise.
Rule has been tedious to her all her reign,
And dangerous too.
   Margarita.   Make it less dangerous, make it
Less tedious.
   Durazzo.   She has chosen the duke Otho
To sit above thy husband, and all else.   50
   Margarita. I think my husband is as brave as he.
   Durazzo. I think so too: yet people doubt.
   Margarita.   Indeed!
   Durazzo. And doubt they will, unless the truest knight
Of Margarita takes to horse, and scours
Her gransire's realm of foreners like Otho.
   Margarita. If you do that, you must displease our aunt.
   Durazzo. Perhaps so: and hast never thou displeas'd her?
   Margarita. Never; although I sometimes did what might.
   Durazzo. I cannot disappoint the Holy Father.
   Margarita. Nay, God forbid! But let me no more see her,   60
To hear her tell me all she did for me!
I can bear anything but evil tongues.
   Durazzo. Then let us slink away and live obscurely.   [*Going.*
   Margarita. Come back again . . Now! would you leave me so?
I have been thinking I must think no more
About the matter . . and am quite resolved.
   Durazzo. My sweetest! you have several female cousins;
What are they?
   Margarita.   Duchesses.
   Durazzo.   But are they queens?
   Margarita. No indeed; and why should they be? They queens?
   Durazzo. I know but one well worthy of the title.   70
   Margarita. Now, who can possibly that be, I wonder!
   Durazzo. She on whose brow already Majesty
Hath placed a crown which no artificer
Can render brighter, or fit better, she
Upon whose lip Love pays the first obeisance.   [*Saluting her.*
   Margarita. I know not how it is that you persuade

---

45 honor] honour *1846.*   55 gransire's] grandsire's *1846.*   foreners] foreigners
1846.   59 cannot] can not *1846.*

FRA RUPERT

So easily . . not very easily
In this, however: yet, if but to teaze
And plague a little bit my sweet dear cousins,
Writing the kindest letters, telling them   80
That I am stil, and shall be, just the same,
Their loving cousin; nor in form alone;
And if I write but seldom for the future,
'Tis only that we queens have many cares
Of which my charming cousins can know nothing.
   Durazzo. What foresight, friendliness, and delicacy!
   Margarita. Nothing on earth but these, in the idea
Of vexing . . no, not vexing . . only plaguing
(You know, love! what I mean) my sweet dear cousins,
Could make me waver . . and then you, sad Carlo!   90
   Durazzo. To please me . .
   Margarita.   Now, what would you have me say?

        81 stil] still *1846.*

     [ACT I.] SCENE V. NAPLES.

   PAGE. GIOVANNA. AGNES. MAXIMIN.

   Page. Fly, O my lady! Troops are near the city.
   Giovanna. There always are.
   Page.   But strangers. People say
Durazzo . . .
   Giovanna. What of him?
   Agnes.   Now then confess
I knew him better. No reports have reacht us
These several days: the roads were intercepted.
   Giovanna. I will fear nothing: Otho watches over us.
Insects, that build their tiny habitations
Against sea-cliffs, become sea-cliffs themselves.
I rest on Otho, and no storm can shake me.
   Agnes. How different this Durazzo!
   Giovanna.   All men are: 10
But blame not without proof, or sign of proof,
Or accusation, any man so brave.
   Page. Lady! his soldiers on Camaldoli
Wave the green banner and march hitherward.
   Giovanna, after a pause. It cannot be! my Carlo! my Carlino!
What! he who said his prayers with hands comprest
Between my knees, and would leap off to say them?

       15 cannot] can not *1846.*

                 55

Impossible! He may have been deterred
From helping me: his people, his advisers,
May have been adverse . . but . . make war upon me!   20
O they have basely slandered thee, my Carlo!
   Agnes. He has been with the Holy Father lately.
   Giovanna. This would relieve me from all doubt, alone.
   Agnes. So kind as you have been to him! a mother!
   Giovanna. Remind me not of any benefit
I may have done him: tell me his good deeds,
Speak not (if some there may have been) of mine:
'Twould but disturb the image that has never
Yet fallen from my breast, and never shall.
He was my child when my own child indeed,   30
My only one, was torne away from me.
   Agnes. And you have brooded o'er a marble egg,
Poor darkling bird!
   Giovanna.   O Agnes! Agnes! spare me.
Let me think on . . . how pleasant 'twas to follow
In that Carlino, in that lovely boy,
The hidings of shy love, its shame, its glee,
Demurest looks at matters we deem light,
And, well worth every lesson ever taught,
Laughter that loosens graver, and that shakes
Our solemn gauds into their proper place.   40
   Maximin (out of breath). The castle-gates are open for one moment . .
Seize them and enter . . Crowds alone impede
Durazzo, and not arms.
   Agnes.   Do you believe
His treason now?
   Giovanna.   Peace, peace! 'tis hard, 'tis hard!

31 torne] torn 1846.

ACT II.

SCENE I. RUPERT'S CELL.

RUPERT *and* MAXIMIN.

   Rupert, alone. I've dogged him to the palace: there's some treachery.
Giovanna . . and that witch too, Agatha . .
Why not all three together? Sixty miles
From Naples there is Muro. Now, a word
Was dropt upon it. We must be humane.
But, one more trial first to make him serve

FRA RUPERT

In stablishing the realm. I fain must laugh
To think what creatures stablish realms, and how.

(MAXIMIN *enters.*)

Well, Maximin! We live for better days
And happier purports. Couldst thou not devise   10
Something that might restore the sickened state,
And leave our gracious king the exercise
Of his goodwill, to give them companies
Who now are ensigns? Ah brave Maximin!
I do remember when thou wert but private.
Psein, Klapwrath, Zinga, marcht, and made thee way.
Nothing in this our world would fain stand still.
The earth we tread on labors to set free
Its fires within, and shakes the mountain-heads;
The animals, the elements, all move,   20
The sea before us, and the sky above,
And angels on their missions between both.
Fortune will on. There are whom happiness
Makes restless with close constancy; there are
Who tire of the pure air and sunny sky,
And droop for clouds as if each hair were grass.
No wonder then should more aspiring souls
Be weary of one posture, one dull gloom
All the day through, all the long day of life.
   Maximin gapes. Weary! ay am I. Can I soon be captain?   30
   Rupert. Why not?
   Maximin.   And then what service?
   Rupert.   Queen Giovanna
Is blockt up in the castle, as thou knowest;
Was not my counsel wise, to keep thee out?
Famine had else consumed thee; she spares none.
Charles of Durazzo, our beloved king,
Presses the siege; and, when the queen gives up,
Thou art the man I prophecy to guard her.
There are some jewels: lightly carried in,
A thousand oxen cannot haul them forth;
But they may drop at Muro, one by one,   40
And who should husband them save Maximin?
   Maximin, pretending alarm. I will not leave my sister out of sight:
She ne'er must fall again.

---

7 stablishing] 'stablishing *1846.*   8 stablish] 'stablish *1846.*   13 goodwill]
good will *1846.*   18 labors] labours *1846.*

Rupert.   Forefend it, heaven!
I might be weak! She would indeed be safe
Where the queen is! But who shall have the heart
To shut her up? What has she done? Her brother
Might be a comfort to her; and the queen
And some few ladies trust her and caress her.
But, though the parks and groves and tofts around,
And meadows, from their first anemonies   50
To their last saffron-crocuses, though all
Open would be, to her, if not to them,
And villagers and dances, and carousels
At vintage-time, and panes that tremble, partly
By moon-ray, partly by guitar beneath,
Yet might the hours, without street-views, be dull.
    Maximin. Don't tell her so. Get her once there. But how?
Beside, the queen will never trust Hungarians.
There would be mortal hatred. Is there fire
Upon the hearth?
    Rupert.   None.
    Maximin.   Why then rub your hands?   60

50 anemonies] anemones *1846*.   53 carousels] carousals *1846*.

[ACT II.] SCENE II. CASTEL-NUOVO.

GIOVANNA *and* AGNES.

Giovanna. 'Tis surely wrong that those who fight for us
So faithfully, so wretchedly should perish;
That thriftless jewels sparkle round your temples
While theirs grow dank with famine.
    Agnes.   Now I see,
O my poor queen! the folly of refusal,
When they had brought us safety.
    Giovanna.   Not quite that,
To me at least, but sustenance and comfort
To our defenders in the castle here.
    Agnes. Will you now take them?
    Giovanna.   If some miracle
Might turn a jewel to a grain of corn,   10
I would: my own were kneaded into bread
In the first days of our captivity.
    Agnes. And mine were stil witholden! Pardon me,
Just Heaven!
    Giovanna.   In words like those invoke not Heaven.

13 stil] still *1846*.

FRA RUPERT

If we say *just*, what can we hope? but what
May we not hope if we say *merciful?*
   Agnes. And yet my fault is very pardonable.
We, at our time of life, want these adornments.
   Giovanna. We never want them. Youth has all its own;
None can shed lustre upon closing days,   20
Mockers of eyes and lips and whatsoever
Was prized; nor can they turn one grey hair brown,
But, skilfully transmuted, might prolong
The life and health and happiness of hundreds.
   Agnes. Queens may talk so.
   Giovanna.   Not safely, but to friends.
   Agnes. With power and pomp . .
   Giovanna.   Behold my pomp, my power!
These naked walls, cold pavements, grated windows.
   Agnes. Let me share these with you. Take all my jewels.
   Giovanna. Forbear, forbear, dear Agnes!
   Agnes.   Earth then, take them!
                     Throwing them from her.

[ACT II.] SCENE III. CASTEL-NUOVO.

DURAZZO. RUPERT. GIOVANNA. AGNES.

   Durazzo. Upon my knees I do entreat of you
To hear me. In sincerity, the crown
(Now mine) was forced upon me.
   Giovanna.   Carlo! Carlo!
Know you what crowns are made of?
   Durazzo, rising.   I must wear one,
However fitly or unfitly made.
   Giovanna. The ermine is outside, the metal burns
Into the brain.
   Durazzo.   Its duties, its conditions,
Are not unknown to me, nor its sad cares.
   Giovanna. 'Tis well Maria my sweet sister lives not
To see this day.
   Durazzo.   But Margarita lives,   10
Her beauteous daughter, my beloved wife.
She thinks you very kind who let her go
And join me, when strange rumours flew abroad
And liars call'd me traitor.
   Giovanna.   With my blessing
She went, nor heard (I hope) that hateful name.

         1 entreat] intreat *1846.*

Durazzo, negligently. My cousin Agnes! not one word from you?
Agnes. Charles of Durazzo! God abandons thee
To thy own will: can any gulph lie lower!
Durazzo. 'Twas not my will.
Agnes.   No!
Durazzo.   What I did, I did
To satisfy the people.
Agnes.   Satisfy   20
Ocean and Fire.
Durazzo.   The Church too.
Agnes.   Fire and Ocean
Shall lie together, and shall both pant gorged,
Before the Church be satisfied, if Church
Be that proud purple shapeless thing we see.
Durazzo to Rupert. Show the pope's charter of investiture.
Rupert. 'Tis this. May it please our lady that I read it.
Giovanna to Durazzo. Reasons where there are wrongs but make
   them heavier.
Durazzo to Agnes. When the whole nation cries in agony
Against the sway of Germans, should I halt?
Agnes. No German rules this country; one defends   30
And comforts and adorns it: may he long!
The bravest of his race, the most humane.
Durazzo. Quell'd, fugitive, nor Germany nor France
Afford him aid against us.
Giovanna.   Sir! he hoped
No aid from France.
Agnes.   Does any? What is France?
One flaring lie, reddening the face of Europe.
Durazzo. French is Provenza.
Agnes.   There our arts prevail,
Our race: no lair of tigers is Provenza.
I call that France where mind and soul are French.
Durazzo. Sooner would he have graspt at German arms.   40
Giovanna. God hold them both from Italy for ever!
Durazzo. She shall want neither. The religious call
Blessings upon us in long-drawn processions.
Agnes. Who are the men you please to call religious?
Sword-cutlers to all Majesties on earth,
Drums at the door of every theatre
Where tragedies are acted: that friar knows it.
Rupert. Such is the fruit of letters sown in courts!
Peaches with nettle leaves and thistle crowns!

Upon my faith! kings are unsafe near them.   50
  Durazzo, to Agnes. May-be we scarcely have your sanction, lady?
Am I one?
  Agnes.   No.
  Durazzo.   What am I?
  Agnes.   What! an ingrate.
  Durazzo, scoffingly. Is that to be no king? You may rave on,
Fair cousin Agnes: she who might complain
Absolves me.
  Agnes.   Does the child she fed? the orphan?
The outcast? does he, can he, to himself,
And before us?
  Durazzo.   I, the king, need it not.
  Agnes. All other blind men know that they are blind,
All other helpless feel their helplessness.   59

57 it] misprinted it it 1840.

[ACT II.]   SCENE IV.   UNDER CASTEL-NUOVO.

DURAZZO and RUPERT.

  Rupert. Remarkt you not how pale she turn'd?
  Durazzo.   At what?
  Rupert. I said kings were unsafe. She knew my meaning.
  Durazzo. No man alive believes it: none believed it,
Beside the vulgar, when Andrea died.
  Rupert. Murdered he was.
  Durazzo.   Mysteriously. Some say . .
  Rupert. What do some say?
  Durazzo.   I never heeded them.
I know thee faithful: in this whole affair
I've proved it. He who goes on looking back
Is apt to trip and tumble.   *[Goes.*
  Rupert, alone.   Why this hatred?
Are there no memories of her far more pleasant?   10
I saw her in her childish days: I saw her
When she had cast away her toys, and sate
Sighing in idleness, and wishing more
To fall into her lap; but what? and how?
I saw her in the gardens, stil a child,
So young, she mockt the ladies of the court,
And threw the gravel at them from her slipper,
And ran without if they pursued, but stopt
And lept to kiss the face of an old statue

15 stil] still 1846.   19 lept] leapt 1846.

61

Because it smiled upon her: then would she 20
Shudder at two wrens fighting, shout, and part them.
Next came that age (the lovely seldom pass it)
When books lie open, or, in spite of pressing,
Will open of themselves at some one place.
Lastly, I saw her when the bridal crown
Entwined the regal. Oh! that ne'er these eyes
Had seen it! then, Andrea! thou had'st lived,
My comfort, my support. Divided power
Ill could I brook; how then, how tolerate
Its rude uprooting from the breast that rear'd it! 30
And must I now sweep from me the last blossoms
That lie and wither in the walk of life?
Fancies! . . mere fancies! . . let me cease to waver.
Who would not do as I did? I am more
A man than others, therefor I dare more,
And suffer more. Such is humanity:
I cannot halve it. Superficial men
Have no absorbing passions: shallow seas
Are void of whirlpools. I must on, tho' loath. 39

35 therefor] therefore *1846.*   37 cannot] can not *1846.*

[ACT II.] SCENE V. PALACE-GARDEN.

MAXIMIN *and* AGATHA.

Maximin. Courage! or start and leave me. Sobs indeed!
Pack those up for young girls who want some comfits.
Nay, by my soul, to see grown women sob it,
As thou dost, even wert thou not my sister,
Smites on me here and whets my sword at once.
It maddens me with choler . . for what else
Can shake me so? I feel my eyes on fire.
He shall pay dear for it, the cursed Frate.
Agatha. Why, Maximin, O why didst thou consent
To meet the friar again?
Maximin.   To make him serve thee. 10
Agatha. Poverty rather! want . . even infamy.
Maximin. Did'st thou not pity, would'st not serve, the queen?
Agatha. Oh might I! might I! she alone on earth
Is wretcheder: my soul shall ever bend
Before that sacredest supremacy.
Maximin. Come with me: we will talk about the means.
Agatha. But, be thou calm.

62

FRA RUPERT

Maximin.   A lamb.

                    He little thinks   [*Aside.*
To see the lamb turn round and bite the butcher.

Agatha! Agatha! while I repeat
Thy name again, freshness breathes over me.   20
What is there like it? Why, 'tis like sweet hay
To rest upon after a twelve hour's march,
Clover, with all its flowers, an arm's length deep.

22 hour's] hours' *1846.*

[ACT II.] SCENE VI. NAPLES. PALACE OF BUTELLO.

BUTELLO *and* RUPERT.

Butello reads. We, Urban, by the grace of God . .
Rupert.   Well, well;
That is all phrase and froth; dip in the spoon
A little deeper; we shall come at last
To the sweet solids and the racy wine.
    Butello. Patience, good Frate, patience!
    Rupert.   Now, Butello,
If I cried *patience,* wouldst not thou believe
I meant *delay?* So do not cry it then.
Read on . . about the middle. That will do . .
Pass over *love, solicitude, grief, foresight,*
Paternal or avuncular. Push on . .   10
There . . thereabout.
    Butello.   Lift off thy finger, man,
And let me, in God's name, read what wants reading.
    Rupert. Prythee be speedy . . Where thou seest my name . .
    Butello reads. If that our well-beloved Frate Rupert
Shall, by his influence thereunto directed
By the blest saints above, and the good will
Which the said Frate Rupert ever bore us,
Before the expiration of one month,
So move the heart of Carlo of Durazzo
That the said Carlo do invade and seize . .   20
    Rupert. What would his Holiness have next?
    Butello.   Wait, wait.
Naples, a kingdom held by our permission . .
    Rupert. Ho! is that all? 'Tis done.
    Butello.   Hear me read on.
From those who at this present rule the same . .

63

Rupert. This present is already past. I've won.

Butello. And shall consign a princely fief thereof,
Hereditary, to our foresaid nephew
Gieronimo Butello, We, by power
Wherewith we are invested, will exalt
Our trusty well-beloved Frate Rupert   30
Unto the highest charge our Holy Church
Bestows upon her faithful servitors.

Rupert. Would not one swear those words were all engrossed,
And each particular letter stood bolt-upright,
Captain'd with taller at the column-head?
What marshal'd files! what goodly companies!
And, to crown all, the grand heaven-sent commission
Seal'd half way over with green wax, and stiff
With triple crown, and crucifix below it.
Give me the paper.

    Butello.   Why?

    Rupert, impatient.   Give me the paper.   40

    Butello. His Holiness hath signed it.

    Rupert.   Let me see.

    Butello. Look.

    Rupert.   Nay but give it me.

    Butello.   A piece of paper!

    Rupert. . . Cannot be worth a principality.

    Butello, giving it.   There then.

    Rupert.   What dukedom has the grandest sound?

    Butello. Dukedom! the Pope says principality.

    Rupert. Thou soon shalt blazon.

    Butello.   I relie on you:
Adieu, my lord!

    Rupert.   My prince, adieu!

                   (Alone.) Who knows
If this will better me! Away from court?
No; never. Leave the people? When he leaves it,
The giant is uplifted off the earth   50
And loses all his strength. My foot must press it.
Durazzo, in things near, is shrewd and sighted:
I may not lead him. If I rule no more
This kingdom, yet ere long my tread may sound
Loud in the conclave, and my hand at last
Turn in their golden wards the keys of heaven.

36 marshal'd] marshall'd *1846.*   43 Cannot] Can not *1846.*   46 relie] rely *1846.*

FRA RUPERT

GIOVANNA *and* AGATHA.

Giovanna. Both mind and body in their soundest state
Are always on the verge of a disorder,
And fear encreases it: take courage then.
Agatha. There is an error in the labyrinth
Of woman's life whence never foot returns.
Giovanna. Hath God said that?
Agatha.   O lady! man hath said it.
Giovanna. He built that labyrinth, he led that foot
Into it, and there left it. Shame upon him!
I take thee to my service and my trust.
To love the hateful with prone prudent will   10
Is worse than with fond unsuspiciousness
To fall upon the bosom of the lovely,
The wise who value us, the good who teach us,
The generous who forgive us when we err.
Agatha. Oh! I have no excuse.
Giovanna.   She stands absolved
Before her God who says it as thou sayst it.
I have few questions for thee: go, be happier.
I owe thy brother more than I can pay,
And would, when thou hast leisure, hear what chance
Rais'd up a friend where the ground seem'd so rough.   20
Agatha. Leave me no leisure, I beseech of you:
I would have cares and sorrows not my own
To cover mine from me: I would be questioned,
So please you, I may else be false in part,
Not being what eyes bedim'd with weeping see me.
Giovanna. You come, 'tis rumour'd here, from Hungary.
My infant was torne from me by his uncle
And carried into Hungary.
Agatha.   I saw it.
Giovanna. Saw it! my infant! to have seen my infant,
How blessed! Was it beautiful? strong? smiling?   30
Agatha. It had mild features and soft sun-bright hair,
And seem'd quite happy.
Giovanna.   No, poor thing, it was not;
It often wanted me, I know it did,
And sprang up in the night and cried for me,
As I for it .. at the same hour, no doubt.

3 encreases] increases *1846.*   27 torne] torn *1846.*

It soon soon wasted .. And you saw my child!
I wish you would remember more about him ..
The little he could say you must remember ..
Repeat it me.
    Agatha.   Ah lady! he was gone,
And angels were the first that taught him speech.   40
    Giovanna. Happier than angels ever were before!
    Agatha. He happier too!
    Giovanna.   Ah! not without his mother!
Go, go, go .. There are graves no time can close.

ACT III.

SCENE I. NAPLES. PALACE.

DURAZZO. RUPERT. HERALD. OFFICERS.

    Durazzo. I thought I heard a trumpet. But we reel
After we step from shipboard, and hear trumpets
After we ride from battle. 'Twas one. Hark!
It sounds again. Who enters?
    Officer.   Please your Highness!
A herald claims admittance.
    Durazzo.   Let him in.
    Rupert. Now for disguises; now for masks; steel, silk;
Nothing in these days does but maskery.
Pages talk, sing, ride with you, sleep beside you,
For years: behold-ye! some fine April-day
They spring forth into girls, with their own faces,   10
Tricks, tendernesses .. ne'er a mark of saddle!

             (HERALD *enters.*)
Bacco! this is not one of them, however!
    Durazzo. Well, sir, your message.
    Herald.   Herald from duke Otho,
I bring defiance and demand reply.
    Durazzo. I know duke Otho's courage, and applaud
His wisdom. Tell duke Otho from king Carlo,
I would in his place do the very same:
But, having all I want, assure your lord
I am contented.
    Rupert.   Blessed is content.
    Durazzo. Now, should duke Otho ever catch the reins   20
(For all things upon earth are changeable)
He cannot well refuse the turn he tries,

But will permit me to contend with him
For what at present I propose to keep.
   Herald. If then your Highness should refuse the encounter,
Which never knight, and rarely king, refuses . .
   Durazzo. Hold, sir! All kings are knights. The alternative?
   Herald. None can there be where combat is declined.
He would not urge in words the queen's release,
But burns to win it from a recreant knight.   30
   Durazzo. Did Otho say it?
   Herald.   Standing here his herald,
I have no voice but his.
   Durazzo.   You may have ears:
Hear me then, sir! You know, all know at Naples,
The wife and husband are as near at present
As ever, though the knight and lady not.
She, when she married him, declined his love,
And never had he hers: Taranto won it,
And, when he squandered it, 'twas unretrieved.
   Herald. Is this, sir, for my ears or for my voice?
My voice (it is a man's) will not convey it.   40
   Durazzo, to guards. Escort the herald back with honors due.
                                 to RUPERT.
What think you, my lord bishop of Nocera?
   Rupert. Troublesome times! troublesome times indeed!
My flock, my brethren at Nocera, will,
Must, want me: but how leave my prince, a prey
To tearing factions, godless, kingless men!
   Durazzo. Never mind me, good father!
   Rupert.   Mind not you?
I cannot go; I would not for the world.
   Durazzo. The world is of small worth to holy men.
   Rupert. I will not hence until the storm be past.   50
   Durazzo. After a storm the roads are heavier.
Courage! my good lord bishop! We must speed
And chaunt our *Veni Domine* at Nocera.
   Rupert. Then would your Highness . .
   Durazzo.   Not corporeally,
But, where my bishop is, I am in spirit.   *(Goes.)*
   Rupert, alone. So! this is king . . and wit too! *that's* not kingly.
Can he be ignorant of who I am?
They will show fragments of this sturdy frock,
Whence every thread starts visible, when all

            22, 48 cannot] can not *1846.*

The softer nappery, in its due descent,
Drops from the women, Carlo, to the moths.

[ACT III.] SCENE II. APARTMENT IN THE CASTLE OF MURO.

MAXIMIN *and* AGATHA.

Maximin. How fares thy lady?
Agatha.   As one fares who never
Must see the peopled earth, nor hear its voice
Nor know its sympathy; so fares Giovanna;
But, pure in spirit, rises o'er the racks
Whereof our world is only one vast chamber.
Maximin. Dost thou enjoy the gardens, fields, and forests?
Agatha. Perfectly.
Maximin.   Hast a palfrey?
Agatha.   Had I ever?
Reading and needlework employ the day.
Maximin. Ah! our good mother little knew what pests
Those needles and those books are, to bright eyes;   10
Rivals should recommend them, mothers no.
We will ride out together.
Agatha.   On what horses?
Maximin. One brought me. Are the queen's at grass?
Agatha.   We have none.
Maximin. Thou art hale, Agatha, but how enjoy
Perfectly, as thou sayest, these domains?
Agatha. By looking out at window with the queen.
Maximin. All the day thro'?
Agatha.   I read to her: and then,
If she suspects it tires me, she takes up
The volume, and pretends great interest
Just there, and reads it out.
Maximin.   True history?   20
Agatha. History she throws by.
Maximin.   Then sweet-heart songs,
Adventures?
Agatha.   Some she reads, and over some
Tosses her work, rises, and shuts the cover.
Maximin. I would not shut the song-book. There are others
That show within them gold-and-purple saints,
Heads under arm, eyes upon platter, laughing
At her who carries them and lately wore them.
Agatha. Such are not wanting.

68

FRA RUPERT

Maximin.   Pleasant sights enough!
I would fain see them.
   Agatha.   Quite impossible.
   Maximin. On feast-days?
   Agatha.   All are in her bedroom-closet.   30
   Maximin. So! the best books then must be out of sight,
As all the best things are! What are her pictures?
   Agatha. Chiefly her own lost family, and those
She loved the most in it.
   Maximin.   O for a glimpse!
Tell me at least who are they.
   Agatha.   Good king Robert,
Whose face she often kisses.
   Maximin.   None more worth it?
   Agatha. There are the two Marias: one elate
With merriment, her eyes orbs wing'd with flame;
Long deep and dark the other's, and within
Whose cooler fountains blisfully might bathe   40
A silenter and (haply) purer love.
   Maximin. I should be glad to look at them, but rather
At the kind queen herself.
   Agatha.   That thou mayst do.
   Maximin. When?
   Agatha.   Now; I think; for having heard who 'twas
That warned her of her danger when the duke
Rode in, she wisht to thank thee. Come with me:
I must first enter and announce your name.
   Maximin. I thought you said she knew it. Take your course.

40 blisfully] blissfully 1846.   43 mayst] mayest 1846.

[ACT III.] SCENE III. CHAMBER AT MURO.

GIOVANNA. MAXIMIN. AGATHA.

   Giovanna. Accept my too few thanks, sir, for your zeal. . .
   Maximin. Fine air, my lady queen, in this high tower;
Healthy as Hungary; may you enjoy it
These many days!
   Giovanna, bending. I fancied Hungary
Was moister, leveler, than hereabout.
   Maximin. We have a plain in Hungary on which,
Just in the middle, all of Italy's
You shall pin down nor see them from the sides.
And then what cattle! horse, ox, sheep! God's blessing

Upon hard-working men, like furlough soldiers,   10
And rare sport at the foray, when the Turk
Might seize them if we sent them not to quarters.
Here too seems nothing wanting.   (*Looking round.*)
   Giovanna.   A few friends
Were welcome, could they but return, whose pen
And conversation lighten'd former hours.
   Maximin. Learned ones; ay?
   Giovanna.   The learned came around me.
   Maximin. Whistle, and they are at the barley-corns,
Wing over wing, beak against beak, I warrant.
I knew two holy friars, as holy men
As ever snored in sackcloth after sinning,   20
And they were learned. What now was the upshot?
I should have said one's crucifix was white,
The other's black. They plied mild arguments
In disputation. *Brother*, was the term
At first, then *sir*, then nothing worse than *devil*.
But those fair words, like all fair things, soon dropt.
Fists were held up, grins in the face grew rife,
Teeth (tho' in these one had the better of it
By half a score) were closed like money-boxes
Against the sinner damn'd for poverty.   30
At last the learned and religious men
Fell to it mainly, crucifix in hand,
Until no splinter, ebony or linden,
Was left, of bulk to make a toothpick of.
   Agatha. Brother! such speech is here irreverent.
   Giovanna. Let him speak on: we are not queens all day.
Soldiers are rivals of the hierarchs,
And prone to jealousy, as less at ease,
Less wealthy, and, altho' the props of power,
Less powerful and commanding.
   Maximin.   Never queen   40
Spoke truer. I bear lusty hate to them.
   Agatha. Again? O Maximin! before our princes
We never hate nor love.
   Maximin.   Then, lady, I
Am your worst vassal.
   Giovanna.   How?
   Maximin.   Being taught to hate you .
God pardon me! None but the frockt could teach
So false a creed. But now the heart let loose

FRA RUPERT

Swings quite the other way. Folks say they love
Their princes: sure they must have wrong'd them first.
I turned away mine eyes from your young beauty,
And muttered to my beard, and made it quiver   50
With my hard breathing of hard thoughts: but now
Conspirators shall come in vain against you:
Here is the sill they tread upon who enter.   (*Striking his breast.*)

[ACT III.] SCENE IV: RUPERT'S CLOISTER.

Rupert, alone. Fealty sworn, should I retract so soon?
I will live quiet . . no more crimes for me . .
When this is fairly over . . for a crime
It surely is . . albeit much holier men
Have done much worse and died in odor after.
They were spare men, and had poor appetites,
And wanted little sleep. 'Twont do with me.
Beside, I must get over this bad habit
Of talking to myself. One day or other
Some fool may read me, mark me, and do hurt.   10
And furthermore . . when highest dignities
Invest us, what is there to think about?
What need for cleverness, wit, circumspection,
Or harm to any . . who keep still, submiss,
And brush not in attempting to pass by.

1 Fealty] Fëalty *1846.*   5 died] lived *1840 (corr. in errata).*   odor] odour *1846*

[ACT III.] SCENE V.

STEPHEN [STOURDZA] *enters.*

So, Stephen! we Hungarians are sent off.
Stephen. Your Reverence is made bishop, we hear say:
As for all us . .
Rupert.   Lupins . . . when times are good.
Ah! thou hast bowels; thou canst pity others.
Stephen. I can myself.
Rupert.   I all my countrymen.
I have been lately in that happy realm
Our native land.
                    (*whispers.*) Her kings should govern here.
Stephen. And everywhere. What loyal subject doubts
His prince's right over all other princes?
Rupert. Here are sad discontents. The prince Butello,   10
Nephew of His Beatitude the Pope,

Cannot yet touch his principality.
Durazzo, our sharp king, snatches it back,
Altho' the kingdom was bestowed on him
Under this compact.
    Stephen.   He will bring down bull
And thunder on his crown. The pope's own nephew!
    Rupert. No less a man.
    Stephen.   If there 's pope's blood in him
He wont stand robbery.
    Rupert.   We owe obedience
To kings . . unless a higher authority
Dissolves it.
    Stephen.   Doubtless: but what kings? our own   20
Say I.
    Rupert. O Stephen! say it, say it softly.
Few ears can open and can close like mine.
    Stephen, aside. Ah! how good men all over are maligned!
    Rupert. I would not trust another soul on earth . .
But others must be trusted. Lucky they
Who first bring over to right ways the brave,
First climb the pole and strip the garland off
With all its gold about it. Then what shouts!
What hugs! what offers! dowers, in chests, in farms . .
Ah! these are worldly things too fondly prized!   30
But there are what lie deeper; the true praise
Of loyalty, of sanctity.
    Stephen, pondering. 'Tis pleasant
To look into warm chest with well-wrought hinges
That turn half-yearly. Pleasant too are farms
When harvest-moons hang over them, and wanes
Jolt in the iron-tinged rut, and the white ox
Is call'd by name, and patted ere pull'd on.
    Rupert. These are all thine. I have lived many days
And never known that man unprosperous
Who served our holy church in high emprize.   40
    Stephen. If so, I wish I could.
    Rupert.   Wish we had kings
Who keep their words like ours of Hungary.
    Stephen. Just.
    Rupert.   I have half a mind to let Elizabeth
Know what a zealous subject, what a brave,
Her daughter has at Naples.
                  12 Cannot] Can not *1846.*   his] this *1846.*

Stephen. Would she give me
(For thanks in these hard times are windy) money?
Think you?
    Rupert. Don't squander all away. Few know
Its power, its privilege. It dubs the noble,
It raises from the dust the man as light,
It turns frowns into smiles, it makes the breath   50
Of sore decrepitude breathe fresh as morn
Into maternal ear and virgin breast.
    Stephen. Is that all it can do? I see much farther.
I see full twenty hens upon the perch,
I see fat cheese moist as a charnel-house,
I see hogs' snouts under the door, I see
Flitches of bacon in the rack above.
    Rupert. Rational sights! fair hopes! unguilty wishes!
I am resolved: I can refrain no longer:
Thou art the man for prince to rest upon,   60
The plain, sound, sensible, straitforward man,
No courtier . . or not much of one . . but fit
To show courts what they should be. Hide this letter.
Mind! if thou losest it, or let'st an eye
Glance on it, I may want the power again
To serve thee: thou art ruin'd. The new king
Might chide and chafe should Rupert ask another
To forward any suit he would prefer
For friend or kindred. Since thou must return
To Hungary, thou shalt not go ill-fed.   70
'Tis to the queen's confessor; look at it;
Now put it up; now, godson of our Saint!
Take this poor purse, and, honest soul! this blessing.
Guides thou shalt have all the first day, and rules
How to go forward on the road: so speed thee!

ACT IV.

SCENE I. CASTLE OF MURO.

GIOVANNA. AGATHA.

Giovanna. Long have we lived in one imprisonment;
Our tears have darkened many a thread about
Each distaff, at the whitening half-spent fire
On winter-night; many a one when deep purple
Cloath'd yonder mountain after summer-day,
And one sole bird was singing, sad though free.

Death, like all others, hath forgotten me,
And grief, methinks, now growing old, grows lighter.
   Agatha. To see you smile amid your grief, consoles me.
   Giovanna. I never wanted confidence in you,   10
Yet never have I opened my full mind,
Keeping some thoughts secreted, altho' bent
To draw them out before you. They have lain
Like letters which, however long desired,
We cover with the hand upon the table
And dare not open.
   Agatha.   If relief there be,
Why pause? if not, why blame your diffidence?
   Giovanna. Fostered too fondly, I shot up too tall
In happiness: it wasted soon. Taranto
Had my first love; Andrea my first vow,   20
And warm affection, which shuts out sometimes
Love, rather than embraces it. To lose him
Pained me, God knows! and worse (so lost!) than all
The wild reports Hungarians spread about me.
My first admirer was my first avenger.
He, laying at my feet his conquering sword,
Withdrew. Two years elapst, he urged the dangers
That stil encompast me; recall'd our walks,
Our studies, our reproofs for idling, smiled
By (O kind man!) the granfather of both.   30
I bade him hope. Hope springs up at that word
And disappears; Love, radiant Love, alights.
Taranto was my joy; my heart was full:
Alas! how little can the full heart spare!
I paus'd .. because I ill might utter it ..
In time he turn'd his fancies to another.
Wretchedest of the wretched was I now;
But gentle tones much comforted my anguish,
Until they ended; then loud throbs confused
The treasured words; then heavy sleep opprest me.   40
I was ashamed .. I *am* ashamed .. yet (am I
Unwomanly to own it?) when he loved
One only, I was driven to despair;
When more .. *Adieu Taranto!* cried my heart
And almost sank thro' sorrow into peace.
O that fresh crimes in him should solace me!
My life of love was over, when his spirit

   28 stil] still *1846.*   30 granfather] grandfather *1846.*   34 spare!] spare? *1846.*

FRA RUPERT

Flew from my lips, and carried my forgiveness
On high, for Heaven's.
                        Wars burst forth again;
He who defended me from their assaults   50
Saw in me what to love, but whom to love
He found not in me.
                        "*If my confidence,
My gratitude,*" said I, "*suffice thee, Otho,
Here is my hand.*"
                        He took it, and he wept.
Brave man! and let me also weep for thee!
    Agatha. Not beauteous youth enrobed in royal purple
And bright with early hope, have moved you so.
    Giovanna. Record not either; let me dwell on Otho;
The thoughts of him sink deeper in my pillow;
His valiant heart and true one bleeds for me.   60

[ACT IV.] SCENE II. COURT-YARD OF MURO.

MAXIMIN *and* STEPHEN [STOURDZA].

Stephen. Maximin! art thou close?
Maximin.   Yea, close enough,
Altho I have the whole court-yard to cool in.
    Stephen. I meant not that.
    Maximin.   A baton to a pike
Thou didst not; else thou hadst not spoken it.
    Stephen. Some folks think better of my understanding.
    Maximin. None of thy heart: give me thy fist then, Stephen.
    Stephen. That sets all right.
    Maximin.   What brought thee hither?
    Stephen.   What?
    Maximin. Hast secrets?
    Stephen.   None worth knowing.
    Maximin.   No man has:
They never did one any good.
    Stephen.   They may.
Maximin! hast commands for Hungary?   10
    Maximin. For Hungary?
    Stephen.   What! is there no such place?
    Maximin. No, by my soul! nor ever will for me.
Were not my sister here about her duty,
I could knock out my brains against the wall
To think of Hungary.
            9 one any] anyone *1846.*

75

Stephen. Yet thou hast there
No croft, no homestead, pullet, chick.
   Maximin. Hast thou?
   Stephen. I am a man at last. Wert thou but one!
   Maximin. Stephen, we will not quarrel.
   Stephen. I am rich
I meant to say.
   Maximin. So far so well: however, 20
Not some bold thief who stands some ages back
(Tho' better there than nearer) nor some bolder
Who twists God's word and overturns his scales,
Nor steel, nor soil in any quantity,
Nor gold, whose chain encompasses the globe,
Nor even courage, Stephen, is sufficient
To make a man: one breath on Woman's wrongs,
Lifting the heart, does that.
   Stephen. And other things.
   Maximin. Chick, pullet, homestead, croft; are these our makers?
   Stephen. I have them in this lining, one and all.
   Maximin, suspecting. Stephen! I could show thee the duplicate 30
In the same hand. He who fixt me at Muro
Will fix thee too in some such place as firmly.
What! hast no heart for castles? art low-minded?
How! with chick, pullet, homestead, croft? Sit down:
Thou didst not sweat so after all thy walk
As thou dost now. What ails thee, man?
   Stephen. What ails me!
Nothing.
   Maximin. But did Fra Rupert, did he truly
Clap thee up here? Cleverly done! Don't blame him.
   Stephen. Blame him! if friar he were not, and moreover
The tadpole of a bishop, by the martyr! 40
I would run back and grapple with his weazon.
   Maximin. He is too cunning for us simple men.
   Stephen. For thee, it seems, he has been . . but for me,
I, man or child, was never yet out-witted.
   Maximin. Ah! we all think so; yet all are, by weaker.
And now about the letter.
   Stephen. Thee he trusted;
I know he did; show me the duplicate.
   Maximin. Duplicates are not written first nor shown first.
How many men art good against?
   Stephen. One only.

Maximin. Then five might overmaster thee and gag thee.　　50
And five are ready in the Appennines;
If I knew where exactly, I would tell thee.
　Stephen. A fiend of hell in frock!
　Maximin.　　　　　　No, not so bad:
He, without blame or danger on thy part,
Shall build thy fortune.
　Stephen.　　　　He? I scorn the thief . .
Beside . . he would not.
　Maximin.　　　　Would or not, he shall.　　(*Stephen hesitates.*)
Am I an honest man?
　Stephen.　　　Why! as men go.
　Maximin. Give me the letter then, and, on my life,
It shall do more and better for thee much
Than placed in any other hands but mine.　　　　60
　　　　　　(*An Officer passes.*)
Ho! captain! see an honest man at last,
　　　　　(*Giving him the letter.*)
And you the very man he came about.
　Stephen, threatening Maximin. Traitor!
　Maximin.　　　　　　A traitor, with a vengeance, is he.
　Stephen. Hangman!
　Maximin.　　　　Thou needst not call him; he will come
Presently.　　　　　　　　(*To the Officer.*)
　　　　This poor hind hath saved the prince
From insurrection, from invasion. Read.
　　　　　　(*Officer reads.*)
The royal favour will shine warm upon
One friend of mine.
　Officer.　　　Be sure: he will be made.
'Tis but our service . . We must not complain . .
Tho there are things, of late, which soldier's crops　　70
Swell high against. We captains . .
　Maximin.　　　　　　Ay, we captains!.
　Officer. I must be gone to Naples; so must thou
My gallant grey-coat.　　　　(*Goes out.*)
　Maximin.　　　　Tell me how thou camest
To Muro, of all places in the world,
It lies so wide of any road to Hungary.
　Stephen. Fra Rupert bade me follow at mid-day

51 Appennines] Apennines *1846.* 63 *threatening*] *threating* 1840 (*mispr.*) 70 soldier's] soldiers' *1846.*

77

A band of holy mendicants, due south,
To baffle all suspicion: the next morn
To cross the mountains on my left, and turn
Northward, and then take boat by Pesaro.   80
While they were stretcht along the levelest tiles
In the best chamber . . being mendicants . .
Each on his sheepskin . . for they love soft lying . .
Of grand farm-house; and while nighthawk and grillo
Fought for it which should sing them first to sleep;
And while aside them, in brass pot unfathomed,
The rich goat-whey was ripening for next breakfast,
I thought of my far sheep and my near friend;
My near friend first; and so, by luck, here am I.
    Maximin. But how didst dream that thou shouldst find me here? 90
    Stephen. Who, in the Virgin's name, should first step up,
After I bade the mendicants good-bye,
Who but Augustin!   Much about our country,
Mops, wakes, fairs, may-poles, gipsey-girls, and fortunes,
When suddenly, as one that knew them all,
He whispered thou wert at this Muro here,
Some twenty miles, or near upon it, off.
I must fain see thee. After three hour's walk
I ask the distance: twenty-five miles scant.
At night I supt and slept with an old shepherd: 100
His dog soon crope betwixt us; so genteely,
I should have never known it, but his nose
Was cold against my ear, and, when I turn'd,
A snag or two was at it . . without harm.
Morning blew sharp upon us from the hills.
How far are we from Muro, my good man?
Said I, and dipt my olive in the salt.
"*Scant thirty miles.*" Let never man believe
In luck! I overturned the salt, alert
To hurry on; yet here thou seest me, rich . .   110
Sleeping six hours in winter, five in summer.
    Maximin, pondering. Augustin told thee I was here! Augustin!
How should he know? One only knew beside
The friar: he never would have told: she told him.
                          (*Walks about impatiently.*)
Augustin has smooth locks and fresh complexion,
And heels for dance and voice for dulcimer,
Rare articles at finding secrets out:
      94 gipsey-girls] gipsy-girls *1846.*   98 hour's] hours' *1846.*

But, with thy slanting face, and arm curl'd round
The inside canework of a padded chair,
And leg oblique slid negligently under,   120
If thou wouldst keep them nicely in repair
Ferret no more my secrets out, Augustin!
 Officer (returned). Ready? my dapple grey! ready for Naples?
 Stephen. Not without Maximin. By his advice
I call'd you in to help us: he shall have
His share.
 Maximin. When our blythe king sniffs up the wind
And sees the clouds roll mainly from the north,
And finds Giovanna's enemies advance,
He may be kinder to her: so, commander,
If you believe I did my duty now,   130
Let me confirm the letter you convey.
 Officer. Canst thou add aught?
 Maximin.   Much, were there much required.
 Officer. Come then along: we will drink gold tomorrow.

[ACT IV.] SCENE III. MONASTERY GARDEN.

 Rupert, alone. I must have peace: I cannot live without it:
Only few years (who knows) may yet remain.
They shall not hurt the queen: in part the harm
Would be my doing. But then Maximin . .
He too . . yet why not let him die in battle?
Battles there will be: kings are all tenacious
Of their king-life: Italians are astute,
Hungarians valiant: two stout swords must clash
Before one break.
    That Agatha, that Agatha
Troubles me most of all! Suppose she comes   10
Into my very palace at Nocera,
And tells the people what the bishop did!
Never was blow cruel like this since Herod.
Giovanna must then live, if for her sake
Alone; for such her tenderness, her truth,
She 'll not abandon her while life remains.

GARDEN] GARDENS *1846.* 1 cannot] can not *1846.* 8 Hungarians]
Hugarians *1840 (misp.).*

DRAMAS AND DRAMATIC SCENES

[ACT IV.] SCENE IV. PALACE IN NAPLES.

DURAZZO. CHANCELLOR. PRIVY-COUNSELLORS.

Durazzo. Speak, my lord chancellor: you now have redd
The letter thro': can doubt remain upon it?

(Chancellor shakes his head.)

Gentlemen! you have heard it: what think you?

First Counsellor. Traiterous, if there be treason.

Second Counsellor. Sentence then.

Chancellor. Powerful is Rupert: many think him saintly,
All know him wise and wary: he has friends
In every house, and most among the women.
Such men are dangerous to impeach: beside,
Being now bishop . .

Durazzo. Not quite yet: appointed.
Not seated.

Chancellor. This quite changes the whole aspect.   10
Once bearing that high dignity, once throned . .

Durazzo. I like no thrones that narrow mine too much,
And wonder wherefor clergymen should mount them.

Chancellor. However, sir, since such hath been the custom
From barbarous times . .

Durazzo. Til times herein as barbarous . .

Chancellor. . . We must observe the usage of the realm
And keep our hands from touching things held sacred.
Few days ago for lighter crimes the friar
Might have been punisht with severity.

First Counsellor. Even now, altho' his legs begin to sprout   20
With scarlet plumage, we may crop his crest;
But better on the beam than in the yard.

Third Counsellor. It would put by much bickering.

Fourth Counsellor. There are many
Expectants, holy men, who would condemn
In any court ecclesiastical
Appeal so manifest to foren force,
And strip him to the skin to wash him clean.

Fifth Counsellor. And there are civil laws which tread on velvet
And leave no scandal when they pass the door;
Modest and mild and beautifully drest,   30
And void of all loquacity, all pomp,

1 redd] read *1846*.   4 Traiterous] Traitorous *1846*.   10 This quite] No?
This *1846*.   13 wherefor] wherefore *1846*.   15 Til] Till *1846*.   26 foren]
foreign *1846*.

80

They, should you ask them what they are, reply
We are not laws; we are prerogatives.
    Carlo. Paoluccio! wit may give the best advice.
Far be from me all violence. If the criminal
Be strong and boisterous, the ecclesiastical
Craving and crafty, swift or slow at pleasure,
At least our civil laws are excellent,
And what you call prerogatives are civil.
    Paoluccio. I class them so.
    Many at once.   They are the best of all.   40
    Carlo. I will pursue this counsel.
                  You may rise.

ACT V.

SCENE I. CASTLE OF MURO.

GIOVANNA. AGATHA. OTHO. OFFICERS.

    Giovanna. What shouts are those? whose voice above them all,
Above the neighing horse and trumpet's clang,
Calls to the rescue? Can I doubt? . .
                    My Otho!
My Otho! rush not rashly into fight,
Thou canst not free me.
    Agatha.   He has beat them off . .
He enters.
    Officer.   Yes, he enters.
    Otho, wounded mortally.   Take the ransom . .
'Tis small . . 'tis only one worne life . . and loose her.
    Giovanna. Not from thy neck, my Otho, while thou livest,
Or while I live.
    Otho.   Giovanna hath embraced me . .
I now have lived . . life should be over now.   10
    Officer. His breath is gone: bear him away: the king
May have commands for her.   *(Points to the queen, who swoons.)*
    Agatha.   My queen! my queen!
My friend! my comforter! Oh! *that* no more.   [*Falls.*

    7 worne] worn *1846.*   12 *stage direction comes in* 1846 *after* king, *l.* 11.

[ACT V.] SCENE II. PALACE. NAPLES.

MARGARITA. DURAZZO.

    Margarita. I cannot see what mighty things indeed
My aunt Giovanna ever did for me,
Can you?
        1 cannot] can not *1846.*

Durazzo.   They long are over, if she did.
Margarita. Beside . .
Durazzo.   Now what beside?
Margarita.   I had almost
Said such a foolish thing!
Durazzo.   You! Margarita!
Margarita. I was about to say she did no more
For me than you. If she loved *me*, she loved me
Because she loved my mother, her own sister;
Where is the wonder? where the merit?
Durazzo.   None.
Margarita. She even loved another sister, her   10
Whom people call'd *Fiammetta;* God knows why ;
No Christian name, nought Christian-like about it.
She was the one of Sicily, who fancied
(O shame upon her) somebody a writer.
Durazzo. What writer?
Margarita.   Is not that enough? a writer!
Durazzo. There is not much to thank her for, if all
Partake of her affection, even those
Who sink so low.
Margarita.   She played with *you* the most;
Perhaps because she thought you like her child.
She did show pleasure when she fondled *me;*   20
But 'twas not to make *me* the happier,
Altho' it did so, but herself, herself.
Yet, Carlo, would you think it! there are times
When I am ready to desire of you
That you would let her out of such a den
At Muro.
Durazzo. Had you mentioned it before,
As wishing it . . why, then indeed . .
Margarita.   So, then
You would have let her out? how very kind!
Durazzo. If we could have persuaded her to go.
Margarita. Persuaded her? what! out of prison?
Durazzo.   Do not   30
Term it so harshly: who can bear to hear
Of prisons?
Margarita. Is the tower indeed not lockt
Nor bolted?
Durazzo.   People would run into it

14 somebody a] somebody   a *1846.*   27 So, then] So, then, *1846.*

And trouble her devotions. At this time
She needs them most particularly.
    Margarita.   Why?
    Durazzo. Her health declines.
    Margarita.   Is she in danger?
    Durazzo.   Some.
    Margarita. Imminent?
    Durazzo.   There are fears.
    Margarita.   About her life?
    Durazzo. Men shake their heads.
    Margarita.   O Carlo! O my Carlo!
I have . . (will God forgive me?) been ungrateful.
And all this time! . . when but one moment of it . .   40
My hand in her's, or her's upon my head . .
    Durazzo. Hush! Margarita! thou'rt a queen: be calm,
And worthy of the station we enjoy.   (*Leads her out.*)

    41 her's . . . her's] hers . . . hers *1846.*   *After l.* 43 *Leads*] *He leads 1846.*

[ACT V.] SCENE III. PALACE. NAPLES.

HIGH STEWARD. CHAMBERLAIN. CHANCELLOR. DURAZZO.

    Chamberlain. Wary and slow is this our chancellor,
Where title-deeds are fluttering in suspense;
The peril'd life and honor of his queen
He passes as he would a wretch in chains
On the road-side, saying, *So ! there thou art !*
    Lord High Steward. We want such men's religion, their sound sense,
Coolness, deliberation, ponderous front,
Broad and dark eyebrow. Much of dignity
Reverence and awe, build on these crags alone.
    Lord Chamberlain. Ye have them all in one. I hear his foot: 10
The king steps lighter: both advance.
    Lord High Steward.   Who come
Behind? for there are many.

        (*Durazzo, Chancellor, Counsellors, enter.*)

    Durazzo.   Take your seats.
Gentlemen! ye have heard with indignation
The rash attempt against my peace and yours,
Made by the Suabian, husband of Giovanna.
    Lord Chamberlain. We hear, by Heaven's protection of your High-
        ness,
It fail'd.

    3 peril'd] perill'd *1846.*

Lord High Steward.   And that he fell in the attempt.

Durazzo. Desperate, he cut his way, tho' wounded, thro'
My bravest troops, but could not force the gate;
Horsemen are weak at walls nine fathoms high;   20
He had scarce twenty with him.

Chancellor.   There he paid
His forfeit life, declared already traitor.

Durazzo. On this we are not met, but to deliberate
On the state's safety. My lord chancellor,
Is the queen guilty?

Chancellor starts.   We must try her first,
Privately; then decide.

Durazzo.   Yea, privately;
So pleaseth me. Take then your secretaries
And question her; decorously, humanely.

[ACT V.] SCENE IV. CASTLE OF MURO.

GIOVANNA. CHANCELLOR. HIGH STEWARD. CHAMBERLAIN.
SECRETARIES.

Chancellor. Lady! we have heard all, and only ask
(For the realm's weal) your Highness will vouchsafe
To sign this parchment.

Giovanna, taking it.   What contains it?

Chancellor.   Peace.

Giovanna. I then would sign it with my blood; but blood
Running from royal veins never sign'd peace.   (*Reads.*)
It seems I am required to abdicate
In favor of duke Carlo of Durazzo.

Chancellor. Even so.

Giovanna, to the others. To you I turn me, gentlemen!
If ever you are told that I admitted
His unjust claims, if ever you behold   10
Sign'd, as you fancy, by my hand the parchment
That waves our kingdom from its rightful heir,
Believe it not: only believe these tears,
Of which no false one ever fell from me
Among the many 'twas my fate to shed.
I want not yours; they come too late, my friends;
Farewell then! You may live and serve your country;
These walls are mine, and nothing now beyond.

                 12 waves] waives *1846*.

84

FRA RUPERT

MAXIMIN. STEPHEN.

Maximin. Among the idle and the fortunate
Never drops one but catafalc and canopy
Are ready for him: organ raves above,
And songsters wring their hands and push dull rhymes
Into dull ears that worse than wax hath slopt,
And cherubs puff their cheeks and cry half-split
With striding so across his monument.
Name me one honest man for whom such plays
Were ever acted.
     They will ne'er lay Otho
With kindred clay! no helm, no boot beside   10
His hurried bier! no stamp of stately soldier
Angry with grief and swearing hot revenge,
Until even the paid priest turns round and winks.
I will away: sick, weary . .
      (Stephen enters.)
Stephen.   Hast thou heard
The saddest thing?
Maximin.   Heard it? committed it,
Say rather. But for thee and thy curst gold,
Which, like magician's, turns to dust, I trow,
I had receiv'd him in the gate, and brought
The treasure of his soul before his eyes:
He had not closed them so.
Stephen.   Worst of it all   20
Is the queen's death.
Maximin.   The queen's?
Stephen.   They stifled her
With her own pillow.
Maximin.   Who says that?
Stephen.   The man
Runs wild who did it, through the streets, and howls it,
Then imitates her voice, and softly sobs
Lay me in Santa Chiara.

MAXIMIN. DURAZZO.

Maximin.   Gallant prince!
Conqueror of more than men, of more than heroes!
What may that soldier merit who deserts
His post, and lets the enemy to the tent?

85

Durazzo. Death is the sentence.
Maximin.   Sign that sentence then.
I shall be found beside a new-made grave
In Santa Chiara.
Durazzo.   Art thou mad?
Maximin.   I shall be
If you delay.
Durazzo, to guards. See this man into Hungary.

[ACT V.] SCENE VII. NAPLES. MONASTERY GARDEN.

RUPERT, *alone.*

There are some pleasures serious men sigh over,
And there are others maniacs hug in chains:
I wonder what they are: I would exchange
All mine for either, all that e'er were mine.
I have been sadly treated my whole life,
Cruelly slighted, shamefully maligned:
And this too will be laid upon my shoulders.
If men are witty, all the wit of others
Bespangles them; if criminal, all crimes
Are shoveled to their doors.
                  God knows how truly   10
I wisht her life; not her imprisonment
More truly. Maximin and Agatha
In the queen's life would never have come forth.
  Men of late years have handled me so roughly,
I am become less gentle than I was.
Derision, scoffs and scorns, must be rebuft,
Or we can do no good in act or counsel.
Respect is needful, is our air, our day,
'Tis in the sight of men we see ourselves,
Without it we are dark and halt and speechless.   20
Religion in respect and power hath being,
And perishes without them. Power I hold:
Why shun men's looks? why my own thoughts? afraid?
No, I am not afraid: but phantasies
Long dwelt on let us thro'.
                  If I do quail,
'Tis not the mind, the spirit; 'tis the body.
  A Monk, entering. Father! I come from Muro, where a woman
(Sickly before) for days refused all food,
And now is dead.

         23 thoughts? afraid?] thoughts? . . afraid *1846.*

FRA RUPERT

Rupert.   What is her name?
Monk.   One Agatha.
Rupert. Did she receive the holy Sacrament?   30
Monk. You must have known she did, else why such joy?
She would receive nought else.
Rupert.   Then she is safe.
Monk. We trust in God she is: yet she herself
Had pious doubt.
Rupert.   Of what was her discourse?
Monk. Her mind, ere she departed, wandered from her.
Rupert. What did she talk about? dost hear?
Monk.   She said,
Rupert, if he could see me, might be . . .
Rupert.   What?
Monk. Her mind, observe, was wandering.
Rupert.   Thine is too.
Tell me the very word she uttered.
Monk.   Saved.
Blessings upon her! your uplifted hands   40
And radiant brow announce her present bliss.
Rupert. Said she no more?
Monk.   *Since he 's not here, take these,*
And let the friar and his brotherhood
Say masses for my soul: it may do good
To theirs no less.
          I stoopt the holy taper,
And through her fingers and her palm could see
That she held something: she had given it
But it dropt out of them: this crucifix,
From which the square set jewels were removed,
And this broad golden piece, with its long chain   50
Of soft dark hair, like our late queen Giovanna's.
Rupert. Her medal . . *anno primo* . . All goes right.
Monk. Your blessing!
Rupert.   Take it, prythee, and begone.   (*Monk goes.*)
Nothing has hurt me: none have seen me. None?
Ye saints of heaven! hath ever prayer been mist?
Penance, tho' hard, been ever unperform'd?
Why do ye then abandon me? like one
Whom in your wrath ye hurl aside; like one
Scathed by those lightenings which God's sleepless eye
Smites earth with, and which devils underneath,   60

55 mist] miss'd 1846.   59 lightenings] lightnings *1846*.

Feeling it in the abysses of the abyss,
Rejoice was not for them.
                  Repent I did ..
Even of Agatha I did repent.
I did repent the noble friends had fallen.
Could they not have been wiser, and escaped,
By curbing evil passions, pride, distrust,
Defiance? It was wrong in them: in me
'Twas not quite well: 'twas harsh, 'twas merciless:
Andrea had not done it: wrong'd, betray'd,
Andrea had not done it.
                Have my words   70
Sorcery in them? do they wake the dead?
Hide thy pale face, dear boy! hide from my sight
Those two dark drops that stain thy scanty beard,
Hide those two eyes that start so! Curse me, kill me;
'Twere mercy, 'twere compassion, not revenge;
Justice, the echo of God's voice, cries *More!*
I can endure all else.
              I will arise,
Push off this rack that rends me, rush before him
And ask him why he made me what I am.

Enter Officers.

First Officer. Traitor! the king hath traced all thy devices.   80
Rupert. Without them he had ne'er been what ye style him.
Second Officer. Avowest thou thy perfidy?
Rupert.   And his.
Third Officer. Murderer! thou shalt confess.
Rupert.   'Twere royal bounty.
Third Officer. And die.
Rupert.   'Twere more than royal.
First Officer.   Come thy way.
Rupert. My way? my way? .. I've travel'd it enough,
With or without thee I will take another.
Second Officer. Whither?
Rupert points to the window. Look yonder! There it lies.
                                (Stabs himself.)
                                Andrea!

First Officer, after a pause. Merciful God! end thus his many crimes?
Third Officer, after a pause. What moans and piteous wailings from
    the street!

        85 travel'd] travell'd *1846.* 87 Whither?] Whither! *1846.*

Second Officer. Can they arise for him so suddenly? 90
First Officer. There are too many. None hath told the deed
Beyond this spot, none seen it.
Third Officer. Now you hear
Distinctly; if distinctly may be heard
The wail of thousands.
Second Officer. Their queen's name they cry . .
Third Officer. With blessings.
First Officer. Now, at last, ye know Giovanna;
And now will Rupert too be known, tho' late.

THE END.

THE SIEGE OF ANCONA

[Published in 1846; reprinted 1876.]

No event in the history of Italy, including the Roman, is at once so tragical and so glorious as the Siege of Ancona; nor shall we find at any period of it, two contemporary characters so admirable for disinterested valour and prompt humanity, as William degli Adelardi of Marchesella, and the Countess of Bertinoro. The names of those who sustained the siege are, for the most-part, forgotten: but Muratori has inserted in his imperishable work the narratives of contemporary and nearly contemporary authors; and Sismondi has rendered many of the facts more generally known.—*Hist. des Repub. Ital.*, tome ii. ch. xi.

MALE CHARACTERS.

THE CONSUL OF ANCONA.
[*Christian*] THE ARCHBISHOP OF MENTZ [*ob.* 1153].
THE BISHOP OF ANCONA.
ANTONIO STAMURA.
FATHER JOHN.
MINUZZI.

COSTANZIO.
CORRADO, *brother of Costanzio.*
PAOLUCCI, *formerly Consul.*
MARCHESELLA [*Guglielmo degli Adelardi ob. 1183*].
Herald, Senators, Officers, Priests, People.

FEMALE CHARACTERS.

ERMINIA, *the Consul's daughter.*
NINA, *her companion.*
ANGELICA, *mother of Antonio Stamura.*
[The Lady] MALASPINA.

COUNTESS OF BERTINORO [*Aldruda degli Frangipanni.*]
MARIA, *attendant on Erminia.*

[DATE 1174]

ACT I. SCENE I.

On the steps of the cathedral, commanding a view of the country. Many of all ages are leaving the church and looking at the approach of the Archbishop, just beyond the walls, descending the hill.

Erminia. Nina! see what our matin prayers have brought us.
O what a sight! The youth and maidens fly,

Introduction. Not a quotation but Landor's synopsis, with comment, of Sismondi's story of the siege. The reference (here corrected) is misprinted, *1846*, tome xi. ch. i. For *De obsidione Anconæ* by Boncompagnus Fiorentinus see Muratori, *Rerum Italic. Script.*, vol. xvi. [W.]

CHARACTERS. *Words within brackets not in original text.* Clovio Fizzarelli (*Act II, Sc.* 5) is not named here. [W.]

MARIA [in List of Characters] *mispr.* MARCA *in 1846.*

Some to the city, others up the hills,
With the fresh tale each for the one loved best.
   Nina. They are afraid to meet so many horses;
I would not scud away so, were I there,
Would you?
   Erminia. My dress would show the dust; or else . .
I run to tell my father: go, tell yours.

[ACT I.] SCENE II. CONSUL'S HOUSE.

CONSUL *and* ERMINIA.

   Erminia. Father! why are not all the bells set ringing?
   Consul. What should the bells be ringing for to-day?
   Erminia. Such a procession comes along the road
As never was: some bishop at the head:
And what a horse is under him! and what
Beautiful boys . . they really are but boys,
Dear father . . hold the bridle on each side!
Scarlet and gold about their surplices,
And waving hair; not like church servitors,
But princes' sons. I would give all the world   10
To see their faces . . not quite all the world . .
For who would care about boys' faces, father?
Beside, they are too distant, very far.
   Consul. Art thou gone wild, Erminia?
   Erminia.   Come and see.
   Consul (*Listening, and rising*). What means this tumult?

Senators *enter*.

Consul! we are lost.

   Consul. How so?
   First Senator.   The archbishop comes, from Barbarossa,
Against the city.
   Consul.   What archbishop comes?
   Second Senator. Of Mentz.
   Consul.   Then close the gates, and man the walls,
And hurl defiance on him. Bring my robe,
Erminia! I will question this proud prelate.   20
Gasparo, lift my armour from the wall
In readiness.
   Officer.   A herald, sir, claims entrance.

Herald *enters*.

   Consul. What would your master with his perfidy?
   Herald. My master is the emperor and king.

THE SIEGE OF ANCONA

Consul. The more perfidious. Binds him not his oath
To succour Italy? Is slavery succour?
Tell the false priest thou comest from, that priest
Who took the name of *Christian* at the font,
'Twere well he held not in such mockery
The blessed one he bears it from. But wealth   30
And power put Wisdom's eyes out, lest she rule.
   Herald. Sir Consul! if the archbishop never preaches,
Pray why should you? It ill becomes my office
To bandy words: mine is but to repeat
The words of others: and their words are these:
"The people of Ancona must resign
Their lawless independence, and submit
To Frederic, our emperor and king."
   Consul. Brief is the speech: and brief is the reply.
The people of Ancona will maintain   40
Their lawful independence, and submit
No tittle, sir, to emperor or king.
   Herald. Is this the final answer?
   Consul.   Lead him forth.
   Officer (Enters). Sir! ere you hasten to the walls, look once
Toward the harbour.
   Consul.   Gracious Heaven! What sails
Are those? Venetian?
   Officer.   Yes; and they take soundings.
   Consul. Venice against us? Freedom's first-born child,
After the deluge that drown'd Italy.
Alas! the free are free but for themselves;
They hate all others for it. The first murderer   50
(Their patron) slew his brother. Thus would they.   [*To the* Officer.
Merluccio! hasten, man! call back again
Our mariners to leave the battlements
And guard their sisters and their mothers here.
   Officer. Mothers and sisters follow'd them, to bring
Munition up the towers.
   Consul.   Bid them return:
The beach is open: thither is my road
Until more hands arrive.
   Messenger (Enters).   Sir! they weigh down
Machines for storming.
   Consul.   Go thou, tell Campiglio
To intercept them, if he can, before   60
They join the Germans on the hills above.

Erminia. O father! here are none beside ourselves:
And those few people hauling in the boats
Can help us little; they are so afraid.
    Consul. Think not they are afraid because they pull
The oars with desperate strength and dissonance:
Who knows if they have each his loaf at home,
Or smallest fish set by from yesterday?
The weather has been rough; there is a swell
From the Adriatic. Leave me now, Erminia!   70
    Erminia. Alone, dear father?
    Consul (*Placing his hand on the head of* ERMINIA). He who watches over
The people, never is alone, my child!
    Erminia (*Running back*). Here come the men who were debarking.

MINUZZI *and others.*

    Minuzzi.   Hail,
Sir Consul! All our fears then were but vain?
    Consul. So! you *did* fear?
    Minuzzi.   Ay did we. The Venetians
Ride in huge galleys; we ply boats for trade.
But since, Sir Consul, you expected them,
We are all safe. I did not much misgive
When one in gallant trim, a comely youth,
Outside the mole, but ready to slip in,   80
Beckon'd me from his boat, and gave me, smiling,
This letter, bidding me deliver it
Into no other hand beside the consul's,
And adding, "All will soon be well again."
I hope it may. But there was cause for doubt!
The galleys have cast anchor.
    Consul.   Sure enough
They join our enemies.
    Minuzzi.   How! One free state
Against another! Slaves fight slaves, and kings
Fight kings: so let them, till the last has bled:
But shall wise men (and wise above the wise,   90
And free above the free are the Venetians)
Devastate our joint patrimony . . freedom?
I fear not him who falls from such a highth
Before he strikes me. At him! my brave boys!
At him! the recreant! We have borne too much
In seeing his attempt. Could not we cut
The cables?

THE SIEGE OF ANCONA

Stamura. Rare, rare sport for us!

Consul.   Stamura!
If wise Minuzzi deems it feasible,
Ye shall enjoy the pastime, while the wind
Sits in this quarter, blowing from due-east   100
Hard into port: else must ye to the walls,
To meet full twenty thousand, well approved
In arms the most-part, all athirst for plunder.

Minuzzi. Where are they posted?

Consul.   At the battlements.

Minuzzi. Lads! we must lose no time.

Sailor.   Now let us see
Whether we too may not be mischievous
As they could wish us, this fine April morn.

Minuzzi. Each bring his hatchet. Off! and quickly back.   [*They go.*

FATHER JOHN (*Enters*).

One word, sir Consul, ere we part, this one:
My wife sits nigh the old church porch, infirm   110
With many watchings; thro' much love for me,
True-hearted! Should the waters wash me home,
Stiffen'd a little more than is convenient,
Let none displace her from that low stone seat.
Grant me my suit, unless I fail in duty.

Consul (Presses his hand). And these are breasts despotic power would
    crush!

          [MINUZZI *going, meets* FATHER JOHN, *who had listened.*

Father John. Talk ye of hatchets?

Consul.   Father John! good day!

Father John. Yea, with God's blessing, we will make it so.

Consul. I want your counsel on a perilous move.
Father! you were a diver in time past.   120

Father John. And in time present may be one again.

Minuzzi. Ah! could you join us in our enterprize!

Father John. What is it?

Minuzzi.   Why, to dive and cut the cables
Of yon Venetians dancing there so gaily,
And bowing in bright pennons to each other.

Father John. Is this the Doge's wedding-day with Adria?
No dame in Venice ever played him falser
Than she will do, and haply before night.

123 dive] *so in 1876, mispr.* drive *1846.*

93

Ye spoke of hatchet! 'Twould but do poor work
Against a cable.
    Stamura.   We can hold our breath   130
A good while on such business.
    Consul.   Father John,
Could you devise some fitter instrument?
    Minuzzi. Ah! what inventions have not priests devised!
We all of us are what we are thro' them.
    Father John. I love this reverence, my grey boy! and aptly
Hast thou believed that Father John could frame
What will perform the work, else difficult.
I thought of Turks and Saracens, and flags
Bearing the crescent, not the winged lion,
When I prepared my double-handed sickle   140
To reap the hemp-field that lies under water.
I will dive too, and teach you on the way
How ye shall manage it. So fare you well,
Sir Consul!
                                        [*To the* Man.

                  We have all the day before us
And not long work (tho' rather hard) to do.

[ACT I.] SCENE III.

CONSUL *and* ERMINIA.

    Consul. Erminia! read this letter. Wait awhile . .
Repress thy curiosity . . First tell me,
Erminia! would'st thou form some great alliance?
    Erminia. Yes, father! who would not?
    Consul.   I know that none
Hath won that little heart of thine at present.
    Erminia. Many, many have won it, my dear father!
I never see one run across the street
To help a lame man up or guide a blind man
But *that* one wins it: never hear one speak
As all should speak of you, but up my arms   10
Fly ready to embrace him!
    Consul.   And when any
Says thou art beautiful, and says he loves thee,
What are they ready then for?
    Erminia.   Not to beat him
Certainly: but none ever said such things.
They look at me because I am your daughter,

THE SIEGE OF ANCONA

And I am glad they look at me for that,
And always smile, tho' some look very grave.

Consul. Well now, Erminia, should his Holiness
The Pope have sent his nephew with this letter,
Would you receive him willingly?

Erminia.   Most willingly.   20

Consul. Nay, that is scarcely maidenly, so soon.

Erminia. I would not if you disapprove of it.

Consul. I do suspect he came aboard the gallies.

Erminia. O then, the gallies are not enemies.

Consul. Not if thou givest him thy hand. What say'st thou?

Erminia. I never saw him.

Consul.   But suppose him handsome.
Indeed I hear much of his comeliness.

Erminia. Is that enough?

Consul.   And virtues.

Erminia.   That alone
Is not enough, tho' very, very much.
He must be handsome too, he must be brave,   30
He must have seen me often, and must love me,
Before I love or think of him as lover:
For, father, you are not a king, you know,
Nor I a princess: so that all these qualities
(Unless you will it otherwise) are necessary.

Consul. Thou art grown thoughtful suddenly, and prudent.

Erminia. Do not such things require both thought and prudence?

Consul. In most they come but slowly; and this ground
Is that where we most stumble on. The wise
Espouse the foolish; and the fool bears off   40
From the top branch the guerdon of the wise:
Ay, the clear-sighted (in all other things)
Cast down their eyes and follow their own will,
Taking the hand of idiots. They well know
They shall repent, but find the road so pleasant
That leads into repentance.

Erminia.   Ah, poor souls!
They must have lost their fathers: then what wonder
That they have lost their way!

Consul.   Now, in few words,
Erminia, for time presses, let me tell thee,
The Pope will succour us against our foe   50
If I accept his nephew for a son.

95

Erminia. O father! does that make our cause more righteous?
Or more unrighteous theirs who persecute us?
  Consul. No, child: but wilt thou hear him? Rank and riches
Will then be thine. Altho' not born a princess,
Thou wilt become one.
  Erminia.   I am more already;
I am your daughter; yours, whom not one voice
Raised over all, but thousands.
  Consul.   I resign
My station in few days.
  Erminia.   O stay in it
Until the enemy is beaten back,   60
That I may talk of it when I am old,
And, when I weep to think of you, may dry
My tears, and say, *My father then was Consul.*
  Consul. The power may be prolonged until my death.
  Erminia. O no: the laws forbid it: do they not?
  Consul. He who can make and unmake every law,
Divine and human, will uphold my state
So long, acknowledging his power supreme;
And laying the city's keys before his feet.
  Erminia. Hath he not Peter's? What can he want more? 70
O father! think again! I am a child
Almost, and have not yet had time enough
Quite to unlearn the lessons you enforced
By precept and example. Bear with me!
I have made you unhappy many times,
You never made me so until this hour:
Bear with me, O my father!
  Consul.   To my arms,
Erminia! Thou hast read within my breast
Thy lesson backward, not suspecting guile.
Yes, I was guileful. I would try thy nature: 80
I find it what is rarely found in woman,
In man as rarely. The Venetian fleet
Would side with us; their towers, their catapults
Would all be ours, and the Pope's nephew thine,
Would but thy father place the power supreme
Within his hands, becoming his vicegerent.
I turn aside from fraud, and see how force
May best be met, in parley with the German.

THE SIEGE OF ANCONA

SCENE IV. THE ENCAMPMENT AND TENT OF THE ARCHBISHOP
UNDER THE WALLS.

CONSUL *and* ARCHBISHOP.

Archbishop. I do presume from your habiliments
You are the consul of this petty state.
Consul. I am.
Archbishop.   You may be seated. Once again . .
Will you surrender unconditionally?
Consul. Nor unconditionally nor conditionally.
Archbishop. I sent for you to point where lies your duty.
Consul. It lies where I have left it, in the town.
Archbishop. You doubt my clemency.
Consul.   Say rather *"honour."*
Archbishop. Doubt you a soldier's honour?
Consul.   Not a soldier's   10
But when the soldier and the priest unite,
Well may I doubt it. Goats are harmless brutes;
Dragons may be avoided; but when goat
And dragon form one creature, we abhor
The flames and coilings of the fell chimæra.
Archbishop. And therefore you refused a conference
Unless I pitch my tent beneath your walls,
Within an arrow's shot, distributing
Ten archers on each side; ten mine, ten yours?
Consul. No doctor of divinity in Paris
Is cleverer at divining. Thus it stands.   20
Archbishop. Ill brook I such affronts.
Consul.   Ill brook, perhaps,
Florence and Pisa their ambassadors
Invited to a conference on peace,
And cast in prison.
Archbishop.   Thus we teach the proud
Their duty.
Consul.   Let the lame man teach the lame
To walk, the blind man teach the blind to see.
Archbishop. Insolent! Unbecoming of my station
Were it to argue with a churl so rude.
Rise: look before you thro' the tent: what see you?
Consul. I see huge masses of green corn upheaved   30
Within a belt of palisades.

20 Is] In *1846* (*mispr.*).   22 ambassadors [In 1173 the magistrates of Pisa and Florence, invited by Archbishop Christian to a conference, were seized and imprisoned.—W.]

Archbishop. What else?

Consul. Sheep, oxen, horses, trampling them.

Archbishop. No more?

Consul. Other huge masses farther off are smoking,
Because their juices quench the faggot-fire.

Archbishop. And whence come these?

Consul. From yonder houseless fields,
Of crops, and even of boundaries, bereft.

Archbishop. Whose were they?

Consul. Whose? The church's, past a doubt:
It never takes what is not freely given.

Archbishop. Proud rebels! ye have brought upon your heads
This signal vengeance from offended Cæsar. 40

Consul. And must ten thousand starve because one man
Is wounded in that part which better men
Cut from them, as ill-sorted with our nature?
If Satan could have dropt it, he were saved.

Archbishop. What meanest thou? What cast they from them?

Consul. Pride.
It clings round little breasts and masters them,
It drops from loftier, spurn'd and trodden down.
Is this, my lord archbishop, this your Eden?
Is this the sacrifice of grateful herbs
Ye offer to your Gods? And will the next 50
Be more acceptable? Burnt-offerings raised
In your high places, and fossed round with blood!

Archbishop. Blasphemer! I am here no priest; I come
Avenger of insulted majesty.
But, if thou mindest Holy Writ, mind this,
The plainest thing, and worthiest of remembrance: . .
Render to Cæsar what is Cæsar's, man!

Consul. God will do that for us. Nought owe we Cæsar
But what he sent us when he sent you hither,
To cut our rising wheat, our bleeding vines, 60
To burn our olives for your wild carousals . .

Archbishop. The only wood that will burn green: it blazes
Most beautifully, and no smell from it.
But you Anconites have poor olive grounds,
We shall want more by Sunday.

Consul. May the curse
Of God be on you!

Archbishop. We are not so impious:
It *is* on you: it were a sin to wish it.

98

THE SIEGE OF ANCONA

Consul. Prince and archbishop! there are woes that fall
Far short of curses, though sore chastisements;
Prosperities there are that hit the mark,   70
And the clear-sighted see God's anger there.
    Archbishop. Are *we* constrain'd to drag and vex the sea
And harrow up the barren rocks below
For noisome weeds? Are household animals
Struck off the knee to furnish our repast?
    Consul. Better endure than cause men this endurance.
    Archbishop. Clearly ye think so: we think otherwise.
'Tis better to chastise than be chastised,
To be the judge than be the criminal.
    Consul. How oft, when crimes are high enough to strike   80
The front of Heaven, are those two characters
Blended in one!
    Archbishop.   I am not to be school'd
By insolence and audacity.
    Consul.   *We* are,
It seems: but fortitude and trust in God
Will triumph yet. Our conference is closed.

ACT II.

SCENE I. AT THE RAMPARTS.

ANGELICA, STAMURA, *and* Soldiers.

Angelica. See ye those towers that stride against the walls?
    Soldier. See you this arrow? Few were not more fatal
That flew from them: but this arrests my arm
Perhaps beyond to-morrow.
    Angelica (to others).   Fight amain.
    Soldier. The widow of Stamura is below,
And, slender tho' her figure, fair her face,
Brave as her husband. Few her words: beware
Of falling back, lest they increase and shame us.
    Another Soldier. Long live Stamura! She hath crost already
The sallyport.
    Another Soldier. What held she in her hand?   10
    Another Soldier. A distaff.
    Soldier.   Hush! what cries are those?
    Another Soldier.   All German.
    Soldier. What dust is over-head?
    Another Soldier.   Is not it smoke?
Hurrah! flames mount above the battlements.

H 2   99

Soldier. It was her deed.
Another Soldier.   But whose those cries behind us,
Along the harbour?
    Soldier.   Those are all Italian.
    Another Soldier. Look! How yon tower curls outward, red and
      reeling!
    Soldier. Ay; it leans forward as in mortal pain.
    Another Soldier. What are those things that drop?
    Soldier.   Men, while we speak,
Another moment, nothing.
    Another Soldier.   Some leap down;
Others would keep their desperate grasp: the fire   20
Loosens it; and they fall like shrivell'd grapes
Which none will gather. See it, while you can;
It totters, parts, sinks. What a crash! The sparks
Will blind our archers.
    Another Soldier.   What a storm of fire!

[ACT II.] SCENE II. THE CONSUL'S HOUSE.

CONSUL, ERMINIA.

Erminia. The men you spoke with in the port have pass'd
The window, and seem entering.
    Consul.   Friends, come in.
    Minuzzi (Entering with STAMURA *and others).* Sir Consul! we are here
      inopportunely.
Our work is done: God prosper'd it. Young lady!
We come no feasters at a consul's board.
    Consul. Erminia! coverest thou our scanty fare
Because 'tis scanty, and not over-nice?
Child! thou hast eaten nothing.
    Erminia.   Quite enough.
    Consul. No wonder thou hast lost thy appetite,
And sighest.
    Erminia.   I am sure I did not sigh;   10
Nor have I lost my appetite.
    Consul.   Then eat:
Take off the napkin.
    Erminia.   Father! you well know
What is beneath it.
    Consul.   Half a cake.
    Erminia.   Of beans,

Of rye, of barley, swept from off the manger:
My little horse had eaten them ere now,
But . .
    Consul. The child weeps. Even such flesh must serve.
Heaven grant us even this a few days hence.
    Erminia (To STAMURA). Signor Antonio! do not look at me,
I pray you, thinking of my greediness;
Eat, eat! I kept it . . If the sea's fresh air   20
Makes hungry those who sail upon it, surely
It must . . after such toil . .
    Stamura.   Such toil 'twas not.
    Erminia. Father! could you persuade him?
    Stamura.   Pray excuse me!
I want no food.
    Consul.   Take what there is, and wine.
Wine we have still in plenty, old and strong.
    Stamura. Grant me this one half-beaker.
    Erminia.   Let me run
And rinse it well.
    Stamura.   Forbear! forbear!
    Consul.   We have
No man or maiden in the house; they all
Fight or assist the fighting.
    Erminia.   He has taken
And drank it every drop! Poor, poor Antonio!   30
O how he must have thirsted!
                     [*To* STAMURA.
          'Twas half water.
    Stamura. It was not very strong.
    Minuzzi.   And yet the colour
Mounts to his eyes as 'twere sheer wine of Crete.
    Consul. I am impatient (you must pardon me)
To hear what you have done. Pour out the wine,
Erminia! that can cause but short delay.
             [*They drink, all but* STAMURA.
    Cries in the street. Long live Stamura!
    Stamura.   Call they me? why me?
    Cries again. Long live the brave Angelica.
    Stamura.   My mother!
    Minuzzi. Now for the wine! The boy will faint.
    Erminia.   Help! father!
    Officer. Sir! saw you not the flames along the sky?   40
        39 *Erminia*] *Angelica* 1846, 1876 (both wrongly).

Has no one told you how that noble lady
Burnt down the tower with all its galleries,
Down to the very wheels?
   Stamura.   Who minds the tower?
Sirs! is she safe? unhurt?
   Officer.   Sir! the ram's head,
Blacken'd with smoke, lean'd prone against the wall,
Then seem'd to shudder as 'twere half-alive.
Then fell the iron mass. It made no sound
Among the ashes. Had it made a loud one
There were much louder from the wretches crusht
Beneath it and its tower; some tearing off   50
Their burning armour agonised with pain,
And others pierced with red-hot nails that held
The rafters; others holding up their arms
Against the pitch and sulphur that pour'd down.
It was a sight! Well might it have detain'd,
Those who beheld it, from their duty here.
Up flew, not sparks alone, but splinters huge,
Crackling against the battlements, and drove
More men away than all their arrows could.
   Stamura. Sir Consul! I must warm myself with fighting   60
After this dip.
              Nor see my mother first?   [*Aside.*
She would be first to blame me if I did.   [*Goes.*
   Consul. God prosper thee, brave youth, God prosper thee!
   Erminia (Aside). Discourteous man! he said no word to me!
He even forgot my father.

              FATHER JOHN *enters.*

   Minuzzi.   Here comes one
Who can relate to you the whole exploit
Better than we.
   Father John. Where is Antonio?
   Minuzzi.   Gone
This instant. How was it ye did not meet?
   Father John. Ha! I am this time caught in my own net.
I knew the knave would run away at seeing me;   70
He told me if I came he would be gone,
Fearing to hear my story. So, sir Consul,
I stole in softly through the stable-door.
I can not keep my breath beneath the surface
So long as boys can. They are slenderer,

Less buoyant too, mayhap. Oft as I rose
My pilot-fish was with me; that Stamura
Would never leave me.
    Erminia.   Father John! your blessing!
You always used to give it me.
    Father John.   There, take it.
How the girl kisses my rough hand to-day!   [*Aside.* 80
Forgetful, heedless, reckless of himself
He held a shapeless shield of cork before me,
Wherefrom a silent shower of arrows fell
From every galley, amid shouts like hunters'
As they caught sight of us. The bright steel points
Rebounding (for not one of them bit through)
Glistened a moment as they clove the water.
Then delved into the uneven furrow'd sands.
Surely the lustrous and unclosing eyes
Of well-poised fishes have enjoy'd to-day   90
A rarity; they never saw before
So many feathers sticking all upright
Under the brine so many fathoms deep.
    Consul. Father! your gaiety will never fail you.
    Father John. Not while it pleases God to use my arm
Or wits, such as they are, to serve my country.
But this I tell you: had the boy been less
Assiduous, or less brave, the fish had seen
Another sight they oftener see, and then
No Father John had blest that maiden more.   100
    Minuzzi. Stamura saved our country, saving you.
    Father John. And you too, both of you, did well your duty.
    Minuzzi. Aground are five good galleys, and their crews
Await your mercy.
    Father John.   Did Stamura bring
His captive, that spruce Roman-spoken gallant?
    Consul. He brought none hither.
    Minuzzi.   Now our tale is told,
A little fighting will assuage the toil
And cold of diving. Brave Stamura toss'd
The net above his forehead fifty times
And drew it off and shoved it back again,   110
Impatient for his mother. He will knead
(I trow) a pasty German ere he see her;
We too may lend a hand. Come, Father John!
Shrive as if we should need it.

Consul.   Fare ye well.
Thank God! I am not rich; but this one day,
My friends, I would be richer, to reward you.
The ships are yours: let none else claim one plank.   117

[ACT II.] SCENE III. THE QUAY.

PEOPLE. STAMURA.

Stamura. Stand off! The stores within the barks belong
Alike and equally to all. Much grain
Will there be spilt unless a steady hand
Conveys it, and divides it house by house.
Horses no fewer than three-score are dragged
Within the gates, from the last charge against us:
What would ye? Wait another charge, and take it.
People. Brave, brave Antonio!   8

[ACT II.] SCENE IV. ARCHBISHOP'S TENT.

ARCHBISHOP. *The Brothers* COSTANZIO *and* CORRADO.

Archbishop. Could ye not wait for death within the walls,
But must rush out to meet it?
Costanzio.   We could wait
As others do.
Corrado.   And fight we could as others.
Archbishop. Costanzio and Corrado! I am grieved
That you should war against your lawful prince,
Your father being most loyal.
Costanzio.   So are we.
Archbishop. What! when he serves the emperor and king,
And you the rabble?
Corrado.   Who made men the rabble?
Archbishop. Will not your treason and your death afflict him?
Costanzio. Our treason would: God grant our death may not.   10
Corrado. We never took the oaths that he has taken,
And owe no duty but to our own land.
Archbishop. Are ye Anconites?
Corrado.   No, sir, but Italians,
And in Ancona lies the cause of Italy.
Archbishop. Pernicious dreams! These drive young men astray;
But when they once take their own cause, instead
Of ours who could direct them, they are lost:
So will ye find it. As ye were not born
In this vile city, what, pray, could have urged you
To throw your fortunes into it when sinking?   20

THE SIEGE OF ANCONA

Costanzio. Because we saw it sinking.
Corrado.   While it prosper'd
It needed no such feeble aid as ours.
Marquises, princes, kings, popes, emperors,
Courted it then: and you, my lord archbishop,
Would have it even in its last decay.
Archbishop. There is a spirit in the land, a spirit
So pestilential that the fire of heaven
Alone can purify it.
Costanzio.   Things being so,
Let us return and die with those we fought for.
Archbishop. Captious young man! Ye die the death of traitors. 30
Corrado. Alas! how many better men have died
That death! alas, how many must hereafter!
Archbishop. By following your example. Think of that;
Be that your torture.
Costanzio.   As we never grieved
At following our betters, grant, just Heaven!
That neither may our betters ever grieve
At following us, be the time soon or late.

                                   [*To the* Guards.

Archbishop. Lead off these youths. Separate them.
Corrado.   My lord!
We are too weak (you see it) for resistance;
Let us then, we beseech you, be together   40
In what is left of life!
Archbishop.   One hour is left:
Hope not beyond.
Corrado.   We did hope more; we hoped
To be together, tho' but half the time.
Archbishop. It shall not be.
Costanzio.   It shall be.
Archbishop.   Art thou mad?
I would not smile, but such pride forces me.
Costanzio. God, in whose holiest cause we took up arms,
Will reconcile us. Doubt it not, Corrado,
Altho' such men as that man there have said it.   48

[ACT II.] SCENE V. CONSUL'S HOUSE.
STAMURA. ERMINIA.

Stamura. Lady! you need not turn your face from me.
I leave the town for aid. But one perhaps
May bring it, if you listen to him

Erminia.   Who?
Stamura. I made a captive.
Erminia.   So I hear.
Stamura.   I come
Seeking the consul: he expected me
Erminia. And *him?*
Stamura.   Him also.
Erminia.   Know you what he asks?
Stamura. I know it.
Erminia.   And you wish it? *you*, Stamura?
Stamura. I have no voice in it.
Erminia.   True. Go. I know it.
                                      [STAMURA *goes.*

Shameless! to ask him! Never did we meet
But, if his eye caught mine, he walk'd aside: 10
Yet, by some strange occurrence, we meet daily.

            The CONSUL *enters.*

Consul. Erminia! didst thou send away Stamura?
Erminia. He went away: no need for me to send him.
Consul. Knowest thou whom he made his captive?
Erminia.   Yes:
That insolent young Roman.
    Consul.   Speak not thus
Before thou seest him.
    Erminia.   I will never see him.
Consul. Nay, I have promised scarce five minutes since
That thou shalt hear him.
    Erminia.   Has he then found favor
With you so suddenly?
    Consul.   Stamura speaks
Much in his favor.
    Erminia.   Are they friends already?   20
Consul. Hardly; we must suppose. But here they come.

     STAMURA. CLOVIO. CONSUL. ERMINIA.

Clovio. Sir Consul! I am Clovio Fizzarelli.
Have you received the letter?
    Consul.   I received it.
    Clovio. On bended knee permit me to salute
The lady who shall rule my destiny,
Your fair Erminia.
    Erminia.   You are the Pope's nephew,

Sir Clovio! I have heard; and you come hither
Most strongly recommended.
    Clovio.   True, sweet lady!
But I do trust, with all humility,
There may be a mere trifle in myself,   30
Not to engage you in the first half-hour,
But so to plead for me, that in a day
Or two, or three at farthest . .
    Erminia.   Sir, your pleader
Stands there; you are his captive, and not mine.
    Clovio. He knows me well. He threw my whole boat's crew
(Four of them) overboard, but found his match
In me.
    Erminia. It seems so: does it not, Antonio?
    Stamura. More; how much more!
    Clovio.   There! He could not deny it.
    Erminia. And now he has persuaded my kind father
To grant you audience.
    Clovio (to STAMURA*).* She is proud: I'll tame her.   40
    Stamura (Angrily). Sir!   [*Aside.*
              No: he is my prisoner and my guest.
    Erminia. This gentleman, who is so confidential
With you, and whom you whisper to for counsel,
May give my hand away . . and will most gladly.
I doubt not . . for my father can refuse
Nothing to one who made so great a prize,
Beside the preservation of the city.
    Clovio. Speak then, my worthy friend, if thus the consul
Honours your valour; speak for me; and let me
Who owe my life, owe more than life to you.   50
    Stamura. The consul knows what suits his honour best,
And the young lady seems not ill disposed
To shower his favour on such high desert.
I have my duties; but this is not one.
Let the young lady give her hand herself.
If I had any wish . . but I have none . .
It should be, Sir, that you had won it first
By a brave action or a well-tried love.
But, what is love? My road lies toward the walls.   [*To the* CONSUL.
With your permission, Sir! I have yours, lady!   60
                  [STAMURA *goes.*

    Erminia. Father! I am unwell. This gentleman
Comes unexpectedly, demands abruptly . .

Clovio. Impatiently, but not abruptly.
Erminia.   Sir!
I will not marry: never, never, never.   [ERMINIA *goes.*
  Clovio. Ha! ha! all women are alike, Sir Consul.
Leave her to me.
  Consul.   Sir Clovio Fizzarelli!
I will do more than what you ask of me.
I grant you freedom. Go aboard the pinnace
Which bore you into port; and say at Rome
That you have seen men starving in the streets,   70
Because his Holiness refused us help
Unless a father gave a daughter up;
And say the daughter would not sell her heart,
Much less her country; and then add, Sir Clovio,
(O were it true!) "All women are alike."

ACT III.

SCENE I. EPISCOPAL PALACE.

BISHOP *of* ANCONA *and* FATHER JOHN.

Bishop. I have been standing at my terrace-wall
And counting those who pass and cry with hunger.
Brother! the stoutest men are grown effeminate;
Nay, worse; they stamp and swear, even in my presence,
And looking up at me.
  Father John.   Sad times indeed!
  Bishop. I calculate that giving each an ounce
Only one day, scarce would a sack remain
In my whole garner; I am so reduced.
  Father John. I come to beg your lordship for one ounce
Of your fine flour, to save a child; to save   10
A mother, who loathes ordinary food . .
Not ordinary, but most bitter lupin:
She has no other in the house.
  Bishop.   No other?
Poor soul! This famine is a dreadful thing!
Pestilence always follows it! God help us!
I tremble; I start up in sleep.
  Father John.   My lord!
An ounce of meal, a single ounce, might calm
These tremblings, well applied. The nurse that should be
Can be no nurse: the mother very soon
Will be no mother, and the child no child.   20

THE SIEGE OF ANCONA

Bishop. You know not how things stand, good brother John!
This very morning, as I hope for grace,
I paid three golden pieces for the head,
Think you, of what? an ass!
 Father John (Aside). The cannibal!
    [*To the* BISHOP.]
Ah, my good lord! they bear high prices now.
 Bishop. Why brother! you yourself are grown much thinner.
How can you do your duty?
 Father John. Were I not
Much thinner, I should think I had not done it.
 Bishop. My cook assures me that with wine and spice
Elicampane, cumin, angelica,   30
Garlic, and sundry savory herbs, stored by
Most providentially, the Lord be praised!
He can make that strange head quite tolerable . .
The creature was a young one . . what think you?
 Father John. They are more tolerable than the old.
 Bishop. The sellers take advantage of bad times,
Quite without conscience, shame, respect for persons,
Or fear of God. What can such men expect?
You must have seen sad sights about our city:
I wonder you are what you are.
 Father John.   Sad sights   40
Indeed!
 Bishop. But all will give their confessor
Part of their pittance; and the nearer death
The readier; knowing what the church can do.
Tell me now, for my entrails yearn to hear it,
Do they not take due care of you?
 Father John.   No meals
Have now their stated hour. Unwillingly
I enter houses where the family
Sits round the table at the spare repast.
Sometimes they run and hide it.
 Bishop.   Most unmannerly!
Inhuman, I would add unchristianlike.   50
 Father John. Sometimes they push toward me the untasted
And uninviting food, look wistfully,
Press me; yet dread acceptance. Yesterday
A little girl, the youngest of the five,
Was raising to her lips a mealy bean
(I saw no other on the unsoil'd plate)

And, looking at my eyes fixt hard on hers,
And thinking they were fixt upon the morsel,
Pusht it between my lips, and ran away.

 Bishop. Brother! I should have call'd her a good child;   60
I should myself have given the benediction
With my own hand, and placed it on her head:
I wonder you don't praise her. Brother John!
I have my nones to run thro'; so, good-by.

 Father John. Just God! does this house stand? Dark are thy ways,
Inscrutable! Be thy right hand our guide!

[ACT III.] SCENE II.   SENATE-HOUSE.

SENATORS.   CONSUL.

 Consul. Senators! ye have call'd me to debate
On our condition.

 Senator.   Consul! we are lost.

 Consul. All are who think so.

 Second Senator.   Even the best want food.

 Consul. The bravest do.

 Third Senator.   How shall men fight without it?

 Fourth Senator. Concord and peace might have return'd.

 Consul.   By yielding,
Think ye? Not they: contempt and sorrow might.
Can there be ever concord (peace there may be)
Between the German and Italian? None.
Remember how that ancient city fell,
Milano. Seven whole years resisted she   10
The imperial sword: she listened to conditions
And fell. The soldiers of His Majesty . .
His soldiers, ay, his very court . . shed tears
At such affliction, at such utter ruin,
At such wide wails, such universal woe.
They all were equal then; for all were slaves,
Scatter'd, the poor, the rich, the brave, the coward,
Thro' Bergamo, Pavìa, Lodi, Como,
The cities of the enemy. There stood
No vestige of the walls, no church to pray in . .   20
And what was left to pray for? What but Cæsar?
Throw rather all your wealth into the sea
Than let the robber priest lay hold upon it,

10 Milano] *see scene iii, l. 45.* [W.]

THE SIEGE OF ANCONA

And, if ye die of famine, die at least
In your own houses while they *are* your own.
But there are many yet whose hearts and arms
Will save you all: to-day you all can fight,
The enemy shall feed you all to-morrow.
Were it no shame a priest should seize the prey
That kings and emperors dropt with broken talon? 30
The eagle flew before your shouts; and now
A vulture must swoop down! but vultures keep
From living men and from warm blood; they revel
(And most the Roman vulture) in corruption.
Have ye forgotten how your fathers fought,
When Totila with Goths invincible
Besieged you; not with priests and choristers;
When twenty-seven ships assail'd your port
And when eleven only ever left it?
Rome fell before him twice; not once Ancona. 40
Your fathers saved the city . . ye shall save her.
    Senator. Weapons are insufficient; courage, vows,
Avail not. We are unprepared for war:
Scanty was our last harvest: and these winds
Are adverse. They know that who now defy us,
Blockading us alike by sea and land.
    Consul. We some are poor, we some are prosperous,
We all alike owe all we have: the air
Is life alike to all, the sun is warmth,
The earth, its fruits and flocks, are nutriment, 50
Children and wives are comforts; all partake
(Or may partake) in these. Shall hoarded grain
Or gold be less in common, when the arms
That guard it are not those that piled it up,
But those that shrink without it? Come, ye rich,
Be richer still: strengthen your brave defenders,
And make all yours that was not yours before.
Dares one be affluent where ten thousand starve?
Open your treasuries, your granaries,
But throw mine open first. Another year 60
Will roughen this equality again,
The rich be what they were; the poor . . alas!
What they were too perhaps . . but every man
More happy, each one having done his duty.
    Senator (*To another*). Hark! the young fools applaud! they rise
      around;

They hem him in; they seize and kiss his hand;
He shakes our best supporters.
  Another.   Give the sign
To those without.

                    [PEOPLE *enter.*]

  Consul.   Who called you hither?   [*Various voices.*
  First.   Want.
  Second.   Famine.
  Third.   Our families.
  Fourth.   I had three sons;
One hath been slain, one wounded.
  Fifth.   Only one   70
Had I: my loss is greatest.
  Sixth.   Grant us peace.
Sir Consul, peace we plead for, only peace.
  Consul. Will peace bring back the dead? will peace restore
Lost honour? will peace heal the wounds your sons
And brothers writhe with? They who gave those wounds
Shall carry home severer, if they live,
And never in my consulate shall laugh
At those brave men whom men less brave desert.
True, some have fallen: but before they fell
They won the field; nor now can earthly power   80
Take from their cold clencht hands the spoil they grasp;
No mortal spoil, but glory. Life, my sons,
Life may lose all: the seal that none can break
Hath stampt their names, all registered above.
  Senator (To a Man *near).* Speak; you poor fool! speak loudly, or
      expect
From me no favour . . and tell that man next.
  Man. Oh! we are starving.
  Consul.   Better starve than serve.
  Another. He has no pity.
  Consul.   What is that I hear?
I have no pity. Have I not a daughter?
  Another. O what a daughter! How compassionate!   90
How charitable! Had she been born poor
She could not more have pitied poverty.
  Consul. Two ounces of coarse bread, wine, which she loathes,
And nothing more, sustain her.
  Another.   God sustains her;
He will not leave his fairest work to perish.

THE SIEGE OF ANCONA

Consul. Fight then, fight bravely, while ye can, my friends!
In God have confidence, if none in me.
      [*Shouts of applause. Part of the* People *leave the* Senators.]
   Senator (To another). Seducer of the people! shall it end
Thus vilely?   [*To the* CONSUL.]
         You have stores at home, Sir Consul!
You have wide lands.
   Another Senator. You should support your order.   100
   Consul. My order! God made one; of that am I.
Stores, it appears, I have at home; wide lands;
Are those at home too? or within my reach?
Paternal lands I do inherit; wide
They are enough, but stony, mountainous,
The greater part unprofitable.
   Senator.   Some
The richest in rich wine.
   Consul.   Few days ago
Nearly a hundred barrels were unbroached.
   Another Senator. A hundred loaves, tho' small indeed and dry,
Would they be worth in such distress as ours.   110
We could raise half among us.
   Consul.   Shame upon you!
Had not your unwise laws and unfair thrift
Prohibited the entrance of supplies
While they *could* enter, never had this famine
Stalked through the people.
   Senator.   But the laws are laws.
   Consul Yours; never theirs.
   Another Senator.   Why thus inflame the people?
   Consul. Who brought the people hither? for what end?
To serve you in your avarice; to cry *peace!*
Not knowing peace from servitude.
   Senator.   For quiet,   120
Spare them at least a portion of the wine.
   Consul. Nor them nor you; nor price nor force shall gain it.
   People. Are we to perish? Hunger if we must,
Let us be strengthen'd by a draught of wine
To bear it on.
   Senator.   Wine is the oil of life,
And the lamp burns with it which else were spent.
   People. Sir Consul! we forbear; we honour you,
But tell us, ere we sink, where one flask lies.
   Consul. Go ask the women labouring of child,

Ask those who nurse their infants, ask the old,
Who can not fight, ask those who fought the best,   130
The wounded, maim'd, disabled, the Anconites.
Sirs! if ye find one flask within our cellar,
Crack it, and throw the fragments in my face.
 People. Let us away.   *[Shouts of applause.*
 Consul.   Follow me to the walls;
And you, too, senators, learn there your duty.
 People. We swear to do our best.
 Consul.   Sworn wisely! Life
Is now more surely to be won by arms
Than death is, and the sword alone can win it.
I lead the way; let who will lag behind.

[ACT III.] SCENE III. THE CITY.

PAOLUCCI, Officers, Citizens.

 Officer. The consul has been wounded. Who is left
To lead us? and what leader would suffice?
The strongest sink with famine, lying down
Along the battlements, and only raised
When sounds the trumpet.
 First Citizen.   And most fall again.
 Second Citizen. Our day is come, the day of our disgrace.
 Paolucci. Ours never was that day, and never shall be.
Ye may have lost your consul (let us hope
He is not lost to us) but we are sure
His memory and example yet remain   10
With all their life in them.   *[To the* People.]
     Young men! perhaps
Ye know me not: your fathers knew me well;
Their fathers better. Three-score years ago
I was your consul: none then preached surrender;
And let none now: yet there were those around
Who would have pinfolded the quiet flock
As gladly as yon shepherd at the gate.
 People. We can resist no longer. Who can count
The slain?
 Paolucci. Say, rather, who can praise the slain?
Glorified souls! happy your sleep! ye hear   20
No shameful speech from brethren!
 People.   Arms alone
Should not subdue us: famine has: we starve.

    20 souls!] souls? *1846 (mispr.).*

THE SIEGE OF ANCONA

Paolucci. While life remains life's sufferings will arise,
Whether from famine or from sharper sting
Than famine; upon every hearth almost
There creeps some scorpion never seen till felt.
But until every arm that guards our walls
Drop helpless at the starting ribs, until
That hour, stand all united. Ye despair
Untimely. He who rules us rules us well,⁣   30
Exciting no false hope, as bad men do
When they have led where none can extricate.
I was your consul while the king Lothaire
Besieged the city, proud as any prelate,
Swearing he would reduce it. Other kings
Have sworn the same . . and kept their word like kings . .
Cursing and flying. We have met brave foes;
But they met braver. Fly; and let the crook
Drag a vile flock back from its flight to slaughter.
  All. We scorn the thought. But where lies human help?   40
  Paolucci. I may be spared to seek it, spared to try
If one brave man breathes yet among the powerful.
Who knows not Marchesella?
  Officer.   Brave he is,
But mindful of the emperor. He saw
Milano, which had stood two thousand years,
Sink;* every tree, on hill or vale, cut down,
The vine, the olive, ripe and unripe corn
Burnt by this minister of God. Throughout
There was no shade for sick men to die under,
There was no branch to strow upon the bier.   50
  Another Officer. His father was courageous, why not he?
  A third Officer. Above all living men is Marchesella
Courageous: but pray what are our deserts
With him, that he should hazard for our sake
His lordly castles and his wide domains?
Perhaps his fame in arms! 'Twere mad to hope it.
Prudence, we know, for ever guides his courage.
  Paolucci. If generous pity dwells not in his house,
As once it did, with every other virtue,
Seek it, where brave men never seek in vain,   60
In woman's breast: away to Bertinoro:

---

* Ancona was besieged 1162, 1174. [L.] Incorrect. Milan was destroyed by
Frederick Barbarossa in 1162; Ancona was besieged by him in 1167 and by his lieu-
tenant, Archbishop Christian, in 1174. See *Sc.* ii, *l.* 10. [W.]

Take heart: the countess is a Frangipani:
There are a thousand trumpets in that name:
Methinks I hear them blowing toward Ancona.
Old men talk long: but be not ye so idle:
Hie to the walls: I will sue her. To arms!
To arms! the consul of past years commands you.

[ACT III.] SCENE IV. CONSUL'S HOUSE.

PAOLUCCI. CONSUL. ERMINIA.

Paolucci. Consul! how fare you?
Consul.   Not amiss.
Paolucci.   But wounded?
Consul. There was more blood than wound, they say who saw it.
Erminia. My father, sir, slept well all night.
Paolucci.   All night
An angel watched him; he must needs sleep well.
Consul. I drove away that little fly in vain,
It flutter'd round the fruit whose skin was broken.
Erminia. Sweet father! talk not so; nor much at all.
Paolucci. Consul! I have not many days of life,
As you may see; and old men are in want
Of many little things which those in power   10
Can give: and 'twere amiss to hold them back
Because unclaim'd before.
Consul.   I well remember,
Though then a child, how all this city praised
Your wisdom, zeal, and probity, when consul.
Ancona then was flourishing; but never
Were those compensated who served their country,
Except by serving her; 'twas thought enough;
We think so still. Beside, the treasury
Is emptied, that it may procure us food
And troops. Be sure the very first that eats   20
The strangers' corn (if any reach our port)
Shall be no other than yourself: your age
And virtue merit from us this distinction.
Paolucci. Sir Consul! I want more than that.
Consul.   Receive it
And welcome from the father and the man,
Not from the consul. Now would you yourself
Act differently (I ask) on this occasion?
Paolucci. More kindly, no; but differently, yes.

THE SIEGE OF ANCONA

Consul. What would you from me?

Paolucci.   High distinction, consul!

Consul. I will propose it, as I justly may,   30
And do regret it has been so deferred.

Paolucci. May I speak plainly what ambition prompts?

Consul. I hear all claims.

Paolucci.   Those sacks hold heavy sums.

Consul. Avarice was never yet imputed to you.

Paolucci. 'Tis said you can not move them from the town.

Consul. Difficult, dangerous, doubtful, such attempt.
The young Stamura loves bold enterprizes,
And may succeed where others would despair:
But, such the lack of all that life requires
Even for a day, I dare not send one loaf   40
Aboard his bark. Hunger would urge the many
To rush and seize it.

Paolucci.   They would not seize *me*.
One loaf there is at home: that boy shall share it.

Erminia. He would not, though he pined.

Consul.   A youth so abstinent
I never knew.

Paolucci.   But when we are afloat . .

Consul.   We shall not be:
We think not of escape.

Paolucci.   No: God forbid!
We will meet safety in the path of honor.

Consul. Why say *afloat* then?

Paolucci.   Only he and I.
This is the guerdon I demand, the crown
Of my grey hairs.

Erminia.   Alas! what aid could either   50
Afford the other? O sir! do not go!
You are too old; he much too rash . . Dear father!
If you have power, if you have love, forbid it!

Paolucci. It was advised that younger ones should go:
Some were too daring, some were too despondent:
I am between these two extremes.

Consul.   But think
Again!

Paolucci. I have no time for many thoughts,
And I have chosen out of them the best.

Erminia. He never will return! he goes to die!
I knew he would!

DRAMAS AND DRAMATIC SCENES

Consul.   His days have been prolonged   60
Beyond the days of man: and there goes with him
One who sees every danger but his own.

[ACT III.] SCENE V. SEASIDE. NIGHT.

PAOLUCCI, STAMURA.

Paolucci. I feel the spray upon my face already.
Is the wind fair?
Stamura.   'Tis fiercely fair.
Paolucci.   The weather
Can not be foul then.
Stamura (*Lifting him aboard*). Sit down here. Don't tremble.
Paolucci. Then tell the breeze to wax a trifle warmer,
And lay thy hand upon those hissing waves.
She grates the gravel . . We are off at last.

ACT IV.

SCENE I. CASTLE OF BERTINORO.

COUNTESS OF BERTINORO, MARCHESELLA, PAOLUCCI, *and* STAMURA.

Page. My lady! here are two such men as never
Enter'd a palace-gate.
Countess.   Who are they?
Page.   One
Older than anything I ever saw,
Alive or dead; the other a stout youth,
Guiding him, and commanding all around
To stand aside, and give that elder way;
At first with gentle words, and then with stern.
Coarse their habiliments, their beards unshorn,
Yet they insist on entrance to my lady.
Countess. Admit the elder, but exclude the other.   10
Wait.   [*To* MARCHESELLA.
          If the younger be his son, what little
Of service I may render to the father
Will scarce atone for keeping him apart.   [*To the* Page.
Go; bid them enter; both.
                    [STAMURA, *having led* PAOLUCCI *in, retires.*
Paolucci.   I come, O countess!
Imploring of your gentleness and pity,

ACT IV.] *thus correctly numbered in 1876. mispr.* III. *1846.*

118

THE SIEGE OF ANCONA

To save from fire and sword, and, worse than either,
Worse, and more imminent, to save from famine
The few brave left, the many virtuous,
Virgins and mothers (save them!) in Ancona.
Countess. Nay, fall not at my knee. Age must not that . .   20
Raise him, good Marchesella!
Paolucci.   You too, here,
Illustrious lord?
Marchesella. What! and art thou still living,
Paolucci? faithful, hospitable soul!
We have not met since childhood . . mine, I mean.
Paolucci. Smile not, my gentle lord! too gracious then,
Be now more gracious; not in looks or speech,
But in such deeds as you can best perform.
Friendship another time might plead for us;
Now bear we what our enemy would else
Seize from us, all the treasures of our city,   30
To throw them at your feet for instant aid.
Help, or we perish. Famine has begun . .
Begun? has almost ended . . with Ancona.
Countess. Already? We have been too dilatory.
Marchesella. I could not raise the money on my lands
Earlier; it now is come. I want not yours:
Place it for safety in this castle-keep,
If such our lady's pleasure.
Countess.   Until peace.
Marchesella. My troops are on the march.
Countess.   And mine not yet?
Repose you, sir! they shall arrive with you,   40
Or sooner. Is that modest youth your son?
Paolucci. Where is he? gone again?
Countess.   When first you enter'd.
Paolucci. Some angel whisper'd your benign intent
Into his ear, else had he never left me.
My son? Who would not proudly call him so?
Soon shall ye hear what mother bore the boy,
And where he dash'd the gallies, while that mother
Fired their pine towers, already wheel'd against
Our walls, and gave us time . . for what? to perish.
Marchesella. No, by the saints above! not yet, not yet.   50
                              [*Trumpet sounds.*
Countess. Merenda is announced. Sir, I entreat you

51 Merenda] *Italian: mid-day repast.*

DRAMAS AND DRAMATIC SCENES

To lead me! Grant one favour more; and hint not
To our young friend that we have learnt his prowess.   [*To a* Page.
Conduct the noble youth who waits without.

[ACT IV.] SCENE II.

COUNTESS, MARCHESELLA, PAOLUCCI, STAMURA, *at Table.*

Countess (*to* STAMURA). Sir, there are seasons when 'tis incivility
To ask a name; 'twould now be more uncivil
To hesitate.
Stamura. Antonio is my name.
Countess. Baptismal. Pray, the family?
Stamura.   Stamura;
But *that* my honour'd father gave in marriage
To her who wears it brighter day by day:
She calls me rather by the name he bore.
Countess. It must be known and cherisht.
Stamura.   By the bravest
And most enduring in my native place;
It goes no farther: we are but just noble.   10
Countess. He who could head the tempest, and make serve
Unruly ocean, not for wealth, nor harm
To any but the spoiler, high above
That ocean, high above that tempest's wing,
He needs no turret to abut his name,
He needs no crescent to stream light on it,
Nor castellan, nor seneschal, nor herald.
Paolucci. Ha! boy, those words make thy breast rise and fall,
Haply as much as did the waves. The town
Could ill repay thee; Beauty overpays.   20
Countess. Talk what the young should hear; nor see the meed
Of glorious deeds in transitory tints,
Fainter or brighter.
Paolucci.   I was wrong.
Countess.   Not quite:
For beauty, in thy native town, young man,
May feel her worth in recompensing thine.
Stamura (*aside*). Alas! alas! she perishes! while here
We tarry.
Paolucci (*overhearing*). She? Who perishes?
Stamura.   The town.
Paolucci. How the boy blushes at that noble praise!

11 head] heed *mispr. 1876.*

120

THE SIEGE OF ANCONA

Countess. They blush at glory who deserve it most.
. . Blushes soon go: the dawn alone is red . .   30
Stamura. We know what duty, not what glory is.
The very best among us are not rich
Nor powerful.
    Countess.   Are they anywhere?
    Paolucci.   His deeds,
If glorious in themselves, require no glory.
Even this siege, those sufferings, who shall heed?
    Countess. He gives most light by being not too high.
Remember by what weapon fell the chief
Of Philistines. Did brazen chariots, driven
By giants, roll against him? From the brook,   40
Striking another such, another day,
A little pebble stretcht the enormous bulk
That would have fill'd it and have turn'd its course.
And in the great deliverers of mankind
Whom find ye? Those whom varlet pipers praise.
The greatest of them all, by all adored,
Did Babylon from brazen-belted gate,
Not humble straw-rooft Bethlehem, send forth?
We must not be too serious. Let us hear
How were the cables cut.
    Paolucci.   I saw the shears
That clipt them. Father John, before he went,   50
Show'd me them, how they workt. He himself held
The double crescent of sharp steel, in form
Like that swart insect's which you shake from fruit
About the kernel. This enclaspt the cable;
And two long handles (a stout youth, at each
Extremity, pushing with all his strength
Right forward) sunder'd it. Then swiftly flew
One vessel to the shore; and then another:
And hardly had the youths or Father John
Time to take breath upon the upper wave,   60
When down they sank again and there swang round
Another prow, and dasht upon the mole.
Then many blithe Venetians fell transfixt
With arrows, many sprang into the sea
And cried for mercy. Upon deck appeared
The pope's own nephew, who ('tis said) had come
To arbitrate. He leapt into a boat
Which swam aside, most gorgeously array'd,

And this young man leapt after him and seized him.
He, when he saw a dagger at his throat,   70
Bade all his crew, four well-built men, surrender.

  Stamura. They could not have feared *me:* they saw our archers.

  Countess. And where is now your prisoner?

  Stamura.   He desired
An audience of the consul.

  Countess.   To what end?

  Stamura. I know not: I believe to court his daughter.

  Countess. Is the girl handsome? Is that question harder
Than what I askt before? will he succeed?

  Stamura. Could he but save from famine our poor city,
And . . could he make her happy . .

  Countess.   Pray go on.
It would delight you then to see him win her?   80

  Stamura. O that I had not saved him! or myself!

  Countess. She loves him then? And you hate foreigners.
I do believe you like the fair Erminia
Yourself.

  Stamura. She hates me. Who likes those that hate him?

  Countess. I never saw such hatred as you bear her:
If she bears you the like . .

  Stamura.   She can do now
No worse than what she has done.

  Countess.   Who knows that?
I am resolved to see.

  Stamura.   O lady Countess!
How have I made an enemy of you?
Place me the lowest of your band, but never   90
Affront her with the mention of my name.
When the great work which you have undertaken
Is done, admit me in your castle-walls,
And never let me see our own again.

  Countess. I think I may accomplish what you wish;
But, recollect, I make no promises.

[ACT IV.] SCENE III. OPEN SPACE NEAR THE BALISTA GATE IN
ANCONA.

The LADY MALASPINA, *her* Infant, *and a* Soldier.

  Soldier. I am worn down with famine, and can live
But few hours more.

ACT IV.] *om. 1876.* SCENE III.] *thus correctly in 1876, incorrectly* SCENE I, *1846.*

THE SIEGE OF ANCONA

Lady Malaspina. I have no food.
Soldier.   Nor food
Could I now swallow. Bring me water, water!
  Lady Malaspina. Alas! I can not. Strive to gain the fountain.
  Soldier. I have been nigh.
Lady Malaspina.   And could not reach it?
  Soldier.   Crowds
I might pierce through, but how thrust back their cries?
They madden'd me to flight ere half-way in.
Some upright . . no, none that . . but some unfallen,
Yet pressing down with their light weight the weaker.
The brows of some were bent down to their knees,   10
Others (the hair seized fast by those behind)
Lifted for the last time their eyes to heaven;
And there were waves of heads one moment's space
Seen, then unseen for ever. Wails rose up
Half stifled underfoot, from children some,
And some from those who bore them.
  Lady Malaspina.   Mercy! mercy!
O blessed Virgin! thou wert mother too!
How didst *thou* suffer! how did *He!* Save, save
At least the infants, if all else must perish.
Soldier! brave soldier! dost thou weep? then hope.   20
  Soldier. I suffer'd for myself; deserve I mercy?
  Lady Malaspina. He who speaks thus shall find it. Try to rise.
  Soldier. No: could I reach the fountain in my thirst,
I would not.
  Lady Malaspina. Life is sweet.
Soldier.   To brides, to mothers.
  Lady Malaspina. Alas! how soon may those names pass away!
I would support thee partly, wert thou willing,
But my babe sleeps.
  Soldier.   Sleep, little one, sleep on!
I shall sleep too as soundly, by and by.
  Lady Malaspina. Courage, one effort more.
  Soldier.   And tread on children!
On children clinging to my knees for strength   30
To help them on, and with enough yet left
To pull me down, but others pull down them.
God! let me bear this thirst, but never more
Bear that sad sight! Tread on those tiny hands
Clasping the dust! See those dim eyes upturn'd,
Those rigid lips reproachless! Man may stir,

Woman may shake, my soul; but children, children!
O God! those are thine own! make haste to help them!
Happy that babe!

Lady Malaspina. Thou art humane.

Soldier.   'Tis said
That hunger is almost as bad as wealth   40
To make men selfish; but such feebleness
Comes over me, all things look dim around,
And life most dim, and least worth looking after.

Lady Malaspina. I pity thee. Day after day myself
Have lived on things unmeet for sustenance.
My milk is failing .. Rise ..

        (*To the* Child) My little one!
God will feed *thee!* Be sleep thy nourisher
Until his mercies strengthen me afresh!
Sink not: take heart: advance: Here, where from heaven
The Virgin-mother can alone behold us,   50
Draw some few drops.   [*The tocsin sounds.*

Soldier.   Ha! my ears boom thro' faintness.
What sounds?

Lady Malaspina. The bell.

Soldier.   Then they are at the gate ..
I can but thank you .. Give me force, O Heaven!
For this last fight! .. and keep from harm these twain!

        MALASPINA *and* Child *alone.*

Lady Malaspina. And still thou sleepest, my sweet babe! Is death
Like sleep? Ah, who then, who would fear to die?
How beautiful is all serenity!
Sleep, a child's sleep, O how far more serene,
And O, how far more beautiful than any!
Whether we breathe so gently or breathe not,   60
Slight is the difference. But the pangs, the rage
Of famine who can bear? .. unless to raise
Her child above it!

        (*Two* Priests *are passing.*)

First Priest.   Who sits yonder? bent
O'er her dead babe? as many do within
Their houses!

Second Priest. Surely, surely, it must be
She who, not many days ago, was praised
For beauty, purity, humility,
Above the noblest of Anconite dames.

THE SIEGE OF ANCONA

First Priest. The Lady Malaspina?
Second Priest.   But methinks
The babe is not dead yet.
    First Priest.   Why think you so?   70
    Second Priest. Because she weeps not over it.
    First Priest.   For *that*
I think it dead. It then could pierce no more
Her tender heart with its sad sobs and cries.
But let us hasten from the place to give
The dying their last bread, the only bread
Yet unconsumed, the blessed eucharist.
Even this little, now so many die,
May soon be wanting.
    Second Priest.   God will never let
That greater woe befall us.   [*The* Priests *go.*
    Lady Malaspina.   Who runs hither?
                    [*The* Soldier *falls before her.*
Art thou come back? So! thou couldst run, O vile!   80
    Soldier. Lady! your gentleness kept life within me
Until four fell.
    Lady Malaspina. Thyself unwounded?
    Soldier.   No;
If arms alone can wound the soldier's breast,
They toucht me not this time; nor needed they;
Famine had done what your few words achieved.
    Lady Malaspina. They were too harsh. Forgive me!
    Soldier.   Not the last.
Those were not harsh! Enter my bosom, enter,
Kind pitying words! untie there life's hard knot,
And let it drop off easily! How blest!
I have not robb'd the child, nor shamed the mother!   90
                         [*He dies.*
    Lady Malaspina. Poor soul! and the last voice he heard on earth
Was bitter blame, unmerited! And whose?
Mine, mine! Should they who suffer sting the sufferer?
O saints above! avenge not this misdeed!
What doth his hand hold out? A little crate,
With German letters round its inner rim . .
And . . full of wine! Yet did his lips burn white!
He tasted not what might have saved his life,
But brought it hither, to be scorn'd and die.
    [*Singers are heard in the same open space before an image.*]
Singers! where are they? My sight swims; my strength   100

125

Fails me; I can not rise, nor turn to look;
But only I can pray, and never voice
Prays like the sad and silent heart its last.

OLD MEN.

The village of the laurel grove *
Hath seen thee hovering high above,
Whether pure innocence was there,
Or helpless grief, or ardent prayer.
O Virgin! hither turn thy view,
For these are in Ancona too.
Not for ourselves implore we aid,   110
But thou art mother, thou art maid;
Behold these suppliants, and secure
Their humbled heads from touch impure!

MAIDENS.

Hear, maid and mother! hear our prayer!
Be brave and aged men thy care!
And, if they bleed, O may it be
In honour of thy Son and thee!
When innocence is wrong'd, we know
Thy bosom ever felt the blow.
Yes, pure One! there are tears above,   120
But tears of pity, tears of love,
And only from thine eyes they fall,
Those eyes that watch and weep for all.

[They prostrate themselves.

Lady Malaspina. How faintly sound those voices! altho' many:
At every stave they cease, and rest upon
That slender reed which only one can blow.
But *she* has heard them! Me too *she* has heard.
Heaviness, sleep comes over me, deep sleep:
Can it, so imperturbable, be death?
And do I for the last time place thy lip   130
Where it may yet draw life from me, my child!
Thou, who alone canst save him, thou wilt save.

[She dies: the child on her bosom still sleeping.

* The *House of Loreto* was not yet brought thither by the angels. [L.]

[ACT IV.] SCENE IV. NIGHT: THE MOLE OF ANCONA.

CONSUL.   SENATOR.

Senator. Sir consul, you have heard (no doubt) that fires
Have been seen northward all along the sky,
And angels with their flaming swords have sprung

Act. IV] *om. 1846, 1876.* SCENE IV.] *thus correctly in 1876.* SCENE II. *incorrectly 1846.*

From hill to hill. With your own eyes behold
No mortal power advancing. Host so numerous
No king or emperor or soldan led.
    Consul. A host, a mighty host, is there indeed?
    Senator. It covers the whole range of Falcognara.
    Consul. Methinks some fainter lights flit scatter'dly
Along the coast, more southward.
    Senator.   The archbishop   10
Hath seen the sign, and leads away his troops.
    Consul. We are too weak to follow. Can then aid
Have come so soon? 'Tis but the second night
Since we besought it.
    Senator.   In one hour, one moment,
Such aid can come, and *has* come. Think not, consul,
That force so mighty and so sudden springs
From earth. And what Italian dares confront
The German?
    Consul.   What Italian! All, sir; all.

ACT V.

SCENE I. TENT OF MARCHESELLA, NEAR ANCONA. EARLY MORNING.

MARCHESELLA. OFFICERS. PAOLUCCI.

    Officer. My general! easily I executed
Your orders.
    Marchesella. Have they fled, then?
    Officer.   Altogether.
    Marchesella. And could you reach the gate?
    Officer.   And enter too.
Paolucci's seal unbarr'd it; not until
I held two loaves above my head, and threw
My sword before me.
    Marchesella.   And what saw you then?
    Officer. There is a civil war within the city,
And insolence and drunkenness are rife.
Children, and old and middle-aged were reeling,
And some were slipping over, some devouring   10
Long-podded weeds with jagged edges, cast
Upon the shore.
    Paolucci.   Famine had gone thus far
(Altho' with fewer) ere we left the mole.
The ancient garden-wall was overthrown
To get the twisted roots of fennel out;

The fruit-tree that could give no fruit gave buds;
The almond's bloom was withering, but whoe'er
Possest that treasure pierced the bark for gum;
The mulberry sent her tardy shoot, the cane
Her tenderer one; the pouting vine untied   20
Her trellised gems; the apple-tree threw down
Her load of viscous mistletoe: they all
(Little it was!) did all they could for us.
    Marchesella. The Germans (look!) have left their tents behind:
We will explore them; for your wary soldiers
Suspect, and well they may, some stratagem.

[ACT V.] SCENE II. ERMINIA'S CHAMBER.

ERMINIA. MARIA.

                    [MARIA *is going.* ERMINIA *calls her back.*
    Erminia. Maria, is the countess very fair?
    Maria. Most beautiful. But you yourself must judge.
She sent me for you in the gentlest tone,
And far more anxious to see *you,* than you
(It seems) are to see *her.*
    Erminia.   I am afraid
To see her.
    Maria.   *You* afraid! Whom should *you* fear?
Beautiful as she is, are not you more so?
    Erminia. So you may think; others think otherwise.
    Maria. She is so affable! When many lords
Stood round about her, and the noblest of them   10
And bravest, Marchesella, who would give
His lands, his castles, even his knighthood for her . .
Whom do you think she call'd to her? . . the youth
Who cut the cables, and then hid himself
That none might praise him . . him who brought in safety
Your lover to the shore.
    Erminia (angrily).   Whom?
    Maria.   Whom? Stamura.
    Erminia. What heart could he not win . . not scorn . . not break?
    Maria. I do not hear those shy ones ever break
A woman's heart, or win one. They may scorn;
But who minds that?
    Erminia.   Leave me.
    Maria.   And tell the countess   20
You hasten to her presence?

THE SIEGE OF ANCONA

Erminia.   Is *he* there?
Maria. Who?
Erminia.   Dull, dull creature!
Maria.   The brave Marchesella?
Erminia. Are there none brave but he?
Maria.   O! then, Stamura.
No: when he led her from the mole again,
And she had enter'd the hall-door, he left her.
   Erminia. I fear'd he might be with her. Were he with her,
What matter! I could wait until . . Wait! why?
He would not look at me, nor I at him.
   Maria. No; I can answer for him. Were he born
Under the waves, and never saw the sun,   30
He could not have been colder. But you might
Have lookt at him, perhaps.
   Erminia.   Not I indeed.
   Maria. Few men are like him. How you hug me!
   Erminia.   Go . .
I will run first . . Go . . I am now quite ready.

[ACT V.] SCENE III. CHAMBER IN THE CONSUL'S HOUSE.

COUNTESS and ERMINIA.

Countess. The depths of love are warmer than the shallows,
Purer, and much more silent.
   Erminia (*aside*).   Ah! how true!
   Countess. He loves you, my sweet girl; I know he does.
   Erminia. He says not so.
   Countess.   Child! all men are dissemblers:
The generous man dissembles his best thoughts,
His worst the ungenerous.
   Erminia.   If, indeed, he loves me . .
   Countess. He told me so.
   Erminia.   Ah! then he loves me not.
Who, who that loves, can tell it?
   Countess.   Who can hide it?
His voice betray'd him; half his words were traitors . .
To him, my sweet Erminia! not to you.   10
What! still unhappy!   [ERMINIA *weeps.*
   Erminia.   Let me weep away
A part of too much happiness.
   Countess.   I wish
One more could see it. From these early showers
What sweets, that never spring but once, arise!

DRAMAS AND DRAMATIC SCENES

[ACT V.] SCENE IV.

Consul *enters.*

Consul. Before you leave us, since you part to-day,
From our full hearts take what lies deepest there,
And what God wills beyond all sacrifice . . .
Our praises, our thanksgivings. Thee we hail,
Protectress! But can words, can deeds, requite
The debt of our deliverance?
 Countess.   What I ask
Should not infringe your freedom. Power is sweet,
And victory claims something. I am fain
To exercise a brief authority
Within the walls, appointing you my colleague.   10
 Consul. Lady! this very night my power expires.
 Countess. And mine, with your connivance, shall begin.
 Consul. Lady! all power within the walls is yours.

[ACT V.] SCENE V.   ARCH OF TRAJAN ON THE MOLE.

CONSUL, MARCHESELLA, COUNTESS, SENATORS, &c.

Consul. We have no flowers to decorate the arch
Whence the most glorious ruler of mankind
Smiles on you, lady! and on you, who rival
His valour, his humanity, his bounty.
Nor are there many voices that can sing
Your praises. For, alas! our poor frail nature
(May it be seldom!) hears one call above
The call of gratitude. The famishing
Devour your bread. But, though we hear no praises,
There are who sing them to their harps on high,   10
And He who can alone reward you both
Listens in all his brightness to the song.
I do entreat you, blemish not your glory.
No exercise of might or sovranty
Can ever bring you such content again
As this day's victory, these altar-prayers
From rescued men, men perishing; from child
And parent: every parent, every child,
Who hears your name, should bless you evermore.
 Countess. I find, sir, I must win you through your daughter.   20
 Consul. The girl is grateful: urge her not too far:
I could not, without much compunction, thwart her.
Erminia! go: we meet again to-morrow.

THE SIEGE OF ANCONA

Countess. Come hither, my sweet girl! Coy as thou art,
I have seen one, once in my life, as coy.
Stand forth thou skulking youth! Here is no sea
To cover thee; no ships to scatter. Take
This maiden's hand . . unless her sire forbid . .
Holdest thou back? after confession too!
I will reveal it.

[*To* ERMINIA.

              And art thou ashamed?   30
Erminia. I am ashamed.
Countess.   Of what? thou simpleton!
Erminia. I know not what . . of having *been* ashamed.
Consul. Antonio! if thou truly lovedst her,
What, after deeds so valiant, kept thee silent?
Stamura. Inferior rank, deep reverence, due fear.
I know who rules our country.
Consul.   *I, who* saved her.

[FATHER JOHN *enters.*

Father John. What! and am I to be without reward?
Consul. Father! be sure it will be voted you.
Marchesella. And may not we too make our pious offerings,
For such they are, when such men will receive them.   40
Father John. I claim the hand of the affianced. Girl!
Shrink not from me! Give it to God!
Erminia.   'Tis given:
I can not, would not, will not, take it back.
Father John. Refractory! hast thou not dedicated
To God thy heart and soul?
Erminia.   I might have done it
Had never this day shone.
Father John.   And that youth's deeds
Outshone this day, or any day before.
When thou didst give thy hand to the deliverer
Whom God had chosen for us, then didst thou
Accomplish his great work, else incomplete.   50
I claim to pour his benediction on you
And yours for ever. Much, much misery,
Have I inflicted on the young and brave,
And can not so repent me as I should;
But 'twas in one day only my device
Ever wrought woe on any man alive.   [PAOLUCCI *enters.*
Consul. Who enters?
Paolucci.   Who? The bridesman.

Marchesella (embracing him).   My brave friend!
My father's!

Paolucci. Ay, thy grandfather's to boot.
And there was one, about my age, before him,
Sir Stefano, who wore a certain rose,   60
Radiant with pearls and rubies and pure gold,
Above the horse-tail grappled from the Turk.

Marchesella. We have not in the house that ornament.

Paolucci. I do believe he wears it in the grave.

Countess. There is a sword here bright enough to throw
A lustre on Stamura. Marchesella!

Marchesella. Kneel, sir!   *[He kneels to* ERMINIA.

Countess.   Not there.

Marchesella.   Yes, there; what fitter place?
We know but one high title in the world,
One only set apart for deeds of valour,
And palsied be the hand that ill confers it.   70
Here is the field of battle; here I knight thee.   *[Knights him.*
Rise, my compeer! Teach him his duties, lady,
Toward the poor, the proud, the faith, the sex.

Countess (smiling). Stamura! would you enter now my service?

Stamura. Yes, lady, were you wrong'd, this very hour;
Then might I better earn the bliss I seek.

GUZMAN AND HIS SON

[Published in 1846; reprinted 1876. See note at end of volume.]

[Scene. Tarifa in Southern Spain, A. D. 1296.]

[CHARACTERS]
[DON ALONZO PEREZ DE GUZMAN, Governor of Tarifa.
GUZMAN'S son, aged fifteen.]

Son. O father! am I then within thy arms
Once more? O yes; what other heart beats so?

Guzman. Son! art thou free? How couldst thou have escaped?

Son. God, God alone hath moved our enemy.

Guzman. He will perfect his work; he needs not us.

Son. I shall then hold my sister's eyes again
Within my own, her palm around my head!
Hence let us, while we may.

Guzman.   What speakest thou?

132

GUZMAN AND HIS SON

Son. If thou wilt only bid the war to pause,
I then am free.
    Guzman.   Free? then thou art not yet?   10
    Son. Unless our soldiers are withdrawn, not death
Alone awaits me.
    Guzman.   Mercy! mercy! God!
Without thy voice, without thy helping hand,
We stagger, weak as infants, from our duty.
Child! child! what can I do?
    Son.   Hath not God spoken?
And hath he ceast to speak?
    Guzman.   The brave man's breast
Is God's pure tabernacle: thro' the world,
Its storms, its deserts, we must carry it.
For Him against the infidel I war;
No peace, no truce, unless at his command.   20
    Son. God doth not always speak in thunder-clouds.
Even in the rain and dew, on the weak herb
That bends before them, there too is a voice
Breathing from Him. God is not always wroth;
He pities too, and most delights in pity.
    Guzman. Art thou afraid?
    Son.   Father! O father! no.
Shame me not thus. But to have felt thy lips
Upon my brow, upon my eyes, my mouth,
And to have breathed his breath who gave me life
Now sixteen years ago . . O father! save me!   30
    Guzman. Another would have said thou wert too rash;
How many fathers, of their sons, have said it,
Ay, and of brave ones, and for being brave;
I never said it, even when I lost thee,
Thee, my first-born, my only living son,
Precious as life . . almost, almost, as honour.
Son! thou art going into God's own glory,
And wouldst thou that thy father at one breath
Be spoil'd of his, and thine?
    Son.   No, father, no!
Fight on; and think of my worst fault no more.   40
They shout.
    Guzman (*to his trumpeters*). Reply.

                     [*Flourish of trumpets.*
             Thus my last groan is drown'd.

DRAMAS AND DRAMATIC SCENES

THE CORONATION

[Published in 1846; reprinted 1876. See note at end of volume.]

[Scene. Naples, 1830.]

FEBE. GRISELDA. ROMOALDA. ARMIDA. FRA PEPE.

Febe. Our good king Ferdinand, altho' I say it,
He is the bravest king that ever trod
Upon neat's leather, with a star to brisket.
  Griselda. Death, a dog's death, to whosoe'er denies it!
  Febe. He 's just like one of us, as kings should be.
  Griselda. Ay, he has bowels.
  Febe.   Faith! has he: I saw
His Majesty hold up a string of paste
Three palms in length, and down his throat it slid,
Just like the sword down that great conjuror's.
  Griselda. And then he claspt his hand on t'other side,   10
So natural!
  Febe.   And laught as heartily
As any pickpocket when purseless wight
Cries *thief*, and points him out to some near sbirro,
Who looks all ways but that, and will hear first
What has been lost, and where are witnesses.
  Griselda. Gnats, rats, and rogues, are bred in every city,
But only ours rears Ferdinands.
  Febe.   Here comes Fra Pepe.
  Fra Pepe. What now want ye? What hath brought ye
Into this crowd, among these men and horses?
  Griselda. Father! do shrive us ere we face such perils;   20
Trumpeters, poets, heroes, harlequins,
And overhead vast tottering catafalcs,
Choak-full, and mountain-high; ten thousand arms
Around ten thousand waists, and scarce can save them.
  Fra Pepe. I have no time to shrive ye.
  Febe.   God forbid
That we should urge it! But yon tripe smells bravely,
And we keep many Fridays in the week;
Do not turn this fine Tuesday into one.
  Fra Pepe. Knowest thou what tripe is?
  Febe.   From ancient records
And faint remembrances.
  Fra Pepe.   Hast tasted it?   30
  Griselda. Why should we not, on some rare festival?

134

THE CORONATION

Fra Pepe. Luxury will creep downward, and seize souls.
Who pampered you at this enormous rate?
    Griselda. We are not young ones now, but heretofore
We have had lovers, and have seen carlinos
Spin upon table; and the change was ours.
    Fra Pepe. O shame upon ye!
    Febe.   Shame is called upon us
When we are old and needy; they who brought
Shame and old age upon us, call it loudest.
    Fra Pepe. Thou talkest foolishly indeed, good woman!   40
    Febe. We all talk our best things when teeth are flush.
    Griselda. Wit is not wanting while the cheek wears roses
And coral lips are ready to impart it.
    Romoalda. I doubt now whether all this tripe be real.
    Ermida. They got it cheap, or would not give so largely;
An ounce, two ounces, to one family.
    Febe. What! kings mere hucksters! better say they stole it.
    Griselda. Such glorious ones would scarcely steal the cattle,
Much less what some call offal. Rob poor farmers!
Come, Febe, if we listen to her talk   50
We may do penance in a stiller place.
    Febe. Never say *"come away,"* my good Griselda!
While they are forking it from pans and kettles
Wide as the crater and as piping-hot.
O father Pepe! could you touch, see, smell it!
Bees may make honeycombs; what bee could ever
Make honeycomb like tripe? Ah fat! ah pith!
Soft, suctionable, savory.
    Fra Pepe.   Out upon thee!
    Griselda. See there now! Off he goes!
    Febe.   No fault of mine.
    Griselda. Yes; thy shrill squally shouts, and rubbing down   60
Of mouth, with one arm first, and then the other,
And then the apron. Who beside thyself
Would talk so touchingly, so near mid-day?
A qualm came over *me;* I felt half-famisht;
No monk on earth could stand it; not the best
That ever faced the devil in the desert.
    Romoalda. Between you, pretty work! the frate gone!
    Febe. Follow him: who detains you? We want nothing
With you, signora!
    Armida.   Let those vulgar women
Talk about tripe; we can buy liver, *buy* it,   70

Drink the half-flask, doze the half-hour, again
Be young, then shrive us. One night scores not deep.
There 's, by my reckoning, mother Romoalda,
Only one night between us and to-morrow.
    Romoalda (striking her stomacher). The best church-clock lies under
    this red canvas,
And points, within a trice, to dinner-time.
    Griselda. You totter about sadly, neighbour Febe!
    Febe. No wonder; they have thrown so many pulps
And peels of melon on the ground, I know
My feet are wet, and my whole stockings, with them   80
And plashy daffodils, like artichokes
In size, knee-deep, and palm-leaves long as boats:
So, were there room for falling, fall I must.
    Griselda. May-hap you tasted a cup's rim at starting?
    Febe. Before we met, one little broken one
I sipt. They never told me 'twas so strong:
And then they took advantage of me.
    Griselda.   Men
Always do that with us poor lonely women.
    Febe. 'Twas not the wine nor men: a fig for them!
This hubbub has confounded me, this crowd;   90
Soldiers and monks, and mummers fill the street,
And candles bigger than the priests that bear them,
And saucy boys running aside the candles
To catch the drops, leaving one hand for mischief;
And then the bells are making such a coil,
Saint against saint, from Mole to Capo-monte,
We can not hear the loudest voice cry *gara*
If horse or mule tramp muzzling into us.
In vain, Griselda, lift we up our shoulders
And whisper in God's ear we think it hard.   100
    Griselda. Well, Febe, by stout shoving we are now
Beyond the mob. What ails thee?
    Febe.   Many things
Ail me; vexations and infirmities;
Beside a tiny matter of an infant
I dropt into the sea through awkwardness.
    Griselda. Did not the child cry out, as children should?
    Febe. It did. Well, well! I made an angel of it.

---

85 *a comma after* broken one *is deleted in Landor's own copy of 1846, but retained in 1876.*

Griselda. Then say no more about it.
    Febe.   'Tis in heaven,
Among the other angels: but I fear
That when they say, "Sing! sing, my little one!"   110
It may give answer, "Five hard fingers here
Have spoilt my singing."
    Griselda.   They who make an angel
Make more than they who make ten penitents,
And yet to make one penitent wins heaven.
    Febe. I sometimes wish 'twere back again.
    Griselda.   To cry?
    Febe. Ah! it *does* cry ere the first sea-mew cries;
It wakes me many mornings, many nights,
And fields of poppies could not quiet it.
    Griselda. Febe! we must not think of it to-day.
Sorrow is most offensive to the great,   120
And nobody should grieve when kings are near.
This, above all days, is a day of joy;
Another king is given to the world,
And our first duty is to guard his throne.
    Febe. And drink a little beaker to his health.
We, mother Romoalda! with Christ's help,
Will, against all his enemies, support him.
O! I am thirsty with the dust! beside,
I was so worried by that odious mob,
The people seem to push against me still.   130

DRAMAS AND DRAMATIC SCENES

[BEATRICE CENCI]

FIVE SCENES

BY WALTER SAVAGE LANDOR

I. COUNT CENCI AND CONFESSOR.
II. BEATRICE AND HER AJA MARGARITA.
III. COUNT, STEWARD, PEASANTS, BEATRICE.
IV. BEATRICE AND POPE CLEMENT VIII.
V. DEATH OF BEATRICE.

[Published in full in *Fraser's Magazine*, January, 1851; reprinted 1853, 1876. Scene IV had been published separately in *The Keepsake for 1851* (issued 1850). See notes at end of volume. Text *Fraser's Magazine*, 1851.]

PREFACE.

POETRY is not History. In features they may resemble; in particulars, in combinations, in sequences, they must differ. History should "tell the truth, the whole truth, and nothing but the truth." Poetry, like all the fine arts, is eclectic. Where she does not wholly invent, she at one time amplifies and elevates; at another, with equal power, she simplifies, she softens, she suppresses. This part of her prerogative has fallen much into desuetude. Many a rich proprietor is a bad husbandman. The system of deep draining, or even of carrying off the surface-water, is but partially introduced. We have, however, seen tragedians, of late, who bear the pall and sceptre "right royally."   10

The author of the *Five Scenes* assumes no place among them: he stands only just near enough to make his plaudit heard. These scenes interfere very little with Shelley's noble tragedy. Two names are the same; one character, by necessity, is similar; Count Cenci, the wickedest man on record. His benefactions to the Papacy, under the rubric of penalties or quit-rents for crimes, amounted to three hundred thousand crowns; so that after Saint Peter, King Pepin, and Countess Matilda, the Roman See was under greater obligations to him than to any other supporter. Crimes in the Papal States are as productive to *Government* as vines and olives: no wonder then his death was so cruelly avenged. His life had been its *gaudy-day;* and his loss was the severest it ever had sustained in one person. Yet, so little of gratitude is there in high places, his funeral was unattended by the Cardinals and Court; and, what is more remarkable, no poet wrote an elegy to deplore or an epitaph to praise him.

Title. Beatrice Cenci and Pope Clement VIII, *Keepsake, 1851.*
Sub-title. By . . . Landor *om. 1853. Scene headings,* I. II. III. V., *not in Keepsake, 1851.*
Preface. not in *Keepsake, 1851.*   *l.* 17 Pepin and Countess] For Pepin's "splendid donation" to the Papacy, see Gibbon, *Roman Empire,* Chap. 49; and Hallam, *Middle Ages,* Chap. 3, for the "famous Countess Matilda's" grant to the Holy See of the reversion of all her possessions. [W.]

BEATRICE CENCI

SCENE I.

COUNT CENCI *and* CONFESSOR, *in Rome.*

Confessor. Our thoughts, my lord, are not entirely ours:
The Tempter hath much influence over them,
And sways them to and fro.
    Count.   More often to
Than fro, methinks.
    Confessor.   Prayer can do much, and more
Confession, most goodwill toward the Church.
Nieces and uncles, aunts and nephews, meet
In holy matrimony; but beyond,
The Church forbids; nor grants even these without
Due cause, in alms and Petropatrimonials.
    Count. If one may do it, why may not another?   10
    Confessor. Only the great may do it; only princes.
Sovrans may ride where common men must walk,
And may with safety and with seemliness . .
With seemliness! aye more . . . with acclamation,
And dance and bonfire, leap across the sheepwalk
Where sheep and shepherd humbly creep along.
    Count. Such are their doings in the Church and Court
And other places, for example-sake
No doubt.
    Confessor. No doubt whatever. Great the good
Arising from the wealth they thus disburse.   20
The Church, thus aiding and thus aided, throws
Her sackcloth from her, and sits up elate,
Triumphant, glorified, the spouse of Christ,
Born in the manger but to mount the throne.
None but the fool and the ungodly doubt
These saving truths.
    Count.   None but the fool, most surely;
For who beside the fool would pour his broth
Upon the threshing-floor at noontide hour
When he is hungry and may take his fill?
About the ungodly you know more than I,   30
Who never have held converse with the knaves,
For, to my mind, they must be fools as well;
Sure to be losers at our table here,
And doubtful of revenge another day.
    Confessor. They dare not meet confession face to face,
As honester and braver sinners do,

Like you, my lord, who ask before you take,
Ready to pay the penalty of guilt,
And weighing both in steady even scales.
    Count. You always comfort the few qualms that rise   40
Within my breast, too empty or too full.
The present sometimes puzzles me; the past
Is past for ever.
    Confessor.   But beyond the grave . . .
    Count. I am short-sighted, and would spare my eyes;
Too much light hurts them: you wear spectacles,
And take them off and put them on again,
To read or not to read, as suits you best.
    Confessor. Your lordship has paid dearly for some sins!
    Count. Churchmen may get them cheaper; they can whirl
The incense round and sweeten one another.   50
    Confessor. Count! we are friends; but this sounds rather free.
    Count. My speech is free, and free too is my hand.
Three paoli is the price of masses now
To the poor man; the citizen pays five;
The noble seven; but often bargaining
For thirteen to the dozen: I meanwhile
Reckon but twelve, and pay my crown a-piece,
Ay, for a thousand, father, for a thousand . .
If this won't save me, what the devil can?
    Confessor. Do not be angry; let us hope it will;   60
But matters, awkward matters, lie between . .
We say no masses for the soul on earth.
    Count. Yet here it hath its troubles as down yonder;
Masses might oil them over on the spot
And supple the sting's barb; it lies not deep.
    Confessor. No, no; far different is their ordinance.
    Count. Well, I believe it: let us say no more.
    Confessor. Best so, my son! Sweet, sweet is resignation.
Three hundred thousand crowns have overlaid
Some gross enormities: stifled they lie,   70
No whisper over them: the Pope's right hand
Hath wiped the record from the Book of Life.
    Count. Are you quite sure?
    Confessor.   Infallibility
Declares it.
    Count.   Bless infallibility!

37 lord] Lord *1853*.   54 citizen pays] citizens pay *1853*.

BEATRICE CENCI

Confessor. Sin not, my son! but, sinning, strait confess
And stand absolved.
    Count.   Plague me no more. I have
Confest. The wish . . again I swear . . is odious.
    Confessor. The very thought confounds and petrifies me.
Ten yokes of oxen, fifty casks of wine
(Were it Orvieto), scarcely would efface   80
Such scandal.
    Count.   I have played away the worth
Of those ten yokes, those fifty casks, but lately,
And therefore have not now wherewith . . .
    Confessor.   The sin
Of gambling is, alas! worse . . worse than all.
(*After a pause.*) If you will have the peach . . why, have the peach;
But pay for it: the crab and sloe come cheaper.
Costly or vile, 'tis better to abstain.
                  [CONFESSOR *goes out, the* COUNT *remains.*
    Count (*alone*). There must be (since all fear it) pains below.
But how another's back can pass for mine,
Or how the scourge be softened into down   90
By holy water, puzzles me: no drop
Is there; and nothing holy. Doubt I will.
Now, can these fellows in their hearts believe
What they would teach us? Yes; they must. Methinks
I have some courage: I dare many things,
Most things; yet were I certain I should fall
Into a lion's jaws at close of day
If I went on, I should be loth to go,
Altho some nightcap from some booth well barr'd
Opens a window, crying *Never fear!*   100
Is there no likeness? Theirs is the look-out.
They toss my sins on shoulder readily;
Are they quite sure they can as readily
Shuffle them off again? They catch our pouch.
The price, the stipulated price, I pay;
Will the receiver be as prompt to them?
May not he question them? Well! there are gone
Three hundred thousand crowns; and more must go;
I shall cry *quits* . . but what will their cry be?
When time is over, none can ask for time;   110
Payment must come . . and these must pay, not I.

        90 softened] soften'd *1853.*

'Three hundred thousand crowns,' runs my receipt,
'Holiness and Infallibility'
At bottom. I am safe: the firm is good.
If the wax burn their fingers, let them blow
And cool it: there it sticks: my part is done.   116

SCENE II.

BEATRICE CENCI *and her* AJA MARGARITA.

Margarita. Blessed be Saint Remigio! This day year,
This his own day, was held the marriage-feast
Within our castle-walls, which always frown'd
Till then, and never since smiled heartily.
Beatrice. We have been very happy, Margarita,
Before and since.
Margarita.   I want another feast;
I yearn; and you must give it, lady mine.
Beatrice. My father can alone ordain a feast
Other than what this pleasant vintage-time
Always brings round.
Margarita.   Things are got ready soon.   10
Your sister for her bridal festival
Borrowed some vases filled with citron-trees
From those who brought the chaplets. Signor Conte
Has not one citron-tree, one orange-bush,
One lemon, one train'd jessamine: he never
Has prickt his finger with bare lavender,
To curse it. Flowers and music he abhors.
And how he hated those dull nightingales!
Indeed they are too tiresome: what think you?
Beatrice. If their sweet sorrow overshadows mine   20
I ought to love them for it, and I do.
I have not always thought them melancholy;
'Tis but of late; and gayer things are worse.
Margarita. You were less childish when you were a child.
However, flowers you cull as formerly
And put them in your bosom.
Beatrice.   They are cool.
Margarita. Are they? Some too are sweet. The Count is caught
By fragrance; not their vulgar fragrance; gloves,
Gloves I have seen (no matches though) that smelt

1 This day] *St. Remigio's day, October 1.* [W.]   12 Borrowed . . . filled] Bor-
row'd . . . fill'd *1853.*

Deliciously, about his private room. 30
But music! we keep music to ourselves,
And close the door upon it, like the plague.
Make last year this. I did believe, I did
Indeed, that you could better understand
My meaning.
    Beatrice.   I have understood it well,
But dare not ask my father anything;
It·is undaughterly, unmaidenly,
To ask for a carousal or a dance.
My sister and my brother may suggest
More properly what might entice our friends. 40
    Margarita. I doubt it. One enticement, one alone,
Depends on you. Marry, my pretty dove!
    Beatrice. Marry? and whom?
    Margarita.   Have you forgotten all
Who drank the vintage of the year before
To make (they said) room for last year's?
    Beatrice.   In truth
I hardly know their names. I sat not with 'em
At supper or at dinner or at dance . .
Although at dance I was, but placed apart,
With you beside me, pleas'd not quite so well.
    Margarita. May-be. But you saw all, and all saw you. 50
    Beatrice. May-be that too. I saw them all, and lookt
With joy upon them: whether they saw *me*
I know not, heed not: 'twas enough that joy
Seem'd universal.
    Margarita.   But among the guests
Could not you name one name?
    Beatrice.   Perhaps I could,
And more than one, give me but time to think.
    Margarita. None yet? none? Let me call them over then.
Don Beppo, Don Olinto, Don Olimpio,
Don Prospero-Leonzio Buffalmacco,
Don Cane della Scala, Don Gatteschi, 60
Don Tissaferne, Don Ambrogio,
Don Michel-Angiolo, Don Angiolo
Without the Michel . . .
    Beatrice.   Take your breath, dear Aja.
They weary you. Suppose we leave the rest.
    Margarita. Don Carlo, Don Ferrante, Don Camillo,
Don Agostino Pecore, Don Gallo,

Don Pio-Maria-Giuseppe Squarcialupi,
Don Innocenzio-Flavio Cinghialone,
Don Neri, Don Petruccio, Don Giuliano,
Don Tito, Don Trajano, Don Aurelio,   70
Three pretty brothers, save Aurelio's eye,
A little red about it, and Trajano's
Swerving a little, but as black as jet,
And bright as dagger drawn out overnight
And seen to, and fresh-whetted for revenge.
Your noble father hath such furniture,
Stored where you children might not hurt yourselves,
Not in the armoury, but close behind
Old breviaries and missals, and among
The holy relics that preserve the house,   80
Frightening the demons from it night and day.
    Beatrice. Oh! rather run through fifty names than tell
Such stories.
    Margarita.   Fifty! aye, there were threescore,
Or near upon it . . *men*, I mean; we women
Here count for nothing.
    Beatrice.   Not in dance?
    Margarita.   They all
Had partners; that is certain; but what then?
    Beatrice. You seem to have collected a whole host
Of the young men; the ladies you forget.
    Margarita. Even less worth remembrance.
    Beatrice.   Some were lovely.
    Margarita. I saw no loveliness; and why should you,   90
Whom such girls envy?
    Beatrice.   Envy *me?* I shared
No partner. Only one, and she but once
Lookt at me: 'twas when I had clapt my hands
After that pretty song; which then she bade
Her lover bring me, and you snatcht away.
    Margarita. Such silly words!
    Beatrice.   Yes; but sung plaintively.
I wish I sang as well.
    Margarita.   Try then once more.
    Beatrice. You call them silly; so indeed they are.
    Margarita. Songs sound the sweeter in the solitude
Of sense.
    Beatrice. Who wrote them?
    Margarita.   Some young idle boy,   100

Who should be whipt for his effrontery.
Begin; or you will have more ears about.
   Beatrice. I have no heart to sing it.
   Margarita.   Then will I.

> What says the dove on yonder tree?
>   *Coo coo* . . and only a *coo coo?*
> I hear as plain as plain can be,
>   Poor restless bird! *come! come! do! do!*
>   The words I often said to you.

> If blushes pain not, be ashamed
>   A bird hath caught the sounds from me,   110
> While you, by that mild teacher blamed,
>   Have yet to learn by heart what he
>   Repeats so well, so tenderly.

   Beatrice. O thank you! dearest Margarita, thank you!
You sang them with such tenderness; you made
The most of them.
   Margarita.   I made them all they are.
Let me go on while memory is at hand,
Or half the signors will slip through my fingers.
   Beatrice. How good you are! but are you not quite tired?
   Margarita. Now you have put me out. Peace! let me try.   120
Don Sigismondo with his twin Goffredo,
Don Serafino, Don Serafico,
Don Sant-Elizabetta, Don Sant-Anna,
Don Beatifico, Don Ipsilante . .
   Beatrice. O Aja!
   Margarita.   So! the shoe then pinches there?
   Beatrice. Rather go on than say it. Who is he?
   Margarita. No very proper man. I might have run
A furlong further with more likelihood.
Don Biagio, Don Cristofano, Don Bino,
Don Agostino, Don Teodosio,   130
Don Mario, Don Bastiano, Don Eufemio,
Don Giorgio, Don Giorgione, Don Silvestro,
Don Gasparo, Don Stefano, Don Gino.
   Beatrice. O what a river-full of sparkling bubbles!
Will the stream never end?
   Margarita.   Not yet awhile.
Don Cinque-Pesci, Don Maria-Balbo,
Don Romolo, Don Cino, Don Gieronimo,
Don Tertulliano (Teresina's brother),

123 Sant-Anna] Santa-Ann *text 1853*, Santa-Anna *corrigenda 1853.*

Don Opobalsamo-di-Caritade,
Don Romualdo, Don Ricupero,   140
Don Unigenito Gino Cappone,
Don Amoroo-Galateso Stella,
Don Braccioforte, Don Pacifico,
Don Bacio-Santa-Croce Cicciaporci,
Don Carl-Onofrio-Gru de' Beccafichi.
 Beatrice. O the strange names!
 Margarita.   Men never choose their own,
But take them as they're given, to show Saint Peter,
Who knows their water-mark and lets them pass.
 Beatrice. No doubt of that . . and we may let them too.
 Margarita. Wait, wait a moment: here are some few more. 150
Don Luca, Don Abele, Don Marino,
Don Sosimo, Don Zeno, Don Camillo,
Don Loretano (heir of Don Fulgenzio),
Don Curio de Montaspro, Don Pasquale.
 Beatrice. What an interminable waste of names!
Are not the grilli of last year gone by?
 Margarita. Nearly. Sandrino, Piero, and Cirillo;
The two first are, the other should be, poor,
Noble, but wanting pride, and shunning friends.
 Beatrice. Cirillo! sure 'twas he that sate beside 160
The little girl whose arms and face were burnt
So sadly.
 Margarita. Hideously, most hideously.
Her mother left her by the fire alone
In infancy.
 Beatrice. Alone he sate with her
On a long barrel.
 Margarita.   Heeding not who laught
Outrageously.
 Beatrice.   I saw them, I saw *him* . .
And could have kist him . . had he been my brother . .
 Margarita. And rather handsomer.
 Beatrice.   Could he be that?
 Margarita. So! Does the pin stick there? aye, to the head.
 Beatrice. I ought to love him: but we never love 170
(I do believe) the only men we ought,
Or not as we should love them if we might.
 Margarita. He would not join the party; no, not he,
Nor offer, where' twas proper, one salute:

161 face] legs 1853.

That ugly barrel and that uglier child
Besotted him; he staid there to the last.
Pride! no; 'twas worse; 'twas sheer rusticity.
Thinking of him, six better men escaped me.
Don Marlo, Don Virgilio, Don Matteo,
Don Beppo, Don Simoni, Don Marziale,   180
Brother of Donna . . stay . . Donna Lucrezia,
Who ran away from home, and was pursued
Somewhat too late, caught, and let loose again,
A virgin, a pure virgin, to the last.
Ready to swear it were three witnesses,
Her father, and her husband, and herself:
No law-court can refuse three witnesses.
   Beatrice. One surely is enough where honour is.
Prythee no more about her.
   Margarita.   Don Marziale
Call'd out the vile betrayer, but in vain;   190
He fled; and that same week another won
The lovely prize, and wears it to this day,
At least a part of it, a husband's part.
   Beatrice. O Aja! what is this? what words are those?
But . . hath she turn'd her face to God, and God
His face to her? May it be thus! Forgive,
O blessed Saint Remigio! and do thou
Thrice-blessed Virgin, purer than Heaven's light,
My wicked thought! Thy countenance was turn'd
One moment from me. In one moment sin   200
Bursts through our frail embankment, and engulphs
All superstructure human strength can raise.
   Margarita. Mad art thou, or inspired.
   Beatrice.   Mad, mad, I was,
But now, with contrite heart, am calm again.
   Margarita. I do believe I am as good as most,
If you are better, I am wiser, child!
I say as many prayers, and know more ways
Of happiness. Among these vacant I
Choose one . . or two at most. There are indeed
Who think *one* better; and they may be right.   210
Our mother Church, long-suffering and indulgent,
Would rather tie two knots than sever one.
You ponder on these things without one word.
   Beatrice. I dare not utter one; I scarce dare ponder.

    188 honour] honor *1853.*   203 inspired.] inspired ? *1853.*

                   L 2

Margarita. It is all right, if we will only think so.
Beatrice. True, true . . but do not make me think about it.
Margarita. No, child, while there are those who think for us,
And have much broader backs and tougher hides,
Fireproof, and tongues that charm the devil off.
I like to take all good men at their word,   220
Without a scruple or suspicion. Thought
Is uphill work; many its paths, few smooth;
Let others trudge 'em while we two sit still . .
Sit still we may, but not sit quite so grave.
I must not let you look at me demurely
On such a day as this. My lord last year
Admitted, as all other lords are wont,
His contadini, married and unmarried,
To dance upon the terrace with the great.
Will he to-night?
    Beatrice.   I hope he may.
    Margarita.   Why hope it?   230
The great are absent.
    Beatrice.   Yet without the great
The lowly may be happy, at small cost.
Good-morrow brightens the whole day to them,
Good-night brings early rest and hopeful dreams :
A friendly word, a gentle look, is more
From one above than twenty truer ones
From those who merit best the peasant's love.
    Margarita. Whimsical girl! whimsical more than ever!
I have seen tears fall on this dimpled hand
When it had graspt the sunburnt hairy one,   240
And would not let it go, altho' I chided;
I have seen you stand a-tip-toe to return
The kiss imprinted on it, when the face
Was decently averted, whether man's
Or woman's; for the Count had been enraged.
    Beatrice. Stern he may be; but cruel no, not that.
    Margarita. Propriety! maintain propriety!
Minor transgressions every one forgives.
We must not let the humble spring too high.
    Beatrice. Nor sink too low. God gave us hearts for theirs   250
To rest upon, and form'd them not of stone.
    Margarita. This now, this brings me back again. Come, talk
Rationally with me . . In this afternoon
My lord your father, as you know, returns.

BEATRICE CENCI

Beatrice. Happier I may be; not much happier:
For when he saw me last, now some months since,
He took me on his knee, then pusht me off,
Suddenly, strangely; stampt, and left the room.
   Margarita. Is this worth crying for?
   Beatrice.   I think it is.
   Margarita. He may have thought of somebody at Rome   260
As pretty in his eyes, and not unlike.
   Beatrice. Should he not love me more then for her sake?
   Margarita. Men are odd creatures; what they should they don't,
And what they should not, sure enough, they do.
How would you like a stepmother?
   Beatrice.   If young
I should so like her! We would play together
All day, all night.
   Margarita.   Simpleton!
   Beatrice.   We would toss
Roses in summer, daffodils in spring,
Into each other's faces: if they struck
The eyes, O then what kisses! what protests   270
We were not hurt! The saints would all forgive.
I know the names of many good to us
Young girls, and mindful they were girls themselves.
   Margarita. What fancy strikes you now?
   Beatrice.   One strange and wild.
Some say my mother lives. It can not be;
I have not seen her many many days,
A year almost.
   Margarita.   *Stepmother*, you should say.
   Beatrice. Stepmother! what can that be else than mother?
She loved me, and wept over me. She rests,
(I trust) with God. Another may console me,   280
If she prevail with Him to send another.
My own, who waved me in her arms to sleep,
Could not have loved me better than the last.
When did she die? and where? Not here, we know;
No funeral was here; no sadder looks
Than usual in the poor good villagers . .
Tell me: it happen'd while I was away?
   Margarita. Useless to ask for what we cannot know,
And what, if we could know it, might do harm.
Nobody here dares stir where the Count's feet   290
Move softly, nobody his steps espy.

Beatrice. How prudent and how gentle the reproof!
But . . could I hear my mother were alive!
Margarita. Your brothers, both are living, tho' afar,
She may be too, and nearer.*
Beatrice.   Grant it, Heaven!
Was it not wicked then to think of joy
With one who soon might take her vacant place;
To think of smiles and games where tears were shed,
Perhaps for me too, since mine also fell?
O! it *was* wicked. Mother! pray for me!   300
Both mothers! pray for me! Let not my grief
Disturb your bliss! bear up my prayer on yours!
Margarita. Make me not dismal. Prayers are excellent
In the right place. Seven are the sacraments,
And of all seven, marriage is the best:
This lies before you; some are past, some wait.
Let us return to thoughts far pleasanter;
I do not mean of saints and patronesses . .
Another, and no saint, but a mama,
Might wish you married; sure your father would.   310
Beatrice. If ever I should marry . . but I feel
I never shall . . so let me say no more.
Margarita. Were my ears open to catch wind and cold
Like this, my Lady Beatrice? Speak;
Say something; to the purpose, if you can,
But something.
Beatrice.   Should one love me, may that one
Be better, wiser, older!
Margarita.   Hush! hush! hush!
Wiser, and no harm done. Older! God's peace!
Well, certainly sixteen is somewhat young
For bridegroom . . but no help for it, no harm,   320
Past all endurance.
Beatrice.   I may hope to live
A few years longer; and should Heaven bestow
One many older yet, who truly loves,
He will love wisely: he will see in me
Much to correct with calmer eyes than mine.
Margarita. Aye; some old creature. He would find out faults,
Or make them for you. Never let young blood
Be frozen, or (Madonna!) it will burst

---

* She lived imprisoned. The whole family was [were *1853*] kept separated. [L.]
294 tho'] tho *1853*.

With such a crack as never shepherd heard
In early spring o'er tarn on Appennine. 330
Beatrice. We will not talk about what will not be.
Margarita. Hark! Was not that the bugle? There again!
Haste, haste upstairs . . dress yourself handsomely . .
The Count is coming.
Beatrice.　　　　I will dress myself
To please him; but with arms about his neck
First crave his blessing. Loose me; let me run.

SCENE III.

COUNT, STEWARD, PEASANTS, BEATRICE.

Count. They might do something better, I should think,
Than sing o' Sundays. I am quite dog-tired
With this hard ride.
Steward.　　　　Indeed, my lord, you seem,
Despite of youth as ever on your side,
Wearied and ill at ease. The ride is long:
Strong as they are, alert as are the grooms,
The horses must have suffered this hot day.
Count. My horses are half-dead as well as I:
Bravely they mounted the last hill, however,
At sight of stable: all that was not smoke 10
Was froth; the bits had burnt your hand to touch.
Steward. Too weak to battle with the flies, outstretcht
Lies every groom, his hat upon his face,
In the thin shade dropt from the grange's eaves.
Count. Swill'd with unwatered wine.
Steward.　　　　　　No time or heart
Had they to lift the bucket from the well.
Count. I have a mind to whip them up again.
Their liveries look already like the litter,
The silver tarnisht, and the scarlet dim
As the last musty medlar of the year. 20
What can those idlers yonder want of me?
What do they here?
Steward.　　　My gentle lord, permit
Those who have laboured all the week apart,
To meet upon the blessedest of days
After due service; to inquire how fares

7 suffered] suffer'd *1853.*　　15 unwatered] unwater'd *1853.*　　23 laboured]
labour'd *1853.*

The sick at home; to slip the thin brass coin
Into the creviced box their priest shakes round,
That the soul suffer not for lack of mass.
What other day for distant friends to hear
The weal or woe that swells the breast with joy   30
Or sinks with grief? In either case, it pours
Its fulness forth before His awful throne
Whose will they are.
    Count.   No preaching, sir, for me.
A mass, and welcome . . twice or thrice a-year . .
The Church requires it: what the Church requires
I do . . or pay for what is left undone.
                [Tuning of instruments is heard.
Crack me those strings! stop me that fellow's breath
Who blows his fife so fitfully! To hear
Those chords and canes, sure were enough without
What they call tuning: that is worst of all . . .   40
    Steward. Most gracious Signor Conte! it may please
My Lady Beatrice.
    Count.   Let the fools
Tickle their strings, and twist their lips. Set on!
        [Steward gives a sign. Peasants chant.

Can any be both great and gay?
    Then may our lord be all his life:
We halve it with him this one day,
    Who bring the lute to wed the fife.

We wish no feast: above our heads
    Swell the rich clusters of the vine:
No lamps wish we: behold, there spreads   50
    Her robe of stars the jessamine.

We have not many songs to sing,
    And those we have are sadly dull;
The livelier all were made for spring,
    When hopes are fresh and hearts are full.

We must not mind the cruel tale
    Old rhymers from old books relate,
About the blood on nightingale,
    Who comes each year and sings her fate.

She now is gone; but happier love   60
    Attends the bird that yet remains;
Attends the chaste, the constant dove,
    And soothes (if pains she know) her pains.

Sweet were the flowers May rear'd for June
    To kiss, and you to find and cull;
Sweeter the fruits the vintage-moon
    Ripens, with gold-red radiance full.

BEATRICE CENCI

O lady! much is yours to grant . .
  Bride-cake, and ribands, rest within! . .
A smile to rule our dance we want,   70
  A nod to tune our violin.

To-morrow we prepare to heap
  With heavy grapes the creaking wane;
The hearts the last year's bride made leap,
  For you this year shall leap again.

Beatrice. Kind friends! my father would not lose both daughters
So near together. Some years yet must pass
Before we think about it.
  Count.   Send them off.
What insolence! to mix in my concerns!
My Beatrice! thou wert ever fond   80
Of chattering with the peasants. Very wrong:
Whimper not; but look up.
  Beatrice.   Could it be wrong?
  Count. Early in childhood very wrong 'twere not,
And more another's fault than thine, perhaps . .
Nay, be not vext, my prettiest, overmuch.
  Beatrice. Kind father! this is, yes, indeed, too kind.
  Count (to STEWARD). I would not have them look upon me now,
Or they might think me weak. They may have heard
The idle name I call'd her. Spake I loud?
Did they; dost thou imagine?   Plagues upon 'em!   90
  Steward. All call her so.
  Count.   How dare they?
  Steward.   They all love her;
Fathers the most of all, I do believe.
  Count. Send them away. Off with them all. Begone!
Off with you!
(*To the* STEWARD). Give the fools some bread and wine,
And send them back.
  Beatrice.   Dear father! let them stay
A little while. They may do more than I
In cheering you! They may remind you, sir,
Of last year's festival. Look now, and see
If you miss any.
  Count.   Oxen, horses, mules,
We count.
  Beatrice. Dear creatures! yes.
  Count.   Enough, if those.   100
  Beatrice. Here only two are wanting, girls I mean.

153

Beppina you permitted to be married,
And poor Cristina wastes away . .
    Count.   For love,
No doubt . . Let her too go.
    Beatrice.   Alas! alas!
She will be gone, and soon. She caught the fever
From her old mother.
    Count.   Of what name?
    Beatrice.   Her own,
The lame Cristina, who brought strawberries
From the hill-side, when sister and myself
Lay, as she lies, in fever.
    Count.   Was it she
Who made the butter?
    Beatrice.   O, how glad I am   110
You recollect her!
    Count.   If her girl is sick
She can not make it: if she could, for me
No butter from a house where folks are sick.
Return we, Beatrice; I am tired;
I have not slept since dinner.
    Beatrice.   Father dear!
May sleep refresh you more than dinner did,
And not be sent away from you so soon!

SCENE IV.

BEATRICE *and the* POPE.

    Clement. Who art thou? and what art thou?
    Beatrice.   What I am
I dare not utter, holy father! Tears
The bitterest ever shed from sleepless eye
Announce me: none so wretched! none so lost!
    Clement. Thy name?
    Beatrice.   'Tis Beatrice.
    Clement.   Thy surname?
    Beatrice.   Was . . .
    Clement. Speak, thou sobbing fool! Then speak will I.
Cenci. No doubt thou gladly wouldst forget
Thy father's name; it burns into thy soul;
Thou canst not shake it off, thou canst not quench it.
Thou, ere thou camest hither, didst forget   10
Thou wert his child. What wouldst thou urge thereon?

BEATRICE CENCI

Beatrice. Never did I forget he was my father;
He did forget . . forget . . I was his child.
    Clement. Passionate tears drop from unholy lids
More often than from holy. The best men
May chide their children; may dislike; may hate . . .
    Beatrice. Oh, had he hated me!
    Clement.   Perverse! perverse!
Bold interrupter of my speech, vouchsafed
To lead thee from the wandering of thy thoughts.
I would have said, where daughters are untoward,   20
Chiefly where they are wanton, sires may hate.
    Beatrice. Urge not that fault, O holy father! spare it!
    Clement. I thought so. I *will* spare it. There are more.
Not only hast thou with that little hand
Transfixt the breast which cherisht thee . . Ay, shriek!
Stamp, spread the floor as 'twere with yellow straw . .
Here are no youths to gather that fine gold,
And treasure it, and gloat on it unseen.
Not only hast thou done so, but hast torn
Thy ancient house from its foundation. Crime,   30
Like lightning, at one stroke pierces the roof
And penetrates the obscurest stone below.
Ay, writhe, groan, beat thy bosom, dim the light
Of those vain ringlets with those tears as vain;
All, all, shall not avail thee.
    Beatrice.   Naught avail'd
They all, nor ever can avail me now.
    Clement. I said it. But thy house must suffer shame,
Which timely full confession may avert.
    Beatrice. Alas! alas! no, holy father! no,
But darken it for ever. Save a branch   40
From the sad rot that eats into it; bid
My sister live, my brother be absolved.
    Clement. Thou fearest an impeachment of thy guilt
From kindred tongues.
    Beatrice.   Fear is too weak to reach
An agony like mine. I once did fear,
And when that fear was over, courage came
With heavenly power; courage that showed the tomb,
But not dishonour opening it.
    Clement.   Again?
Maniac! again? Well shriekest thou *dishonour*,

      47 showed] show'd *1853.*   49 *dishonour*] *dishonor 1853.*

And turnest (what none ever did before) 50
Thy back on me. Shame, shame, thou insolent!
I have no patience with a wench so wild,
So wicked . . setting this last scorn aside . .
Enough that I have heard thee; to forgive
Were impious.
  Beatrice. Yet the Son of God besought
The Father to forgive his murderers.
  Clement. Darest thou utter the word *Father*, wretch?
  Beatrice. Yes, yes, *that* Father; and *that* Father hears:
That Father knows my innocence.
  Clement.   He knows it,
And I, and all the city. What then brought thee 60
Before this footstool, at our throne of grace?
For pardon? pardon of a parricide?
And opens not the earth beneath thy feet!
  Beatrice. The earth, O holy Father! opened not
Beneath the cross, beneath man's impious feet,
When God's own Son was murdered.
  Clement.   And thy tongue
Can speak of murder?
  Beatrice. Could it were I guilty?
Ah! for that death none grieves so bitterly
As I do. Gone! gone! O unhappy man,
With all his sins upon his head . . the last, 70
Worst, unrepented.
  Clement. *Thou* shalt have good time
For *thy* repentance of one worse than all . .
Parricide.
  Beatrice. Holy father! say not so!
It tortures me.
  Clement. Worse tortures there await
Thy dainty limbs.
  Beatrice. Worse tortures they have caused
Already than man's wrath can now inflict.
  Clement. We shall see that, thou murderous miscreant!
  Beatrice. Spare, holy father! spare reproachful words.
  Clement. Audacious! vengeance, not reproach, is mine.
Justice, God's justice, I pronounce against thee. 80
  Beatrice. Ah! be it but God's justice! be it His,
And there is mercy; else what soul could live?

   64 opened] open'd *1853*.   66 murdered] murder'd *1853*.

BEATRICE CENCI

Clement. Audacious! here none argues. When I speak,
I breathe God's spirit and proclaim His law.
  Beatrice. Forgive an inadvertence in a girl
Who hath not graspt the flowers of sixteen springs,
Nor held sweet converse with the riper age
Of girls two fingers higher, nor learnt the ways
Of courtly life; but ever bent the head
O'er breviary, and closed the gayer leaves   90
Left open to engage her, which had taught
Perhaps some better customs than appear'd.
  Clement (pondering abstractedly). An inadvertence peradventure yea,
Never a parricide . . Peace! peace! Within
These walls unseemly are such ecstacies.
  Beatrice. Pity me, blessed Virgin! pity me!
There is none other careth for my grief,
Thou carest for all sorrowers. Hear me, hear me,
In my last anguish.
  Clement.   This is not thy last.
Halters and pulleys may uplift those arms   100
Again, which thou upliftest impiously
To the most blessed. Hope from her is none
Before confession of thy heinous crime.
I, I myself will hear it (out of grace
To that nobility thy father bore)
And may remit, in part, the penalty.
Confess, thou obstinate!
  Beatrice.   I will not bear
False witness . . no, not even against myself . .
For God will also hear it.
  Clement.   Get thee gone,
Parricide! hie thee from my sight. The rack   110
Awaits thee.
  Beatrice.   Holy father! I have borne
That rack already which tears filial love
From love parental. Is there worse behind?
  Clement. Questionest thou God's image upon earth?
  Beatrice. Sire! I have questioned God himself, and askt
How long shall innocence remain unheard?
  Clement. Say thou art guilty, and thy bonds are loose.
  Beatrice. Oh, holy father! guilty I am not.
  Clement. Die in thy sin then . . unrepentant, curst!

83 Audacious] Simpleton *Keepsake, 1851.*   86 sixteen] fifteen *Keepsake, 1851.*

Beatrice. My sins are washt away, not by the blood   120
Of him whose name to utter were opprobrious,
But by His blood who gives you power to rule
And me to suffer.
            God! Thy will be done!

SCENE V.

CITIZENS *at a distance from the scaffold.*

Citizen. Wouldst thou not rather look than talk, good man?
Old Man. I can talk yet, my sight grows somewhat dim;
Beside, 'tis said that they who see an angel
Live not long after. Surely there stands one
In purest white, immovable as heaven,
Her hair resplendent, not with stars, but suns . .
I would, but dare not . . yes, once more must gaze.
Another Citizen. Do they still torture her? At times she quakes,
While they seem only speaking very mildly.
Another. Ay, they speak mildly when they torture most.   10
Another. I catch no pulley near, no red-hot iron.
The Next. The pulley may have crackt, the iron cool'd,
And they alone who suffer it must see it.
Woman. How pale she looks!
Another.   She always did look pale,
They tell me; all the saints, and all the good,
And all the tender-hearted, have lookt pale.
Upon the Mount of Olives was there one
Of dawn-red hue even before that day?
Among the mourners under Calvary
Was there a cheek the rose had rested on?   20
Old Woman. Is she alive or dead? Oh! I would give
Half my day's meal to be as tall as you,
And see her over all those heads. Speak, tell me.
Another. She looks so pale, so calm, she may be dead.
Third. But can the dead sit upright? Tell me that.
Another. When they are bound, ankles and throat, they may.
Nardi, who stole the Virgin's rosary
From her own fingers, stood right up, although
Ribs were alone of all his bones unbroken,
But every muscle making their amends,   30
Doubled in size, and swell'd like snakes about them.
Woman. To rob the Virgin of her rosary!
O what a thief was he!
Another Woman.   Those were true snakes

That lookt like muscles coiling round his bones,
And whence they came, at dead of night, we know.
Ave Maria! were I rich as thou,
Thou shouldst not long look for thy rosary.
    Fourth (*to a Citizen*). Were there blood-spots about her? couldst thou
        spy?
    Citizen. There were blood spots about the blessed cross;
Yea; but whose were they? Woe betide the spillers!   40
    Third Woman. O the good man! he thinks upon the cross!
Then thou couldst see her?
    Citizen.   I could see no more
Than marble statue sees; my eyes were stiff.
Prythee now let them drop their heaviness
Upon this waste, this scorching waste, of woe;
Nor stop them, woman, with that idle tongue.
    Third Woman. O the rude man!
    Fourth Woman.   His huge arms scatter us,
Thick as we stand, beating that brawny breast.
Murrain upon those priests!
    Citizen.   They stood around,
As these do here.
    Fourth Woman. Murrain on these, on all   50
Tapsters of children's blood.
    Third Woman.   Save good priest Aldi;
He lets me off for little week by week.
O what a wail! Could it be hers? It fills
The streets, it overflows the city walls,
The churches and their altars, with one wave,
Huge as the Red Sea heav'd upon the host
Of that proud king . . who was he? . . Now again
What silence!
    Another.   Break it not. Let man's tears fall,
Reverently let them fall, never in shame,
On woman's blood: were yon feet still which stamp,   60
From agony of grief and anger, mine
In this dread pause were heard to splash the stones.
Could not, O Christ! thy saving blood save hers?
                [Outcries before the scaffold: bell.
Are those shrieks hers?
    Another Citizen.   Which shrieks, among ten thousand?
Fool! when all daughters, mothers, fathers, cry
In this whole piazza, thinkest thou a few
Expiring shrieks and sobs can come distinct?

Another. Those must be . . hers must those be.
Another. So far off,
She could not make us hear.
Another. Yet, Heaven is farther,
And hears her, the sweet innocent! Again!   70
Oh! that sound must have been the scourge that smote her.
Another Woman. O Christ! O crucified Redeemer! hear,
Hear that long cry lessening for lack of breath!
Another. The very priests, the very cardinals,
Are hardly mute.
Citizen. They curse the cruelty,
Thro' fear, not thro' compunction. O that each
Partook her sufferings. One poor girl hath borne
More than enough to crack the joints of all,
Cased as they are in fatness. But their day
May come, even upon earth.
Another Citizen. One day will come,   80
Not upon earth . . one day for them and her!
Woman. Poor soul! her prayers will save them.
Another Woman. God is just:
His mercy is but for the merciful.
Hush! Holy Virgin! the poor child is dead!
Another Woman. Is that the passing-bell?
Another Woman. Down on your knees
All of you!
Another Woman. What a silence! every stroke
Clear as within the belfry: sighs are heard
Half a street off. Now there is voice for prayer;
And hundreds pray who never prayed before . .
Another Woman. For they have children. Shower, ye saints above,
Blessings upon her! Comfort her among you!   91
Many cry. Blessings upon her!
Citizen. Curses!
Another. Upon whom?
Citizen. Him who condemn'd her.
Fourth Citizen. 'Twas the holy father.
Third Citizen. Were it the devil I would curse the devil.
Fourth Citizen. The stroke that fell on her may fall on you.
Third Citizen. Speed it! I should be saved in following her;
Even I might kiss those beauteous feet, and weep . .
Alas! . . on that rackt corse, in Paradise.
Sbirro. Silence! insensate! reprobate! Come out;

89 prayed] pray'd 1853.

Thy words, thou knowest, violate God's image   100
Here upon earth.
   Third Citizen.   My words? Your deeds, say rather.
Behold it.   [*The corpse is carried by.*
         Rest, O daughter! rest in peace!
   Another Citizen. Spake she no words at all?
   Another.   These words she spake,
Caught by the nearest, then the farthest off,
And striking every breast throughout the square,
Rapid as lightning, withering too like that.
   Another. Well, well . . the words?
   Reply.   Hast thou alone not heard?
Hear now then. No confession; not a breath.
   Old Woman. Poor sinful soul!
   Citizen.   They urged: she only said . .
And scarcely one or two could hear the sound,   110
It was so feeble . . for her heart was broken
Worse than her limbs . .
   Former Citizen.   What said she?
   Last Citizen.   Wouldst thou torture
Worse than yon paid ones?
   Former Citizen.   Hold thy peace! The two
Confessors urged her on each side to speak
While time was left her, and while God might hear,
And leave the rest to them. She thus replied . .
'My father's honour will'd my father's death:
He could not live; no, nor could I. Now strike.
Strike, and let questioning's worse torture cease.'
The vizor'd struck: a dull sound shook the block: 120
The head roll'd from it. Mercy on her soul!
Men have been brave, but women have been braver.

117 honour] honor 1853.

DEATH OF BLAKE

[Published in *The Examiner*, May 13, 1854; reprinted 1858, 1876. See note at end of volume.]

[Scene: Off Plymouth, August 7, 1657.]

   Blake. The pillow is too soft; my head sinks in;
Raise me up higher: that will do, my men!
But where is England? Are they cliffs or clouds
That rise before me?

Captain Hardy.   There are both, sir, both
Ahead of us. But you without your glass
See better than the best of us.
   Blake.   How so?
I could not read my Bible in the sun,
Nor see the porpoises that played below
But yesterday. My sight grows worse and worse . . .
My hearing too . . . I catch your words by halves . . .   10
I cannot hear the water. Do we move?
   Captain Hardy. Ay, sir, and homeward.
   Blake.   *My* home lies, methinks,
Nearer than thine.
   Captain Hardy (*aside*). God help him! he forgets
That we are neighbours in our pleasant vale,
That he has caught me up and twitcht my chin
When I would run into the house for shame.
   Blake. Look out, men! Level with the shrouds, nay lower,
The mists loom over-head; the cliffs are close;
Beware; mind each his business; leave me here,
And say no more; for I am faint . . at heart   20
Not very . . yet there too.
                 O restless soul,
So soon to leave me with my God alone,
Why sickenest thou? He will support my steps
To His own house and rest me with His own.
   Captain Hardy. General! He hears you; He hath heard our prayer.
   Blake. I thought . . but I was wrong . . that my command
Was *Let all leave me.* Once none disobeyed;
Now, alas! now . . O Robert Blake! thy voice
Is weak indeed; it was not so, time past.
   Captain Hardy. Sir! the most duteous is the only one   30
Who here hath disobeyed. Forgive this fault,
The first in Edward Hardy you have blamed.
   Blake. I dare not blame it. How much greater faults
Have I committed when thy years were mine!
Yet they were all forgiven, else the Lord
Would not have rais'd me from my low estate
To gain His battles, with true men like thee.
   Ah surely I am haler than I was,
And much of fever hath abated in me,
For I feel moisture on my hand and cheek.   40

6 best] rest *1858.*   11 cannot] can not *1858.*   14 neighbours] neighbors
1858.   15 twitcht] twicht *1858.*

DEATH OF BLAKE

What! groanest thou at this? Wouldst wish me dead
Because in battle 'twas not mine to die?
   Captain Hardy. O sir! my tears have wetted you! they may
Do mischief!
   Blake.   There are tears that brave men shed
And brave men only; thine have done me good;
Squander no more of them; reserve the rest
For better . . *men* I would have said, but *men*
Is not the word . . for woman . . spouse and widow.
   Where are we now?
   Captain Hardy.   The Lizard is in sight.
   Blake. Happy, O England! he who meets thee safe,   50
Mistress of nations, mistress of thyself . .
Be this thy glory!
   Captain Hardy. No small part is yours,
My general!
   Blake.   Hush, thou babbler! without more
As bold, as self-devoted . . Am I proud?
I, who should now grow humbler . . without those
Nothing were done for England's Commonwealth:
Long, long as ye deserve it, may it last!
Edward! I think no better word, if any,
Will follow. Lower my head. Thanks; thanks; goodbye.

> Thus sank the wisest of the godly-brave,   60
> And England's own high heart sank too . . how deep!
> She saw his bones, yet moist with their own clay,
> Amid the giggles of the fouly fair
> And smirks of prelates in like lawn arraid,
> A drunken king dig from the grave and spurn.
>   Britain! take up thy spear; the morn is fresh;
> A brood of the same beasts is prowling round
> In packs: prick onward; let not one escape,
> Growler or whiner: thou hast limbs as strong
> As those who fought with Blake and died for thee..   70

Walter Savage Landor.

59 goodbye] good-bye *1858.*

DRAMAS AND DRAMATIC SCENES

ANTONY AND OCTAVIUS

SCENES FOR THE STUDY.

[Published separately 1856; reprinted, without the Dedication, 1876. See notes at end of volume.]

THESE SCENES

ARE DEDICATED TO

EDWARD CAPERN,

POET AND DAY-LABORER AT BIDEFORD, DEVON.

We are fellow-laborers; you work in two fields, I in one only; you incessantly, I intermittently. Well do I know the elevation of your mind above your worldly condition, and that in Christian humility there walks with you a spirit conscious of its divine descent. This shall not deter me from offering what may be eventually of some service, however small; and I offer it with confidence, because it is not personally to yourself, but to your children. Should there be at the close of the year any small profit accruing from the sale of this first, and perhaps last, edition of *Scenes for the Study*, accept it for their benefit. Little is to be expected from so old-fashioned and obsolete a style of composition, and that little will be owing to the virtues and genius, not of the author, but of EDWARD CAPERN. Rely on your own exertions, and on that Supreme Power whence is derived whatever is worth possessing. Depend not on the favor of Royalty; expect nothing from it; for you are not a hound or a spaniel or a German prince.

PREFACE.

Few have obtained the privilege of entering Shakespeare's garden, and of seeing him take turn after turn, quite alone, now nimbly, now gravely, on his broad and lofty terrace.

Let us never venture where he is walking, whether in deep meditation or in buoyant spirits. Enough is it for us to ramble and loiter in the narrower paths below, and to look up at the various images which, in the prodigality of his wealth, he has placed in every quarter.

Before you, reader, are some scattered leaves gathered from under them: carefuller hands may arrange and compress them in a book of their own, and thus for a while preserve them, if rude children do not finger them first and tamper with their fragility.

Dedication. om. 1876. [See "Poems, by Edward Capern, Rural Postman, 1856". Among the subscribers were Tennyson, Dickens, Charles Kingsley, and Landor. In 1857 Capern, on Palmerston's recommendation, was granted a civil list pension. He died in 1894. *D.N.B.*]

ANTONY AND OCTAVIUS

SCENE THE FIRST.

[Near Actium, 31 B.C.]

SOOTHSAYER AND ANTONY.

Soothsayer. Speak it I must. Ill are the auguries.
Antony. Ill ever are the auguries, O priest,
To those who fear them: at one hearty stroke
The blackest of them scud and disappear.
Now, not a word of any less than good
To Cleopatra.
    Soothsayer.   'Twas at her command
I hasten'd to consult them.
    Antony.   Rightly done
To follow her commands; not rightly comes
Whate'er would grieve her; this thou must withhold.
    Soothsayer. Not this, not this: her very life may hang   10
Upon the event foretold her.
    Antony.   What is that?
Announced then is the accursed augury
So soon?
    Soothsayer. She waited at the temple-door
With only one attendant, meanly drest,
That none might know her; or perhaps the cause
Was holier; to appease the offended Gods.
    Antony. Which of them can she ever have offended?
She who hath lavisht upon all of them
Such gifts, and burnt more incense in one hour
Before her Isis, than would wrap in smoke   20
A city at mid-day! The keenest eye
Of earth or heaven could find in her no guile,
No cruelty, no lack of duty.
    Soothsayer.   True;
Yet fears she one of them, nor knows she which,
But Isis is the one she most suspects.
    Antony. Isis! her patroness, her favourite?
    Soothsayer. Even so! but they who patronize may frown
At times, and draw some precious boon away.
    Antony. I deem not thus unworthily of Gods;
Indeed I know but Jupiter and Mars;   30
Each hath been ever on my side, and each
Alike will prosper me, I trust, to-morrow.
    Soothsayer. But there are others, guardian Gods of Egypt;
Prayers may propitiate them, with offerings due.

165

Antony. I have forgotten all my prayers.
Soothsayer. No need,
When holier lips pronounce them.
Antony. As for offerings,
There shall be plenty on the day's success.
Soothsayer. Merit it.
Antony. Do your Gods or ours mind that?
Merit! and where lies merit?
Soothsayer. In true faith
On auguries.
Antony. Birds hither thither fly, 40
And heard there have been from behind the veil
Voices not varying much from yours and mine.

SCENE THE SECOND.

[Before the battle of Actium (September 2), 31 B.C.]

SOOTHSAYER AND CLEOPATRA.

Soothsayer. Our lord Antonius wafts away all doubt
Of his success.
Cleopatra. What! against signs and tokens?
Soothsayer. Even so!
Cleopatra. Perhaps he trusts himself to Hercules,
Become of late progenitor to him.
Soothsayer. Ah! that sweet smile might bring him back; he once
Was flexible to the bland warmth of smiles.
Cleopatra. If Hercules is hail'd by men below
For strength and goodness, why not Antony?
Why not succede as lawful heir? why not
Exchange the myrtle for the poplar crown? 10

ANTONY *enters.* SOOTHSAYER *goes.*

Cleopatra. Antony! is not Cæsar now a god?
Antony. We hear so.
Cleopatra. Nay, we know it. Why not thou?
Men would not venture then to strike a blow
At thee: the laws declare it sacrilege.
Antony. Julius, if I knew Julius, had been rather
First among men than last among the Gods.
Cleopatra. At least put on thy head a kingly crown.
Antony. I have put on a laurel one already;
As many kingly crowns as should half-cover
The Lybian desert are not worth this one. 20

ANTONY AND OCTAVIUS

Cleopatra. But all would bend before thee.
  Antony. 'Twas the fault
Of Cæsar to adopt it; 'twas his death.
  Cleopatra. Be then what Cæsar is.
              O Antony!
To laugh so loud becomes not state so high.
  Antony. He is a star, we see; so is the hair
Of Berenice: stars and Gods are rife.
What worth, my love, are crowns? Thou givest pearls,
I give the circlet that encloses them.
Handmaidens don such gear, and valets snatch it
Sportively off, and toss it back again.   30
  Cleopatra. But graver men gaze up with awful eyes . .
  Antony. And never gaze at that artificer
Who turns his wheel and fashions out his vase
From the Nile clay! 'Tis easy work for him;
Easy was mine to turn forth kings from stuff
As vile and ductile: he stil plies his trade,
But mine, with all my customers, is gone.
Ever by me let enemies be awed,
None else: bring round me many, near me few,
Keeping afar those shaven knaves obscene   40
Who lord it with humility, who press
Men's shoulders down, glue their two hands together,
And cut a cubit off, and tuck their heels
Against the cushion mother Nature gave.
  Cleopatra. Incomprehensible! incorrigible!
O wretch! if queens were ever taught to blush,
I should at such unseemly phrase as thine.
I think I must forgive it.
            What! and take
Before I grant? Again! You violent man!
Will you for ever drive me thus away?   50

      43 heels] *so in errata 1856,* knees *in text.*

SCENE THE THIRD.

[After the battle of Actium.]

ANTONY AND CLEOPATRA.

Antony. What demon urged thy flight?
  Cleopatra. The demon Love.
I am a woman, with a woman's fears,

A mother's, and, alas O Antony!
More fears than these.
 Antony.   Of whom?
 Cleopatra.   Ask not *of* whom
But ask *for* whom, if thou must ask at all,
Nor knowest nor hast known. Yes, I did fear
For my own life . . ah! lies it not in thine?
How many perils compast thee around!
 Antony. What are the perils that are strange to me?
 Cleopatra. Mine thou couldst not have seen when swiftest oars, 10
Attracted by the throne and canopy,
Pounced at me only, numerous as the waves;
Couldst not have seen my maidens throwing down
Their fans and posies (piteous to behold!)
That they might wring their hands more readily.
I was too faint myself to still their cries.
 Antony (aside). I almost thought her blameable.

     (*To* CLEOPATRA.) The Gods
So will'd it. Thou despondest . . too aware
The day is lost.
 Cleopatra. The day may have been lost,
But other days, and happier ones, will come. 20
 Antony. Never: when those so high once fall, their weight
Keeps them for ever down.
 Cleopatra.   Talk reasonably,
And love me as . . til now . . it should be more,
For love and sorrow mingle where they meet.
 Antony. It shall be more. Are these last kisses cold?
 Cleopatra. Nor cold are they nor shall they be the last.
 Antony. Promise me, Cleopatra, one thing more.
 Cleopatra. 'Tis promist, and now tell me what it is.
 Antony. Rememberest thou this ring?
 Cleopatra.   Dost thou remember
The day, my Antony, when it was given? 30
 Antony. Day happiest in a life of many happy,
And all thy gift.
 Cleopatra. 'Tis call'd the richest ruby,
The heaviest, and the deepest, in the world.
 Antony. The richest certainly.
 Cleopatra.   And not the deepest
And broadest? Look! it hides all this large nail,
And mine are long ones, if not very wide;

168

ANTONY AND OCTAVIUS

Now let me see if it don't cover yours
As wide again! there! it would cover two.
Why smile you so?
   Antony.   Because I know its story.
   Cleopatra. Ha! then you have not lost all memory quite.   40
I told it you. The king of Pontus sent it
When dying to my father, warning him
By letter that there was a charm in it
Not to be trifled with.
   Antony.   It shall not be.
   Cleopatra. But tell me now the promise I must make;
What has the ring to do with it?
   Antony.   All, all.
Know, Cleopatra, this is not one ruby.
   Cleopatra. The value then is smaller.
   Antony.   Say not so,
Remark the rim.
   Cleopatra.   The gold is thin, I see.
   Antony. And seest thou it will open? It contains   50
Another jewel, richer than itself.
   Cleopatra. Impossible! my Antony! for rubies
Are richer than all other gems on earth.
   Antony. Now, my sweet trifler, for thy promise.
   Cleopatra.   Speak.
By all the Powers above and all below,
I will perform thy bidding, even to death.
   Antony. To death it goes; not until after mine.
   Cleopatra. I kiss the precious charm. Methinks an odor
Of almond comes from it. How sweet the flower
Of death!
   Antony. 'Tis painless death, 'tis sudden too.   60
   Cleopatra. Who could wish more, even were there more to wish?
With us there is not.
   Antony.   Generous, pious girl!
Daughter of Ptolemies! thou hast not won
A lower man than they. Thy name shall rise
Above the pyramids, above the stars,
Nations yet wild shall that name civilize,
And glorious poets shake their theaters,
And stagger kings and emperors with applause.
   Cleopatra. I was not born to die; but I was born
To leave the world with Antony, and will.   70
   Antony. The greatest of all eastern kings died thus,

169

The greater than all eastern kings thus died.
O glorious forgeman who couldst rivet down
Refractory crowds by thousands, and make quake
Scepters like reeds! we want not here thy voice
Or thy example. Antony alone
And queenly pride, tho' Love were dumb, would do.

SCENE THE FOURTH.

[*At Alexandria, after arrival of Octavius, 30 B.C.*]

CLEOPATRA. CHARMIAN. IRAS.

Cleopatra. At the first entrance of your lord, before
He ordered you, before he spake a word,
Why did ye run away?
    Charmian.   I was afraid,
Never so in my life; he lookt so fierce
He fear'd his own wild eyes, he placed one hand
(His right) across them on lowered brow, his left
Waved us away as would a hurricane
A palm-tree on the desert.
    Cleopatra (*to* IRAS).   And wert thou,
Iras, so terrified?
    Iras.   Not I indeed;
My lady, never man shall frighten *me*.   10
    Cleopatra. Thou silly creature! I have seen a mouse
Do it.
    Iras. A mouse is quite another thing.
    Charmian (*hesitating*). Our lord and master . .
    Cleopatra.   What of Antony?
    Charmian. Octavius . .
    Cleopatra.   Who? Our lord and master he?
He never shall be mine . . that is to say . .
    Charmian. What! lady?
    Cleopatra.   I forget . . 'twas not worth saying.
Charmian! where hast thou been this last half-hour?
    Charmian. In my own room.
    Cleopatra.   So fearful?
    Charmian.   Far more sad.
    Cleopatra. Where, Iras, thou?
    Iras.   I wanted to report
To my sweet lady what I might espy.   20
    Cleopatra. And what have those long narrow eyes espied?
    Iras. All.

ANTONY AND OCTAVIUS

Cleopatra. 'Twas done speedily; but what is all?
Army and fleet from any terrace-roof
Are quite discernible, the separate men
Nowhere.
    Iras. My heart had told me what delight
Its queen would feel to hear exactly how
The leaders look.
    Cleopatra.   And how then did they look?
Tell me: some might have ridden near enough
The town to judge by, where the sight is sharp.
    Iras. Merciful Isis! ridden! and so close!   30
Horses are frightful, horses kick and rear
And whinny, full of wickedness; 'twere rash
To venture nigh them.
    Cleopatra.   There are things more rash.
    Iras. Quieter creatures than those generals are
Never were seen.
    Cleopatra.   Barbarians! not a word
About them, Iras, if thou lovest me;
They would destroy my city, seize my realm,
And ruin him we live for.
    Iras.   Surely no;
It were a pity; none are so unkind;
Cæsar the least of all.
    Cleopatra.   Ah simple child!   40
Thou knowest not his heart.
    Iras.   I do indeed.
    Cleopatra. No, nor thy own.
    Iras.   His better; for of mine
I never askt a question. He himself
Told me how good he would be.
    Cleopatra.   He told *thee?*
What! hast thou seen him?
    Iras.   Aye, and face to face,
Close as our lord's to yours.
    Cleopatra.   O impudence!
    Iras. But he would have it so; just like our lord.
    Cleopatra. Impudent girl! thou shalt be whipt for this.
    Iras. I am too old; but lotuses don't hurt
Like other things; they cool the strokes they give.   50
    Cleopatra. I have no patience with thee. How I hate
That boy Octavius!
               Dared he touch thy cheek?

Iras. He could; he only whispered in my ear,
Holding it by the ring.
  Cleopatra.   Whispered? what words?
 Iras. The kindest.
  Cleopatra.   Ah! no doubt! but what were they?
 Iras. He said, The loveliest creature in the world . .
 Cleopatra. The vulgar brute! Our ferrymen talk so:
And couldst thou listen, Iras, to such speech?
 Iras. Only when people praise our gracious queen.
 Cleopatra. Me? this of me? Thou didst thy duty, child: 60
He might have fail'd in what he would express.
The birds have different voices, yet we bear
To hear those sing which do not sing the best.
Iras! I never thought thee half so wise.
And so, he said those gentle words of *me?*
 Iras. All, and forgot to kiss me when I vow'd
I would report them faithfully.
  Cleopatra.   Is there
Resemblance in him to that marble image
I would have broken, but my Antony
Seiz'd both my hands?
  Iras.   Alas! that image wants 70
The radiant eyes, and hair more radiant stil,
Such as Apollo's may have been if myrrh
Were sprinkled into its redundant waves.
 Cleopatra. He must be tenderer than I fancied him
If this be true.
  Iras. He spoke those very words.
 Cleopatra. Iras! 'tis vain to mind the words of men;
But if he lookt as thou hast said he lookt,
I think I may put trust in him.
  Iras.   And see him?
 Cleopatra. I am not hasty.
  Iras.   If you could but see him!
 Cleopatra. Call Charmian: I am weary: I must rest 80
Awhile.
 Iras. My sweetest lady! could not I,
Who have been used to it almost a year,
Help you as well as Charmian? While you sleep
Could I not go again and bid him haste
To comfort you?
  Cleopatra. Is the girl mad? Call Charmian.

ANTONY AND OCTAVIUS

(To C<small>HARMIAN</small>.)

Charmian! hath Iras tickled thee away
From moping in thy chamber? thou hast sped.
   Charmian. Iras is growing bold.
   Cleopatra.   I was bold too
While I was innocent as Iras is.
   Charmian. Our lady looks more flurried than deprest.   90
   Cleopatra. I am not flurried, I am not deprest.
[After a pause.
Believest thou in Cæsar's generosity?
   Charmian. I know it.
   Cleopatra.   In what matter?
   Charmian.   Half the guards
And half the ministers of state have shown
Signs of his bounty to the other half.
   Cleopatra. Gifts are poor signs of bounty. Do not slaves
Slip off the gold-black pouches from their necks
Untied but to buy other slaves therewith?
Do not tame creatures lure into the trap
Their wilder brethren with some filthy bait?   100
All want companions, and the worst the most.
I am much troubled: even hope troubles me.
   Charmian. I dare not ask our lady why she weeps.
   Cleopatra. Cæsarion, my first-born, my dearest one,
Is safely shielded by his father's name:
He loves his brothers, he may save them both,
He only can: I would fain take the advice
Of Dolabella, fain would venture him
In Cæsar's camp: the father's voice and look
Must melt him, for his heart is not so hard   110
That he could hurt so beautiful a child;
Nay, what man's is?
   Charmian.   But trust not the two younger;
Their father will not help them in their need.
   Cleopatra. Cæsarion in fit hour will plead for them.
Charmian, what ponderest thou? what doubtest thou?
   Charmian. Cæsar I doubt, and Dolabella more;
And what I pondered were your words: *It may be
That givers are not always benefactors.*
   Cleopatra. I have one secret, but keep none from thee:
He loves me!

104 Cæsarion] son of Julius Cæsar and Cleopatra, born 47 B.C.—[W.]

Charmian. All do.

Cleopatra.   Yes, but some have power. 120

Charmian. Power, as most power is, gain'd by treachery.

Cleopatra.   Whom,
In Egypt, Europe, Asia, can I trust?

Charmian. Few, nor those few too far, nor without watch.

Cleopatra. Not Charmian?

Charmian.   Bid her die; here; now; and judge.

SCENE THE FIFTH.

Octavius. [C. Cilnius] Mecænas. [C. Cornelius] Gallus.

Octavius. Is Dolabella to be trusted?

Mecænas.   Youth
There is on Dolabella's side; with youth
Comes always eloquence where women are.

Octavius. Gallus is honester and prudenter.

Mecænas. But Gallus is the older by some years.

Octavius. A poet says, Love at odd hours hath smiled
And covered with his pinions sportively,
Where he espied some hairs that seem'd like Time's
Rather than his.

Mecænas.   There must have been but few,
Or else the poet dreamt it.

Octavius.   Who comes hither? 10

Mecænas. Not Dolabella, but the better man.

Octavius. Welcome, brave Gallus, opportunely met.
We were debating how to lure that dove
Of Antony's, now in her cote, a tower,
From which we would not frighten her away,
But tempt her down.

Gallus.   It might be difficult.

Octavius. Unless thou aidest us, indeed it might.

Mecænas. What sport 'twould be to see her mate descend
And catch him too!

Gallus.   Nor this more easily.

Octavius. To Gallus all is easy.

Mecænas.   Pleasant too 20
Would such task be.

---

1 Dolabella] P. Cornelius Dolabella was at Alexandria with Octavius.—[W.]   4 Gallus] After the battle of Actium, Gallus was sent in pursuit of Antony and burnt many of his ships.—[W.]

ANTONY AND OCTAVIUS

Gallus.   No better judge of pleasures
Than Cilnius here; but ours are not alike.
  Octavius. Gallus! one word apart. We need thee much.
  Gallus. What! after Egypt won?
  Octavius.   Antony lives!
  Gallus. Beaten, disgraced, imprisoned, his own jailer.
  Mecænas. Defying us, however, by the power
The queen his mistress gives him with her name . .
  Gallus. Worthless as his.
  Mecænas.   Were she within our reach
We soon might bring him down.
  Gallus.   What! lower?
  Octavius.   Even yet?
  Gallus. She might succumb, and must, by promising   30
That Cæsar's son, after her death, shall reign.
  Mecænas. A prudent thought. But will she give up Antony
Unless she hear it from the giver's mouth?
There is one anxious to deserve the grace
Of princes. Dolabella could persuade
The queen to trust herself to him for Cæsar.
  Gallus. I doubt it.
  Mecænas.   Doubt his honor, not his skill.
He could not keep the secret that he loves
And that he often in times past hath seen her.
  Gallus. He loves her? then, by all the Gods! he never   40
Will win her for another than himself.
Beside, he was the friend of Antony
And shared with him the toils at Mutina.
Altho' no eagle, he would soar aloft
Rather than bow for others, like an owl,
The smallest of the species, hooded for it.
Who knows not Dolabella?
  Mecænas.   Thou hast sense,
Comeliness, courage, frankness. Antony
Tore from thy couch the fairest girl in Rome.
  Gallus. And let him have her, let him have her, man.   50
What then?
  Mecænas.   There are who would retaliate.
  Gallus. The girl hath left no mark upon my memory . .
  Mecænas. Or mine, beside a few soft lines; but mine

43 Mutina] now Modena. Antony was defeated there 43 B.C.—[W.]   49 fairest
girl] Lycoris, who deserted Gallus for Antony. See Virgil, *Eclogue X*, parts of which
are imitated in *ll.* 56–71.—[W.]

Retains them, mindful of a friend who sang,
Unless my singing mars the harmony,

> I thought it once an idle tale
> That lovely woman's faith could fail;
> At last I said, It may be true,
> Lycoris, of them all but you.
> And now you leave me! and you go   60
> O'er pinnacles of Alpine snow.
> Another leads you (woe is me!)
> Across that grim and ghastly sea!
> Let him protect those eyes from sleet,
> And guide and chafe those tender feet,
> And fear for every step you tread,
> Then hardly will I wish him dead.
> If ice-barb'd shafts that ring around
> By his neglect my false one wound,
> O may the avenging Gods for this   70
> Freeze him to death in the abyss!

Gallus. They have reserved him for a sadder fate.
Sleep, without painful dreams that crush the breast,
Sleep, without any joyous ones that come
Only to mock the awaken'd, comes unfelt
And unsolicited among those cliffs
Of ice perennial.
                Antony hath dreamt
His broken dream, and wakened to despair:
I never wisht him that; the harm I wisht him
Was when my youth was madder than his age.   80
He stood a prouder and a better man
At Mutina, when Famine walkt the camp,
When I beheld him climb up painfully
A low and crumbling crag, where servises
Hung out above his head their unripe fruit:
That was my day. Some grains of sodden maize
I brought and offered him: he struck them down.
    Octavius. Rejoice at pride so humbled.
    Gallus.   I rejoice
At humbled pride, at humbled valor no.
    Octavius. But those avenging Gods whom thou invokedst   90
Stand now before thee and demand why call'd.
    Gallus. They know: they pardon such irresolution
As pity, and not cowardice, persuades.
One woman has betraid me; not one woman
Will I betray.

                90 avenging] offended *1876*.

ANTONY AND OCTAVIUS

Mecænas. O that poetic mind!

Gallus. Where others sneer, Mecænas only smiles.

Mecænas. Such is my nature, and I widely err,
Gallus, if such be not thy nature too.

Octavius. Did then Lycoris, that wild girl, prefer
The unworthy to the worthy, the most rude   100
To the most gentle, scampering beyond reach?
Let her repair her fault: no danger here
That angry skies turn coral lips to slate
Or icicles make limp the runaway.

Gallus. Those days are over. He who won the prize
May say as much and add a little more.

Octavius. Laughest thou not to see the tables turn'd?
The little queen who fascinates her fool
Is now as lovely as Lycoris was,
And never ran away from any man: 110
Fain would I see that roysterer's spirit broken,
And she alone can do it: help her on.

Gallus. In any such attempt, in such a place
Fortune would baffle me.

Octavius.   Then baffle *her*;
She baffles only those who hesitate.

Gallus. The queen, we hear, takes refuge in the depths
Below the palace, where but reptiles lie.

Octavius. Indeed! what! scorpions, serpents?

Gallus.   Haply these.

Octavius. Poor woman! they may bite her! let my fears
Prove not prophetic!

                  Now, my friend, adieu!   120
Reflect upon our project; turn it over.   [GALLUS *goes.*
These poets look into futurity
And bring us glimpses from it more than dreams.
Asps! But the triumph then without the queen!
Alas! was ever mortal so perplext!
I doubt if your friend Gallus can be won.

Mecænas. All may be won, well handled; but the ear
Is not the thing to hold by. Show men gold,
Entangle them in Gallic torquises,
Tie stubborn necks with ropes of blushing pearls,   130
Seat them on ivory from the realms of Ind,
Augur them consulates, proconsulates,
Make their eyes widen into provinces,
And, gleaming further onward, tetrarchies.

Octavius. It strikes me now that we may offer Gallus
The prefecture of Egypt.
  Mecænas.   Some time hence:
Better consult Agrippa.
  Octavius.   None more trusty.
Yet our Agrippa hath strange whims; he dotes
Upon old Rome, the Rome of matted beards
And of curt tunics; of old Rome's old laws,   140
Worm-eaten long, now broken and swept off.   [*Pausing.*
He stands forth high in station and esteem.
  Mecænas. So should the man who won the world for thee.
  Octavius. I must not play with him who won so much
From others; he might win as much from me:
I fear his fortunes.
  Mecænas.   Bind them with your own.
Becoming are thy frowns, my dear Octavius,
Thy smiles alone become thee better: trust
Thy earliest friend and fondest: take not ill
My praises of Agrippa, tried in war   150
And friendship.
  Octavius.   And for this wouldst thou, my Cilnius,
Send him away from me?
  Mecænas.   Thyself did fear
His popularity: all Rome applauds
His valor, justice, moderation, mercy.
  Octavius. Not one word more.
  Mecænas.   One word I have to speak,
And speak it I will now. He must away.
  Octavius. Can Cilnius then be jealous of Agrippa?
  Mecænas. No; crown him king and give him provinces,
But give him not to clench the heart of Rome.
  Octavius. I could make kings and unmake kings by scores,   160
But could not make nor unmake one Agrippa.
  Mecænas. Well spoken! wisely! worthily! No praise
Can equipoise his virtues, kings may lay
Their tributes on the carpet of his throne
And cities hope to honor whom they serve,
The royal mantle would obscure Agrippa.
  Octavius. I would be generous, but be cautious too.
  Mecænas. Then grant him all beyond the sight of Rome;
Men's eyes would draw him thither tho' his will
Hung back: thus urged the steddiest might give way.   170
  Octavius. I hate suspicion and suspicious men.

Gallus I fancied was the bitterest foe
Of Antony, his rival, and successful,
Then he should hate him worse than I.
    Mecænas.   But empire
Is more worth hatred than a silly girl,
Every day to be won and lost again.
    Octavius. Our Gallus is weak-minded to forgive
So easily.
    Mecænas. I find that on the hearth
Where lie love's embers there lie hatred's too,
Equally cold and not to be stir'd up.   180
    Octavius. I do not think, my Cilnius, thou hast felt
Love but for me; I never knew thee hate.
    Mecænas. It is too troublesome; it rumples sleep,
It settles on the dishes of the feast,
It bites the fruit, it dips into the wine;
Then rather let my enemy hate *me*
Than I hate him.
    Octavius.   We must look round. What think you?
Is Dolabella to be trusted?
    Mecænas.   Try.
    Octavius. I wish this country settled, us return'd.
Resolved am I to do what none hath done,   190
And only Julius ever purposed doing;
Resolved to render Rome, beneath my rule,
A second Alexandria. Corinth, Carthage,
One autumn saw in stubble; not a wreath
Enough to crown a capital was left,
Nor capital to crown its pillar, none;
But here behold what glorious edifices!
What palaces! what temples! what august
Kings! how unmoved is every countenance
Above the crowd! And so it was in life.   200
No other city in the world, from west
To east, seems built for rich and poor alike.
In Athens, Antioch, Miletus, Rhodes,
The richest Roman could not shelter him
Against the dogstar; here the poorest slave
Finds refuge under granite, here he sleeps
Noiseless, and, when he wakens, dips his hand
Into the treasured waters of the Nile.
    Mecænas. I wish, Octavius, thou wouldst carry hence
For thy own worship one of those mild Gods,   210

Both arms upon the knees: 'tis time that all
Should imitate this posture.
 Octavius.   We will close
The gates of Janus.
 Mecænas.   Janus looks both ways;
He may like best the breezy air abroad
And knock too hard against the bolted brass.
 Octavius (to a Guard). Call Gallus hither.
 Gallus.   Cæsar! what commands?
 Octavius. I would entrust a legion, more than one,
To our friend Gallus: I would fix him here
In Egypt: none is abler to coerce
The turbulent.
 Gallus. Let others flap their limbs   220
With lotus-leaves when Sirius flames above,
Give me the banks of Anio, where young Spring,
Who knows not half the names of her own flowers,
Looks into Summer's eyes and wakes him up
Alert, and laughs at him until he lifts
His rod of roses and she runs away.
 Octavius. And has that lovely queen no charms for thee?
 Gallus. If truth be spoken of her, and it may,
Since she is powerless and deserted now,
Tho' more than thrice seven* years have come and stolen 230
Day after day a leaf or two of bloom,
She has but changed her beauty; the soft tears
Fall, one would think, to make it spring afresh.
 Octavius. And not for Gallus? Let one brave man more
Ascend the footstool of the regal bed.
 Gallus. As the Gods will! but may they not will *me*!

* History and poetry do not always well agree. Julius Cæsar had left Egypt before
the birth of Cæsarion, at which time Cleopatra was about fourteen. That she retained
her freshness seven or eight years longer may be attributed in part to the care she took
of it, and in a greater to her pure Macedonian blood. Beside, Alexandria is not sultry;
and the architects of antiquity knew how to keep up an equable and healthy tem-
perature. [L.] According to the best authorities Cleopatra was born about the end of
69 B.C. or in 68 B.C. That she was born, as Landor held, in 61 or 60 B.C. is less likely.—[W.]

SCENE THE SIXTH.

ANTONY AND DOLABELLA.

 Antony. Welcome, my Dolabella! There is none
From yonder camp I would embrace beside.
My little queen hath given at last an audience
To thy persuasive tongue?

ANTONY AND OCTAVIUS

Dolabella.   Most graciously.
Antony. I never thought she would permit Cæsarion
To leave her side; hardly can I myself
Bear separation from that brave young boy;
I love him as my own.
Dolabella.   Your own thus stand
Safe from all peril.
Antony.   Is not it disgrace?
A boy save *me*? for to save them is *me*.   10
Dolabella. Create a generosity of soul
In one whom conquest now hath made secure;
Bid him put forth his power, it now is greater
Than any man's: consider what a friend
Cæsarion hath in Julius, all whose wounds
Will bleed afresh before the assembled tribes
On the imperial robe thy hands outsprad
With its wide rents, for every God above
And every Roman upon earth to number.
Antony. Ah! those were days worth living o'er again.   20
Dolabella. Live them again then.
Antony.   Never, stript of power,
Of dignity, of Rome's respect, of theirs
Who compass me, who fix before these eyes
The very eagles which adorn'd my tent.
Dolabella. Brave thoughts! but are none weaker intermixt?
Antony. Smile, Dolabella! Oh, could but that smile
Kill as it pierces me! But tread the ground
Softly and lightly where her feet have moved.
My Cleopatra! never will we part,
Thy son shall reign in Egypt.
Dolabella.   Much I fear'd,   30
O Antony, thy rancour might prevail
Against thy prudence. Cæsar bears no rancour.
Antony. Too little is that heart for honest hatred.
The serpent the most venomous hath just
Enough of venom for one deadly wound,
He strikes but once, and then he glides away.
Dolabella. Octavius strikes not Antony.
Antony.   One man
Alone dares strike the man whom thou hast named.
But let me hear the phrase of fraudulence.
Dolabella. Cæsar's, I trust, will not deserve that name,   40
He says his reign shall be the reign of peace.

181

Antony. Peace! what is that? a pleasant room to sit
Or walk about in, nor could heart desire
A cooler place wherein to spread the cates:
First, bring these cates; bring liberty, the salt
That seasons with true relish all things else.
    Dolabella. We sometimes leave but little, when we rise
From its enjoyment, for those servitors
Who toil'd for us throughout the heat of day:
Reckless we riot: never can spilt wine   50
Enter the golden cup it sparkled in:
Harpies above defile the half-eaten fruit.
Rome now would rest awhile.
    Antony.   Yea, long will be
Her rest; the scourge of Earth will be the scorn.
    Dolabella. We must submit.
    Antony.   Thou must; thou hast submitted;
But never I; what I have been I am.
    Dolabella. Less prosperous than once, thy fortunes may
Be yet restored.
    Antony.   I would not take them back,
By any man, least by that man, bestow'd;
I would not have my portion of the world,   60
No, nor the whole of it, if that glib tongue
Call'd every God to ratify the gift.
Show me the foe he ever fairly met,
The friend he hath embraced, and not betray'd,
And tell me, Dolabella, for thou canst,
Who murder'd Hirtius; by whose agency
Poison was dropt into the wound of Pansa.
    Dolabella. Of this ask Glyco, ask Aquilius Niger
Of that.
    Antony. Both know the secret, both have told it:
And now will I tell thee one.
                    At the noon   70
Of yesterday, when fruit is most refreshing,
A countryman who brings the yellow figs
His queen is fond of, brought a basketful,
Saying to Iras:
             "These my little daughter,
Whom once you used to play with in the garden,

66, 67 [The consuls Hirtius and Pansa lost their lives in the fighting round Mutina. According to Suetonius, Aquilius Niger said that Glyco the physician poisoned Pansa's wound.—W.]

ANTONY AND OCTAVIUS

Bids me to give into your hands; she thinks
The queen requires some frolic; you alone
Can venture so far with her. Place within
The smooth cool linen of her bed this basket
Of cane-leaves and of rushes intertwined, 80
With all the fruit below, the leaves a-top;
You see it is but shallow, scarce a palm,
Mind it lie flat; yet she will find it out
Tho' it be always dusky in that room."
What is there in the tale that thou shouldst stare?
   Dolabella. Enough. An idle rumor reacht the camp
That Cleopatra stung herself to death,
Vexing two asps held close against her bosom.
   Antony. Are Romans all so ignorant of the asp
That two are wanted? that he must be vext? 90
That, like domestic animals, he bites?
He bites not, but he strikes with upper jaw
As other vipers do, and the black lid
Drops, and he crawls away; one pang, one shriek,
Death hears it, nor delays: the hind knows that.
An earlier story now. So exquisite
In luxury, my queen dissolved a pearl
Above all price, and drank it in her wine.
Bid thou the tatler of the tale expound
How that same acid which dissolved the pearl 100
Darken'd no tooth, abbreviated no smile,
But gave her spirits for the festive song.
Ah! had she done so, Medicine had run up
In vain to help her; Death had interposed.
   Dolabella. Another tale, alike incredible.
'Tis said she shook from off her coronal
Poison into your cup, dashing it down
Just at the lip, and proving its effect
On household beast before you, thus to show
How easy were the deed to one who will'd. 110
   Antony. Is such a fiction workt by homespun yarn?
I doubt it: surely some Greek needle wrought
The quaint device, for poet to adorn
By metaphor, and sage by apologue.
Thou hast among thy friends one capable,
In man's attire, fresh-blooming from Hymettus,
Handmaid of Cilnius the rich Aretine.
O Romans! are your ears to falsities

Wide open, and your mouths agape for them
As are the callow sparrows for their food,   120
Hour after hour? Ye little know that asps
Are not mere worms of one span-length, one cubit,
But longer than the vipers in your fields,
So hideous that no woman, young or old,
Or rustic, or well train'd to monkey-gods,
But must abhor them. Your credulity
Will urge the whisper in each other's ear
That she, the daintiest of all womankind,
Would handle them, now plague them, now caress
And hug them as she might a tender babe . .   130
Yet even the serious may believe the tale,
For what in Rome is not believed . . but truth?
   Dolabella. To me the queen said nothing of this snare.
   Antony. Nothing she knows of it.
                        I heard a scream
From Iras, and rusht in. She threw herself
Before my feet, prayed me to strike her dead,
And ran toward the corner, where I saw
The beasts coil'd up, and cut them thro' and thro'.
Then told she all; but not until her prayer
For death was fruitless, not until I warn'd her   140
Her life and death, while yet we live, are ours.
   Dolabella. Might I advise . .
   Antony.   Not me: I never took
Any advice, in battle or debate:
   Dolabella. Cæsar hath urged thee sorely, and may worse;
What wouldst thou do with him were he the vanquisht?
   Antony. Do with him? throw him to the fishermen
To bait their hooks with and catch crocodiles,
If crocodile feeds upon crocodile.
Take him these words: we keep no secrets here.
   Dolabella. Cæsar is lenient.
   Antony.   Never let that word   150
Glide o'er thy lips, no word is it for me.
Tell him no friend of mine shall ask my life,
No enemy shall give it. I am lord
Of my own honor; he has none to lose:
The money-changer's granson calculates
But badly here. He waits for thee: depart.

141 Her] *so in errata 1856 and text 1876*; How *in text 1856.*

ANTONY AND OCTAVIUS

SCENE THE SEVENTH.

ANTONY AND AGRIPPA.

Antony. And so, the victor comes to taunt the vanquisht!
Is this well done, Agrippa?
  Agrippa.   'Twere ill done,
And never done by me.
               There have been some
Who carried to the forum and there cast
The tags and rags of mimes, and tarnisht spangles
Bag'd from the dusthole corner; gravity
Becomes me better and plain Roman garb
In action and in speech; no taunt is mine.
  Antony. What then demands the vanquisher?
  Agrippa.   I come
To ask a favor, ask a gift, of thee.   10
Give me thy children.
  Antony.   To adopt?
  Agrippa.   To save:
They may have enemies; they shall have friends
If thou accedest to my last request:
Lose we no time; we shall be soon at Rome.
  Antony. Ventidius may prevent it.
  Agrippa.   He hath serv'd thee
Faithfully, and is steddy to thy cause:
The sea is closed to him, the river closed,
Wide as the desert is, it is not open,
And half his army, more than half, is ours.
  Antony. But many yet are left me, brave and true.   20
  Agrippa. When Fortune hath deserted us, too late
Comes Valor, standing us in little stead.
They who would die for us are just the men
We should not push on death or throw away.
  Antony. Too true! Octavius with his golden wand
Hath reacht from far some who defied his sword.
How little fire within warps loosen'd staves
Together, for the hoop to hold them tight!
I have too long stood balancing the world
Not to know well its weight: of that frail crust   30
Friends are the lightest atoms.
  Agrippa.   Not so all.

Sc. 7. Characters. M. Vipsanius Agrippa commanded the fleet which defeated
Antony's at Actium.—[W.]   15 Ventidius] P. Ventidius Bassus, Antony's legate in
campaigns against the Parthians. See Plutarch's life of Antony.—[W.]

Antony. I thought of Dolabella and the rest.
Ventidius and Agrippa, these are men
Romulus might have wrestled with nor thrown.
I have proved both.

Agrippa. One thou shalt prove again,
In guise more friendly than when last we met.

Antony. To me well spoken hast thou for Ventidius,
Speak for him in that manner to another,
Tell him that he has done against the Parthian
What Julius might, perhaps might not, have done. 40
Triumph must follow. I shall never see it,
Nor shall I see, nor shalt thou either, one
On which cold eyes, dim even in youth to beauty,
Look forward.

Are there not kings left enow
To drag, by brace or leash, and back to back,
Along the *Sacred Way*?

Vile wretch! his steeds
Shall never at the cries of Cleopatra
Prance up against their trappings stiff with gold.

Agrippa. Sad were the sight.

Antony. Too far hath Dolabella
Prevail'd with her.

Agrippa. Hath Dolabella come
Within these walls? 50

Antony. Hast thou not seen him then
Leave them within the hour?

Agrippa. Indeed not I.
My station is the harbor where the ships
Are riding, his lies nearer to the town.
Thou musest, Antony!

Antony. And well may muse.
He was my friend .. *is* he. Away with doubt!

Agrippa. He was the friend of Tullius, friend of Brutus,
Friend too of Lepidus, akin to each,
And yet betraid he them.

Give me the boys;
With me they enter Rome.

Antony. Take, take them; both? 60
Yes; both are safer, both are happier so.
I loved them; but I might have loved them more;
Now is too late.

Take them; be kind to them ..

Nay, look not back. Tears scorch the father's eyes,
The Roman should extinguish them . . and shall.
Farewell! farewell!
     But turn thy face aside . .
No . . one word more.
 Agrippa.   Thy gladness gladdens me,
Bursting so suddenly. What happy change!
 Antony. Thou hast a little daughter, my old friend,
And I two little sons . . I had at least . .   70
Give her the better and the braver one,
When by thy care he comes to riper age.
 Agrippa. O Antony! the changes of our earth
Are suddener and oftener than the moon's,
On hers we calculate, not so on ours,
But leave them in the hands of wilful Gods,
Inflexible, yet sometimes not malign.
 Antony. They have done much for me, nor shall reproach
Against them pass my lips: I might have askt,
But never thought of asking, what desert   80
Was mine for half the blessings they bestow'd.
I will not question them why they have cast
My greatness and my happiness so low;
They have not taken from me their best gift,
A heart for ever open to my friends:
It will be cold ere long, and one will grieve.

SCENE THE EIGHTH.

OCTAVIUS. AGRIPPA. CÆSARION. MECÆNAS.

 Octavius. What said that obstinate and proud old thief?
Couldst thou not draw him from his den, Agrippa?
 Agrippa. I tried not.
 Octavius.   Nor perhaps desired.
 Agrippa.   'Tis true,
I entered not by stealth, and broke no confidence;
Tatius, who knew and once fought under me . .
 Octavius. And would not he who knows thy power, and who
Admitted thee within the royal hold,
Do more?
 Agrippa. Not even this would he have done
For any other, nor for me without
Permission from his general; this obtain'd,   10
I enter'd.

Octavius. His audacity, no doubt,
Abated with his fortunes, and he droopt
As droops a lotus when the water fails.
    Agrippa. Neither in life nor death will that man droop;
He holds down Fortune, stil too strong for her.
    Octavius. We must then starve him out, or slay his sons
Before his eyes.
    Agrippa.   Thus nothing will remain
For him to fear, and every honest sword
Will skulk within its scabbard for mere shame.
This may not be the worst . . when brave men fall   20
By treachery, men like them avenge the blow;
Antonius did it . . was Antonius blamed?
    Octavius. But who will answer for our own dear lives
If these boys live?
    Agrippa.   I will . . the boys are mine.
    Octavius. Cæsarion is secure.
    Agrippa.   I do rejoice
At this.
    Octavius. I wonder he hath not arrived.
    Agrippa. Rescued from Egypt is the Roman lad?
I long to see him.
    Octavius.   Wait then, and thou shalt.
    Agrippa. Women and eunuchs and Greek parasites
Educate ill those who may one day rule.   30
    Octavius. True, very true . . we will bear this in mind.
    Agrippa. He must learn better soon.
    Octavius.   Be sure he shall.
    Agrippa. What are those sistrums and those tamborines
That trifle with the trumpet and intrude?
    Octavius. The very things thou wouldst provide against.
Heigh! who commanded such obstreperous shouts?
    Agrippa. The man who gave us Egypt, sir, and thee.
The sound bursts louder from his hollow tomb:
Such are the honors which attend his child.
    Octavius. Hark! the arms strike the ground!
    Agrippa.   Soldiers, well done!
Already do they know whom they salute.   41
    Cæsarion. Hail! hail! my cousin!
                          Let me kiss that hand
So soft and white. Why hold it back from me?
I am your cousin, boy Cæsarion.
    Octavius. Who taught you all this courtesy?

ANTONY AND OCTAVIUS

Cæsarion. My heart.
Beside, my mother bade me wish you joy.
   Octavius. I would myself receive it from her.
   Cæsarion. Come,
Come then with me; none see her and are sad.
   Octavius. Then she herself is not so?
   Cæsarion. Not a whit,
Grave as she looks, but should be merrier stil.   50
   Octavius. She may expect all bounty at our hands.
   Cæsarion. Bounty! she wants no bounty.
                    Look around;
Those palaces, those temples, and their gods
And myriad priests within them, all are hers;
And people bring her ships, and gems, and gold.
  O cousin! do you know what some men say,
(If they do say it) that your sails ere long
Will waft all these away?
               I wish 'twere true
What else they talk.
   Octavius. What is it?
   Cæsarion. That you come
To carry off her also.
            She is grown   60
Paler, and I have seen her bite her lip
At hearing this. Ha! well I know my mother;
She thinks it may look redder for the bite.
  But will you really carry us to Rome
In triumph? thro' the streets, and up the hill,
And over arches .. foolish folks say under ..
With flowers all round them? O! what joy to see
The people that once loved my father so!
   Octavius. We will do all that may oblige the queen.
   Cæsarion. And yet she shudders at the very thought   70
Of those fresh honors which delight my heart.
   Octavius. For her, or for yourself?
   Cæsarion. We boys, you know,
Think of ourselves the first; and yet, and yet,
If my sweet mother is averse to change,
And weary of it, I would pass my days
With her; yes, even in that lonely tower
(Which to my eyes looks like a sepulcher)
Whence she protests the Gods alone shall take her.

      51 She] See *mispr. 1876.*

Octavius (*to a* Guard). See due attention paid this royal guest.
Cæsarion. Unwillingly I part from one so kind.   80
Octavius (*to* AGRIPPA). Agrippa, didst thou mark that comely boy?
Agrippa. I did indeed.
Octavius.   There is methinks in him
A somewhat not unlike our common friend.
    Agrippa. Unlike? There never was such similar
Expression. I remember Caius Julius
In youth, altho' my elder by some years;
Well I remember that high-vaulted brow,
Those eyes of eagle under it, those lips
At which the senate and the people stood
Expectant for their portals to unclose;   90
Then speech, not womanly but manly sweet,
Came from them, and shed pleasure as the morn
Sheds light.
    Octavius. The boy has too much confidence.
    Agrippa. Not for his prototype. When he threw back
That hair in hue like cinnamon, I thought
I saw great Julius tossing his, and warn
The pirates he would give them their desert.
    My boy, thou gazest at those arms hung round.
    Cæsarion. I am not strong enough for sword and shield,
Nor even so old as my sweet mother was   100
When I first rioted upon her knee
And seiz'd whatever sparkled in her hair.
Ah! you had been delighted had you seen
The pranks she pardon'd me. What gentleness!
What playfulness!
    Octavius.   Go now, Cæsarion.
    Cæsarion. And had you ever seen my father too!
He was as fond of her as she of me,
And often bent his thoughtful brow o'er mine
To kiss what she had kist, then held me out
To show how he could manage the refractory,   110
Then one long smile, one pressure to the breast.
    Octavius. How tedious the boy grows!
                        Lead him away,
Aufidius!
                There is mischief in his mind,
He looks so guileless.

97 pirates] Julius Cæsar was captured by pirates off Miletus in 76 B.C. Landor also referred to the incident in the imaginary conversation, 'Lucullus and Cæsar'.—[W.]

Agrippa. He has lived apart
From evil counsellors, with grey-hair'd men
Averse to strife, and maidens of the queen.
 Octavius. This makes me think . .
       We will another time
Consider what is best.
     Here comes Mecænas.

     (*To* Mecænas.)
Cilnius! you met upon the stairs that boy?
 Mecænas. I did.
 Octavius.   What think you of him?
 Mecænas.   At one glance   120
'Twere rashness to decide.
 Octavius.   Seems he not proud?
 Mecænas. He smiled, and past me by.
 Octavius. What insolence! quite insupportable!
 Mecænas. Perhaps he knew me not; and, if he knew me,
I have no claim on affability
From Cæsar's enemies.
 Agrippa (to himself). By Jove! the man
At first so calm begins at last to chafe.
O, the vain Tuscan of protuberant purse!
 Octavius. What said Agrippa?
 Agrippa.   That our friend here chafes,
Altho' the mildest of all mortal men.   130
 Octavius. Excepting one; one whom no wrongs can ruffle.
I must give orders for some small affairs,
And will rejoin you soon.
 Agrippa.   My gentle Cilnius!
Do save this lad! Octavius is so calm,
I doubt he hath some evil in his breast
Against the only scion of the house,
The orphan child of Julius.
 Mecænas.   Think, Agrippa,
If there be safety where such scion is,
Safety for you and me.
 Agrippa.   The mother must
Adorn the triumph, but that boy would push   140
Rome, universal Rome, against the steeds
That should in ignominy bear along
The image of her Julius. Think; when Antony
Show'd but his vesture, sprang there not tears, swords,

Curses? and swept they not before them all
Who shared the parricide? If such result
Sprang from torn garment, what must from the sight
Of that fresh image which calls back again
The latest of the Gods, and not the least,
Who nurtured every child within those walls,
And emptied into every mother's lap   150
Africa, Sicily, Sardinia, Gaul,
And this inheritance of mighty kings.
No such disgrace must fall on Cæsar's son.
Spare but the boy, and we are friends for ever.
   Mecænas. Friends are we, but Octavius is our master.
   Agrippa. Let him brush kings away and blow off queens,
But there are some of us who never struck
At boys, nor trampled on a prostrate head;
Some of us are there too who fain would see   160
Rome better than they left her, with high blood
Bounding along her veins; enough hath flowed.
   Mecænas. Here comes Octavius. We attend his will.
   Octavius. Enough that I know yours, my truest friends!
I look into your hearts and find my own.
Thy wishes, O Agrippa, I divine.
Antony was thy comrade in the wars
Of Julius; Fulvia was thy enemy
And mine: her children to the Infernal Gods
Devote I, but the born of Cleopatra   170
Thou shalt have saved: Cæsarion shall rest here.

168 Fulvia] widow of Clodius, married to Antony 46 B.C. and by him divorced before his marriage to Octavia.—[W.]

SCENE THE NINTH.

DOLABELLA. CÆSARION. SCOPAS.

Dolabella. Where hast thou put Cæsarion?
Scopas.   Nigh at hand.
Dolabella. What is he doing?
Scopas.   Just what lads like most;
Munching a water-melon.
            There is good,
At least good-nature, in that simple soul.
While most were sleeping in the night of noon
I brought him hither. Thirsty were we both

And wine I offer'd him: he pusht it by
And said, "I drink no wine; bring water-melons."
I brought him one: he cut it fairly thro',
And gave me half before he toucht the other,   10
Saying, "but keep the seeds, the round and black,
That I may plant them, when we get to Rome,
With my own hands in garden all my own."
   Dolabella. Poor innocent!
   Scopas.   I could not help but smile.
   Dolabella. For once I envy thee.
                         But call him in.
   Scopas. Ho! youngster! here!
   Cæsarion.   What means that loud rude speech?
This man seems civiler; I may converse
With him, but never more, thou churl, with thee.
   Dolabella. I would, my fair young friend, his voice less rough,
But honest Romans are sometimes abrupt.   20
Scopas is sorry.
   Cæsarion.   Honest! sorry too!
I then was wrong, and am more vext than he.
   Scopas. Boy! I could wish I never saw thy face
Nor heard thy tongue.
   Cæsarion.   What can he mean?
   Dolabella.   He feels
The offence he gave.
   Cæsarion.   Good man, be comforted,
And let my hand atone for face and tongue.
   Scopas (to DOLABELLA). That smile disarms me.
   Dolabella.   My sweet prince, observe
How he repents.
                I have some words to speak
In private to him: but I first would hear
How fare your little brothers.
   Cæsarion.   They are gone,   30
Both gone: two maidens carried them away
Before a noble-looking man they call
Agrippa.
   Dolabella. Gone? say you? and with Agrippa?
O that I could have seen them ere they went!
   Cæsarion. No matter; I will tell you all about them,
It is not much, if you desire to know.
One can not talk, the other talks all day,
One smiles at me, the other pulls my hair,

But he smiles too, and then runs off as fleet
As my gazelle, yet easier to be caught.   40
You have heard all, and now will I return
And leave you, as you wish: I know my way.
    Dolabella. The duty must be done; 'tis Cæsar's will.
    Scopas. Then done it shall be.
    Dolabella.   Take this token: here;
Take this too; ninety golden of like weight
Lie in the leather.
    Scopas.   Thanks; the deed is done.   [*Alone.*
What do these letters, bright and sharp, denote?
CÆSAR DICTATOR; and what else beneath?
PERPETUO.
                Gods above! PERPETUO too!
Ashes may be perpetual: nothing more   50
Remains of our dictator. Take the urn,
Empty it, weigh its inwards: poise the two,
This inch-broad coin with it; and what I toss
On my forefinger is the solider.
    I must go in.
    Cæsarion.   'Tis very kind in you
To visit me again: you bear no malice.
I know at once who loves me.
    Scopas.   And do I?
    Cæsarion. One moment yes, one moment no. My handsome
And gentle cousin does not love me quite;
I wish he did, I want so to love *him*.   60
How cool and quiet is this small dim room!
It wants no cushion: I begin to think
The hard stone-seat refreshes more the limbs.
Will you not try?
    Scopas.   Not yet; but presently.
    Cæsarion. My mother is not here; you need not mind.
People must not sit down before a queen;
But before boys, whatever boys they are,
Men may, and should.
              Oh! what can I have done?
And did you strike me? Would you strike again?
What runs into my sandals from my breast?   70
Oh! it begins to pain me .. sadly, sadly!
    Scopas. By all the Gods and Goddesses above!
I have no strength to strike the boy again.
    Cæsarion. O father! father! where is now that face

ANTONY AND OCTAVIUS

So gravely fond that bent o'er your Cæsarion?
And, mother! thou too gone! In all this gloom
Where shall I find thee? Scopas! Scopas! help!
  Scopas. Away with me! Where is the door? Against it
Stands he? or follows he? Crazed! I am crazed!
O had but he been furious! had he struck me!   80
Struggled, or striven, or lookt despitefully!
Anything, anything but call my name
So tenderly. O had that mild reproach
Of his been keener when his sense return'd,
Only to leave him ever-lastingly,
I might not have been, what I now am, frantic.
Upturn'd to me those wandering orbs, outspred
Those quivering arms, falling the last of him,
And striking once, and only once, the floor,
It shook my dagger to the very hilt,   90
And ran like lightning up into my brain.

SCENE THE TENTH.

Eros and Antony.

  Antony. Eros! I speak thee welcome.
  Eros.   Hail, our lord!
  Antony. Thou hast been ever faithful to thy trust,
And spoken freely, but decorously,
On what concern'd the household and the state.
My glory is gone down, and life is cold
Without it. I have known two honest men
Among the senators and consulars . .
  Eros. None among humbler?
  Antony.   By the Powers above!
I thought but of the powerful, men of birth.
  Eros. All men are that. Some sink below their cradle,   10
Others rise higher than parental roof,
And want no scepter to support their steps.
  Antony. Such there may be whom we have all past by.
  Eros. Men cast long shadows when their life declines,
Which we cross over without noticing;
We met them in the street and gave not way,
When they were gone we lifted up both hands,
And said to neighbors *These were men indeed!*
  Antony. Reflections such as thine had wearied me

Erewhile, and from another even now;   20
But what is that thou bringest me wrapt up,
Tardy in offering it as worth too little?
Eros. I bring a ruby and a hollow ring
Whereon it fitted.
Antony.   Gods of Rome! at last
Ye make me grateful. Thanks, and thanks alone,
Have I to give, and one small sacrifice;
I vow it you before this hour is past.
My heart may beat against its bars awhile,
But shall not leave me yet.
                          Go, Eros, go,
I must lie down and rest, feeble and faint.   30
But come back presently.
Eros (after some absence). How fares our lord?
Antony. Recovered, sound again, more sound than ever.
Eros. And yet our lord looks more like other men.
Antony (smiling). We can not always swagger, always act
A character the wise will never learn:
When Night goes down, and the young Day resumes
His pointed shafts, and chill air breathes around,
Then we put on our own habiliments
And leave the dusty stage we proudly trod.
I have been sitting longer at life's feast   40
Than does me good; I will arise and go.
Philosophy would flatten her thin palm
Outspred upon my sleeve; away with her!
Cuff off, cuff out, that chattering toothless jade!
The brain she puzzles, and she blunts the sword:
Even she knows better words than that word *live.*
Cold Cato, colder Brutus, guide not me;
No, nor brave Cassius.
                      Thou hast brought me balm.
Eros. Our lord may have some message for the giver,
Which will console her.
Antony.   She expected none: 50
I did; and it is come.
                      Say, lookt she pale?
Spake she no word?
Eros.   Alas, most noble sir,
She would not see me. Charmian said her face
Was indeed pale, yet grew less pale than usual
After she gave the ring, and then she spake

196

ANTONY AND OCTAVIUS

Amid some sighs (some spasms too interposed)
More cheerfully, and said she fain would sleep.
   Antony. The fondest heart, the truest, beats no more.
She listened to me, she hath answered me,
She wanted no entreaty, she obeyed,   60
She now commands: but no command want I.
Queen of my soul! I follow in thy train,
Thine is the triumph.
                Eros, up! rejoice!
Tears, man! do tears become us at this hour?
I never had too many; thou hast seen
(If thou didst see) the last of them.
                    My sword!
I will march out becomingly.
   Eros.   O sir!
Enemies watch all round, and famine waits
Within.
   Antony. Thou knowest not the prudent sons
Of Egypt; corn and wine have been supplied   70
Enough for many years, piled underground.
Tho' stiffened by the sludge of barbarism,
Or indolent and overgorged at home,
Briton or German would take heed that none
Who fought for him should perish for the lack
Of sustenance: the timid bird herself
Will hover round and round until she bring
The grain cried out for in the helpless nest.
Give me my sword! Is the point sharp?
   Eros.   In vain
To trust it now!
   Antony.   Come, bring it; let me try it.   80
   Eros. O heavens and earth! Help! help! no help is nigh,
No duty left but one: less worthily
Than willingly this duty I perform.   *[Stabs himself.*
It pains not: for that blood I see no more.

DRAMAS AND DRAMATIC SCENES

SCENE THE ELEVENTH.

[Alexandria. August, 30 B.C.]

OFFICER. OCTAVIUS. MECÆNAS. GALLUS.

Officer. News! glorious news! news certain! Dead as Death!
Octavius. Who dead?
Officer.   The master of the horse to Julius,
Master too, but this morning, of this realm,
The great . .
Mecænas. Halt there! and know, where Cæsar is
There is none great but Cæsar!
Officer.   Pardon! true!
Octavius. And nought about his paramour?
Officer.   The queen?
Octavius. Yes, fellow, yes.
Officer.   Surely our emperor knows
Of her; the story now is some days old.
The queen was poisoned by two little worms
Which people here call asps, most venomous things,   10
Coil'd in a yellow fig around the seeds.
Her maidens wail'd her loudly; men and maidens
Alike mourn'd over . . I had nearly slipt.
Octavius. Many have done the same.
                                  Art thou a Roman?
Officer. I have the honor, sir, to be a Gaul,
A native of Massilia, that famed city
Inhabited by heroes, built by Gods,
Who entered it again with Caius Julius.
Mecænas. And didst thou see them enter?
Officer.   Not distinctly,
There were a few between: one told it me   20
Who saw them; which, ye know, is just the same.
Octavius. Retire, my brave! go sure of a reward.
Lucretia hath escaped us after all!
But there is wax in Egypt, there are Greeks
Who model it, and who can bear to look
On queen or asp; this model'd to the life,
The other more like what they work upon.
No trouble in thus carrying her to Rome.

Sc. xi *sub-title.* August 29, 30 B.C. is generally given as the date of Cleopatra's suicide. According to Plutarch, Cæsarion was put to death soon afterwards and not, as in Scene 9, a few days earlier. Plutarch also states that before killing herself Cleopatra wept over Antony's grave.—W.

Gallus! thou lookest grave: thou art the man
Exactly to compose an epitaph.   30
No matter which died first: I think the asps
Rather have had the start: I may be wrong,
A bad chronologist, a worse astrologer.
   Mecænas. Where Cæsar smiles, all others smile but Gallus.
   Gallus. Not even Cæsar's smiles awaken mine
When every enemy has dropt away,
And he who made so many safe, is safe.
   Mecænas. I wish thou wert more joyous.
   Gallus.   Kind the wish,
Almost enough to make me so.
   Mecænas.   Come! come!
I know you poets: any wager now   40
Thou hast already forced the weeping Muse
To thy embraces. Tell us honestly;
Hast thou not turn'd the egg upon the nest
Ready for hatching?
   Octavius.   Guilty; look at him,
He blushes, blushes from cheekbone to beard.
Now, Gallus, for the epitaph.
   Mecænas.   Recite it.
   Gallus. Epitaphs are but cold and chisel'd words,
Or mostly false if warmer: quite unfit
Are mine for marble or for memory.
I thought of her . . another would have said   50
He wept: I wept not, but I know I sigh'd.
   Mecænas. And wrote? For poet is half sigh half flame:
Sigh out thy sigh.
   Gallus.   Would Cæsar hear it?
   Octavius.   Yea.
   Gallus. I have not ventured to pronounce the name
Of her I meditated on.
   Caesar.   My friend
Is here judicious as in all things else.
   Gallus.

> "Thou hast been floating on the o'erswollen stream
>   Of life these many summers; is thy last
> Now over? hast thou dreamt out every dream?
>   Hath horn funereal blown the pageant past?   60
> Cæsar! thou too must follow: all the rods
>   Of sternest lictor cannot scare off Death;
> She claims the earth for heritage; our Gods
>   Themselves have seen their children yield their breath."

Cæsar. Gallus! I always thought thee a brave soldier,
Never a first-rate poet: I am right.
   Gallus. Cæsar! I never heard of one who gain'd
A battle and a kingdom who was not.
   Cæsar. If there be anything on earth I know
Better than other things, 'tis poetry.   70
   Mecænas. My sweet Octavius! draw not under nose
The knuckle of forefinger. Gallus aim'd
A harmless arrow: Love in sport hath done it
Often and often.
              Gallus, seize his hand.
Now sing a pæan; sing a prophet's; sing
Egypt! thy pyramid of power is closed.
   Gallus. I would; but want the breath: I have but strength
For elegy: here is the last of mine.

> "The mighty of the earth are earth,
>   A passing gleam the brightest smile,   80
> In golden beds have sorrows birth,
>   Alas! these live the longer while."

   Octavius. Unless we haste to supper, we shall soon
Forfeit our appetites. Come, my two friends!

SCENE THE TWELFTH.

OCTAVIUS AND OCTAVIA.

   Octavius. Embrace me, sister; we have won; thy wrongs
Are now avenged.
   Octavia.   Speak not of wrong, but right,
And bring Rome peace and happiness once more.
'Tis kind in thee (but thou wert always kind)
To come so soon to greet me, while the altar
Is warm and damp with incense for thy safety.
   Octavius. Octavia! I have brought thee from the Nile
Two pretty little serpents.
   Octavia.   Of all beasts
The serpent is the beast I most abhor.
Take them away.
   Octavius.   I have not brought them here,   10
Be not afraid; beside, they are so young
They can not bite.
   Octavia.   But send them off.
   Octavius.   I will.
What thinkest thou are these two reptiles call'd?
   Octavia. I know not, nor can guess.

ANTONY AND OCTAVIUS

Octavia.   *Lucius and Marcus,*
The brood of Antony. O Heaven! she faints!
Rise, sister! let me help thee up; be sure
They shall not hurt thee. Grasp not thus my wrist,
And shoot not up those leaden bolts at me,
For such are thy stiff eyes. I said, and swear,
The little monsters never shall hurt *thee.*   20
I do not like those tears; but better they
Than the cold flint they fall from, and now melt.
    Octavia. Brother, I know thy purpose. On my knees . .
    Octavius. Arise! There wants not this to seal their doom.
    Octavia. This is my fault, not theirs, if fault there be.
    Octavius. I want, and I will have, security.
    Octavia. What is there now on earth to apprehend?
    Octavius. I dread lest he who guards them should adopt.
    Octavia. Let him! O let him! if an honest man.
Frown not, debate not, struggle not against   30
Thy better Genius ; argue with him thus,
"Octavius! has there not been blood enough
Without the blood of children?"
    Octavius.   Is my safety
Not dear to thee?
    Octavia.   Thy glory, thy content,
Are . . no, not dearer, but almost as dear.
Hast thou not suffer'd pangs at every head
That fell?
    Octavius. They fell that mine might not.
    Octavia.   But children
Strike not so high.
    Octavius.   Are children always children?
    Octavia. O brother! brother! are men always men?
They are full-grown then only when grown up   40
Above their fears. Power never yet stood safe;
Compass it round with friends and kindnesses,
And not with moats of blood. Remember Thebes:
The towers of Cadmus toppled, split asunder,
Crasht: in the shadow of her oleanders
The pure and placid Dirce stil flows by.
What shatter'd to its base but cruelty,
(Mother of crimes, all lesser than herself)
The house of Agamemnon king of kings?
    Octavius. Thou art not yet, Octavia, an old woman;   50
Tell not, I do beseech thee, such old tales.

Octavia. Hear later; hear what our own parents saw.
Where lies the seed of Sulla? Could the walls
Of his Præneste shelter the young Marius,
Or subterranean passages provide
Escape? he stumbled through the gore his father
Had left in swamps on our Italian plains.
We have been taught these histories together,
Neither untrue nor profitless; few years
Have since gone by, can memory too have gone? 60
Ay, smile, Octavius! only let the smile
Be somewhat less disdainful.
    Octavius.   'Tis unwise
To plant thy foot where Fortune's wheel runs on.
    Octavia. I lack not wisdom utterly; my soul
Assures me wisdom is humanity,
And they who want it, wise as they may seem,
And confident in their own sight and strength,
Reach not the scope they aim at.
                         Worst of war
Is war of passion; best of peace is peace
Of mind, reposing on the watchful care
Daily and nightly of the household Gods. 70

THE END [OF ANTONY AND OCTAVIUS].

SCENE

JAMES I. OF SCOTS, EARL OF ATHOL, SIR ROBERT STEWART, HIS GRANDSON, AND GRAHAM

[Published in 1863; reprinted 1876. See notes at end of volume.]

Scene:—A bed-chamber in the Dominican Convent, Perth.
[February 20, 1437]

King James. Uncle! and thou too with these murderers!
Nay, hide not thy grey head behind that door
Half broken down. See I thee, cousin Robert?
Thee, with a dagger in thy grasp! the intent
Is plain. I ask no grace of thee, for thou
Who never hast known love canst not know pity.
    Earl of Athol. If thou hadst not, this realm had never stoopt
Before a scepter in a stranger's hand.

Title. James II of Scotland and Assassins, *1876. See note at end of volume.*

JAMES I. OF SCOTS

Sir Robert Graham. We come to vindicate our country's rights
And have no time to parley.
  Earl of Athol.   Thou, my liege,   10
Hast injured all of us. What lord is safe
In his own castle from thy vengeful laws?
  Graham. Answer us that.
  King James.   What honest traveler
Is safe from rapine where your wide domains
And power usurpt from soverainty extend.
  Graham. Are there no ladies in this land of ours
Worthy to mate with any king?
  King James.   Yea, many.
  Graham. Why then should England force upon the throne
An alien brood.
  King James. Cease, villain! I was free.
So are ye all in this; rich, poor, alike;   20
Are kings alone debarr'd? I chose a mate
Of royal blood, not for her royalty,
Unless such royalty as God imparts
When he gives grace and virtue; these are Jane's.
Would ye slay her too?
  Earl of Athol. We war not with women.
  King James. Ye war against them when ye strike the breast
They cling to.
  Earl of Athol. Thou shouldst have been stil her minstrel.
Is it becoming in a king to ride
About the country with a single groom,
And crouch thro' half-rooft cottages, and ask   30
The creatures to complain of aught amiss?
As if they had not plenty to blab out
Against their lords; are they not our born serfs?
Answer us that.
  King James. I am God's bailiff, sir,
Not yours, to Him alone I give account.
  Graham. That shalt thou speedily; the book is closed;
Take it him.
  Earl of Athol. Well done, Graham, strike again.
  Graham. He folds his cloak around him so, and lifts
So high both upright arms, there is no place.
  Earl of Athol. Well, well, methinks we have done enough to-day. 40
He speaks tho'.
  King James. Robert! art *thou* here?

   30 half-rooft] rush-rooft *MS. emendation.*

Sir Robert Stewart.   **My liege!**
Here am I. What may be our lord's commands?
King James. Thou at least art no robber . . . take my ring . . .
Give it to *her* . . but first wipe off the blood
If there be any on it.
    Graham.   She has one,
And can not want another: ruby rings
Suit ill for marriages, and worse for deaths.
    Sir R. Stewart. Peace, Graham, peace!
                        Sire, thy behest is sacred.
King James. Robert! thou art again for this half-hour
What thou wast when we both were only boys.   50
    Sir R. Stewart. Sire, your breath fails you.
                 (*Aside*) Faith! and mine fails too.
King James. Give it her . . . call some holy man . . haste . . . go.

48 thy] your 1876.

DIANA DE POICTIERS AND CAILLETTE

[Printed here from a manuscript. A version with variants noted below and a few
others of no significance was published in 1876. See notes at end of volume.]

[CHARACTERS.

DIANA DE POICTIERS, wife of the Grand Seneschal of Normandy and afterwards
    Duchesse de Valentinois (*ob.* 1566).
CAILLETTE, The King's Fool.
KING FRANCIS I.
CHANCELLOR. (Antoine du Prat, afterwards Archbishop and Cardinal.)]

DATE 1523.

Diana. Caillette! by those lower'd eyes I often thought
Thou lovedst me.
    Caillette.   Madame! where we dare not love
We may adore.
    Diana.   Speak plainly; dost thou love me?
Rise, simpleton! If thou dost love me, save
My father, whom a shameful death awaits;
The king hath sworn it.
    Caillette.   If the king hath sworn
My lord shall die, why then my lord is safe.

    Title. Three scenes not for the stage *with present title as sub-title, 1876.*   List of
Characters and date not in MS.   2 Thou lovedst] You loved *1876.*   5 shameful
death] cruel doom *1876.*   6 If . . . sworn *not in 1876 which after it has:* and the
king hath said   7–8 *not in 1876.*

DIANA DE POICTIERS AND CAILLETTE

Diana. Caillette! Caillette! His Majesty declares
"Truth, if it leave the world, should rest with kings."
   Caillette. Is this encouragement to plead for pardon   10
Against his oath?
   Diana.   Argue not; save my father!
He rais'd thee up and gave thy post* to thee,
And none stands higher in favor.
   Caillette.   None; God knows,
God who will pardon me, that, when the post
Of Fool was forced on me, I seized my dirk
And would have stabb'd myself: unfriendly hand
Seiz'd mine, and left me life, grief, scorn, despair.
   Diana. Thy noble form, thy nobler manners, give
The power of scorn to thee; grief we will share,
Disgrace we never will: the worst disgrace   20
In all men's eyes is that which kings inflict,
Their frown the bravest shudder at, the block
Blackens beneath it; such my father's doom.
   Caillette. Direct me in the way that I must go,
Give me the words, the voice you can not give,
Tears I may find, but other than my own
Would sink more deeply.
   Diana.   Trifle not, nor sigh.
A witticism may win where mercy fails,
Caillette, try these, and we may hope success.
   Caillette. Could Francis see that smile, and kiss the hand   30
I now have kist, and dare to hold, but dare not
(Lest my heart break) release . .
   Diana.   Go; win my suit,
For thou canst win it, and none other can.

* The post of King's Fool. [L.]

---

9 should] shall *1876.*   12 thee up] up thine, *1876.*   thy post] the rank *1876.*
13 None;] Ah! *1876.*   17 scorn, despair] shame, disgrace *1876.*   22 bravest]
gravest *1876.*   *For ll.* 24–9 *1876 substitutes three lines (continuing Diana's speech):*
       Give the king verses, let him call them his;
       Give him witticisms; they win where pity fails;
       Try thou but these and we may hope success.
30 smile . . . the] look . . . that *1876.*   33 *after* can. *1876 has:*
       Go, tarry not.
       Caillette.   The word wings me away;
       For the first time I go hence willingly.

SECOND SCENE.

DIANA AND CAILLETTE.

Diana. Well hast thou sped, Caillette! It ill becomes
To show my gratitude within these walls;
Beside, I hasten to the court, to thank
Our gracious monarch for his clemency;
To thee I owe it all.
    Caillette.   'Tis only *Fools*
Who plead for mercy to an angry prince;
I of all Fools am the most fortunate;
Merry are others, few of them are happy,
I am, for life.
           I will ask one more grace.
    Diana. Ask any.
    Caillette.   None from you, my sovran lady,   10
One from my sovran lord.
    Diana.   What can that be?
    Caillette. Freedom from court, from courtiers, and from king.
O! would God grant me evermore to kneel
Upon these fragrant rushes, close before
The tapestry where rest your slender feet! . .
    Diana. Hark! hear you not the horses tramp the stones
Below the archway? many days of rest,
Since my disquietude hath kept them in,
Make them impatient to prance forth again.
I see thee in thy fit habiliments
Ready to come with me.   20
    Caillette.   To follow.
    Diana.   Nay;
To sit in front of me, that I may see
The face of him who saved my father's life.

1 becomes] beseems *1876.*   6 prince] king *1876.*   8 Merry are others] Many are merry *1876.*   9 grace] favour *1876.*   15 rest your] tread these *1876.*   16 Hark] Hush *1876.*   17 Below] Under *1876.*

THIRD SCENE.

FRANCIS, DIANA, CAILLETTE, CHANCELLOR.

King Francis. What means this whispering at the folding doors,
Behind the curtain and before it?
    Chancellor.   Sire!
Caillette, your Majesty's appointed Fool

DIANA DE POICTIERS AND CAILLETTE

Hath ventured to come forward with a lady
Who, from her father's criminality,
Must have incurr'd your Majesty's ill-will.
Francis. The ill-favor'd can alone incur ill-will
With me.
Chancellor. Too surely she is not ill-favor'd.
Francis. Let her then enter.
                  Never would Caillette
Bring ugly one or cruel one to me.   10

(CAILLETTE *and* DIANA *enter.*)

Diana! troth! I am well-pleas'd to see
Thy beauteous face within this court again.
Thy suit is granted.
   Diana.   Gracious Sire! I come
To offer my most humble thanks for this.
Francis. Thou couldst have won it without intercession.
Well hast thou chosen thy embassador,
No one is worthier of a lady's love.
   Diana. I think it, Sire! He has all mine that God's
And human laws have sanction'd.
   Francis.   And no more?
Diana (turning to CAILLETTE). Caillette! take thou my hand. Before
   the king   20
Take thou, nor fear rebuke, my gratitude.
Chancellor. By heaven! she kisses him! no shame is left!
No fear of scandal! none of Majesty!
Francis. Arch not those eyebrows, saintly Chancellor!
None but a woman more a saint than we
Dared in our presence do this noble deed.

4 lady] dame *1876.*   7 The . . . alone] Ill-favour only can *1876.*   12 court]
hall *1876.*   15 it . . . intercession.] without an intercessor, *1876.*   For *l.* 16
1876 substitutes: But thou hast chosen well in choosing him.   19 human] your
own *1876.*   And . . . more] None else *1876.*   21 Take . . . rebuke,] Before thy
God, accept *1876.*   22 no . . . left] For shame! for shame! *1876.*   *ll.* 23–4 *not*
in 1876.   25 woman . . . we] virtuous woman dared do thus *1876.*   For *l.* 26
1876 substitutes two lines:
               There have been modest poets; Caillette is
               The only modest fool that ever lived.

DRAMAS AND DRAMATIC SCENES

JOAN OF ARC AND HER JUDGE

[Printed from a manuscript and published in *Letters*, &c., 1897.]

Judge. After due hearing in our court supreme
Of temporal and spiritual lords,
Condemn'd art thou to perish at the stake
By fire, forerunner of the flames below.
Hearest thou? Art thou stunn'd? Art thou gone mad?
Witch! think not to escape and fly away,
As some the like of thee, 'tis said, have done.
Joan. The fire will aid my spirit to escape.
Judge. Listen, ye lords. Her spirit! Hear ye that?
She owns, then, to have her Familiar. 10
And whither (*to* JOAN)—whither would the spirit, witch,
Bear thee?
Joan. To Him who gave it.
Judge. Lucifer?
Joan. I never heard the name until thus taught.
Judge. He hath his imps.
Joan. I see he hath.
Judge. My lords!
Why look ye round, and upward at the rafters?
Smile not, infernal hag! for such thou art,
Altho' made comely to beguile the weak,
By thy enchantments and accursed spells.
Knowest thou not how many brave men fell
Under thy sword, and daily?
Joan. God knows best 20
How many fell—may their souls rest in peace!
We wanted not your land, why want ye ours?
France is our country, England yours; we hear
Her fields are fruitful: so were ours before
Invaders came and burnt our yellowing corn,
And slew the labouring oxen in the yoke,
And worried, in their pasture and their fold,
With thankless hounds, more sheep than were devour'd.
Judge. Thou wast a shepherdess. Were those sheep thine?
Joan. Whatever is my country's is mine too— 30
At least to watch and guard; I claim no more.
Ye drove the flocks adrift, and we the wolves.
Judge. Thou shouldst have kept thy station in the field,
As ours do.

JOAN OF ARC AND HER JUDGE

Joan.   Nobles! have I not? Speak out.
In the field, too—the field ye shared with me—
The cause alone divided us.
    Judge.   My lords!
Must we hear this from peasant girl, a witch?
Wolves we are call'd. (*To* JOAN). Do wolves, then, fight for glory?
    Joan. No; not so wicked, tho' by nature wild,
They seek their food, and, finding it, they rest.   40
    Judge. Sometimes the devil prompts to speak a truth
To cover lies, and to protect his brood.
But, *we* turn'd into wolves!—*we* Englishmen!
Tell us, thou knowing one, who knowest well—
Tell us, then, who are now the vanquishers.
    Joan. They who will be the vanquished, and right soon.
    Judge. False prophets there have been, and thou art one,
And proud as he that sent thee here inspired.
Who ever saw thee bend before the high
And mighty men, the consecrate around—   50
They whom our Lord exalted, they who wear
The mitre on their brows?
    Joan.   One—one alone—
Hath seen me bend, and may he soon more nigh,
Unworthy as I am! I daily fall
Before the Man (for Man he would be call'd)
Who wore no mitre, but a crown of thorns
Wore he; upon his hands no jewel'd ring,
But in the centre of them iron nails,
Half-hidden by the swollen flesh they pierced.
    Judge. Alert to play the pious here at last,   60
Thou scoffest Mother Church in these her sons,
Right reverend, worshipful, Beatitude's
Creation, Christ's and Peter's lawful heirs.
    Joan. My mother Church enforced no sacrifice
Of human blood; she never made flames drink it
Ere it boil over. Dear were all *her* sons,
Nor unforgiven were the most perverse.
    Judge. Seest thou not here thy hearers sit aghast?
    Joan. Fear me not, nobles! Ye were never wan
In battle; ye were brave to meet the brave.   70
I come not now in helm or coat of mail,
But bound with cords, and helpless. God incline
Your hearts to worthier service!
    Judge.   Darest thou,

After such outrages on knight and baron,
To call on God, or name his holy name?
'Tis mockery.
  Joan.   'Tis too often, not with me.
When first I heard his holy name I thought
He was my Father. I was taught to call
My Saviour so, and both my parents did
The like, at rising and at setting sun   80
And when they shared the oaten cake at noon.
  Judge. So thou wouldst babble like an infant still?
  Joan. I would be silent, but ye bade me speak.
  Judge. Thou mayst yet pray—one hour is left for prayer.
Edify, then, the people in the street.
  Joan. I never pray in crowds; our Saviour hears
When the heart speaks to him in solitude.
May we not imitate our blessed Lord,
Who went into the wilderness to pray?
  Judge. Who taught thee tales like this? They are forbidden. 90
Hast thou no supplication to the court?
  Joan. I never sued in vain, and will not now.
  Judge. We have been patient; we have heard thee prate
A whole hour by the bell; we have endured
Impiety; we have borne worse affronts.
My lords, ye have been bantered long enough.
The sorceress would have turned us into wolves,
And hunt us down; she would be prophetess.
  Joan. I am no sorceress, no prophetess;
But this, O man in ermine, I foretell: 100
Thou and those round thee shall ere long receive
Your due reward. England shall rue the day
She entered France—her empire totters.
            Pile,
Ye sentinels, who guard those hundred heads
Against a shepherdess in bonds—pile high
The faggots round the stake that stands upright,
And roll the barrel gently down the street,
Lest the pitch burst the hoops, and mess the way.
         (To the court.)
Ye grant one hour; it shall be well employed.
I will implore the pardon of our God   110
For you. Already hath He heard my prayer
For the deliverers of their native land.

SCENES GREEK AND ROMAN

[1]

THE SHADES OF AGAMEMNON AND OF IPHIGENEIA

[Incorporated in *Pericles and Aspasia* 1836, so reprinted 1846, 1876; reprinted as separate piece 1847, 1859. Text 1836.]

Iphigeneia. Father! I now may lean upon your breast,
And you with unreverted eyes will grasp
Iphigeneia's hand.
          We are not shades
Surely! for yours throbs yet.
                   And did my blood
Win Troy for Greece?
               Ah! 'twas ill done, to shrink;
But the sword gleam'd so sharp; and the good priest
Trembled, and Pallas frown'd above, severe.
  Agamemnon. Daughter!
  Iphigeneia.   Beloved father! is the blade
Again to pierce a bosom now unfit
For sacrifice? no blood is in its veins,   10
No God requires it here; here are no wrongs
To vindicate, no realms to overthrow.
You standing as at Aulis in the fane,
With face averted, holding (as before)
My hand; but yours burns not, as then it burn'd;
This alone shews me we are with the Blest,
Nor subject to the sufferings we have borne.
I will win back past kindness.
                Tell me then,
Tell how my mother fares who loved me so,
And griev'd, as 'twere for you, to see me part.   20
Frown not, but pardon me for tarrying
Amid too idle words, nor asking how
She prais'd us both (which most?) for what we did.
  Agamemnon. Ye Gods who govern here! do human pangs
Reach the pure soul thus far below? do tears
Spring in these meadows?
  Iphigeneia.   No, sweet father, no . .
I could have answered that; why ask the Gods?
  Agamemnon. Iphigeneia! O my child! the Earth

Title. . . . and Iphigeneia *1859.*   9 a . . . now] my bosom? 'tis *1846–1859.*
13 standing] are standing *1846–1859.*   16 shews] shows *1846–1859.*   me] that
1847, 1859.

Has gendered crimes unheard-of heretofore,
And Nature may have changed in her last depths, 30
Together with the Gods and all their laws.

    Iphigeneia. Father! we must not let you here condemn;
Not, were the day less joyful: recollect
We have no wicked here; no king to judge.
Poseidon, we have heard, with bitter rage
Lashes his foaming steeds against the skies,
And, laughing with loud yell at winged fire,
Innoxious to his fields and palaces
Affrights the eagle from the sceptred hand;
While Pluto, gentlest brother of the three 40
And happiest in obedience, views sedate
His tranquil realm, nor envies theirs above.
No change have we, not even day for night
Nor spring for summer.
                  All things are serene,
Serene too be your spirit! None on earth
Ever was half so kindly in his house,
And so compliant, even to a child.
Never was snatcht your robe away from me,
Though going to the council. The blind man
Knew his good king was leading him indoors, 50
Before he heard the voice that marshal'd Greece.
Therefore all prais'd you.
                Proudest men themselves
In others praise humility, and most
Admire it in the scepter and the sword.
What then can make you speak thus rapidly
And briefly? in your step thus hesitate?
Are you afraid to meet among the good
Incestuous Helen here?

    Agamemnon.   Oh! Gods of Hell!

    Iphigeneia. She hath not past the river.
                        We may walk
With our hands linkt nor feel our house's shame. 60

    Agamemnon. Never mayst thou, Iphigeneia! feel it!
Aulis had no sharp sword, thou wouldst exclaim,
Greece no avenger .. I, her chief so late,
Through Erebus, through Elysium, writhe beneath it.

    Iphigeneia. Come; I have better diadems than those

---

51 marshal'd] marshall'd *1846–1859.*   54 scepter] sceptre *1846.*   64 Erubus]
Erebos *1846–1859.*

SHADES OF AGAMEMNON AND OF IPHIGENEIA

Of Argos and Mycenai . . come away,
And I will weave them for you on the bank.
You will not look so pale when you have walked
A little in the grove, and have told all
Those sweet fond words the widow sent her child.   70
    Agamemnon. O Earth! I suffered less upon thy shores!
(*Aside.*) The bath that bubbled with my blood, the blows
That spilt it (O worse torture!) must she know?
Ah! the first woman coming from Mycenai
Will pine to pour this poison in her ear,
Taunting sad Charon for his slow advance.
Iphigeneia!
    Iphigeneia. Why thus turn away?
Calling me with such fondness! I am here,
Father! and where you are, will ever be.
    Agamemnon. Thou art my child . . yes, yes, thou art my child.   80
All was not once what all now is! Come on,
Idol of love and truth! my child! my child!
(*Alone.*) Fell woman! ever false! false was thy last
Denunciation, as thy bridal vow;
And yet even that found faith with me! The dirk
Which sever'd flesh from flesh, where this hand rests,
Severs not, as thou boastedst in thy scoffs,
Iphigeneia's love from Agamemnon:
The wife's a spark may light, a straw consume,
The daughter's not her heart's whole fount hath quencht,   90
'Tis worthy of the Gods, and lives for ever.
    Iphigeneia. What spake my father to the Gods above?
Unworthy am I then to join in prayer?
If, on the last, or any day before,
Of my brief course on earth, I did amiss,
Say it at once, and let me be unblest;
But, O my faultless father! why should you?
And shun so my embraces?
                Am I wild
And wandering in my fondness?
                    We are shades!!
Groan not thus deeply; blight not thus the season   100
Of full-orb'd gladness! Shades we are indeed,
But mingled, let us feel it, with the blest.
I knew it, but forgot it suddenly,
Altho' I felt it all at your approach.

        68 walked] walkt *1847, 1859.*

Look on me; smile with me at my illusion . .
You are so like what you have ever been
(Except in sorrow!) I might well forget
I could not win you as I used to do.
It was the first embrace since my descent
I ever aim'd at: those who love me live,   110
Save one, who loves me most, and now would chide me.
   Agamemnon. We want not, O Iphigeneia, we
Want not embrace, nor kiss that cools the heart
With purity, nor words that more and more
Teach what we know, from those we know, and sink
Often most deeply where they fall most light.
Time was when for the faintest breath of thine
Kingdom and life were little.
   Iphigeneia.   Value them
As little now.
   Agamemnon. Were life and kingdom all!
   Iphigeneia. Ah! by our death many are sad who loved us.   120
They will be happy too.
                Cheer! king of men!
Cheer! there are voices, songs . . Cheer! arms advance.
   Agamemnon. Come to me, soul of peace! These, these alone,
These are not false embraces.
   Iphigeneia.   Both are happy!
   Agamemnon. Freshness breathes round me from some breeze above.
What are ye, winged ones! with golden urns?

            THE HOURS.

          (*Descending.*)

    The Hours . . To each an urn we bring.
        Earth's purest gold
        Alone can hold
    The lymph of the Lethean spring.   130

    We, son of Atreus! we divide
    The dulcet from the bitter tide
      That runs athwart the paths of men.

    No more our pinions shalt thou see.
    Take comfort! We have done with thee,
      And must away to earth agen.

     Between *ll.* 120–1 *1846–1859* insert two lines:
         The little fond Electra, and Orestes
         So childish and so bold! O that mad boy!
     136 agen] again *1846–1859.*

SHADES OF AGAMEMNON AND OF IPHIGENEIA

(*Ascending.*)

Where thou art, thou
Of braided brow!
Thou cull'd too soon from Argive bow'rs!
Where thy sweet voice is heard among   140
The shades that thrill with choral song,
None can regret the parted Hours.

CHORUS OF ARGIVES.

Maiden! be thou the spirit that breathes
Triumph and joy into our song!
Wear and bestow these amaranth-wreathes,
Iphigeneia! they belong
To none but thee and her who reigns
(Less chaunted) on our bosky plains.

SEMICHORUS.

Iphigeneia! 'tis to thee
Glory we owe and victory.   150
Clash, men of Argos, clash your arms
To martial worth and virgin charms.

OTHER SEMICHORUS.

Ye men of Argos! it was sweet
To roll the fruits of conquest at the feet
Whose whispering sound made bravest hearts beat fast.
This we have known at home;
But hither we are come
To crown the king who ruled us first and last.

CHORUS.

Father of Argos! king of men!
We chaunt the hymn of praise to thee.   160
In serried ranks we stand agen,
Our glory safe, our country free.
Clash, clash the arms we bravely bore
Against Scamander's God-defended shore.

SEMICHORUS.

Blessed art thou who hast repel'd
Battle's wild fury, Ocean's whelming foam;
Blessed o'er all, to have beheld
Wife, children, house avenged, and peaceful home!

145 wreathes] wreaths *1846–1859*.   161 agen] again *1846–1859*.   165 repel'd]
repell'd *1846–1859*. 166 foam;] So in *1846–1859*, no stop in *1836*.

215

OTHER SEMICHORUS.

We too, thou seest, are now
Among the happy, though the aged brow   170
From sorrow for us we could not protect,
Nor, on the polisht granite of the well
Folding our arms, of spoils and perils tell
Nor lift the vase on the lov'd head erect.

SEMICHORUS.

What whirling wheels are those behind?
What plumes come flaring through the wind,
   Nearer and nearer? From his car
He who defied the heaven-born Powers of war
   Pelides springs! But dust are we
To him, O king, who bends the mailed knee,   180
Proud only to be first in reverent praise of thee.

OTHER SEMICHORUS.

Clash, clash the arms! None other race
Shall see such heroes face to face.
We too have fought; and they have seen
Nor sea-sand grey nor meadow green
Where Dardans stood against their men . .
Clash! Io Pæan! clash agen!
Repinings for lost days repress . .
The flames of Troy had cheer'd us less.

CHORUS.

Hark! from afar more war-steeds neigh,   190
Thousands o'er thousands rush this way.
Ajax is yonder! ay, behold
The radiant arms of Lycian gold!
Arms from admiring valour won,
Tydeus! and worthy of thy son.
'Tis Ajax wears them now; for he
Rules over Adria's stormy sea.

He threw them to the friend who lost
(By the dim judgement of the host)
Those wet with tears which Thetis gave   200
The youth most beauteous of the brave.

179 But dust] Dust, dust *1846–1859*.   180 mailed] *om. 1846–1859*.   187 agen
again *1846–1859*.   199 judgement] judgment *1846–1859*.

In vain! the insatiate soul would go
For comfort to his peers below.
Clash! ere we leave them all the plain,
Clash! Io Pæan! once again!

[2]

THE DEATH OF CLYTEMNESTRA

ORESTES AND ELECTRA.

[Printed privately in *Friendly Contributions*, 1836, and Ablett's *Literary Hours*, 1837;
published in *Pentalogia* 1837; reprinted 1847, 1859; incorporated in *Pericles and Aspasia*
(2nd *ed.*) 1846 and so reprinted 1876. Text *Pentalogia* 1837.]

Electra. Pass on, my brother! she awaits the wretch,
Dishonorer, despoiler, murderer. . . .
None other name shall name him. . . . she awaits
As would a lover . .
　　　　　　　Heavenly Gods! what poison
O'erflows my lips!
　　　　　　　Adultress! husband-slayer!
Strike her, the tigress!
　　　　　　　Think upon our father . .
Give the sword scope . . think what a man was he,
How fond of her! how kind to all about,
That he might gladden and teach *us* . . how proud
Of thee, Orestes! tossing thee above　　　　　　　　10
His joyous head and calling thee his crown.
Ah! boys remember not what melts our hearts
And marks them evermore!
　　　　　　　Bite not thy lip,
Nor tramp as an unsteddy colt the ground,
Nor stare against the wall, but think again
How better than all fathers was our father.
Go . .
　Orestes. Loose me, then! for this white hand, Electra,
Hath fastened upon mine with fiercer grasp
Than mine can grasp the sword.
　Electra.　　　　　Go, sweet Orestes!

Title. The *not in 1836. Ablett and 1859 have* ORESTES AND ELECTRA *as title.*
Sub-title. not in 1836 which has: By Walter Savage Landor, Esq. *1859 has* THE
MADNESS OF ORESTES, THE PRAYER OF ORESTES, PRIESTESS OF APOLLO, THE DEATH
OF ORESTES *as sectional titles.*　　2 Dishonorer] Dishonourer, *1836, Ablett.*　　10 thee
. . . thee] you . . . you *1836.*　　11 thee] you *1836.*　　12, 16 our] *our Ablett.*　　13 thy]
your *1836.*　　14 unsteddy] unsteady *1836, 1846, 1859.*

I knew not I was holding thee .. Avenge him!   20
(*Alone.*) How he sprang from me!

                  .. Sure, he now has reacht
The room before the bath ..

               The bath-door creeks!
.. It hath creakt thus since he .. since thou, O father!
Ever since thou didst loosen its strong valves,
Either with all thy dying weight, or strength
Agonized with her stabs ..

              What plunge was that?
Ah me!

      .. What groans are those?
  Orestes (returning).   They sound through hell
Rejoicing the Eumenides.*

               She slew
Our father; she made thee the scorn of slaves;
Me (son of him who ruled this land and more)   30
She made an outcast . . .

            Would I had been so
For ever! ere such vengeance. . . .
  Electra.   O that Zeus
Had let thy arm fall sooner at thy side
Without those drops! list! they are audible ..
For they are many .. from the sword's point falling,
And down from the mid blade!

            Too rash Orestes!
Couldst thou not then have spared our wretched mother?
  Orestes. The Gods could not.
  Electra.   She was not theirs, Orestes!
  Orestes. And didst not thou . . .
  Electra.   'Twas I, 'twas I, who did it;
Of our unhappiest house the most unhappy!   40

---

* An ancient scholiast has recorded that the name of Eumenides was given to these Goddesses after the expiation of Orestes. But Catullus (called the *learned* by his countrymen) represents Ariadne invoking them by this appellation long before the Trojan war. The verses are the most majestic in the Roman language.

    Eumenides! quarum anguineis [quibus anguino] redimita capillis [capillo]
    Frons expirantes præportat pectoris iras,
    Huc, huc adventate! &c. [L.]

[*See Catullus, lxiv. 193. For the* scholiast *see* Sophocles, *Schol. ad Œdipus Col.* 42.—W.]

   20 thee] you *1836.*   *after* him! *1836 has* (*Orestes rushes out.*).   21 (*Alone.*)] *not in 1836 or Ablett.*   22 creeks] opens *1836, Ablett.* creaks *1846–1859.*   27 *returning*] re-entering *1836,* entering *Ablett.*   32 O] Oh *1836, Ablett.*   40 unhappiest] unhappy *1836.*

THE DEATH OF CLYTEMNESTRA

Under this roof, by every God accurst,
There is no grief, there is no guilt, but mine.
   Orestes. Electra! no!
                'Tis now my time to suffer . .
Mine be, with all its pangs, the righteous deed.   44

   43 time] turn *1836.*

THE MADNESS OF ORESTES

ORESTES AND ELECTRA.

[Printed privately in Ablett's *Literary Hours* 1837 [A]; published in *The Tribute* [T]
and in *Pentalogia* 1837; reprinted 1847, 1859; incorporated in *Pericles and Aspasia*
(2nd *ed.*) 1846, and so reprinted 1876. A portion printed from a MS. in Nicoll and Wise,
Literary Anecdotes [NW]. Text, *Pentalogia* 1837.]

   Orestes. Heavy and murderous dreams, O my Electra,
Have dragged me from myself.
                   Is this Mycenai?
Are we . . . . . . are all who should be . . . . . . in our house?
Living? unhurt? our father here? our mother?
Why that deep gasp? for 'twas not sigh nor groan.
She then . . . . . . 'twas she who fell! when? how? beware!
No, no, speak out at once, that my full heart
May meet it, and may share with thee in all . .
In all . . . but that one thing.
                  It was a dream.
We may share all.
           They live: both live:
                     O say it!   10
   Electra. The Gods have placed them from us, and there rolls
Between us that dark river. . . . .
   Orestes.   Blood! blood! blood!
I see it roll; I see the hand above it,
Imploring; I see *her.*
             Hiss me not back
Ye snake-hair'd maids! I will look on; I will
Hear the words gurgle thro' that cursed stream,
And catch that hand . . that hand . . which slew my father!
It cannot be . . . . how could it slay my father?
Death to the slave who spoke it! . . . . slay my father!

   Title. Orestes Maddened A; Orestes and Electra, Last Scenes. By Walter Savage
Landor, Esq. T.   *Sub-title. om. 1859.*   2 dragged] drag'd A, NW.   3 our]
the T.   6 beware] reply not A, NW.   7 No, no] Yea, yea A, NW.   10 say
it] say that A, say so NW.   19 spoke] said A, NW.

It tost me up to him to earn a smile,   20
And was a smile then such a precious boon,
And royal state and proud affection nothing?
Ay, and thee too, Electra, she once taught
To take the sceptre from him at the door . .
Not the bath-door, not the bath-door, mind that! . .
And place it in the vestibule, against
The spear of Pallas, where it used to stand.
Where is it now? methinks I missed it there.
How we have trembled to be seen to move it!
Both looking up, lest that stern face should frown,   30
Which always gazed on Zeus right opposite.
Oh! could but one tear more fall from my eyes,
It would shake off those horrid visages,
And melt them into air.
                                    I am not your's,
Fell Goddesses! A just and generous Power,
A bright-hair'd God, directed me.
                                    And thus
Abased is he whom such a God inspired!
                              (*After a pause.*)
Into whose kingdom went they? did they go
Together?
        Electra.   Oh! they were not long apart.
        Orestes.   I know why thou art pale; I know whose head   40
Thy flowerlike hands have garlanded; I know
For whom thou hast unbraided all thy love.
He well deserves it . . . . . . he shall have it all.
Glory and love shall crown thee, my brave sister!
        Electra.   I am not she of Sparta. Let me live
(If live I must, Orestes!) not unnamed
Nor named too often. Speak no more of love,
Ill-omen'd and opprobrious in this house . .
A mother should have had, a father had it,
O may a brother let it dwell with him,   50
Unchangeable, unquestioned, solitary,
Strengthened and hallowed in the depths of grief!

Between ll. 20–1 A *inserts one line:*
        Didst thou not tell me, thou who must remember,
23 thee] you T, A, NW.   24 sceptre] scepter A.   *l.* 25 *not in* NW.   26 vestibule]
mispr. veste *1837.*   28 missed it there] saw it not A, NW.   30 stern] grave A.
31 on] at A.   *l. 44 not in* A.   *ll.* 44–68 *not in* T *or* NW.   48 Ill-omen'd] *mispr.*
Ill-open'd *1837.*

THE MADNESS OF ORESTES

Gaze not so angrily . . I dare not see thee,
I dare not look where comfort should be found.
   Orestes. I dare and do behold them all day long,
And, were that face away so like my mother's,
I would advance and question and compell them . .
They hear me, and they know it.
   Electra.   Hear me too,
Ye mighty ones! to me invisible!
And spare him! spare him! for without the Gods   60
He wrought not what he wrought: And are not ye
Partakers of their counsels and their power?
O spare the son of him whom ye and they
Sent against Ilion, to perform your will
And bid the rulers of the earth be just.
   Orestes. And dare they frighten thee too? frighten thee!
And bend thee into prayer?
                   Off, hateful eyes!
Look upon me, not her.
               Ay, thus, 'tis well.
Cheer, cheer thee, my Electra!
                I am strong,
Stronger than ever . . steel, fire, adamant . .   70
But cannot bear thy brow upon my neck,
Cannot bear these wild writhings, these loud sobs,
By all the Gods! I think thou art half-mad . . . . . .
I must away . . . . . . follow me not . . . . . . stand there!

57 compell] compel *1846, 1859.*   62 power] powers A.   *ll.* 66–8 *not in* A.
69 Cheer] Come A. *After* Electra A *and* NW *have:* (*Electra* [*she* NW] *throws herself on*
[*upon* NW] *his neck in great agony.*)   70 steel, fire] fire, steel A, T.   *l.* 70 *not
in* NW.   71 cannot] can not *1847.*   72 Cannot] I cannot A, NW.   Can
not *1847.*   wild] *not in* A *or* NW.

THE PRAYER OF ORESTES

[Published in 1846 when incorporated in second edition of *Pericles and Aspasia*; reprinted as separate piece 1847, and as final part of "Orestes and Electra" in 1859. Text,
1846.]

HERE is the Prayer of Orestes, in his madness, to Apollo; and there
follows, what is not immediately connected with it, the Reply of the
Priestess. [Aspasia to Cleone. *Not in 1847, 1859.*]

Orestes. O king Apollo! god Apollo! god
Powerful to smite and powerful to preserve!
If there is blood upon me, as there seems,

Title. not in 1846; in 1847 as here; as sectional title 1859.

Purify that black stain (thou only canst)
With every rill that bubbles from these caves
Audibly; and come willing to the work.
No; 'tis not they; 'tis blood; 'tis blood again
That bubbles in my ear, that shakes the shades
Of thy dark groves, and lets in hateful gleams,
Bringing me .. what dread sight! what sounds abhorr'd!   10
What screams! They are my mother's: 'tis her eye
That through the snakes of those three furies glares,
And makes them hold their peace that she may speak.
Has thy voice bidden them all forth? There slink
Some that would hide away, but must turn back,
And others like blue lightnings bound along
From rock to rock; and many hiss at me
As they draw nearer. Earth, fire, water, all
Abominate the deed the Gods commanded!
Alas! I came to pray, not to complain;   20
And lo! my speech is impious as my deed!

Priestess of Apollo.

Take refuge here amid our Delphian shades,
    O troubled breast!
Here the most pious of Mycenai's maids
    Shall watch thy rest
And wave the cooling laurel o'er thy brow,
    Nor insect swarm
Shall ever break thy slumbers, nor shalt thou
    Start at the alarm
Of boys infesting (as they do) the street   30
    With mocking songs,
Stopping and importuning all they meet,
    And heaping wrongs
Upon thy diadem'd and sacred head,
    Worse than when base
Œgisthus (shudder not!) his toils outspread
    Around thy race.
Altho' even in this fane the fitful blast
    Thou may'st hear roar,
Thy name among our highest rocks shall last   40
    For evermore.

20 came] come *1847.*   36 Œgisthus] *mispr. in all edd. for* Ægisthus (Αἴγισθος)
Clytemnestra's paramour.   outspread] outspred *1847.*   *Between ll. 41–2 1859*
has: THE DEATH OF ORESTES. *as sectional title.*

THE PRAYER OF ORESTES

Orestes. A calm comes over me: life brings it not
With any of its tides: my end is near.
O Priestess of the purifying God
Receive her!* and when she hath closed mine eyes,
Do thou (weep not, my father's child!) close hers.

* Pointing to his sister. [L.]

[3]

MENELAUS AND HELEN AT TROY

[Published in 1846; reprinted 1847, 1859, 1876.]

HELEN is pursued by MENELAUS up the steps of the palace: an old attendant deprecates
and intercepts his vengeance.

Menelaus. Out of my way! Off! or my sword may smite thee,*
Heedless of venerable age. And thou,
Fugitive! stop. Stand, traitress, on that stair . .
Thou mountest not another, by the Gods!   (*She stops: he seizes her.*)
Now take the death thou meritest, the death
Zeus who presides o'er hospitality,
And every other god whom thou hast left,
And every other who abandons thee
In this accursed city, sends at last.
Turn, vilest of vile slaves! turn, paramour   10
Of what all other women hate, of cowards,
Turn, lest this hand wrench back thy head, and toss
It and its odours to the dust and flames.
Helen. Welcome the death thou promisest! Not fear
But shame, obedience, duty, make me turn.
Menelaus. Duty! false harlot!
Helen.   Name too true! severe
Precursor to the blow that is to fall,
It should alone suffice for killing me.
Menelaus. Ay, weep: be not the only one in Troy
Who wails not on this day . . its last . . the day   20
Thou and thy crimes darken with dead on dead.
Helen. Spare! spare! O let the last that falls be me!
There are but young and old.

* The reader must be reminded that this is no translation from a French tragedy:
such really and truly were the manners of the Greeks in the time of the Trojan war:
they respected age, but disregarded sex. [L. *om. 1847–1876.*]

Introduction Helen ... palace: *om. 1847–1876.*   : an] . An *1847, 1859.*   1 thee*]
thee *without footnote 1847–1859.   Between ll. 4–5 direction* (She ... her.) *om. 1847–1876.*

223

Menelaus.   There are but guilty
Where thou art, and the sword strikes none amiss.
Hearest thou not the creeping blood buzz near
Like flies? or wouldst thou rather hear it hiss
Louder, against the flaming roofs thrown down
Wherewith the streets are pathless? Ay, but vengeance
Springs over all; and Nemesis and Atè
Drove back the flying ashes with both hands.   30
I never saw thee weep till now: and now
There is no pity in thy tears. The tiger
Leaves not her young athirst for the first milk,
As thou didst. Thine could scarce have claspt thy knee
If she had felt thee leave her.
Helen.   O my child!
My only one! Thou livest: 'tis enough:
Hate me, abhor me, curse me . . these are duties . .
Call me but Mother in the shades of death!
She now is twelve years old, when the bud swells
And the first colours of uncertain life   40
Begin to tinge it.
Menelaus (aside). Can she think of home?
Hers once, mine yet, and sweet Hermione's!
Is there one spark that cheer'd my hearth, one left,
For thee, my last of love!
                    Scorn, righteous scorn
Blows it from me . . but thou mayst . . never, never.
Thou shalt not see her even there. The slave
On earth shall scorn thee, and the damn'd below.
Helen. Delay not either fate. If death is mercy,
Send me among the captives; so that Zeus
May see his offspring led in chains away,   50
And thy hard brother, pointing with his sword
At the last wretch that crouches on the shore,
Cry, "She alone shall never sail for Greece!"
Menelaus. Hast thou more words?
                    Her voice is musical
As the young maids who sing to Artemis:
How glossy is that yellow braid my grasp
Seiz'd and let loose! Ah! can then years have past
Since . . but the children of the Gods, like them,
Suffer not age.

30 Drove] Drive *MS. emendation.*   56 yellow] auburn *MS. emendation.*   57 then]
? mispr. for ten.   58 Since . . but] Since but *mispr. 1847–1876.*

Helen! speak honestly,

And thus escape my vengeance . . was it force   60
That bore thee off?
    Helen.   It was some evil God.
    Menelaus. Helping that hated man?
    Helen.   How justly hated!
    Menelaus. By thee too?
    Helen.   Hath he not made *thee* unhappy?
O do not strike.
    Menelaus.   Wretch!
    Helen.   Strike, but do not speak.
    Menelaus. Lest thou remember me against thy will.
    Helen. Lest I look up and see you wroth and sad,
Against my will; O! how against my will
They know above, they who perhaps can pity.
    Menelaus. They shall not save thee.
    Helen.   Then indeed they pity.
    Menelaus. Prepare for death.
    Helen.   Not from that hand: 'twould pain
    you.   70
    Menelaus. Touch not my hand. Easily dost thou drop it!
    Helen. Easy are all things, do but thou command.
    Menelaus. Look up then.
    Helen.   To the hardest proof of all
I am now bidden: bid me not look up.
    Menelaus. She looks as when I led her on behind
The torch and fife, and when the blush o'erspread
Her girlish face at tripping in the myrtle
On the first step before the wreathed gate.
Approach me. Fall not on thy knees.
    Helen.   The hand
That is to slay me, best may slay me thus.   80
I dare no longer see the light of heaven,
Nor thine . . alas! the light of heaven to me.
    Menelaus. Follow me.
                 She holds out both arms . . and now
Drops them again . . She comes . . Why stoppest thou?
    Helen. O Meneläus! could thy heart know mine,
As once it did . . for then did they converse,
Generous the one, the other not unworthy . .
Thou wouldst find sorrow deeper even than guilt.
    Menelaus. And must I lead her by the hand again?

76 o'erspread] o'ersprad 1847, 1859.

Nought shall persuade me. Never. She draws back . .   90
The true alone and loving sob like her . .
Come, Helen!   [*He takes her hand.*
   Helen.   Oh! let never Greek see this!
Hide me from Argos, from Amyclai hide me,
Hide me from all.
   Menelaus.   Thy anguish is too strong
For me to strive with.
   Helen.   Leave it all to me.
   Menelaus. Peace! peace! The wind, I hope, is fair for Sparta.

[4]

DEDICATION OF AN ANCIENT IDYL

TO ROSE.

EUROPA CARRIED OFF.

[Published in *Dry Sticks*, 1858; not reprinted.]

FRIEND of my age! to thee belong
The plaintive and the playful song,
And every charm unites in thee
Of wisdom, wit, and modesty;
Taught hast thou been from early youth
To tread the unswerving path of truth,
And guided to trip lightly o'er
The amaranth fields of ancient lore,
Turn thou not hastily aside
From her who stems the Asian tide,   10
For shores henceforth to bear her name . .
Thine, thine shall be a better fame;
Lands yet more distant shall it reach
Than yonder Hellespontic beach,
Or where the bravest blood now flows
Before perfidious Delhi, Rose!
From boyhood have I loved old times
And loitered under warmer climes.
I never dream such dreams as there . .
Voices how sweet, and forms how fair!   20
The Nymphs and Graces there I find,
The Muses too, and thee behind,
All chiding thee, all asking why
Thou whom they cherish art so shy;

Sub-title. Rose]. Mrs. afterwards Lady Graves Sawle. [W.]

226

DEDICATION OF AN ANCIENT IDYL

They will not listen when I say,
Thou hast some dearer ones than they.
"Ungrateful!" cry they, "can it be?
We have no dearer one than she."

THE ANCIENT IDYL

EUROPA AND HER MOTHER.

[Published in 1858; reprinted 1859, 1876.]

Mother. Daughter! why roamest thou again so late
Along the damp and solitary shore?
Europa. I know not. I am tired of distaf, woof,
Everything.
Mother.   Yet thou culledst flowers all morn,
And idledst in the woods, mocking shrill birds,
Or clapping hands at limping hares, who stampt
Angrily, and scour'd off.
Europa.   I am grown tired
Of hares and birds. O mother! had you seen
That lovely creature! It was not a cow,
And, if it was an ox,* it was unlike   10
My father's oxen with the hair rubb'd off
Their necks.
Mother.   A cow it was.
Europa.   Cow it might be . .
And yet . . and yet . . I saw no calf, no font
Of milk: I wish I had; how pleasant 'twere
To draw it and to drink!
Mother.   Europa! child!
Have we no maiden for such offices?
No whistling boy? Kings' daughters may cull flowers,
To place them on the altar of the Gods
And wear them at their festivals. Who knows
But some one of these very Gods may deign   20
To wooe thee? maidens they have wooed less fair.
Europa. The Gods are very gracious: some of them
Not very constant.
Mother.   Hush!
Europa.   Nay, Zeus himself
Hath wandered, and deluded more than one.

* Bulls are never at large in those countries; Europa could not have seen one. [L.]

Title. THE . . . IDYL *om. 1859–1876 which have* EUROPA AND HER MOTHER *as title.*
20 one] *wrongly om. 1876.*

Mother. Fables! profanest fables!

Europa.   Let us hope so.
But I should be afraid of him, and run
As lapwings do when we approach the nest.

Mother. None can escape the Gods when they pursue.

Europa. They know my mind, and will not follow me.

Mother. Consider: some are stars whom they have loved,   30
Others, the very least of them, are flowers.

Europa. I would not be a star in winter nights,
In summer days I would not be a flower;
Flowers seldom live thro' half their time, torn off,
Twirl'd round, and indolently cast aside.
Now, mother, can you tell me what became
Of those who were no flowers, but bent their heads
As pliantly as flowers do?

Mother.   They are gone
To Hades.

Europa. And left there by Gods they loved
And were beloved by! Be not such my doom!   40
Cruel are men, but crueler are Gods.

Mother. Peace! peace! Some royal, some heroic, youth
May ask thy father for thy dower and thee.

Europa. I know not any such, if such there live;
Royal there may be, but heroic . . where?
O mother! look! look! look!

Mother.   Thou turnest pale;
What ails thee?

Europa.   Who in all the house hath dared
To winde those garlands round that grand white brow?
So mild, so loving! Mother! let me run
And tear them off him: let me gather more   50
And sweeter.

Mother.   Truly 'tis a noble beast.
See! he comes forward! see, he rips them off,
Himself!

Europa. He should not wear them if he would.
Stay there, thou noble creature! Woe is me!
There are but sandrose, tyme, and snapdragon
Along the shore as far as I can see.
O mother! help me on his back; he licks
My foot. Ah! what sweet breath! Now on his side
He lies on purpose for it. Help me up.

Mother. Well, child! Indeed he is gentle. Gods above!   60

EUROPA AND HER MOTHER

He takes the water! Hold him tight, Europa!
'Tis well that thou canst swim.
                                      Leap off, mad girl!
She laughs! He lows so loud she hears not me . .
But she looks sadder, or my sight is dim . .
Against his nostril fondly hangs her hand
While his eye glistens over it, fondly too.
It will be night, dark night, ere she returns.
And that new scarf! the spray will ruin it.

[5]
ACHILLES AND HELENA ON IDA

[Published in 1858. Not reprinted in this form. For a longer version, published in 1859, reprinted 1876, see notes at end of the volume.]

Helena. Stranger! who art thou? why approachest thou
To break my sacred slumber? such it was,
For she who brought me all my joy and grief
Hath brought me hither.
                                      Thou appallest me,
For thou art stern and godlike; and no crook
Nor needful staff of upland wayfarer
Is that thou bearest. O that cruel spear!
Comest thou . . yes, thou comest . . speak . . to slay me?
    Achilles. Helena! fear me not . . I am the son
Of Peleus.
    Helena.   Fear thee not! O hide awhile   10
The glittering point before it strike me dead.
    Achilles. Behold it fixt into the glebe.
    Helena.   It casts
A slitting shadow half across the down.
    Achilles. Now seat thee (but why risen?) as before.
    Helena. Be thou too seated: first look round about;
For there are lions on these lonely hills,
Beside the tamer which are yoked before
The Mother of the Gods, upon whose head
Are towers and cities in one awful crown.
And thou hast come alone.
    Achilles.   Alcides slew   20
His lion, and Alcides was alone.
    Helena. O son of Peleus! didst thou ever see
My two brave brothers?

13 slitting] ? *mispr. for* flitting. *cf.* Pope, *Odyssey*, x 587, "a flitting shade."—[W.]

229

Achilles. In my father's house
I saw them once.
    Helena. And were they not like thee?
Dear Kastor! Polydeukes dearer stil!
Kastor would lift me on his fiercest horse
And laugh at me: but Polydeukes placed
One kindly hand beneath my sinking chin
Upon the swift Eurotas, with the other
Buoying my feet, for I was then a child.
    But tell me, who conducted thee away
From those beleaguered walls into this wild?
    Achilles. Thetis, my mother: she around me threw
A cloud, not dark within, but dark without,
As clouds may be wherein the Gods rejoice.
But what, more wonderful, impel'd thy feet
Hither? so delicate, so like to hers
Who bore me, which are radiant thro' the depth
Of dimmest ocean.
    Helena. All I know is this,
A voice, and it was Aphrodite's voice,
Call'd me: I would have risen at the call,
But wings were over me and underneath,
And, until thou appearedst, left me not;
Nor did sleep leave me.
             O how fresh the flowers
Are breathing round us in this tepid air!
I do love flowers; they look into my eyes
And seem to say fond things to me, in breath
Sweeter than infants.
        O Hermione!
Sweet even as thine. Where art thou, lovely babe?
Who tends thee? who caresses thee? all must;
All but one wretch who left thee in thy sleep.
    Achilles. Sorrow is not unseemly in the breast
Of women: men too (shame on them) have grieved,
Have wept, and not the tears of rage alone.
    Helena. Blame not my weakness then: no rage is mine,
I never felt it. Flowers are comforters
At dawn and sunset on the terraced roof:
Few are they; but the dearest are the few.
    Achilles. Flowers! Inconsiderate! Thinkest thou of flowers
While nations shed their blood, their lives, for thee?
    Helena. They are so fragrant and so beautiful!

30

40

50

60

And what profusion! what variety!
In my own country I have known by name
More than my fingers of both hands could count
Twice over: there was mint and drosera
And serpolet, just as you see are here:
How can I then but love to talk of them?
   Achilles. O Helena! let children love to talk
Thus idly.
   Helena. Ah! that I were yet a child!
But how wilt thou return before the walls?   70
   Achilles. The Gods will care for that: they too who brought
Thee hither will provide for thy return.
   Helena. Couldst not thou?
   Achilles.   Helena! I come to warn thee
Against the rancour of a man incenst:
I hate him; I shall hate him worse if wrath
Urge him to vengeance on thee; for the twins
(Then boys) thy brothers were my father's guests,
And much I loved to hear of them, and hoped
One day to share their glory, sung on earth
For me; for them along the placid waves   80
There where my mother oft repeats the song.
   Helena. I loved songs too.
   Achilles.   Sweetest are those to me
Which Keiron taught me; songs which bring again
To life, and fresher life, the brave of old.
Zeus! grant me but few years, grant only one,
And he who wrongs me, he when such men sing,
The king of Argos shall stand far behind.
   Helena. Ah! thou art strong and irresistable.
But spare . .
   Achilles.   Spare whom?
   Helena.   Alas! I dare not name him.
No fault was his; no fault was mine: the Gods   90
Decreed it. She to whom he gave her prize
Perform'd a promise . . how imperfectly!
And gave him . . O pernicious gift, me! me!
Pity thou him whom even my brothers might
Have pardon'd; him as beautious as themselves
Or thee, almost.
   Achilles.   In this arm lies my beauty,
Smiter in vengeance of the guilty head.
   Helena. Why springest thou upon thy feet, alert

As grasshopper, without a hand to rest
Upon the turf beneath?
    Achilles.   I must be gone.   100
    Helena. And without me?
    Achilles.   It hath not been forbidden,
No; nor commanded.
                  If the Gods so will
Come thou with me.
    Helena.   I dare not. They who led
My way to Ida will direct me hence.
And yet I tremble.
    Achilles.   Take thou heart.
    Helena.   It fails.
For there are other Deities who hate
Me and my guilt. The Mother of the Gods
Inhabits here, and here her temple stands;
Here sound the tymbrels and the cymbals struck
By priests infuriate.
    Achilles.   Fear them not: thy sire   110
Zeus and his daughter will watch over thee.
    Helena. Farewell, O son of Peleus! born to rule
O'er happier realms.
    Achilles.   O Helena! 'tis here,
Far from my birthplace, from my father's tomb,
I die.
        So sang the three who sing but truth.
    Helena. Wretched, thrice wretched me! in this alone
Are we alike. Thou art less stern, more calm,
In speaking of that last sad hour.
                   No word
Of comfort hast thou for me?
    Achilles.   I shall bring
Comfort to those who bore thee truer love   120
Than thou hast borne to others.
    Helena.   Spare me! spare me!
To whom that comfort?
    Achilles.   To thy brethren: they
Have heard my name among the Blest above,
Or they shall hear it.
            I will tell them age
And royalty have loved and pitied thee,
That Priam held thee dearer to his heart
Than his own daughters, that thy tears have washt

Thy stains away; then, that Achilles turn'd
His face aside ashamed of grief for thee.
  Helena. Stay, stay one instant.   130
                  Is this too a dream?
Who lifts my feet from earth and whirls me round?
Children! O fan me with your wings again;
I sink; I fall! help! Aphrodite! help!

[6]

HERCULES, PLUTO, ALCESTIS, ADMETOS

[Published in 1859; reprinted 1876.]

  Hercules. Weepest thou? Weep thou mayst; but not for long.
  Alcestis. Certainly not for long, O Heracles!
So let me weep: this day, if not this night,
Will join me to Admetos.
  Hercules.   Say, what voice
Hath told thee so?
  Alcestis.   The voice within my breast.
  Hercules. It shall be true as was thy heart to him . .
  Alcestis. Who now lies without hope for one hour more
Upon this earth.
  Hercules.   No power have I o'er fate.
  Alcestis. Thou canst not, I can, save him.
  Hercules.   Tell me how.
  Alcestis. I dare not utter my design to thee,   10
For vows are sacred, so conditions are,
And both are, or will soon be, ratified.
The God who rules below will cast him down
Before my steps can reach those horrid realms,
If those are horrid where the faithful meet
To love eternally.
  Hercules.   But wouldst thou not
Rather return with him to the early scenes
Of your betrothal, of your happier hours?
  Alcestis. Alas! alas! not Hades, not Elysion,
Not heaven itself, could ever soothe my soul   20
As those have done . . but when he goes I go . .
O could it but be first!
  Hercules.   The Gods may grant
This wish at thy entreaty.

Alcestis.   They have heard
Already every prayer my heart could frame.
  Hercules. On me they have bestow'd some power to calm
Thy breast, Alcestis!
  Alcestis.   Save with his, mine never.
  Hercules. Be calmer, cheer thee. Every God above
Hath been propitious to me; he below
Shall hear me: not another day shall see
Such faithful hearts apart.
  Alcestis.   No word of thine   30
Was ever false, but how can this be true?
  Hercules. Question me not.
                    I have been told ere now
That heavy grief brings also heavy sleep,
Lighter be thine! but confidently close
Those eyes half-closed already by the weight
That overhangs them.
  Alcestis.   Can I? Do I dream?
  Hercules. No, but thou shalt when Love hath had his way.
  Pluto. Who comes among the Shades and is no Shade?
  Hercules. Thy elder brother's offspring, Heracles.
  Pluto. And sent thee hither he?
  Hercules.   His will it was.   40
  Pluto. And what thy errand?
  Hercules.   Rescue.
  Pluto.   Rescue hence?
There never was, nor shall be.
  Hercules.   Say not so,
Brother of him the mighty and the just.
  Pluto. Just callest thou the brother who usurpt
His father's throne, and thrust these realms on me?
Peopled are mine, 'tis true, far more than his
Or than Poseidon's, with his singing Nymphs
And blowing Tritons in loud choruses
On conchs, and songless speechless multitudes;
Callest thou him the just? mighty he may be   50
On earth, or over earth, but never here.
And thou, who art but mortal, darest come
Invader, to my very throne!
  Hercules.   I came
Speedily as I could, but was outrun
By one who hurried to recall from hence
Him whom ere this she haply hath embraced,

234

Admetos; her own life she gives for his;
And this condition every God approves.
    Pluto. Every? and am not I one? My consent
Neither those gods nor thou shall gain. Return . .   60
For what is she to thee, audacious man?
    Hercules. Alcestis is the daughter of my friend.
    Pluto. If truth has reacht me here (and oftener truth
Is found below than among those on earth)
Many have been the daughters thou hast there
Rescued from spousal and parental bonds.
    Hercules. I bear no shaft of wit so keen as thine,
Nor would confront thee: only give me up
The virtuous bride, then will I reäscend.
    Pluto. What if thy calculation be amiss.   70
The bride I give not up: thou mayest go,
With my goodwill, but must leave her behind.
    Hercules. I would not wrestle with thee.
    Pluto.   Art thou mad?
Wrestle with an Immortal!
    Hercules.   If compell'd,
And grow myself Immortal by that strife.
    Pluto. Cerberos! seize him.
    Hercules.   'Twas not long ago
He lickt the instep of Eurydice
And only growl'd at her deliverer.
Brave dogs are fellow-creatures of brave men,
Not one of his three heads would bark at me.   80
    Pluto. (*Alcestis rushing forward.*) Woman! whence comest? whither
    rushest thou?
    Alcestis. (*Not minding him.*) O Heracles! and art thou also doom'd
To bless earth never more?
    Hercules.   To bless once more
Earth with thy presence come I, nor will go
Until I lead thee back.
    Pluto.   Styx! Phlegethon!
Surround him.
    Hercules.   I will cast thee into them,
God as thou art, if any hurt befalls
Alcestis.
    Alcestis. Leave me, leave me, Heracles!
Never from my Admetos will I part.
    Persephone (*entering*). Nor shalt thou.

             60 shall] shalt *1876.*

Pluto. And thou, too, refractory? 90
Even thou, Persephone!
  Persephone. Thou once didst love me,
O Pluto! love me now; remit, remit
Thy rigid laws . . give me these two. Advance,
Admetos! (*whispers*)
  He may change his mind . . go, go.
  Admetos (*ascending*). I feel afresh the air of heaven; thy kiss
Breath'd it, and do my steps touch earth again?
  Hercules. Yea, firm as mine do.
  But thou stil art faint,
Alcestis! If my shoulder is too high
For thee to lean on, let this arm help his.
  I had no time or thought to look beyond, 100
And I saw nothing of Elysian fields;
If there be any thou shalt find them all
Among those pastures where Apollo fed
Thy herds, Admetos! where another God
(Thou knowest who) Alcestis! drew thee forth
And placed thee on that fond and faithful breast
Whereon thou, undivided, shalt repose.
  Alcestis. Shall we be never, never, parted more?
  Admetos. Let us, my own Alcestis, leave behind
(Since one day both must die) a proof that love 110
May be as happy, if as true, as thine.
Age is before us, be it long before,
And Death not wait for either!
  Hercules. Haste ye home,
And there hold fitter than such grave discourse.
Remember, Hymen is come back again
And follows close, for Hymen hates delay.
Admetos! I was fancying that thy brood
Of gallant coursers, boast of Thessaly,
Will not awaken you tomorrow-morn,
With all their neighings at the palace-gate, 120
To greet ye coming safe and sound again.
Let me forbid the maidens to entwine,
Whatever they may gather in the dew,
Flowers till past noontide: they are ever apt
To speed on such occasions, and to break
The spell descending from the silent moon,
A spell which binds together strong and weak.
They shall sing merrily for honied cates,

236

HERCULES, PLUTO, ALCESTIS, ADMETOS

A guerdon and a symbol not unmeet:
I too would sing among them, but no song   130
Could Orpheus teach me, nor would let me touch
His harp; my fingers, said he, were unfit;
Nor was my voice melodious, tho less harsh
Than when ye heard it in yon place below.

CHORUS OF MATRONS AT MORNING.
Come, little girls who catch the laughter
   And know not what the laughter means,
But who shall know it well hereafter
   Amid less grand and gaudy scenes.
Come, maidens, ye almost as young,
   Ye too whose cheeks are full in bloom,   140
Lay by your wreathes, and sing a song
   To her whose love hath burst the tomb.
Then to the praises of the bold,
   Then of the tender and the true,
A pair whom Hades could not hold . .
   And may such heroes wed with you!

GIRLS' REPLY.
We are too young to think of men,
   Few of us yet are seventeen;
Better to trim the wreathe, and then
   To look and see how looks the queen.   150

[7]
PELEUS AND THETIS

[Published in 1859; reprinted 1876. A prose version, printed as a separate piece in
Imaginary Conversations 1829, was incorporated in the *Conversation* "Epicurus,
Leontion, Ternissa" published 1846, reprinted 1853, 1876.]

Thetis. O Peleus! whom the Gods have given me
For all my happiness on earth, a bliss
I thought too great. . .
   Peleus.   Why sighest thou? why shed
Those tears? why sudden silence? our last tears
Should then have fallen when the Fates divided us,
Saying, earth is not thine; that he who rules
The waters call'd thee. Bitter those that flow
Between the loved and loving when they part,
And ought to be; woe to the inhuman wretch
Who wishes they were not: but such as fall   10
At the returning light of blessed feet
Should be refreshing and divine as morn.

237

Thetis. Support me, O support me in thy arms
Once more, once only. Lower not thy cheek
In sadness; let me look into thine eyes;
Tho the heavens frown on us, they, now serene,
Threaten us no fresh sorrow . . *us?* ah me!
The word of Zeus is spoken: our Achilles
Discovered, borne away in the Argive ships
To Aulis, froward youth! his fearless heart   20
Had bounded faster than those ships to Troy.
Ah! surely there are some among the Gods
Or Goddesses who might have, knowing all,
Forewarn'd thee.
          Were there neither auguries
Nor dreams to shake off thy security,
No priest to prophecy, no soothsayer?
And yet what pastures are more plentiful
Than round Larissa? victimes where more stately?
Come, touch the altar with me.
              Pious man,
Doth not thy finger even now impress   30
The embers of an incense often burnt
For him, for thee?
          The lowing of the herds
Are audible, whose leaders lead them forth
For sacrifice from where Apidanos
Rises, to where Enipeus widens, lost
In the sea-beach: and these may yet avail.
    Peleus. Alas! alas! priests may foretell calamity
But not avert it: all that they can give
Are threats and promises and hopes and fears.
Despond not, long-lost Thetis! hath no God   40
Now sent thee back to me? why not believe
He will preserve our son? which of them all
Hath he offended?
    Thetis.   Yet uncertainties,
Worse than uncertainties, oppress my heart,
And overwhelm me.
    Peleus.   Thetis! in the midst
Of all uncertainties some comfort lies,
Save those which even perplex the Gods on high
And which confound men the most godlike . . love,
Despond not so. Long may Achilles live

28 victimes] victims *1876.*   32 lowing] *rectius* lowings *prose version.*

PELEUS AND THETIS

Past our old-age . . *ours?* had I then forgot,   50
Dazed by thy beauty, thy divinity?
   Thetis. Immortal is thy love, immutable.
   Peleus. Time without grief might not have greatly changed me.
   Thetis. There is a loveliness which wants not youth,
And which the Gods may want, and sometimes do.
The soft voice of compassion is unheard
Above; no shell of ocean is attuned
To that voice there; no tear hath ever dropt
Upon Olympos.
                Fondly now as ever
Thou lookest, but more pensively; hath grief   60
Done this, and grief alone? tell me at once,
Say have no freshly fond anxieties . . .
   Peleus. Smile thus, smile thus anew. Ages shall fly
Over my tomb while thou art flourishing
In youth eternal, the desire of Gods,
The light of Ocean to its lowest deep,
The inspirer and sustainer here on earth
Of ever-flowing song.
   Thetis.   I bless thy words
And in my heart will hold them; Gods who see
Within it may desire me, but they know   70
I have loved Peleus. When we were so happy
They parted us, and, more unmerciful,
Again unite us in eternal woe.
   Peleus. Powerfuller than the elements their will,
And swifter than the light, they may relent,
For they are mutable, and thou mayst see
Achilles every day and every hour.
   Thetis. Alas! how few! . . I see him in the dust,
In agony, in death, I see his blood
Along the flints, his yellow hair I see   80
Darken'd, and flapping a red stream, his hand
Unable to remove it from the eyes.
I hear his voice . . his voice that calls on *me.*
I could not save him; and he would have left
The grots of Nereus, would have left the groves
And meadows of Elysium, bent on war.
   Peleus. Yet Mars may spare him. Troy hath once been won.
   Thetis. Perish he must, perish at Troy, and now.
   Peleus. The *now* of Gods is more than life's duration;
       85 grots of Nereus] caverns of Ocean *prose version.*

Other Gods, other worlds, are form'd within it.   90
If he indeed must perish, and at Troy,
His ashes will lie softly upon hers,
Thus fall our beauteous boy, thus fall Achilles.
Songs such as Keiron's harp could never reach
Shall sound his praises, and his spear shall shine
Over far lands, when even our Gods are mute.
   Thetis. Over his head nine years had not yet past
When in the halls of Tethys these were words
Reiterated oftenest . . *O thou brave*
Golden-hair'd son of Peleus! What a heap   100
Of shells were broken by impatient Nymphs
Because of hoarseness rendering them unfit
For their high symphonies! and what reproofs
Against some Tritons from their brotherhood
For breaking by too loud a blast the slumber
Of those who, thinking of him, never slept.
To me appeard the first light of his eyes,
The dayspring of the world; such eyes were thine
At our first meeting on the warm sea-shore.
   Why should youth linger with me? why not come   110
Age, and then death? The beast of Kalydon
Made his impetuous rush against this arm
No longer fit for war nor for defence
Of thy own people; is the day come too
When it no longer can sustain thy Thetis?
Protend it not toward the skies, invoke not,
Name not, a Deity; I dread them all.
No; lift me not above thy head, in vain
Reproving them with such an awful look,
A look of beauty which they will not pity,   120
And of reproaches which they may not brook.
   Peleus. Doth not my hand now, Thetis, clasp that foot
Which seen the Powers of ocean cease to rage,
Indignant when the brood of Æolus
Disturbs their rest? If that refreshing breath
Which now comes over my unquiet head
Be not the breath of immortality,
If Zeus hath any thunderbolt for it,
Let this, beloved Thetis, be the hour!

ll. 110–115 *spoken by Peleus in prose version.*   115 thy] my *prose version.*
124 Æolus] *so in errata 1859;* Œolus *text 1859.*

8

PENELOPE AND PHEIDO

[Published in 1859; reprinted 1876.]

Pheido. Ha! what strange stories these old people tell!
Will you believe me, gracious lady queen?
Yesterday-eve behind this figtree sate
Melantheus and that idler Iros, he
Who breaks more bread than the best workman earns,
And seem'd contending which should lie the most.
 Penelope. What did they talk about?
 Pheido.   Why, they discourst
About our lord, be sure, as all men do.
Iros, who scratcht his shoulder, said he tried
To shirk the ships that were afloat for Troy.   10
I could well-nigh have smitten him, but thought
So wise a man, with such a queen for wife,
So beautiful, so provident of corn
And oil and wine, must suddenly have lost
His wits, by sun-stroke, or magician's wand
Or witches charm, to leave her willingly.
 Penelope. Willingly not, but duteously; the Gods
Urged him, and he obey'd: the chiefs of Greece
Knew that they wanted much his prudent mind,
Kings tho they were, to counsel them aright.   20
There was no folly in their thinking so.
Brave as he was, he would have staid at home,
But Hellas rose in arms to punish fraud
And rapine. When he left me, tears he shed,
Which he had never done but on that day
When on his mother's breast he cried for milk
And milk was there no longer. He was born
For glory.
 Pheido. O sweet mistress! what is that?
 Penelope. To carry arms, and quell thereby the proud.
 Pheido. Here are no robbers in these blessed realms,   30
Here in our Ithaca no boars, no wolves
No dragons: glory then is gone abroad,
Unless it may be found in cestuses.
 Penelope. But there are monarks, far across the sea,
Proud monarks, and they boast of sons as proud,
Who steal the wives of those who trusted them,
And purple robes therewith and treasured gold
And silver.

4 Melantheus . . . Iros] cf. Ovid, *Heroid.* i. 95. Irus . . . Melanthius. [W.]

Pheido.   May the Gods guide safely home
Our master! Will he bring back purple robes,
Silver, and gold? he should have more than half.   40
But O those purple robes! how they will suit
The lovely shoulders of our gracious queen.
Do thou, Poseidon, let them come unhurt
Upon our shores; for thy salt waves might wash
The colour out; chide them, forbid them thou!
Pray to him, O sweet lady! for your prayers
Will reach him sooner than your handmaid's could;
Beside, the wealthy always can prevail
With gifts; and upon Neritos are kids
And goats in plenty, easy to be caught   50
If they know Gods are waiting.
    Penelope.   We will think
About this matter; but Laertes first
Must be consulted: he knows every kid
And goat upon the rocks there.
                        Now lay by
The yarn, and leave this figtree for yon vines,
Where I can trust thee better than the rest
Of all my maidens; for thy truthful tongue
Never laid blame upon the wasp when gaps
I found among the bunches; go, and cull
The ripest; thou shalt have two figs for each.   60
    Pheido. All the blue figs lie slit upon the wall
For winter use, and little lizards keep,
With never-closing eye and panting heart,
Watch and ward over them against the flies
And ants, and hold those fast with viscous tongue,
Sharp-pointed, swiftly out and swiftly in.
The green and yellow are ungathered yet
Mostly. Telemakos is tall enough
To help me up with hand below my heel,
And shoulder close against the trunk applied.   70
    Penelope. Telemakos plies other work; he mends
The nets to catch those busy birds that hang
Tail downward and inflict sad wounds on fig.
    Away! but come back soon, and then for woof.
Idleness ill befits a royal house:
The husbandman, who labors hard may rest
In the midday, and thereby shorten night.

9

PINDAR AND HIERO

[Published in 1859; reprinted 1876.]

Hiero. Pindar! no few are there among my guests
Who lift up eyebrows archt and rounded eyes
To hear thee talk as they do. Poets grin
And whisper,
        He is one of us, not more,
Tho' higher in . . I think they also add
Our foolish king's esteem.
    Pindar.   In verse I sing
Not always dithyrambics. I may lift
A mortal over an admiring crowd,
And I may hear and heed not their applause,
A part whereof is given to him who fed   10
The steeds, a part to him who drove, a part
At last to me.
    Hiero.   My friend! the steeds are gone,
The charrioteers will follow: Death pursues
And overtakes the fleetest of them all:
He may pant on until his ribs are crackt,
He never shall reach thee. Believe one word
A king hath spoken . . Ages shall sweep off
All lighter things, but leave thy name behind.
    Pindar. I was amused at hearing the discourse
Of our wise judges, when their maws were fill'd,   20
About some poets of the present day.
    Hiero. I did not hear it. I would not surcharge
Thy memory, 'twere unfriendly; but perchance
A tittle of the tattle may adhere
Stil to thy memory, as on amber hairs
That some loose wench hath combed into the street:
If so, pray let me have it.
    Pindar.   An old friend
Of mine had represented the grave sire

Title [Pindar visited Hiero I, Tyrant of Syracuse, *c.* 470 B.C.—W.]   6 *before* verse
text 1859, 1876 has:
                              We do not feed
    On race-horse flesh, nor drive the charriot [chariot *1876*] -wheels
    Upon the table. Even in
We . . . Even *deleted in corrigenda 1859 but retained 1876.*   8 A] *so in corrigenda*
1859. Weak *text 1859, 1876.*

Of poets, in the ile of Ithaca,
Conversing with Laertes.

Hiero.　　　　　　　He was wrong.   30
Homer lived some time after him.

Pindar.　　　　　　　Who knows?
Howbeit, the worst complaint was that a king
Spoke of stale bread, and offered it his guest.

Hiero. Ithaca is not Sicily: the rocks
Of that poor iland bear no crops of wheat;
Laertes might not every day have spared
The scanty brushwood for the oaten cake.
Wine, I will wager, your old friend hath jogg'd
The generous host to lay upon the board.

Pindar. And both converst as other men converse.   40
The poet is no poet at all hours,
The hero is no hero with a friend.

Hiero. The virtuous, the valiant, and the wise,
Have ever been thy friends, and they alone.

Pindar. Few have I found, and fewer have I sought.
Apart I chose to stand. The purest air
Breathes o'er high downs on solitary men.
Thou smilest, O king Hiero, at my words,
Who seest me in thy court.

Hiero.　　　　　　　No, no, my friend!

Pindar. We must not penetrate the smile of kings,   50
There may be secrets in it.

Hiero.　　　　　　　Open mine;
There is but one for thee; and it is this;
'Tis written on no scroll, but on my heart;
Command I dare not call it, though I would . .
Pindar is Pindar, Hiero is but king.

Pindar. Embolden'd when I ought to be abasht,
I venture now to question thee.

Hiero.　　　　　　　Obey.
Sprinkle a drop of Lethe on the fount
Of sparkling Dirce, nor remember Thebes,
Or him alone remember, him whose harp   60
Rais'd up her walls, which harp thou strikest now
With hand more potent than Amphion's was.
Here shalt thou dwell in honor, long thy due,
And sing to us thy even-song of life.

10

PTOLEMY AND THEOCRITOS

[Published in 1859; reprinted 1876.]

Ptolemy. Pleasant art thou, Theocritos! The pair
Thou broughtest forward to our festival
Of yesterday, Praxinoe and Gorgo,
Are worthy pair for Aristophanes,
Had he been living, to have brought on stage:
Even grave Menander, wittiest of the wise,
Had smiled and caught thee by the hand for this.
   Theocritos. Ah! to be witty is hard work sometimes.
'Tis easier to lie down along the grass,
Where there is any, grass there none is here.   10
   Ptolemy. But here are couches where we may repose
And dream as easily. Thy dreams were all
For Sicily, about the Nymphs and swains.
   Theocritos. It seems an easier matter to compose
Idyls of shepherds and of little Gods
Than great heroic men.
   Ptolemy.   Thou hast done both.
   Theocritos. Neither is easy. Grass in Sicily
Is slippery, scant the turf and hard to tread.
The sheep oft wonder, and crowd close, at sight
Of venturous shepherd, putting pipe to lip   20
And, ere he blow it, sprawling heels in air.
I have sung hymns; but hymns with fuller breath
Are chaunted by my friend Kallimakos.
   Ptolemy. *Friend!* O strange man! poet call poet *friend!*
If my good genius brought thee hither, thanks
We both may pay him.
   Theocritos.   Well indeed may I.
   Ptolemy. What! for disturbing dreams of Nymphs and swains,
And whispering leaves of platan and of pine?
Sweet whispers! but with sweeter underneath.
   Theocritos. No; but for banishing far different ones,   30
Such as were facts in our fair Sicily.
Had kings like Ptolemy been living then,
However far removed this empire lies,

3 Praxinoe . . . Gorgo] [*see* Theocritus, Idyl. xv, written between 277 B.C., when
Ptolemy Philadelphus is said to have married Arsinoë, and 270 B.C. when she died.—W.]
23 Kallimakos] [Poet, grammarian, and librarian at Alexandria.—W.]

Phalaris never had shut up within
His brazen bull the bravest and the best.
   Ptolemy. Kings have their duties: it concerns them all
To take good heed that none betray their trust,
Lest odious be the name, and they themselves
Fall thro the crime of one: the crowns they wear
Make some hot-headed, nearly all weak-eyed.   40
   'Tis written how this bull went close behind,
Bellowing his thunders, belching smoke and flame,
Wherever that king went.
   Theocritos.   No fiction, sire,
Of poets, or historians, who feign more.
   Ptolemy. Pleasanter in our Ægypt be thy dreams!
Come, let me hear the latest; speak it out.
   Theocritos. Last night, beneath the shadow of a sphinx
I fancied I was lying, and I dream'd
Only of placid Gods and generous kings.
   Ptolemy. Knave! knave! on neither shall thy dream be vain.   50

[11]

ÆSCHYLOS AND SOPHOCLES

[Published in 1859; reprinted 1876.]

   Sophocles. Thou goest then, and leavest none behind
Worthy to rival thee!
   Æschylos.   Nay, say not so.
Whose is the hand that now is pressing mine?
A hand I may not ever press again!
What glorious forms hath it brought boldly forth
From Pluto's realm! The blind old Œdipos
Was led on one side by Antigone,
Sophocles propt the other.
   Sophocles.   Sophocles
Sooth'd not Prometheus chaind upon his rock,
Keeping the vultures and the Gods away;   10
Sophocles is not greater than the chief
Who conquered Ilion, nor could he revenge
His murder, or stamp everlasting brand
Upon the brow of that adulterous wife.
   Æschylos. Live, and do more.
                 Thine is the Lemnian ile,
And thou hast placed the arrows in the hand

246

ÆSCHYLOS AND SOPHOCLES

Of Philoctetes, hast assuaged his wounds
And given his aid without which Greece had fail'd.
  Sophocles. I did indeed drive off the pest of flies;
We also have our pest of them which buz   20
About our honey, darken it, and sting;
We laugh at them, for under hands like ours,
Without the wing that Philoctetes shook,
One single feather crushes the whole swarm.
  I must be grave.
          Hath Sicily such charms
Above our Athens? Many charms hath she,
But she hath kings. Accursed be the race!
  Æschylos. But where kings honor better men than they
Let kings be honored too.
          The laurel crown
Surmounts the golden; wear it, and farewell.   30

[12]

MARCUS AURELIUS AND LUCIAN

[Published in 1859; recast and expanded 1863, and so reprinted 1876. Text 1859.]

  Marcus Aurelius. Lucian! in one thing thou art ill-advised.
  Lucian. And in one only? tell me which is that.
  Marcus Aurelius. In scoffing, as thou hast done openly,
At all religions: there is truth in all.
  Lucian. Ah! could we see it! but the well is deep.
Each mortal calls his God inscrutable;
And this at least is true: why not stop there?
Some subdivide him; others hold him close,
Forcing the subdivisions to unite.
The worshiper of Mithras lifts his eyes   10
To hail his early rising, for he knows
Who gives the fruits of earth to nourish him;

1 one] *one* 1863.   7 why ... there] then why not stop *1863.*   8 subdivide]
subsidize *1863.*   hold ... close,] split him down *1863.*   *Between ll.* 8–9 *1863* has
one line:
            From nape to navel, others bandage him,
Between ll. 9–10 *1863 has six lines:*
      These should have lived in Saturn's day, his son
      Methinks had found them easier work to do.
      Eclectic are we Romans, yet we run
      (Pardon me, Pontifex!) from bad to worse.
      Those which Fear palsies and which Fraud sustains,
      Not the erect and strenuous, I deride.
10 Mithras] Mothras *text 1863,* Mithras *in corrigenda.*   12 gives ... earth] ripens
all the grain *1863.*

247

Olympus and the Alps are hills alike
To him, and goats their best inhabitants.
Did Epictetus take our rotten staves
To walk with uprightly? did Cicero
Kneel down before our urban deities?
He carried in his mouth a Jupiter
Ready for Senates when he would harangue,
Then wiped him clean and laid him down again.   20
    Marcus Aurelius. Religions, true of false, may lend support
To man's right conduct: some deterr from ill
Thro' fear, and others lead by gentleness,
Benevolence in thought, beneficence
In action, and at times to patriotism
And gallant struggles for their native land.
    Lucian. So much the worse for these. Did Julius spare
The Druid in his grove? no; he wrencht off
The golden sickle from the misleto,
And burnt the wicker basket ere it held   30
Aloft on sacred oak the wretch within.
    Marcus Aurelius. I doubt it: he knew well the use of priests.
Scoffing was not his fault, ambition was;
Yet clemency could over-rule ambition.
    Lucian. This of all vices is the very worst
Where the best men are made the sacrifice.
    Marcus Aurelius. I am accused, I hear, of wanting it.
    Lucian. Yet thou too, Marcus, art ambitious; thou
Wouldst conquer worlds . . with kindness, wouldst instruct
The unwise, controll the violent, and divert   40
From battle-field to corn-field.
    Marcus Aurelius.   This I would,
But never irritate weak intellects
Clinging to a religion learnt by heart
From nurse and mother, thence most justly dear.
    Lucian. Founded on falsehood are not all religions,
All copies, more or less, from older ones?

19 harangue] harang *1863.*   *Between ll.* 20–1 *1863 has forty-six lines, for which see notes at end of vol.*   22 deterr] deter *1863.*   ill] evil *1863.*   23 Thro'] By *1863.* 25–6 at . . . land] *1863 substitutes*:
                    from these springs gratitude,
       Which often widens into patriotism
       Whereby men struggle for their native land.
27 these] them *1863.*   28 no . . . off] our Divus wrencht *1863.*   29 misleto] mistletoe *1863.*   31 Aloft on] Upon the *1863.*   32 he knew well] well he knew *1863.*   33–44 *For these twelve lines 1863 substitutes twenty-three lines, for which see notes at end of vol.*   46 All copies,] And copied *1863.*

MARCUS AURELIUS AND LUCIAN

Some by transfusion purified, and some
Weaken'd, and pour'd again upon the dregs,
Until they first ferment and then turn sour.
    Marcus Aurelius. Yet, Lucian, there is truth in one religion,   50
Truth in that one which rises from a heart
With sweet and silent gratitude o'erflowing.
    Lucian. Weakest of orders is the composite,
Such is the fabric folks walk under here,
Already we have seen part after part
Crack off, and terrify bare scalps below.
    Marcus Aurelius. Leave Rome her quiet Gods.
    Lucian.   Not Saturn though,
Who would have eaten every God ere teetht,
But his first-born disabled him, and made
The little Venus laugh at granpapa.   60
    Marcus Aurelius. We are not going up so far as him.
    Lucian. Fain would I stop at Venus and her son;
It were ungrateful in me to malign
Such gentle Deities; to laugh at them
They now, alas! have left me little power;
Juno has helpt in my discomfiture.
    Marcus Aurelius. Into your Lares I will not intrude:
Temples I enter rarely; not a God
Minds me above those atoms of the earth
Whereof we, low and lofty, are composed.   70
Such is the surest doctrine to uphold,
But to divulge even this may be unsafe.
Have not we known the Sage of Palestine
Derided, persecuted, crucified?
Have we not seen his simple followers
Slaughter'd in this our city, this our Rome,
Some burnt alive, some thrown among wild beasts?
    Lucian. Woefully true! and thieves and murderers
Have sprung up from the ground whereon they bled;
No wicker-basket men, men calling Heaven   80
To help them in their vengeance on a foe
Who puts the left leg where he should the right,
And will not draw it back, but walk strait on.

50–67 *For these eighteen lines 1863 substitutes fourteen lines, for which see notes at end
of vol.*   68 enter rarely] seldom enter *1863.*   69 those] the *1863.*   70 low
and lofty] great and little *1863.*   71 surest] purest *1863.*   73 the Sage] a
sage *1863.*   77 burnt . . . beasts] thrown among wild beasts, some burnt alive
1863.   *l.* 80 *om. 1863.*   81–3 *altered in 1863 and transferred elsewhere: see
notes at end of vol.*

DRAMAS AND DRAMATIC SCENES

Marcus Aurelius. Woefully true this also, but unwise,
Because unsafe, to utter.
    Lucian.   Truth is more
Unsafe than falsehood, and was ever so.
Marcus Aurelius. Well, I would not exasperate by wit's
Sharp point the robb'd and bleeding; stoop thou rather
To heal them.
    Lucian.   They would kick me in the face
If for such office I bend over them.   90
Better to strip the sophists of their rings
And trailing trappings, chaunting boys before,
Waving fat incense up against their beards
Ere they parade in them through every street,
And at the end of Via Sacra halt
To choose an Imperator of their own.
Marcus Aurelius. Friend Lucian! thou art more jocose than ever.
Why not imagine they may take my horse
From under me, then round men's shoulders strap
The curule chair and hoist a priest thereon?   100
    Lucian. Thy depth of wisdom, Marcus, long I knew,
But never knew thee poet til this hour.
Homer feign'd Polypheme, Calypso, Circe,
Imagination left him on the strand
With these; he never saw, even in a dream,
So strange a rider mount a curule chair.

The sentiments of M. Aurelius and of Lucian are here exhibited. That Lucian was
an honest man (if such a scoffer as he and Rabelais, and Cervantes and Dean Swift,
are allowed to be) is probable by so sagacious and virtuous a prince as M. Aurelius
appointing him to an important office in Egypt. There is more of banter than of wit
in his Dialogues. In wit he is far inferior to Molière, Voltaire, Congreve, Swift, Hood,
and some now living. [L. According to some writers it was the Emperor Commodus
who appointed Lucian to be a procurator in Egypt. W.]

85–6 Truth . . . ever so.] *In 1863 spoken by M. Aurelius.*   87–9 Well . . . them.]
1863 substitutes [*M. Aurelius still speaking*]:
              Do not exasperate by pointed wit
              The proud and the morose, but rather stoop
              To raise them up from their infirmities.
89 They would] Poor creatures! they will *1863.*   90 for] at *1863.*   92, chaunting boys
before] femininely loose *1863.*   *Between ll.* 92–3 *1863 has:*
              With chanting boys in marshal'd troops before,
94 *om. 1863.*   95 And . . . Sacra] Soon at the Via Sacra they may *1863, 1876.*
96 To] And *1863.*   *After l.* 100 LUCIAN *om. 1863.*   101 depth of] wit and
1863.   Marcus . . . knew] Lucian, long I've known *1863.*   102 knew . .
hour] found thee poet until now *1863.*   103 Polypheme . . . Circe] Polyphemus
and Calyps *1863.*   105 these;] those: *1863.*   106 mount . . . chair.] on a
seat so strange: *1863.*   *After* strange: *1863 adds one line:*
              Give him my purple, make the scene complete.

250

HOMER, LAERTES, AGATHA

[First published in complete form in 1863; so reprinted 1876. Shorter version with other variants published in 1859. For variants from 1859 see notes at end of volume. Text 1863.]

Homer. Is this Laertes who embraces me
Ere a word spoken? his the hand I grasp?
Laertes. Zeus help thee, and restore to thee thy sight,
My guest of old! I am of years as many,
And of calamities, as thou thyself,
I, wretched man! who have outlived my son
Odysseus, him thou knewest in this house,
A stripling fond of quoits and archery,
Thence to be call'd for counsel mid the chiefs
Who storm'd that city past the farther sea,   10
Built by two Gods, by more than two defended.
Homer. He rests, and to the many toils endur'd
There was not added the worse weight of age.
Laertes. He would be growing old had he remain'd
Until this day, tho' scarcely three-score years
Had he completed; old I seem'd to him
For youth is fanciful, yet here am I,
Stout, a full twenty summers after him:
But one of the three sisters snapt that thread
Which was the shortest, and my boy went down   20
When no light shines upon the dreary way.
Homer. Hither I came to visit thee, and sing
His wanderings and his wisdom, tho' my voice
Be not the voice it was; yet thoughts come up,
And words to thoughts, which others may recite
When I am mute, and deaf as is my grave,
If any grave in any land be mine.
Laertes. Men will contend for it in after times,
And cities claim it as the ground whereon
A temple stood, and worshippers yet stand.   30
Long hast thou travell'd since we met, and far.
Homer. I have seen many cities, and the best
And wisest of the men who dwelt therein,
The children and *their* children now adult,
Nor childless they. Some have I chided, some

ll. 12–21 *printed among* INSERTIONS, *1863; here and in 1876 placed in text as directed.*
21 When] ? *mispr. for* Where. [W.]

Would soothe, who, mounted on the higher sod,
Wept as the pebbles tinkled, dropping o'er
A form outstretcht below; they would not hear
Story of mine, which told them there were fields
Fresher, and brighter skies, but slapping me,   40
Cried worse, and ran away.
    Laertes.   Here sits aside thee
A child grey-headed who will hear thee out.
Here shalt thou arm my son again, in mail
No enemy, no time, can strip from him,
But first I counsel thee to try the strength
Of my old prisoner in the cave below:
The wine will sparkle at the sight of thee,
If there be any virtue left in it.
Bread there is, fitter for young teeth than ours,
But wine can soften its obduracy.   50
At hand is honey in the honeycomb,
And melon, and those blushing pouting buds
That fain would hide them under crisped leaves.
Soon the blue dove and particolor'd hen
Shall quit the stable-rafter, caught at roost,
And goat shall miss her suckling in the morn;
Supper will want them ere the day decline.
    Homer. So be it: I sing best when hearty cheer
Refreshes me, and hearty friend beside.
    Laertes. Voyagers, who have heard thee, carried home   60
Strange stories; whether all be thy device
I know not: surely thou hadst been afraid
Some God or Goddess would have twitcht thine ear.
    Homer. They often came about me while I slept,
And brought me dreams, and never lookt morose.
They loved thy son and for his sake loved me.
    Laertes. Apollo, I well know, was much thy friend.
    Homer. He never harried me as Marsyas
Was harried by him; lest he should, I sang
His praise in my best hymn: the Gods love praise.   70
    Laertes. I should have thought the Gods would more approve
Good works than glossy words, for well they know
All we can tell them of themselves or us.
Have they enricht thee? for I see thy cloak
Is ragged.
    Homer.   Ragged cloak is songster's garb.
    Laertes. I have two better; one of them for thee.

HOMER, LAERTES, AGATHA I.

Penelope, who died five years ago,
Spun it, her husband wore it only once,
And 'twas upon the anniversary
Of their espousal.
   Homer.   Wear it I will not,   80
But I will hang it on the brightest nail
Of the first temple where Apollo sits,
Golden hair'd, in his glory.
   Laertes.   So thou shalt
If so it please thee: yet we first will quaff
The gifts of Bakkos, for methinks his gifts
Are quite as welcome to the sons of song
And cheer them oftener.
        [AGATHA *enters with a cup of wine.*]
                   Maiden! come thou nigh,
And seat thee there, and thou shalt hear him sing,
After a while, what Gods might listen to:
But place that cup upon the board, and wait   90
Until the stranger hath assuaged his thirst,
For songmen, grasshoppers, and nightingales
Sing cheerily but when the throat is moist.
   Homer. I sang to maidens in my prime; again,
But not before the morrow, will I sing;
Let me repose this noontide, since in sooth
Wine, a sweet solacer of weariness,
Helps to unload the burden.
   Laertes.   Lie then down
Along yon mat bestrown with rosemary,
Basil, and mint, and thyme.
                 She knows them all   100
And has her names for them, some strange enough.
Sound and refreshing then be thy repose!
Well may weak mortal seek the balm of sleep
When even the Gods require it, when the stars
Droop in their courses, and the Sun himself
Sinks on the swelling bosom of the sea.
   Take heed there be no knot on any sprig;
After, bring store of rushes and long leaves
Of cane sweet-smelling from the inland bank
Of yon wide-wandering river over-sea   110
Famed for its swans; then open and take out
From the black chest the linen, never used
These many years, which thou (or one before)

Spreadst for the Sun to bleach it; and be sure,
Be sure, thou smoothen with both hands his couch
Who has the power to make both young and old
Live throughout ages.
 Agatha.   And look well through all?
 Laertes. Aye, and look better than they lookt before.
 Agatha. I wish he would make me so, and without
My going for it anywhere below.   120
I am content to stay in Ithaca,
Where the dogs know me, and the ferryman
Asks nothing from me, and the rills are full
After the rain, and flowers grow everywhere,
And bees grudge not their honey, and the grape
Grows within reach, and figs, blue, yellow, green,
Without my climbing; boys, too come at call;
And, if they hide the ripest, I know where
To find it, twist and struggle as they may;
Impudent boys! to make me bring it out,   130
Saying I shall not have it if I don't!
 Laertes. How the child babbles! pardon her! behold
Her strength and stature have outgrown her wits!
In fourteen years thou thyself wast not wise.
 Homer. My heart is freshen'd by a fount so pure
At its springhead; let it run on in light.
Most girls are wing'd with wishes, and can ill
Keep on their feet against the early gale
That blows impetuous on unguarded breast;
But this young maiden, I can prophecy,   140
Will be thy staff when other staff hath fail'd.
 Agatha. May the Gods grant it! but not grant it yet!
Blessings upon thy head!
 Homer.   May they bestow
Their choicest upon thine! may they preserve
Thy comeliness of virtue many years
For him whose hand thy master joins to thine!
 Agatha. O might I smoothen that mild wrinkled brow
With but one kiss!
 Laertes.   Take it. Now leave us, child,
And bid our good Metampos to prepare
That brazen bath wherein my rampant boy   150
Each morning lay full-length, struggling at first,
Then laughing as he splasht the water up

     149 Metampos] ? *mispr. for* Melampos.

Against his mother's face bent over him.
Is this the Odysseus first at quoit and bar?
Is this the Odysseus call'd to counsel kings,
He whose name sounds beyond our narrow sea?
   Agatha. O how I always love to hear that name!
   Laertes. But linger not; pursue the task at hand:
Bethink thee 'tis for one who has the power
To give thee many days beyond old-age.   160
   Agatha. O tell him not to do it if he can:
He cannot make youth stay: the swallows come
And go, youth goes, but never comes again.
   Laertes. He can make heroes greater than they were.
   Agatha. By making them lay by the wicked sword?
How I shall love him when he has done that!
   Laertes. No, but he gives them strength by magic song.
   Agatha. The strength of constancy to love but one?
As did Odysseus while he lived on earth,
And when he waited for her in the shades.   170
   Laertes. The little jay! go, chatterer.
   Agatha to Homer.   Do not think
O stranger, he is wroth; he never is
With Agatha, albeit he stamps and frowns
And shakes three fingers at her, and forbears
To do the like to any one beside.
Hark! the brass sounds, the bath is now prepared.
   Laertes. More than the water shall her hand assuage
Thy weary feet, and lead thee back, now late.

178 now] nor MS. emendation.

HOMER. LAERTES. AGATHA.

In the Morning.

[Published in 1863; reprinted 1876.]

   Homer. Whose is the soft and pulpy hand that lies
Athwart the ridges of my craggy one
Out of the bed? can it be Agatha's?
   Agatha. I come to bring thee, while yet warm and frothy,
A draught of milk. Rise now, rise just half-up,
And drink it. Hark! the birds, two at a time,
Are singing in the terebinth. Our king
Hath taken down his staff and gone afield
To see the men begin their daily work.

Sub-title. Above In ... morning *1876* has: SECOND DAY.

Homer. Go thou to thine: I will arise. How sweet   10
Was that goat's milk!
  Agatha.   We have eleven below,
All milchers. Wouldst thou now the tepid bath?
  Homer. Rather when thou hast laid on the left-hand
My sandals within reach; being colder lymph
To freshen more the frame-work of mine eyes,
For eyes there are, altho their orbs be dark.
  Agatha. 'Tis here; let me apply it.
  Homer.   Bravely done!
Why standest thou so still and taciturn?
  Agatha. The king my master hath forbidden me
Ever to ask a question: if I might,   20
And were not disobedience such a sin,
I would ask *thee*, so gentle and so wise,
Whether the story of that bad Calypso
Can be all true, for it would grieve me sorely
To think thou wouldst repeat it were it false,
And some ill-natured God (such Gods there are)
Would punish thee, already too afflicted.
  Homer. My child! the Muses sang the tale I told,
And they know more about that wanton Nymph
Than they have uttered into mortal ear.   30
I do rejoice to find thee fond of truth.
  Agatha. I was not always truthful. I have smarted
For falsehood, under Queen Penelope,
When I was little. I should hate to hear
More of that wicked creature who detain'd
Her lord from her, and tried to win his love.
I knew 'twas very wrong of me to listen.
  Homer. A pardonable fault: we wish for listeners
Whether we speak or sing, the young and old
Alike are weak in this, unwise and wise,   40
Cheerful and sorrowful.
  Agatha.   O! look up yonder!
Why dost thou smile? everything makes thee smile
At silly Agatha, but why just now?
  Homer. What was the sight?
  Agatha.   O inconsiderate!
O worse than inconsiderate! cruel! cruel!
  Homer. Tell me, what was it? I can see thro' speech.
  Agatha. A tawny bird above; he prowls for hours,
Sailing on wilful wings that never flag

Until they drop headlong to seize the prey.
The hinds shout after him and make him soar   50
Eastward: our little birds are safe from kites
And idler boys.
　　　　　'Tis said (can it be true?)
In other parts men catch the nightingale
To make it food.
　　Homer.　　　　Nay, men eat men.
　　Agatha.　　　　　　　Ye Gods!
But men hurt one another, nightingales
Console the weary with unwearied song,
Until soft slumber on the couch descends.
The king my master and Penelope
Forbade the slaughter or captivity
Of the poor innocents who trusted them,   60
Nor robbed them even of the tiniest grain.
　　Homer. Generous and tender is thy master's heart,
Warm as the summer, open as the sky.
　　Agatha. How true! how I do love thee for these words!
Stranger, didst thou not hear him wail aloud,
Groan after groan, broken, but ill supprest,
When thou recitedst in that plaintive tone
How Anticleia met her son again
Amid the shades below?
　　　　　　　Thou shouldst have stopt
Before that tale was told by thee; that one   70
At least was true, if none were true before.
In vain, O how in vain, I smote my breast
To keep more quiet what would beat within!
Never were words so sweet, so sad, as those.
I sobb'd apart, I could not check my tears:
Laertes too, tho' stronger, could not his,
They glistened in their channels and would run,
Nor could he stop them with both hands: he heard
My sobs, and call'd me little fool for them;
Then did he catch and hold me to his bosom,   80
And bid me never do the like again.
　　Homer. The rains in their due season will descend,
And so will tears; they sink into the heart
To soften, not to hurt it. The best men
Have most to weep for, whether foren lands
Receive them (or stil worse!) a home estranged.
　　Agatha. Listen. I hear the merry yelp of dogs,

And now the ferrel'd staff drops in the hall,
And now the master's short and hurried step
Advances: here he is: turn round, turn round.   90
    Laertes. Hast thou slept well, Mæonides?
    Homer.   I slept
Three hours ere sunrise, 'tis my wont, at night
I lie awake for nearly twice as long.
    Laertes. Ay; singing birds wake early, shake their plumes,
And carol ere they feed. Sound was thy sleep?
    Homer. I felt again, but felt it undisturb'd,
The pelting of the little curly waves,
The slow and heavy stretch of rising billows,
And the rapidity of their descent.
I thought I heard a Triton's shell, a song   100
Of sylvian Nymph, and laughter from behind
Trees not too close for voices to come thro',
Or beauty, if Nymph will'd it, to be seen;
And then a graver and a grander sound
Came from the sky, and last a long applause.
    Laertes. Marvellous things are dreams! methinks we live
An age in one of them, we traverse lands
A lifetime could not reach, bring from the grave
Inhabitants who never met before,
And vow we will not leave an absent friend   110
We long have left, and who leaves *us* ere morn.
    Homer. Dreams are among the blessings Heaven bestows
On weary mortals; nor are they least
Altho' they disappoint us and are gone
When we awake! 'Tis pleasant to have caught
The clap of hands below us from the many,
Amid the kisses of the envious few.
There is a pride thou knowest not, Laertes,
In carrying the best strung and loudest harp.
    Laertes. Apollo, who deprived thee of thy light   120
When youth was fresh and nature bloom'd around,
Bestowed on thee gifts never dim with age,
And rarely granted to impatient youth.
The crown thou wearest reddens not the brow
Of him who wears it worthily; but some

91 Mæonides] Mieonides *mispr. 1863.*   *ll.* 100–5 *printed in* INSERTIONS *1863,*
in text 1876.   *ll.* 112–19 *printed in* INSERTIONS *1863, in text 1876.*   *After l.* 119
Landor wished to insert: That vibrates to deserving hearts alone. *This addition was
sent too late.*

Are snatcht by violence, some purloin'd by fraud,
Some dripping blood, not by the Gods unseen.
To thee, O wise Mæonides, to thee
Worthless is all that glitters and attracts
The buzzing insects of a summer hour.   130
The Gods have given thee what themselves enjoy,
And they alone, glory through endless days.
The Lydian king Sarpedon never swayed
Such sceptre, nor did Glaucos his compeer,
Nor Priam. Priam was about my age,
He had more sorrows than I ever had;
I lost one son, some fifty Priam lost;
This is a comfort, I may rub my palms
Thinking of this, and bless the Powers above.
    Homer. One wicked son brought down their vengeance on him, 140
And his wide realms invited numerous foes.
    Laertes. Alas! alas! are there not cares enow
In ruling nearly those five thousand heads,
Men, women, children; arbitrating right
And wrong, and hearing maids and mothers wail
For flax blown off the cliff when almost bleacht,
And curlew tamed in vain and fled away,
Albeit one wing was shortened; then approach
To royal ear the whisper that the bird
Might peradventure have alighted nigh,   150
And hist upon the charcoal, skinn'd and split.
Bounteous as are the Gods, where is the wealth
To stop these lamentations with a gift
Adequate to such losses? words are light,
And words come opposite, with heavy groans.
    Homer. The pastor of the people may keep watch,
Yet cares as wakeful creep into the fold.
    Laertes. Beside these city griefs, what mortal knows
The anxieties about my scattered sheep?
Some bleeting for lost offspring, some for food,   160
Scanty in winter, scantier in the drought
Of Sirius; then again the shrubs in spring;
Cropt close, ere barely budded, by the goats.
Methinks these animals are over-nice
About their food, else might they pick sea-weeds,
But these foresooth they trample on, nor deign

133 Lydian] Lycian MS. *emendation.*   145 wail] *mispr.* wail; *1863.*   166 fore-
sooth] forsooth *1876.*

To taste even samphire, which their betters cull.
There also are some less solicitudes
About those rocks, when plunderers from abroad
Would pilfer eggs and nestlings; my own folk   170
Are abstinent, without their king's decree.
   Homer. To help thee in such troubles, and in worse,
Where is thy brave Telemakos?
   Laertes.   That youth
Is gone to rule Dulikeon, where the soil
Tho' fitter than our Ithaca for tilth,
Bears only turbulence and idleness.
He with his gentle voice and his strong arm,
Will bring into due train the restive race.
   Homer. Few will contend with gentleness and youth,
Even of those who strive against the Laws,   180
But some subvert them who could best defend,
And in whose hands the Gods have placed the sword.
On the mainland there are, unless report
Belie them, princes who, possessing realms
Wider than sight from mountain-head can reach,
Would yet invade a neighbour's stony croft,
Pretending danger to their citadels
From fishermen ashore, and shepherd boys
Who work for daily and but scanty bread,
And wax the reeds to pipe at festivals,   190
Where the dogs snarl at them above the bones.
   Laertes. What! would the cloth'd in purple, as are some,
Rip off the selvage from a ragged coat?
Accursed be the wretch, and whosoe'er
Upholds him, or connives at his misdeeds.
Away with thoughts that sadden even this hour.
   Homer. I would indeed away with 'em, but wrath
Rings on the lyre and swells above the song.
It shall be heard by those who stand on high,
But shall not rouse the lowlier, long opprest,   200
Who might be madden'd at his broken sleep,
And wrenching out the timbers of his gate
Batter the prince's down.
   Laertes.   Ye Gods forbid!
Thou makest the skin creep upon my flesh,
Albeit the danger lies from me afar.
Now surely this is but a songman's tale,
Yet songman never here discourst like thee,

Or whispered in low voice what thou hast sung,
Striking the lyre so that the strings all trembled.
Are people anywhere grown thus unruly?   210
   Homer. More are they who would rule than would be ruled,
Yet one must govern, else all run astray.
The strongest are the calm and equitable,
And kings at best are men, nor always that.
   Laertes. I have known many who have call'd me friend,
Yet would not warn me tho' they saw ten skiffs
Grating the strand with three score thieves in each.
   Curse on that chief across the narrow sea,
Who drives whole herds and flocks innumerable,
And whose huge presses groan with oil and wine   220
Year after year, yet fain would carry off
The crying kid, and strangle it for crying.
Alas, Mæonides, the weakest find
Strength enough to inflict deep injuries.
Much have I borne, but 'twas from those below;
Thou knowest not the gross indignities
From goat-herd and from swine-herd I endur'd
When my Odysseus had gone far away;
How they consumed my substance, how the proud
Divided my fat kine in this my house,   230
And wooed before mine eyes Penelope,
Reluctant and absconding til return'd
Her lawful lord, true, chaste, as she herself.
   Homer. I know it, and remotest men shall know.
If we must suffer wrong, 'tis from the vile
The least intolerable.
   Laertes.   True, my son
Avenged me: more than one God aided him,
But one above the rest; the Deity
Of wisdom, stronger even than him of war,
Guided the wanderer back, and gave the arms   240
And will and prowess to subdue our foes,
And their own dogs lapt up the lustful blood
Of the proud suitors. Sweet, sweet is revenge;
Her very shadow, running on before,
Quickens our pace until we hold her fast.
   Homer. Rather would I sit quiet than pursue.
   Laertes. Now art thou not, from such long talk, athirst?

ll. 223–46 printed in INSERTIONS *1863, in text 1876.*   223 Mæonides] *mispr*.
Mœonides *1863.*

Split this pomegranate then, and stoop the jar.
Hold! I can stoop it: take this cup . . 'tis fill'd.
   Homer. Zeus! God of hospitality! vouchsafe   250
To hear my prayer, as thou hast often done,
That, when thy lightnings spring athwart the sea,
And when thy thunders shake from brow to base
The Acrokerauneans, thy right hand protect
This Ithaca, this people, and this king!*

   * It has been doubted and denied that Homer and Laertes were contemporary. [L.]

LAERTES. HOMER. AGATHA.

THIRD DAY.

[Published in 1863; reprinted 1876.]

   Laertes. And now, Mæonides, the sun hath risen
These many spans above the awaken'd earth,
Sing me that hymn, which thou hast call'd thy best,
In glory to the God who gives it light.
   First I will call the child to hear thee sing,
For girls remember well and soon repeat
What they have heard of sacred more or less.
I must forbear to join in it, although
That blessed God hath helpt to rear my grain
High as my knee, and made it green and strong.   10
Alas! I cackle when I aim to sing,
Which I have sometimes done at festivals,
But, ere a word were out, methought I felt
A beard of barley sticking in my throat.

(Agatha enters.)

Now, with a trail of honey down the cup
(Agatha, drop it in), commence thy chaunt.
   (*About the 500th verse Laertes falls asleep: awakening he finds Agatha
     in the same state, and chides her.*)
Hast thou no reverence for a song inspired?
   Agatha (*in a whisper*). Hush! O my king and lord, or he may hear.
You were asleep the first: I kept my eyes
Wide open, opener than they ever were,   20
While I do think I could have counted more
Than half a thousand of those words divine,
Had both my hands not dropt upon my lap.
   Laertes. Another time beware of drowsiness

   Sub-title. *Wrongly placed above title in 1863.*   1. Laertes.] *Homer 1863, 1876,
an error here corrected.*

When reverend men discourse about the Gods.
Now lead him forth into the cooler porch,
Entreating him that he will soon renew
His praises of Apollo.
   Agatha.   I will bear
Your words to him; he might care less for mine,
And, sooth to say, I would much rather hear   30
Some other story, where more men than Gods
Shine on the field.
   Laertes.   Of men thou know'st enough.
   Agatha. Too much: then why show Gods almost as bad?
They can not be .. least of all Artemis;
'Twas she directed and preserved Odysseus.
   Laertes. Blessings upon thee! While thou wast a babe
He fondled thee, nor saw when thou couldst walk.
Few love so early or so long: We say
We love the Gods: we lie; the seen alone
We love, to those unseen we may be grateful.   40
   Agatha. But when they are no more before our eyes . . .
   Laertes. That never is, altho' earth come between.
Perplex not thou thy simple little head
With what the wise were wiser to let be.
   Agatha. I go, and will not be again perplext.

                              (Aside.)

He has been dozing while we have converst.
   Mæonides! rise and take this arm
To lead thee where is freshness in the porch.
My master tells me thou another time
Will finish that grand hymn about Apollo.   50
Hast thou no shorter one for Artemis?
   Homer. Such thou shalt have for her, but not to-day.
   Agatha. O, I can wait, so (I am sure) can she.
   Homer. Faint are the breezes here, less faint above;
Gladly then would I mount that central peak
Which overlooks the whole of Ithaca,
That peak I well remember I once clomb
(What few could do) without the help of beast.
   Agatha. Here are sure-footed ones, who weed our thistles,
And give us milk, grey dappled as the dawn: 60
Their large and placid eyes well know that path,
And they will safely bring us to the top
And back again, treading more warily
Than up the ascent.

I will call forth two boys

To lead them, without switches in the fist.
These two can lift thee up; I at thy side
Require no help, and can whisk off the flies.
    Homer. I know not what impels me to retrace
Scenes I can see no more: but so it is
Thro' life.
If thou art able, lead me forth,   70

And let none follow; we are best alone.
    Agatha. Come forward ye.
Now lift up carefully

The noblest guest that ever king received
And the Gods favor most.
Well done! now rest,

Nor sing nor whistle til we all return,
And reach the chesnut and enjoy the shade.
    Homer (at the summit). I think we must be near the highest point,
For now the creatures stop, who struggled hard,
And the boys neither cheer 'em, nor upbraid.
'Tis somewhat to have mounted up so high,   80
Profitless as it is, nor without toil.
    Agatha. Dost thou feel weary?
    Homer.   Short as was the way
It shook my aged bones at every step;
My shoulders ache, my head whirls round and round.
    Agatha. Lean on my shoulder, place thy head on mine,
'Tis low enough.
What were those words? . . I heard

Imperfectly . . . shame on me! Dost thou smile?
    Homer. Child! hast thou ever seen an old man die?
    Agatha. The Gods defend me from so sad a sight!
    Homer. Sad if he die in agony, but blest   90
If friend be nigh him, only one true friend.
    Agatha. Tho' most of thine be absent, one remains;
Is not Laertes worthy of the name?
    Homer. And Agatha, who tends me to the last.
    Agatha. I will, I will indeed, when comes that hour.
    Homer. That hour is come.
Let me lay down my head

On the cool turf; there I am sure to rest.
    Agatha (after a pause). How softly old men sigh! Sleep, gentle soul!
He turns his face to me. Ah how composed!
Surely he sleeps already . . . hand and cheek   100

264

Are colder than such feeble breeze could make 'em.
Mæonides! hearest thou Agatha?
He hears me not . . . Can it . . . can it be . . . death?
Impossible . . . 'tis death . . . 'tis death indeed . . .
Then, O ye Gods of heaven! who would not die,
If thus to rest eternal, he descend?
   O, my dear lord! how shall I comfort thee?
How look unto thy face and tell my tale,
And kneeling clasp thy knee? to be repulst
Were hard, but harder to behold thy grief.*   110

*This poem could not come in time for its proper place. The following note was subjoined:
   Homer's age is uncertain. He may have been, or may not, the contemporary of Laertes. Chronology and poesy are not twins. Two heavy volumes might never have befallen us if their author had consulted *Pericles and Aspasia*. Among the hymns attributed to Homer is one to Apollo, which may well have made an old man and a young girl somnolent. [L. *In 1876 ed. Forster added within brackets*: The "two heavy volumes" were the first two volumes of Mr. Gladstone's work on Homer. "Whatever", said Landor, "is worth noting in them may be found in *Pericles and Aspasia*."—W.]

[14]

THESEUS AND HIPPOLYTA

[Published in 1863; reprinted 1876.]

Hippolyta. Eternal hatred I have sworn against
The persecutor of my sisterhood;
In vain, proud son of Ægeus, hast thou snapt
Their arrows and derided them; in vain
Leadest thou me a captive; I can die,
And die I will.
   Theseus.   Nay; many are the years
Of youth and beauty for Hippolyta.
   Hippolyta. I scorn my youth, I hate my beauty. Go!
Monster! of all the monsters in these wilds
Most frightful and most odious to my sight.   10
   Theseus. I boast not that I saved thee from the bow
Of Scythian.
   Hippolyta. And for what? to die disgraced.
Strong as thou art, yet thou art not so strong
As Death is, when we call him for support.
   Theseus. Him too will I ward off; he strikes me first,
Hippolyta long after, when these eyes
Are closed, and when the knee that supplicates
Can bend no more.

Hippolyta.   Is the man mad?

Theseus.   He is.

Hippolyta. So, thou canst tell one truth, however false
In other things.

Theseus.   What other? Thou dost pause,   20
And thine eyes wander over the smooth turf
As if some gem (but gem thou wearest not)
Had fallen from the remnant of thy hair.
Hippolyta! speak plainly, answer me,
What have I done to raise thy fear or hate?

Hippolyta. Fear I despise, perfidy I abhor.
Unworthy man! did Heracles delude
The maids who trusted him?

Theseus.   Did ever I?
Whether he did or not, they never told me:
I would have chided him.

Hippolyta.   Thou chide him! thou!   30
The Spartan mothers well remember thee.

Theseus. Scorn adds no beauty to the beautiful.
Heracles was beloved by Omphalè,
He never parted from her, but obey'd
Her slightest wish, as Theseus will Hippolyta's.

Hippolyta. Then leave me, leave me instantly; I know
The way to my own country.

Theseus.   This command,
And only this, my heart must disobey.
My country shall be thine, and there thy state
Regal.

Hippolyta. Am I a child? give me my own,   40
And keep for weaker heads thy diadems.
Thermodon I shall never see again,
Brightest of rivers, into whose clear depth
My mother plunged me from her warmer breast,
And taught me early to divide the waves
With arms each day more strong, and soon to chase
And overtake the father swan, nor heed
His hoarser voice or his uplifted wing.
  Where are my sisters? Are there any left?

Theseus. I hope it.

Hippolyta.   And I fear it: theirs may be   50
A fate like mine; which, O ye Gods, forbid!

Theseus. I pity thee, and would assuage thy grief.

Hippolyta. Pity me not; thy anger I could bear.

THESEUS AND HIPPOLYTA

Theseus. There is no place for anger where thou art.
Commiseration even men may feel
For those who want it: even the fiercer beasts
Lick the sore-wounded of a kindred race,
Hearing their cry, albeit they may not help.
  Hippolyta. This is no falsehood: and can he be false
Who speaks it?
                   I remember not the time   60
When I have wept, it was so long ago.
Thou forcest tears from me, because . . because . .
I can not hate thee as I ought to do.

[15]

HIPPOMENES AND ATALANTA

[Published in 1863; reprinted 1876.]

[PROEM.]

Hippomenes and Atalanta strove
To win a race: he lov'd her; but she shunn'd
All lovers, and her royal sire had sworn
That none should marry her unless the one
Swifter of foot, believing none could match
His girl in fleetness, and decreed that all
Should surely die who fail'd in such attempt.
Courageously came forth Hippomenes.
She once beheld him, and she pitied him,
For she had made a vow to Artemis   10
That she would never violate a word
Her father had exacted.
                          Now the hour
Had come to prove her faith; the venturous youth
Stood now before her. Down she cast her eyes,
And cried in broken words, "Rash youth! depart,
The Fates (thou seest them not) are close behind;
Seven brave youths, hardly less brave than thou,
Have fallen for contending in the race
With wretched Atalanta . . . Go."

  Hippomenes.   To live   20
For Atalanta is the first of glory,
To die for her the next: this they enjoyed
In death, the better they bequeathe to me.
  Atalanta. Pity I gave them, do not ask for more,

22 bequeathe] bequeath *1876.*

267

Nor for such cause; let me not weep again,
Let that be the last time.
    Hippomenes.   So may it be!
So shall it; for the Gods have given me strength
And confidence: one name for victory.
Certain I am to win.
    Atalanta.   No, thou rash boy!
If thou must try such hazard . . if thou must . . .
Must? what impels thee? madness! There is time
Yet to turn back; I do implore thee . . go.
Artemis sees me.
    Hippomenes.   Aphrodite sees
Me, and smiles on me, and instructs me how . .
    Atalanta. Cease, cease, this instant: I abhor the name;
My Goddess hates her, should not I? I do.
    Hippomenes. I love all Goddesses, the kindest most,
And I beseech her now to make me grateful.
    Atalanta. All I can hope for is thy swift escape;
Be prompt: I see white sails below the cliff;
My father soon shall know 'twas my command,
He wills obedience, he shall value thine,
And send thee gifts.
    Hippomenes.   I want but one, which one
The king shall give me.
    Atalanta.   What is that?
    Hippomenes.   This hand.
    Atalanta. And snatchest thou my hand? audacious creature!
No man hath dared to touch it until now,
Nor I convert with any half so long.
    Hippomenes. Not half so long have any loved as I.
    Atalanta. Insane! it was but yesterday we met.
    Hippomenes. In yesterday, its day and night, lay years.
    Atalanta. I never was dissembler. I will pass
Unyoked thro' life.
    Hippomenes.   O Atalanta! love
No yoke imposes, he removes the heaviest
The Destinies would throw around the neck
Of youth, who wearies in the dismal way
Of lonely life.
    Atalanta.   I do not comprehend
Those flighty words, they sound like idle song.
    Hippomenes. Scoff not, add not another to the seven,
Without a race for it; my breath is failing.

30

40

50

HIPPOMENES AND ATALANTA

Atalanta. O perfidy! to make me weep again!
Others too may have loved.
   Hippomenes.   But not like me;   60
Else would the Gods have rais'd them to themselves,
Ay, and above themselves, in happiness,
Crowning the best of them with amaranth.
   Atalanta. Zeus holds the scales of weal and woe.
   Hippomenes.   Zeus holds them,
But little Eros with light finger stoops
The balance-bowl: Zeus shakes his head and smiles.
   Atalanta. What wouldst thou?
   Hippomenes.   Thee; thee only; no rich ile,
No far dominion over land and sea.
   Atalanta. Easier to win than what thou seekest here.
Remember last year's fruit; it lies beneath   70
The seven hillocks of yon turf, ill-squared
And disunited yet, on the left hand.
Shame! thus to weaken me in my resolve,
And break my father's heart! no, thou shalt not.
   Hippomenes. I blame not tears for those who bravely fell.
   Atalanta. I never did shed tears, and never will.
Come, let us lose no time, if strive we must.
The sward is level here and sound and soft;
Throw off thy sandals, I will throw off mine.
Start.

[EPILOGUE.]

   They both started; he, by one stride, first,   80
For she half pitied him so beautiful,
Running to meet his death, yet was resolved
To conquer: soon she near'd him, and he felt
The rapid and repeated gush of breath
Behind his shoulder.
           From his hand now dropt
A golden apple: she lookt down and saw
A glitter on the grass, yet on she ran.
He dropt a second; now she seem'd to stoop:
He dropt a third; and now she stoopt indeed:
Yet, swifter than a wren picks up a grain   90
Of millet, rais'd her head: it was too late,
Only one step, only one breath, too late.
Hippomenes had toucht the maple goal
With but two fingers, leaning pronely forth.
She stood in mute despair; the prize was won.

67 ile] isle 1876.

Now each walkt slowly forward, both so tired,
And both alike breathed hard, and stopt at times.
When he turn'd round to her, she lowered her face
Cover'd with blushes, and held out her hand,
The golden apple in it.
             "Leave me now,"   100
Said she, "I must walk homeward."
                      He did take
The apple and the hand.
             "Both I detain,"
Said he, "the other two I dedicate
To the two Powers that soften virgin hearts,
Eros and Aphroditè; and this one
To her who ratifies the nuptial vow."
She would have wept to see her father weep;
But some God pitied her, and purple wings
(What God's were they?) hovered and interposed.

[16]

SAPPHO, ALCÆUS, ANACREON, PHAON

[Published in 1863; reprinted 1876.]

Sappho. I wonder at the malice of the herd
Against us poets. O what calumnies
Do those invent who can invent nought else!
'Tis said, Alcæus, thou hast run away
From battle.
    Alcæus.   Idlers show no idleness
In picking up and spreading false reports.
Nay, 'tis said also (thing incredible)
That women carry them from house to house,
And twirl and sniff them as they would a rose.
Nothing is lighter than an empty tale,   10
Or carried farther on with fresh relays;
No ball do children leap at with more glee,
Catch, and look more triumphant, than do men
At lies: such men, day after day, come here:
Yet, Sappho, which among the worst can say
I love thee not?
    Sappho.   Well, well!
    Alcæus.   To be beloved
By Sappho raises mortal nigh the Gods
In bliss and glory; not to love her sinks
The proudest head below the beasts that perish.

They who look down from heaven into our hearts 20
See truth, how deep! in mine.
    Sappho.   They know the true,
They know the brave, and value them alike.
    Anacreon. Pick up thy shield, man! There was no delay
Upon that meadow, soft to run upon,
Where even the tenderest grass seem'd strong enough
To impede thee like a barrier, every reed
A pointed spear, and every twittering bird
Sounded like trumpet, when two lifted hands
Shielded two ears upright as leveret's.
    Sappho. I never thought Anacreon was so fierce, 30
But even doves are vicious now and then.
    Alcæus. I burn to smite him on the mouth for this.
    Sappho. Sit down, Alcæus; none are angry here.
Do wise men rear and start at sparks of wit?
    Alcæus. Sparks fly up, drop, and die; pure incense burns
Without them.
    Sappho.   Incense usually begins
In smoke, and ends in ashes.
    Alcæus.   Not so mine.
    Sappho. I wish thy voice attuned to notes less grave.
    Alcæus. Ah! can it ever be attuned to thine?
Love checks it.
    Anacreon.   Love, it seems, may check thy tongue, 40
But not thy feet. I wish my verses ran
On feet as light as those which left their soles
Behind them at the clarion's nearer blasts;
The lightest lyre would have been heavy there.
    Sappho. (*Phaon entering.*) Be calm, Alcæus! be less petulant,
Anacreon! Thy persuasive voice, my Phaon,
May harmonize these wranglers.
    Phaon.   Ah! what voice
Could ever harmonize like thine the chords
Of the most rigid breast! a ray of thine
Awakes to song, as the bright Morn awakes 50
Upon the desert sand her Memnon's lyre.
    Anacreon. By Zeus! he beats us both. Sing, sing away,
Alcæus! I will try another time.

                (*To Sappho.*)
Already this brave warrior hath confest
His voice defective in the praise of thee.

DRAMAS AND DRAMATIC SCENES

Alcæus. I did confess it, and will prove it now.

(Sings.)

Glory of Lesbos! where Apollo's hand
Led thee among us mortals, nor withdrew
When Aphroditè claim'd thee for her own,
Over what distant ages shalt thou pass,   60
And thro what distant regions men shall hear
The song of Sappho, and her praise in all.
    Phaon (*to Sappho*). I hate such sing-song from my very soul;
'Tis only proper for hard-fisted girls
Who, crouching on low tressel, milk the goat.
As for that tippler on the other side,
I often hear his verses in the street;
There children stagger, imitating him,
And he runs sidelong after them, and trips.
    Sappho. Why lookest thou so gloomily? say, speak.   70
Surely thou art not jealous, like a poet.
    Phaon. Jealous I am not; but can ill endure
To see a rival wear a gift of thine.
    Sappho. I would not give it hadst thou not been by.
    Phaon. Songsters are ever most importunate.
    Sappho. We like a bird to sing to us sometimes.
    Phaon. Some birds would put their beaks on softer ones.
    Sappho. I have known maidens let their sparrow do it,
Holding the wing on purpose.
                  Thou art cold
And peevish: be what thou hast been till now.   80
Whenever Phaon came, all went away,
As those have done.
    Phaon.   But thou hast given my gift,
If mine it was.
    Sappho.   O cruelest of words!
Were it not thine, and worn till it was dead,
The kitten had been tearing it for play;
I wore it only for thy coming, sure
To have a fresher, so now give it me,
Or lay it on the table: if not, take
Some trouble with it in a fitter place,
Where thou hast often spent much time and tried   90
Contrivances, and tried again, to bend
A riotous curl obedient to thy will.
    Phaon. Forgive me, Sappho. Let me twine it round
Thy sadden'd brow: how hot it is! Had love

And not vexation caus'd it, even then
I might almost have griev'd. Yes! any pain
Thou feelest, I feel more.
  Sappho.   Of love?
  Phaon.   That worst,
Until thy breath wafted it all away.
  Sappho. When thy love perishes, I shall believe
The Gods have perisht too, one only left,   100
And he to laugh and taunt me.
  Phaon.   Truth herself
Shall first leave earth and heaven. Now wipe thine eyes.
  Sappho. Thou shalt then lower thy lips,
  Phaon.   And crush that smile?

103 smile?] *so in errata 1863*: smile. *in text 1863, 1876.*

[17]
THE TRIAL OF ÆSCHYLOS
[Published in 1863; reprinted 1876.]

  Judge. Bring into court the culprit, him accused
Of having, and deliberately, betray'd
The mysteries of Eleusis.
  Æschylos.   Here I stand,
No culprit, and no jailer brings me forth.
  Judge. Hast thou not, Æschylos, divulged the rites
Taught by Demeter?
  Æschylos.   What have I divulged
Beside the truths the Gods to men impart,
And none beside the worthy do they trust.
The human breast they open and they close,
And who can steal their secrets? who shall dare   10
Infringe their laws, or who arraign their will?
Ye men of Athens! before *you* I stand,
Known to ye long ago, nor only here,
But on the plain of Marathon: who flincht
In that fierce fray? did I? and shall I now?
The brave man venerates, the base man fears,
I scorn to supplicate, or even to plead,
For well I know there is a higher court,
A court of last appeal.
  Judge.   We know it not;
Where is it situated?
  Æschylos.   In man's heart.   20

In life it may be barr'd, so dark that none
See into it, not he himself; Death comes,
And then the Furies leave their grove and strike.
    Citizen. He spake no wiser words upon the stage,
Where all men speak their wisest and their best.
    Another Citizen. I wish he had not said a word about
Those Furies; Death is bad enough.
    First Citizen.   Hush! hush!
The Arkon rises up and waves his hand.
    Judge. What say ye, men of Athens, to the charge
Ye heard denounced this morning? Are ye mute?   30
Sadness I see in some, in others wrath,
Wrath ill becomes the seat I occupy;
And even sadness I would fain suppress.
But who can bear irreverence to his Gods?
Their profanation (by your laws) is death.
    Amyntos. (*Rushes forward and bares his brother's scars.*) What have
        these merited? These wounds he won
From Persia, nothing else. Let others show
The purple vestures, stript from satraps slain,
He slew them, and left those for weaker hands
To gather up, and to adorn their wives.   40
                              (*To Æschylos.*)
    Æschylos. Amyntos is my brother, so are ye,
But why display my ragged white-faced scar?
Why show the place where one arm *was*, if one
Keeps yet its own? this left can wield the sword.
    Amyntos. Fling not thy cloak about thee, nor turn round,
Nay, brother, thou shalt not conceal the scars
With that one hand yet left thee.
                         Citizens!
Behold the man, that impious man, who smote
Those who defiled the altars of your Gods.
Look up: is Pallas standing on yon hill?   50
She would not have been standing there unless
Men like the man before ye had well fought
At Marathon, not braver than some here
Who fought with him and bound his shattered limb.
If Æschylos your comrade had profaned
Her mysteries, would Demeter since have blest

---

    36 *Amyntos*] *rectius* Ameinias *younger brother of Æschylos: error repeated throughout the scene.*   40 (*To Æschylos.*)] *rightly om. 1876.*   56 since] *in errata 1863, not in text 1863, 1876.*

THE TRIAL OF ÆSCHYLOS

Your fields with what we call the staff of life,
To give ye strength and courage to protect
Your country, wives, and friends.
                    Ye want him not,
But ye may miss him in the hour of need.   60
If irreligious wretch hath violated
What all hold sacred, Æschylos not least,
To death condemn him.
                    Weep not thou, whoe'er
Thou art, nor stamp thou other, no, nor shout,
Impatient men! impatient as for battle.
If there be any here who deem him guilty,
To death condemn him, or to worse than death,
Drive him from Athens, bid him raise no more
Your hearts and souls, for he no more can fight
To save our country, nor call heroes down   70
To stand before ye, not more brave than he,
Alas! alas! nor more unfortunate.
  Citizen. Truth, by the Gods! thou speakest.
  Judge.   Speak ye too,
Judges who sit beside me.
  Judges.   Thou art absolved
By all the people; we confirm the voice.
Æschylos, go in peace.
  Citizen.   In glory go.
Are there no clarions nigh, to waft him home
With their strong blast? no harp to ring before?
  Another Citizen. No olive? none there had been but for him
In all this land.
  Another Citizen. At least we can raise up   80
Our voices to the hymn they have begun,
And call our children to come forth and kiss
The threshold that our Æschylos hath crost.*

* The trial of Æschylos for ἀσέβεια is said to have taken place 468 B.C., after his defeat
by Sophocles in a tragic contest. [W.]

[18]

DAMOCLES AND HIERA

[Published in 1863; reprinted 1876.]

  Hiera. A kiss, indeed! was ever boy so bold?
Who taught you such bad manners? Run away,
Or presently I may be very angry:

Stay; beg my pardon first. You look ashamed,
And shame becomes the guilty. Kiss, indeed!
Did ever maid or mortal hear the like!
How many summers have you seen above
Twelve at the most? I a whole twelvemonth more.
Learn to revere your elders in your youth.
 Damocles. Shake not my arm, it makes me feel so strange. 10
I do ask pardon, lovely Hiera.
 Hiera. Gods give me power to grant it! I am weak
From such a sudden and severe a blow.
 Damocles. I am not; though I should be: 'twas so wrong.
 Hiera. The Gods take pity on the penitent.
 Damocles. Do maidens never? can they do amiss
In doing what the Gods do?
 Hiera.   You perplex me;
To question so the deeds of those above
Is impious.
 Damocles. I would pray, but first to you,
For you are like them in all other things, 20
Why not in this?
 Hiera.   You talk beyond your years:
Only rude men talk so.
 Damocles.   Give but one sign
Of pardon.
 Hiera. And what sign?
 Damocles.   Dare I repeat
What I implored?
 Hiera.   What was it? I forget.
 Damocles. One kiss; I ask but one.
 Hiera.   You foolish boy!
Well: take it: I don't give it, mind you that.

[EPILOGUE.]

He gave the one; she added twenty more
For his obedience; and he never sued
After that eventide.
    A swain averr'd
That he descried in the deep wood a cheek 30
At first aslant, then lower, then eclipst.
Another said it was not in the wood,
But in the grotto near the water-fall,
And he alone had seen it.
    The dispute
Ran high; a third declared that both were wrong.

19

A MODERN GREEK IDYL

[Published in *The Athenæum*, April 22, 1854; reprinted by Thomas J. Wise for private circulation, 1917. See notes at end of volume.]

[INTRODUCTION.]

In the *Household Words*, a publication which I think will have imparted more of pure pleasure and of useful knowledge than any since the invention of letters, I find the rudiments of a story on which this Idyl is founded. [L.]

Mother, Gregorios, Nikolaos, Demetrios.

Mother. Moping for ever, in the house or out,
I hate the sight of thee, but gladly go
To see thee station'd in a fitter place,
Among yon rocks and brambles, with wild beasts.
    Gregorios. Mother! sweet mother! what hath Mitri done
That he should leave us, leave his home and friends,
And never visit more his father's grave?
    Mother. Silence! Gregorios! Thou rebellest too?
    Gregorios. Speak, Nikolaos! none can hear unmoved
Thy thrilling voice or cross thy winning way.   10
    Nikolaos. O let my tears . .
    Mother.   Child! girl! and tears for *him?*
Knuckling thy knees too? Seest a saint? thou fool!
    Nikolaos. In a son's eyes a mother is a saint,
And saints, O mother! saints are merciful.
    Mother. Shame, shame upon thee! this is blasphemy.
I have been alway, mother, wife, or maid,
A just and virtuous woman, yet no saint.
Hereafter . . maybe . . ah! 'twere sin to say . .
I never hoped it, never thought it I . .
Humility is all I have to boast.   20
    Nikolaos to Demetrios. I can not leave thee mid such tangled brakes,
Such wolf-like haunts, such pining solitudes,
As those before us: he will tend our mother.
    Demetrios. Enter not this dark gorge: here let us part
Where there is sunshine.
                Kind it is in you,
My brothers (but ye always have been kind)
To come so far: we might have said farewell
At the house-door.
             'Tis kinder stil in you,
O mother, who had never come one step
With me these many years, nor spoken word   30

Of gentleness, but wisht me far away.
Ah! far is he away who never sees
A parent's face, nor hopes to see it more.
  Gregorios. Hearest thou? hearest thou thro those thick sobs
The struggling voice in manly pangs emmewed?
Recall him . . there is time, swift as he goes.
  Nikolaos. Recall him, and beyond the lonely porch.
  Mother. He chose it for himself in sun or snow;
He chooses now . . may he enjoy . . the woods.
  Demetrios. Woods, mountains, oceans, separate not hearts;   40
One word, one look, one waft of kindred hand,
One moment's silence in reply, divides
What would cling close, cling ever. But, alas,
When the strong ivy hath been stript away,
And traild along the ground, and trampled on,
How shall it ever climb the wall again?
  Mother! I must have given you much grief
For you to give me what I suffer now.
Mother! we part for ever; may both griefs
Be mine alone henceforth, all mine, all mine,   50
Even to the bitterest dregs that choak the soul
Faint with long suffering.
                  Brothers! ye have loved
Your Mitri; ye have fondled him and cheer'd
In childhood; and it made you feel like men,
When Laos was not stronger much than I.
  Nikolaos. God ever strengthens the protecting arm
And blesses him who rears it o'er the weak.
  Demetrios. Until this day our worst of angry words
Were when we played, and one in play excel'd.
  Gregorios. Ay, then the two held down the conqueror   60
Struggling with kisses til he could escape.
  Demetrios. I have borne all but this: this who can bear
With tearless eyes? tears never fell from mine
Before a second til this saddest hour.
Farewell, my brothers! Think of me sometimes:
Cherish our mother: she will want your aid
When age comes on, which will not come on me
Ever, nor soon on you.
              She looks less stern
On him she loved too little: his warm love
Burst forth perennial over stony ground,   70
And could not wake one blossom from a plant

A MODERN GREEK IDYL

That grew so nigh . . . Yet burst for ever forth
Such wayward love.
                 O mother! doth my sight
Deceive me? do my hopes? or lookest thou
With kindlier look at parting? 'Tis enough:
I could have wisht for more some years ago,
But frowns reproved those wishes; they would rise
Day after day . . day after day cast down.
    Mother. Faintness comes over me. My sons! turn back;
Leave me among these rocks . . but take *him* home.   80
My knees are gone from under me; my sight
Is taken from me, never to return.
Where are ye all? where my Demetrios?
The earth reels round . . Oh! is he safe? is *he?*
    Demetrios. Rise, mother! mother, rise! look up, look up;
Thou hast three children now. We will all strive
Which most shall love thee.
    Mother.   Pardon, gracious God!
The worst of sins, the severance of a bond
Drawn by thy own right-hand across the breast
Of every mother. God! most merciful!   90
Even me thou pardonest . . I feel, I feel
Thy bond restored.
    Demetrios.   O brothers! this one morn
Yield me the place I coveted so long.
Mother! while thou couldst guide my steps thou didst;
Come, let me now, fond as of old, guide thine.

Chorus of maidens to Demetrios at home.

We sing the song we could not sing,
    Demetri! when you went away;
On breaking hearts the coild-up string,
    Heavy with tears, in darkness lay;
Its lyre, that long had ceast to ring,   100
    Sob'd only what despair would say.
Turn! turn . . no . . round thy mother cling . .
    O gloomiest morn! O brightest day!
                   WALTER SAVAGE LANDOR.

DRAMAS AND DRAMATIC SCENES

PYTHAGORAS AND A PRIEST OF ISIS

[Published by Forster in 1869; reprinted 1876.]

Pythagoras. Thou hast inquired of me, and thou hast heard
All I could tell thee of our Deities;
With patience bear me yet awhile, nor deem me
Irreverent, if I ask to know of yours
Which are around me on these sacred walls.
  Priest. Willingly granted; hesitate no more;
Speak.
  Pythagoras. Yonder is an ape, and there a dog,
And there a cat.
  Priest.   Think not we worship these,
But, what is holier even than worshipping,
Gratitude, mindful thro' obscuring years,   10
Urgeth us to look up to them.
                          O guest!
Now tell me what indweller of a town
But shares his substance, nor unwillingly,
With his protectress from invader mouse;
What child but fondles her and is carest;
What aged dame but sees her likeness there
More strikingly than in her dearest child?
  Now to another of these images.
None are such friends as dogs; they never leave
The side of those who only stroke the head   20
Or speak a kindly word to them.
  Pythagoras.   'Tis true.
But may I ask of thee without offence,
What good do apes to any, young or old,
What service render they, what fondness show?
Thou smilest; I rejoice to see that smile.
I wish all teachers could bear questioning
So quietly. Religious men bear least.
  Priest. Pythagoras, they rightly call thee wise,
Yet, like thy countrymen, thou knowest not
Thy origin and theirs, and all on earth.   30
Some of you think, nor quite absurdly so,
That, when the deluge drown'd all creatures else,
One only woman was there left alive,
And she took up two stones and cast behind

Her back those two, whence men and women sprang.
Scraps of the stones seem clinging to the heart
Of that primordial pair.
               We priests of Isis
Acknowledge duly our progenitor,
Whose moral features still remain unchanged
In many, thro' all times.
             Did ever ape,   40
As kindred nations have been doing since,
Tear limb from limb the brother, grin to see
His native bush and his blue babes enwrapt
In flames about the crib for winding-sheet?
  There live in other lands, from ours remote,
The intolerant and ferocious who insist
That all shall worship what themselves indite;
We never urge this stiff conformity.
Forms ever present are our monitors,
Nor need they flesh and blood, nor spill they any.   50
We leave each man his choice, the pictured plank
Or hammer'd block, nor quarrel over ours.

[21]

ENDYMION AND SELENE

(An old discontented love-affair.)

[Published by Forster in 1869; reprinted 1876.]

  Selene. Endymion! sleepest thou, with heels upright
And listless arms athwart a vacant breast?
Endymion! thou art drowsier than thy sheep,
And heedest me as now thou heedest them.
I come to visit thee, and leave a home
Where all is cheerful, and I find a face
If not averted, yet almost as bad.
Rise; none are here to steal away thy reeds.
  Endymion. Thou art immortal; mortal is Endymion,
Nor sleeping but thro' weariness and pain.   10
  Selene. What pains thee?
  Endymion.   Love, the bitterest of pains.
  Selene. Hast thou not mine? ungrateful?
  Endymion.   Thine I have,
O how less warm than what a shepherdess
Gives to a shepherd!

Selene.   Cease thy plaint, rash boy;
I give no warmer to the Blest above,
Yet even the brightest every day pursues
My path, and often listens to my praise,
And takes up his own harp and aids the song.
Few are the youths whose finger never trill'd
An early oat or later lyre for me.   20
Haply thou too, Endymion, shalt be sung
Afar from Latmos if thou meritest,
Nor thy name sever'd, as 'tis here, from mine.
Silence is sweeter at the present hour
Than voice or pipe, or sleep; so pay my due
Ere Morn come on, for Morn is apt to blush
When she sees kisses; let her not see ours.

HELLENICS

PART I: POEMS COLLECTED IN 1846

THE HAMADRYAD

[Published in *The Foreign Quarterly Review*, October, 1842; reprinted 1846, 1847, 1859, 1876. See notes at end of volume. Text 1842.]

Rhaicos was born amid the hills wherefrom
Gnidos the light of Caria is discern'd,
And small are the white-crested that play near
And smaller onward are the purple waves.
Thence festal choirs were visible, all crown'd
With rose and myrtle if they were inborn;
If from Pandion sprang they, on the coast
Where stern Athenè raised her citadel,
Then olive was intwined with violets
Cluster'd in bosses, regular and large.   10
For various men wore various coronals;
But one was their devotion: 'twas to her
Whose laws all follow, her whose smile withdraws
The sword from Ares, thunderbolt from Zeus,
And whom in his chill caves the mutable
Of mind, Poseidon, the sea-king, reveres,
And whom his brother, stubborn Dis, hath pray'd
To turn in pity the averted cheek
Of her he bore away; with promises,
Nay, with loud oath before dread Styx itself,   20
To give her daily more and sweeter flowers
Than he made drop from her on Enna's dell.
   Rhaicos was looking from his father's door
At the long trains that hasten'd to the town
From all the valleys, like bright rivulets
Gurgling with gladness, wave outrunning wave,
And thought it hard he might not also go
And offer up one prayer, and press one hand,
He knew not whose. The father call'd him in,
And said, "Son Rhaicos! those are idle games;   30
Long enough I have lived to find them so."
And, ere he ended, sigh'd; as old men do
Always, to think how idle such games are.

9 intwined] entwined *1847*.   32 ere . . . sigh'd;] here he ended, sighing . *.1847*.

' I have not yet," thought Rhaicos in his heart,
And wanted proof.
                    "Suppose thou go and help
Echion at the hill, to bark yon oak
And lop its branches off, before we delve
About the trunk and ply the root with axe:
This we may do in winter."
                    Rhaicos went;
For thence he could see farther, and see more   40
Of those who hurried to the city-gate.
Echion he found there, with naked arm
Swart-hair'd, strong sinew'd, and his eyes intent
Upon the place where first the axe should fall:
He held it upright. "There are bees about,
Or wasps, or hornets," said the cautious eld,
"Look sharp, O son of Thallinos!" The youth
Inclined his ear, afar, and warily,
And cavern'd in his hand. He heard a buzz
At first, and then the sound grew soft and clear,   50
And then divided into what seem'd tune,
And there were words upon it, plaintive words.
He turn'd, and said, "Echion! do not strike
That tree: it must be hollow; for some God
Speaks from within. Come thyself near." Again
Both turn'd toward it: and behold! there sat
Upon the moss below, with her two palms
Pressing it, on each side, a maid in form.
Downcast were her long eyelashes, and pale
Her cheek, but never mountain-ash display'd   60
Berries of colour like her lip so pure,
Nor were the anemonies about her hair
Soft, smooth, and wavering like the face beneath.

"What dost thou here?" Echion half-afraid,
Half-angry, cried. She lifted up her eyes
But nothing spake she. Rhaicos drew one step
Backward, for fear came likewise over him,
But not such fear: he panted, gaspt, drew in
His breath, and would have turned it into words,
But could not into one.
                    "O send away   70
That sad old man!" said she. The old man went

34 yet,] *so in 1846, 1859*; yet *1847*; yet. *misp. 1842 is now corrected.*   36, 42 53,
64 Echion] Echeion *1859.*   62 anemonies] anemones *1846–1859.*

284

THE HAMADRYAD

Without a warning from his master's son,
Glad to escape, for sorely he now fear'd,
And the axe shone behind him in their eyes.

 Hamadryad. And wouldst thou too shed the most innocent
Of blood? no vow demands it; no God wills
The oak to bleed.
 Rhaicos.   Who art thou? whence? why here?
And whither wouldst thou go? Among the robed
In white, or saffron, or the hue that most
Resembles dawn, or the clear sky, is none   80
Array'd as thou art. What so beautiful
As that gray robe which clings about thee close,
Like moss to stones adhering, leaves to trees,
Yet lets thy bosom rise and fall in turn,
As, toucht by zephyrs, fall and rise the boughs
Of graceful platan by the river-side.
 Hamadryad. Lovest thou well thy father's house?
 Rhaicos.   Indeed
I love it, well I love it, yet would leave
For thine, where'er it be, my father's house,
With all the marks upon the door, that show   90
My growth at every birth-day since the third,
And all the charms, o'erpowering evil eyes,
My mother nail'd for me against my bed,
And the Cydonian bow (which thou shalt see)
Won in my race last spring from Eutychus.
 Hamadryad. Bethink thee what it is to leave a home
Thou never yet hast left, one night, one day.
 Rhaicos. No, 'tis not hard to leave it; 'tis not hard
To leave, O maiden, that paternal home,
If there be one on earth whom we may love   100
First, last, for ever; one who says that she
Will love for ever too. To say which word,
Only to say it, surely is enough:
It shows such kindness! If 'twere possible,
We, at the moment, think she would indeed.
 Hamadryad. Who taught thee all this folly at thy age?
 Rhaicos. I have seen lovers, and have learnt to love.
 Hamadryad. But wilt thou spare the tree?
 Rhaicos.   My father wants
The bark; the tree may hold its place awhile.

  95 Eutychus] Eutychos *1846–1859.*

Hamadryad. Awhile! thy father numbers then my days!   110
Rhaicos. Are there no others where the moss beneath
Is quite as tufty? Who would send thee forth
Or ask thee why thou tarriest? Is thy flock
Anywhere near?
    Hamadryad.   I have no flock: I kill
Nothing that breathes, that stirs, that feels the air,
The sun, the dew. Why should the beautiful
(And thou art beautiful) disturb the source
Whence springs all beauty? Hast thou never heard
Of Hamadryads?
    Rhaicos.   Heard of them I have:
Tell me some tale about them. May I sit   120
Beside thy feet? Art thou not tired? The herbs
Are very soft; I will not come too nigh;
Do but sit there, nor tremble so, nor doubt.
Stay, stay an instant: let me first explore
If any acorn of last year be left
Within it; thy thin robe too ill protects
Thy dainty limbs against the harm one small
Acorn may do. Here 's none. Another day
Trust me: till then let me sit opposite.
    Hamadryad. I seat me; be thou seated, and content.   130
    Rhaicos. O sight for gods! Ye men below! adore
The Aphroditè. *Is* she there below?
Or sits she here before me? as she sate
Before the shepherd on those heights that shade
The Hellespont, and brought his kindred woe.
    Hamadryad. Reverence the higher Powers; nor deem amiss
Of her who pleads to thee, and would repay . .
Ask not how much . . but very much. Rise not:
No, Rhaicos, no! Without the nuptial vow
Love is unholy. Swear to me that none   140
Of mortal maids shall ever taste thy kiss,
Then take thou mine; then take it, not before.
    Rhaicos. Hearken, all gods above! O Aphrodite!
O Herè! let my vow be ratified!
But wilt thou come into my father's house?
    Hamadryad. Nay: and of mine I cannot give thee part.
    Rhaicos. Where is it?
    Hamadryad.   In this oak.

110 Awhile! . . . days!] Awhile ? . . . days ? *1847.*   129 till] til *1859.*   134 heights] hights. *1846,* highth *1859.*   135 Hellespont] *misprinted* Hellespent *1859.*

286

THE HAMADRYAD

Rhaicos.   Ay; now begins
The tale of Hamadryad: tell it through.
   Hamadryad. Pray of thy father never to cut down
My tree; and promise him, as well thou mayst,   150
That every year he shall receive from me
More honey than will buy him nine fat sheep,
More wax than he will burn to all the gods!
Why fallest thou upon thy face? Some thorn
May scratch it, rash young man! Rise up; for shame!
   Rhaicos. For shame I cannot rise. Oh, pity me!
I dare not sue for love . . but do not hate!
Let me once more behold thee . . not once more,
But many days: let me love on . . unloved!
I aim'd too high: on my own head the bolt   160
Falls back, and pierces to the very brain.
   Hamadryad. Go . . rather go, than make me say I love.
   Rhaicos. If happiness is immortality,
(And whence enjoy it else the gods above?)
I am immortal too: my vow is heard:
Hark! on the left . . Nay, turn not from me now,
I claim my kiss.
   Hamadryad.   Do men take first, then claim?
Do thus the seasons run their course with them?

   Her lips were seal'd; her head sank on his breast.
'Tis said that laughs were heard within the wood: 170
But who should hear them? and whose laughs? and why?
   Savoury was the smell, and long past noon,
Thallinos! in thy house; for marjoram,
Basil and mint and thyme and rosemary,
Were sprinkled on the kid's well-roasted length,
Awaiting Rhaicos. Home he came at last,
Not hungry, but pretending hunger keen,
With head and eyes just o'er the maple plate.
"Thou seest but badly, coming from the sun,
Boy Rhaicos!" said the father. "That oak's bark   180
Must have been tough, with little sap between;
It ought to run; but it and I are old."
Rhaicos, although each morsel of the bread
Increast by chewing, and the meat grew cold
And tasteless to his palate, took a draught
Of gold-bright wine, which, thirsty as he was,

156 cannot] can not *1847*.

287

He thought not of until his father fill'd
The cup, averring water was amiss,
But wine had been at all times pour'd on kid,
It was religion.
        He thus fortified,   190
Said, not quite boldly, and not quite abasht,
"Father, that oak is Jove's own tree: that oak
Year after year will bring thee wealth from wax
And honey. There is one who fears the gods
And the gods love . . that one
                  (He blusht, nor said
What one)
        "has promised this, and may do more.
Thou hast not many moons to wait until
The bees have done their best: if then there come
Nor wax nor honey, let the tree be hewn."
    "Zeus hath bestow'd on thee a prudent mind,"   200
Said the glad sire: "but look thou often there,
And gather all the honey thou canst find
In every crevice, over and above
What has been promist; would they reckon that?"

    Rhaicos went daily; but the nymph was oft
Invisible. To play at love, she knew,
Stopping its breathings when it breathes most soft,
Is sweeter than to play on any pipe.
She play'd on his: she fed upon his sighs:
They pleased her when they gently waved her hair,   210
Cooling the pulses of her purple veins,
And when her absence brought them out they pleased.
Even among the fondest of them all,
What mortal or immortal maid is more
Content with giving happiness than pain?
One day he was returning from the wood
Despondently. She pitied him, and said
"Come back!" and twined her fingers in the hem
Above his shoulder. Then she led his steps
To a cool rill that ran o'er level sand   220
Through lentisk and through oleander, there
Bathed she his feet, lifting them on her lap

    192 Jove's] Zeusis' *1859*.   196 has] Has *1846*; Hath *1859*.   196 promised]
promist *1846–1859*.   197 Thou hast not] We have not *1859*.   204 has] hath
1859.   205 but] and *1847*.   was] as *1846–1859*. *In all but the 1842 text the meaning
is utterly lost.* [W.]

THE HAMADRYAD

When bathed, and drying them in both her hands.
He dared complain; for those who most are loved
Most dare it; but not harsh was his complaint.
"O thou inconstant!" said he, "if stern law
Bind thee, or will, stronger than sternest law,
Oh, let me know henceforward when to hope
The fruit of love that grows for me but here."
He spake; and pluckt it from its pliant stem.   230
  Hamadryad. Impatient Rhaicos! why thus intercept
The answer I would give? There is a bee
Whom I have fed, a bee who knows my thoughts
And executes my wishes: I will send
That messenger. If ever thou art false,
Drawn by another, own it not, but drive
My bee away: then shall I know my fate,
And, for thou must be wretched, weep at thine.
But often as my heart persuades to lay
Its cares on thine and throb itself to rest,   240
Expect her with thee, whether it be morn
Or eve, at any time when woods are safe."

Day after day the Hours beheld them blest,
And season after season: years had past,
Blest were they still. He who asserts that Love
Ever is sated of sweet things, the same
Sweet things he fretted for in earlier days,
Never, by Zeus! loved he a Hamadryad.
  The nights had now grown longer, and perhaps
The Hamadryads find them lone and dull   250
Among their woods; one did, alas! She called
Her faithful bee: 'twas when all bees should sleep,
And all did sleep but hers. She was sent forth
To bring that light which never wintry blast
Blows out, nor rain nor snow extinguishes,
The light that shines from loving eyes upon
Eyes that love back until they see no more.

Rhaicos was sitting at his father's hearth:
Between them stood the table, not o'erspread
With fruits which autumn now profusely bore,   260
Nor anise cakes, nor odorous wine; but there
The draft-board was expanded; at which game

Between ll. 230–1 *Hamadryad* om. *1846–1859.*   235 messenger] messager *1847.*
257 until they see] till they can see *1846–1859.*   259 o'erspread] o'erspred *1847.*

Triumphant sat old Thallinos: the son
Was puzzled, vext, discomfited, distraught.
A buzz was at his ear: up went his hand,
And it was heard no longer. The poor bee
Return'd (but not until the morn shone bright)
And found the Hamadryad with her head
Upon her aching wrist, and showed one wing
Half-broken off, the other's meshes marr'd,   270
And there were bruises which no eye could see
Saving a Hamadryad's.
                At this sight
Down fell the languid brow, both hands fell down,
A shriek was carried to the ancient hall
Of Thallinos: he heard it not: his son
Heard it, and ran forthwith into the wood.
No bark was on the tree, no leaf was green,
The trunk was riven through. From that day forth
Nor word nor whisper soothed his ear, nor sound
Even of insect wing: but loud laments   280
The woodmen and the shepherds one long year
Heard day and night; for Rhaicos would not quit
The solitary place, but moan'd and died.
Hence milk and honey wonder not, O guest,
To find set duly on the hollow stone.

THE PRAYER OF THE BEES FOR ALCIPHRON

BY WALTER SAVAGE LANDOR.

[Published in *Hood's Magazine*, April, 1845; reprinted 1846, 1859. See note at end of volume. Text 1845.]

There was a spinner in the days of old,
        So proud, so bold,
She thought it neither shame nor sin
To challenge Pallas to come down and spin.
The goddess won, and forc'd the crone to hide her
Ugly old head, and shrink into a spider.

The bees were frighten'd, for they knew
Within their prudent breasts that few
        Had so much skill as they;
And she who gave the olive might   10
Be angry, if they show'd that light
        As pure and bright
Could shine on mortals any other way.

        Title The prayer ... for] Prayer ... to *1846, 1859.*

PRAYER OF THE BEES FOR ALCIPHRON

So not a syllable said they of wax,
But cover'd it with honey, lest a tax
   Be laid upon it by the Powers above.
Another goddess, no less mighty
Than Pallas, men call Aphroditè,
   The queen of love.

Honey she likes and all things sweet,   20
   And, when she came among the swarms,
They said, "O thou whence love hath all its charms!
   Grant him who saved us what we now entreat.

     "'Tis one whom we
     Are used to see
Among our thyme and ivy flowers
Throughout the matin and the vesper hours,
   Fonder of silence than of talk:
Yet him we heard one morning say,
   'Gardener! do not sweep away   30
   The citron blossoms from the gravel-walk:
   It might disturb or wound my bees;
   So lay aside that besom, if you please.'
"He for whose weal we supplicate is one
Thou haply mayst remember, Alciphron.
We know that Pallas has look'd down
Sometimes on him without a frown,
Yet must confess we're less afraid
Of you than that Hymettian maid.
Give him, O goddess, we implore,   40
Not honey (we can that) but more.
We are poor bees, and cannot tell
If there be aught he loves as well;
But we do think we heard him say
There is—and something in your way.

"Our stories tell us, when your pretty child,
Who drives (they say) so many mortals wild,
Vexed one of our great-aunts until she stung,
     Away he flew, and wrung,
Stamping, his five loose fingers at the smart,   50
     You chided him, and took our part.
May the cross Year, fresh-wakened, blow sharp dust
Into their eyes who say thou art unjust."

42 cannot] can not *1846, 1859*.   48 Vexed] Vext 1846, 1859.

HELLENICS

THRASYMEDES AND EUNÖE

[Published in 1846; reprinted 1847, 1859, 1876.]

Who will away to Athens with me? who
Loves choral songs and maidens crown'd with flowers,
Unenvious? mount the pinnace; hoist the sail.
I promise ye, as many as are here,
Ye shall not, while ye tarry with me, taste
From unrinsed barrel the diluted wine
Of a low vineyard or a plant ill-pruned,
But such as anciently the Ægæan isles
Pour'd in libation at their solemn feasts:
And the same goblets shall ye grasp, embost   10
With no vile figures of loose languid boors,
But such as Gods have lived with, and have led.
　The sea smiles bright before us. What white sail
Plays yonder? what pursues it? Like two hawks
Away they fly. Let us away in time
To overtake them. Are they menaces
We hear? And shall the strong repulse the weak,
Enraged at her defender? Hippias!
Art thou the man? 'Twas Hippias. He had found
His sister borne from the Cecropian port   20
By Thrasymedes. And reluctantly?
Ask, ask the maiden; I have no reply.
　"Brother! O brother Hippias! O, if love,
If pity, ever toucht thy breast, forbear!
Strike not the brave, the gentle, the beloved,
My Thrasymedes, with his cloak alone
Protecting his own head and mine from harm."
"Didst thou not once before," cried Hippias,
Regardless of his sister, hoarse with wrath
At Thrasymedes, "didst not thou, dog-eyed,   30
Dare, as she walkt up to the Parthenon,
On the most holy of all holy days,
In sight of all the city, dare to kiss
Her maiden cheek?"
　　　　　　　　　"Ay, before all the Gods,
Ay, before Pallas, before Artemis,
Ay, before Aphrodite, before Hera,
I dared; and dare again. Arise, my spouse!

　　8 Ægæan] Ægean 1847.　　isles] iles 1859.　　36 Hera] Herè 1847.

THRASYMEDES AND EUNÖE

Arise! and let my lips quaff purity
From thy fair open brow."
                          The sword was up,
And yet he kist her twice. Some God withheld   40
The arm of Hippias; his proud blood seeth'd slower
And smote his breast less angrily; he laid
His hand on the white shoulder, and spake thus:
"Ye must return with me. A second time
Offended, will our sire Pisistratos
Pardon the affront? Thou shouldst have askt thyself
This question ere the sail first flapt the mast."
"Already thou hast taken life from me;
Put up thy sword," said the sad youth, his eyes
Sparkling; but whether love or rage or grief   50
They sparkled with, the Gods alone could see.
Piræos they re-entered, and their ship
Drove up the little waves against the quay,
Whence was thrown out a rope from one above,
And Hippias caught it. From the virgin's waist
Her lover dropt his arm, and blusht to think
He had retain'd it there in sight of rude
Irreverent men: he led her forth, nor spake;
Hippias walkt silent too, until they reacht
The mansion of Pisistratos her sire.   60
Serenely in his sternness did the prince
Look on them both awhile: they saw not him,
For both had cast their eyes upon the ground.
"Are these the pirates thou hast taken, son?'
Said he. "Worse, father! worse than pirates they,
Who thus abuse thy patience, thus abuse
Thy pardon, thus abuse the holy rites
Twice over."
              "Well hast thou performed thy duty,"
Firmly and gravely said Pisistratos.
"Nothing then, rash young man! could turn thy heart   70
From Eunöe, my daughter?"
                          "Nothing, sir,
Shall ever turn it. I can die but once
And love but once. O Eunöe! farewell!"
"Nay, she shall see what thou canst bear for her."
"O father! shut me in my chamber, shut me
In my poor mother's tomb, dead or alive,

45, 60, 69 Pisistratos] Peisistratos *1847*.   52 Piræos] Piræeus *1847*.

293

But never let me see what he can bear;
I know how much that is, when borne for me."
"Not yet: come on. And lag not thou behind,
Pirate of virgin and of princely hearts!80
Before the people and before the Goddess
Thou hadst evinced the madness of thy passion,
And now wouldst bear from home and plenteousness,
To poverty and exile, this my child."
Then shuddered Thrasymedes, and exclaim'd,
"I see my crime; I saw it not before.
The daughter of Pisistratos was born
Neither for exile nor for poverty,
Ah! nor for me!" He would have wept, but one
Might see him, and weep worse. The prince unmoved90
Strode on, and said, "To-morrow shall the people,
All who beheld thy trespasses, behold
The justice of Pisistratos, the love
He bears his daughter, and the reverence
In which he holds the highest law of God."
He spake; and on the morrow they were one.

ICARIOS AND ERIGONÈ

[Published in 1846; reprinted 1847, 1859, 1876.]

Improvident were once the Attic youths,
As (if we may believe the credulous
And testy) various youths have been elsewhere.
But truly such was their improvidence,
Ere Pallas in compassion was their guide,
They never stowed away the fruits of earth
For winter use; nor knew they how to press
Olive or grape: yet hospitality
Sate at the hearth, and there was mirth and song.
Wealthy and generous in the Attic land,10
Icarios! wert thou; and Erigonè,
Thy daughter, gave with hearty glee the milk,
Buzzing in froth beneath unsteady goat,
To many who stopt near her; some for thirst,
And some to see upon its back that hand
So white and small and taper, and await
Until she should arise and show her face.

13 unsteady] unsteddy *1847-1859*.87, 93 Pisistratos] Peisistratos *1847*.

ICARIOS AND ERIGONÈ

The father wisht her not to leave his house,
Nor she to leave her father; yet there sued
From all the country round both brave and rich.   20
Some, nor the wealthier of her wooers, drove
Full fifty slant-brow'd kingly-hearted swine,
Reluctant ever to be led aright,
Race autocratical, autochthon race,
Lords of the woods, fed by the tree of Jove.
Some had three ploughs; some had eight oxen; some
Had vines, on oak, on maple, and on elm,
In long and strait and gleamy avenues,
Which would have tired you had you reacht the end
Without the unshapen steps that led beyond   30
Up the steep hill to where they leaned on poles.
Yet kind the father was, and kind the maid.
And now when winter blew the chaff about,
And hens pursued the grain into the house,
Quarrelsome and indignant at repulse,
And rushing back again with ruffled neck,
They and their brood; and kids blinkt at the brand,
And bee-nosed oxen, with damp nostrils lowered
Against the threshold, stampt the dogs away;
Icarios, viewing these with thoughtful mind,   40
Said to Erigonè, "Not scantily
The Gods have given us these birds and these
Short-bleating kids, and these loose-hided steers.
The Gods have given: to them will we devote
A portion of their benefits, and bid
The youths who love and honour us partake:
So shall their hearts, and so shall ours, rejoice."
The youths were bidden to the feast: the flesh
Of kid and crested bird was plentiful:
The steam hung on the rafters, where were nail'd   50
Bushes of savory herbs, and figs and dates;
And yellow-pointed pears sent down long stalks
Through nets wide-mesht, work of Erigonè
When night was long and lamp yet unsupplied.
Choice grapes Icarios had; and these, alone
Of all men in the country, he preserved
For festive days; nor better day than this
To bring them from beneath his reed-thatcht roof.
He mounted the twelve stairs with hearty pride,

28 strait] straight 1847.

And soon was heard he, breathing hard: he now 60
Descended, holding in both arms a cask,
Fictile, capacious, bulging: cork-tree bark
Secured the treasure; wax above the mouth,
And pitch above the wax. The pitch he brake,
The wax he scraped away, and laid them by.
Wrenching up carefully the cork-tree bark,
A hum was heard. "What! are there bees within?"
Euphorbas cried. "They came then with the grapes,"
Replied the elder, and pour'd out clear juice
Fragrant as flowers, and wrinkled husks anon. 70
"The ghosts of grapes!" cried Phanor, fond of jokes
Within the house, but ever abstinent
Of such as that, in woodland and alone,
Where any sylvan God might overhear.
No few were sadden'd at the ill-omen'd word,
But sniffing the sweet odour, bent their heads,
Tasted, sipt, drank, ingurgitated: fear
Flew from them all, joy rusht to every breast,
Friendship grew warmer, hands were join'd, vows sworn.
Fom cups of every size, from cups two-ear'd, 80
From ivy-twisted and from smooth alike,
They dash the water; they pour in the wine;
(For wine it was,) until that hour unseen.
They emptied the whole cask; and they alone;
For both the father and the daughter sate
Enjoying their delight. But when they saw
Flusht faces, and when angry words arose
As one more fondly glanced against the cheek
Of the fair maiden on her seat apart,
And she lookt down, or lookt another way 90
Where other eyes caught hers, and did the like,
Sadly the sire, the daughter fearfully,
Upon each other fixt wide-open eyes.
This did the men remark, and, bearing signs
Different, as were their tempers, of the wine,
But feeling each the floor reel under him,
Each raging, with more thirst at every draught,
Acastor first (sidelong his step) arose,
Then Phanor, then Antyllos:
                              "Zeus above
Confound thee, cursed wretch!" aloud they cried, 100
"Is this thy hospitality? must all

ICARIOS AND ERIGONÈ

Who loved thy daughter perish at a blow?
Not at a blow, but like the flies and wasps."
Madness had seiz'd them all. Erigonè
Ran out for help: what help? Before her sprang
Mœra, and howl'd and barkt, and then return'd
Presaging. They had dragg'd the old man out
And murdered him. Again flew Mœra forth,
Faithful, compassionate, and seized her vest,
And drew her where the body lay, unclosed   110
The eyes, and rais'd toward the stars of heaven.

Raise thine, for thou hast heard enough, raise thine
And view Böotes bright among those stars,
Brighter the Virgin: Mœra too shines there.
But where were the Eumenides? Repress
Thy anger. If the clear calm stars above
Appease it not, and blood must flow for blood,
Listen, and hear the sequel of the tale.
Wide-seeing Zeus lookt down; as mortals knew
By the woods bending under his dark eye,   120
And huge towers shuddering on the mountain tops,
And stillness in the valley, in the wold,
And over the deep waters all round earth.
He lifted up his arm, but struck them not
In their abasement: by each other's blow
They fell; some suddenly; but more beneath
The desperate gasp of long-enduring wounds.

102 loved] love *1847*.   *Between ll.* 111–12 *1859 inserts*:
Thou who hast listened, and stil ponderest,
118 Listen] Harken *1859*.   121 mountain tops] mountain-top *1847*.

DRIMACOS

[Published in 1846; reprinted 1847, 1859, 1876.]

In Crete reign'd Zeus and Minos; and there sprang
From rocky Chios (but more years between)
Homer. Ah! who near Homer's side shall stand?
A slave, a slave shall stand near Homer's side.
Come from dark ages forth, come, Drimacos!
    O gems of Ocean, shining here and there
Upon his vest of ever-changeful green,
Richer are ye than wide-spread continents,

8 wide-spread] wide-spred *1847*.

Richer in thoughtful men and glorious deeds.
Drimacos was a slave; but Liberty
By him from Slavery sprang, as day from night.
Intolerable servitude o'erran
The isle of Chios. They whose sires had heard
The blind man, and the muse who sat beside,
Constant, as was the daughter to the king
Of Thebes, and comforting his sunless way,
Yea, even these bore stones within their breasts,
Buying by land or capturing by sea,
And torturing too limbs fashion'd like their own,
Limbs like the Gods' they all fell down before.
But Zeus had from Olympus lookt oblique,
Then breath'd into the breasts of suffering slaves
Heroic courage and heroic strength,
And wisdom for their guidance and support.
Drimacos he appointed to coerce
The pride of the enslaver, and to free
All those who laboured and were heavy-laden
With griefs, not even by the avenging Gods
Inflicted, wrongs which men alone inflict
On others, when their vices have scoopt out
A yoke far more opprobrious for themselves.
From field to field the clang of arms was heard;
Fires from the rocks and the hill-tops by night
Collected all the valiant, all the young,
Female and male, stripling and suckling babe,
By mother (then most fond) not left behind.
But many were o'ertaken; many dropt
Faint by the road; thirst, hunger, terror, seiz'd
Separate their prey. Among the fugitives,
In the most crowded and the narrowest path
That led into the thickets on the hill,
Was Amymonè with her infant boy,
Eiarinos. She pray'd the Gods, nor pray'd
Inaudible, although her voice had fail'd.
On Drimacos she called by name; he heard
The voice; he turn'd his head, and cried aloud:
"Comrades! take up yon infant from the arms
That sink with it; and help the mother on."
Far in advance was he; all urged amain;

15 daughter] *sc.* Antigone, daughter of Œdipus. [W.]   19 torturing . . . fashion'd]
torturing limbs fashioned *1847, 1859.*

DRIMACOS

All minded their own household, nor obey'd.   50
But he rusht back amid them till he reacht
The mother, who had fallen under-foot,
Trampled, but not relinquishing her hold.
Scarcely was space to stoop in, yet he stoopt
And rais'd what feebly wail'd among men's legs,
And placed it on his head, that the fresh air
Might solace it: soon it began to play,
To pat the hair of some, of some the eyes,
Unconscious that its mother's soul had fled.
The dust rose lower, for the sultry day   60
Was closing, and above shone Hesperus
Alone. On mossy banks within the brake
The men threw down their weapons snatcht in haste,
Impenetrable woods received their flight,
And shelter'd and conceal'd them from pursuit.
There many years they dwelt; nor only there,
But also in the plain and in the towns
Fought they, and overthrew the wealthier race,
And drove their cattle off and reapt their grain.
Drimacos, strong in justice, strong in arms,   70
Prompt, vigilant, was everywhere obey'd.
He proffer'd the proud Chiots, half-subdued,
Repression of invaders, in return
For their repression of invaders too,
And corn and wine and oil enough for all,
And horned victims to avenger Zeus.
But plenteousness and sloth relaxt his hold
Upon a few, men yearning to partake
The vices of a city: murmurs rose
And reacht the ear of Drimacos, and reacht   80
The wealthy towns and their impatient lords.
Rewards were offered for the leader's head,
And askt perhaps ere offered. When he found
Ingratitude so nigh and so alert,
He listened calmly to the chiefs around,
His firm defenders; then replied:
                                        "My friends!
Already in the days of youth ye watcht
Over the common-weal, but now your eyes
And mine too want repose. Fear not for me,
But guard yourselves. The Gods who placed me here   90

67 plain] plains *1847*.

Call *me* away, not you."

                        They heard, and went,
Sorrowing. Then called he unto him the youth
Eiarinos, who two whole years had fought
Beside him, and fought well.

                       "Eiarinos!
I may have saved thy life ('tis said I did),
In infancy: it now behoves me, boy,
To give thee substance such as parents give.
Alas! 'tis wanting: nought is in the house
Save arms, as thou well knowest; but those men
Who left me now, had talkt with thee before,   100
And there are marks along thy cheek which tears
Leave upon maidens' cheeks, not upon men's.
  Eiarinos spake not, but threw his arms
Around his guardian's neck and shook with grief.
"Thou shalt not be quite destitute, my son!"
Said he, "Thou knowest what reward awaits
Him who shall bring my head within the town.
Here! strike! let never traitor grasp the gold."
Forward he held the hilt and lowered his brow.
"Bequeathest thou to parricidal hand,   110
O father! that accursed gold?" cried he,
And ran against the portal, blind with tears.
But the calm man now caught his arm, and said,
"Delay may bring on both what comes for one.
Inevitable is my death: at least
Promise me this one thing, Eiarinos!
And I release thee: swear that, when I die,
Thou wilt, against all adversaries, bear
My head to those who seek it, pledge of peace."
Calmer, but sobbing deep, the youth replied,   120
"When Zeus the liberator shall appoint
The pastor of the people to depart,
His will be done! if such be his and thine."
He lowered his eyes in reverence to the earth;
And Drimacos then smote into his breast
The unaccepted sword. The pious youth
Fell overpowered with anguish, nor arose
Until the elders, who had gone, return'd.
They comforted the orphan, and implored
He would perform the duty thus enjoined.   130

            102 maidens'] maiden's *1847.*

DRIMACOS

Nor Muse, nor Memory her mother, knows
The sequel: but upon the highest peak
Of Chios is an altar of square stone
Roughened by time, and some believe they trace
In ancient letters, cubit-long, the words
Drimacos and *Eiarinos* and *Zeus*.

ENALLOS AND CYMODAMEIA

[Published in 1846; reprinted 1847, 1859, 1876.]

A vision came o'er three young men at once,
A vision of Apollo: each had heard
The same command; each followed it; all three
Assembled on one day before the God
In Lycia, where he gave his oracle.
Bright shone the morning; and the birds that build
Their nests beneath the column-heads of fanes
And eaves of humbler habitations, dropt
From under them and wheeled athwart the sky,
When, silently and reverently, the youths   10
Marcht side by side up the long steps that led
Toward the awful God who dwelt within.
Of those three youths fame hath held fast the name
Of one alone; nor would that name survive
Unless Love had sustain'd it, and blown off
With his impatient breath the mists of time.
"Ye come," the God said mildly, "of one will
To people what is desert in the isle
Of Lemnos. But strong men possess its shores;
Nor shall you execute the brave emprize   20
Unless, on the third day from going forth,
To him who rules the waters ye devote
A virgin, cast into the sea alive."
They heard, and lookt in one another's face,
And then bent piously before the shrine
With prayer and praises and thanksgiving hymn,
And, after a short silence, went away,
Taking each other's hand and swearing truth,
Then to the ship in which they came, return'd.
Two of the youths were joyous, one was sad;   30
Sad was Enallos; yet those two by none

18 isle] ile *1859.*   19 Lemnos] *mistake for* Lesbos. (*Colvin*).

Were loved; Enallos had already won
Cymodameia, and the torch was near.
By night, by day, in company, alone,
The image of the maiden fill'd his breast
To the heart's brim. Ah! therefore did that heart
So sink within him.
              They have sail'd; they reach
Their home again. Sires, matrons, maidens, throng
The plashing port, to watch the gather'd sail,
And who springs first and farthest upon shore.   40
Enallos came the latest from the deck.
Swift ran the rumour what the God had said,
And fearful were the maidens, who before
Had urged the sailing of the youths they loved,
That they might give their hands, and have their homes,
And nurse their children; and more thoughts perhaps
Led up to these, and even ran before.
But they persuaded easily their wooers
To sail without them, and return again
When they had seiz'd the virgin on the way.   50
Cymodameia dreamt three nights, the three
Before their fresh departure, that her own
Enallos had been cast into the deep,
And she had saved him. She alone embarkt
Of all the maidens, and unseen by all,
And hid herself before the break of day
Among the cloaks and fruits piled high aboard.
But when the noon was come, and the repast
Was call'd for, there they found her. Not quite stern,
But more than sad, Enallos lookt upon her.   60
Forebodings shook him: hopes rais'd *her*, and love
Warm'd the clear cheek while she wiped off the spray.
Kindly were all to her and dutiful;
And she slept soundly mid the leaves of figs
And vines, and far as far could be apart.
Now the third morn had risen, and the day
Was dark, and gusts of wind and hail and fogs
Perplext them: land they saw not yet, nor knew
Where land was lying. Sudden lightnings blaz'd,
Thunder-claps rattled round them. The pale crew   70
Howled for the victim. "Seize her, or we sink."

36 therefore] therefor *1859*.   59 her . . . stern,] her; and they call'd *1859*.
60 But . . . sad,] Enallos: when *1859*.   71 Howled] Howl'd *1847–1859*.

ENALLOS AND CYMODAMEIA

O maid of Pindus! I would linger here
To lave my eyelids at the nearest rill,
For thou hast made me weep, as oft thou hast,
Where thou and I, apart from living men,
And two or three crags higher, sate and sang.
Ah! must I, seeing ill my way, proceed?
And thy voice too, Cymodameia! thine
Comes back upon me, helpless as thyself
In this extremity. Sad words! sad words!   80
"O save me! save! Let me not die so young!
Loving you so! Let me not cease to see you?"
Thou claspedest the youth who would have died
To have done less than save thee. Thus he prayed.
"O God! who givest light to all the world,
Take not from me what makes that light most blessed!
Grant me, if 'tis forbidden me to save
This hapless helpless sea-devoted maid,
To share with her (and bring no curses up   90
From outraged Neptune) her appointed fate!"
They wrung her from his knee; they hurl'd her down
(Clinging in vain at the hard slippery pitch)
Into the whitening wave. But her long hair
Scarcely had risen up again, before
Another plunge was heard, another form
Clove the straight line of bubbling foam, direct
As ringdove after ringdove. Groans from all
Burst, for the roaring sea ingulpht them both.
Onward the vessel flew; the skies again
Shone bright, and thunder roll'd along, not wroth, 100
But gently murmuring to the white-wing'd sails.
Lemnos at close of evening was in sight.
The shore was won; the fields markt out; and roofs
Collected the dun wings that seek house-fare;
And presently the ruddy-bosom'd guest
Of winter, knew the doors: then infant cries
Were heard within; and lastly, tottering steps
Pattered along the image-stationed hall.
Ay, three full years had come and gone again,
And often, when the flame on windy nights 110

82 you ... you] thee ... thee *1859. For ll. 83-4 1859 substitutes:*
    Thus prayed Cymodameia.
        Thus prayed he.

92 pitch] pich *1859.*   96 straight] strait *1847, 1859.*

Suddenly flicker'd from the mountain-ash
Piled high, men pusht almost from under them
The bench on which they talkt about the dead.
Meanwhile beneficent Apollo saw
With his bright eyes into the sea's calm depth,
And there he saw Enallos, there he saw
Cymodameia. Gravely-gladsome light
Environed them with its eternal green:
And many nymphs sate round: one blew aloud
The spiral shell; one drew bright chords across   120
Shell-more expansive; tenderly a third
With cowering lip hung o'er the flute, and stopt
At will its dulcet sob, or waked to joy;
A fourth took up the lyre and pincht the strings,
Invisible by trembling: many rais'd
Clear voices. Thus they spent their happy hours.
I know them all; but all with eyes downcast,
Conscious of loving, have entreated me
I would not utter now their names above.
Behold, among these natives of the sea   130
There stands but one young man: how fair! how fond!
Ah! were he fond to *them!* It may not be!'
Yet did they tend him morn and eve; by night
They also watcht his slumbers: then they heard
His sighs, nor his alone; for there were two
To whom the watch was hateful. In despair
Upward he rais'd his arms, and thus he prayed,
"O Phœbus! on the higher world alone
Showerest thou all thy blessings? Great indeed
Hath been thy favour to me, great to her;   140
But she pines inly, and calls beautiful
More than herself the Nymphs she sees around,
And asks me 'Are they not more beautiful?'
Be all more beautiful, be all more blest,
But not with me! Release her from the sight;
Restore her to a happier home, and dry
With thy pure beams, above, her bitter tears!"
   She saw him in the action of his prayer,
Troubled, and ran to soothe him. From the ground,
Ere she had claspt his neck, her feet were borne.   150
He caught her robe; and its white radiance rose
Rapidly, all day long, through the green sea.
Enallos loost not from that robe his grasp,

ENALLOS AND CYMODAMEIA

But spann'd one ancle too. The swift ascent
Had stunn'd them into slumber, sweet, serene,
Invigorating her, nor letting loose
The lover's arm below; albeit at last
It closed those eyes intensely fixt thereon,
And still as fixt in dreaming. Both were cast
Upon an island till'd by peaceful men,   160
And few (no port nor road accessible)
Fruitful and green as the abode they left,
And warm with summer, warm with love and song.
'Tis said that some, whom most Apollo loves,
Have seen that island, guided by his light;
And others have gone near it, but a fog
Rose up between them and the lofty rocks;
Yet they relate they saw it quite as well,
And shepherd-boys and credulous hinds believe.

159 still] stil *1847, 1859.*   160, 165 island] iland *1859.*   169 credulous]
pious *1859.*

THERON AND ZOE

[Published 1846; reprinted 1847, 1859, 1876.]

Zoe. Changed? very true, O Theron, I am changed.
Theron. It would at least have been as merciful
To hold a moment back from me the briar
You let recoil thus sharply on my breast.
Not long ago, not very long, you own'd
With maiden blushes, which became your brow
Better than corn-flower, or that periwinkle
Trained round it by a very careful hand,
A long while trimming it (no doubt) and proud
Of making its blue blossom laugh at me.   10
Zoe. I could laugh too. What did I own? It seems
(It was so little) you have quite forgot.
Theron. That, since we sate together day by day,
And walkt together, sang together, none
Of earliest, gentlest, fondest, maiden friends
Loved you as formerly. If one remained
Dearer to you than any of the rest,
You could not wish her greater happiness . .
Zoe. Than what?
Theron.   I think you never could have said it . .
I must have dreamt it . .
Zoe. ˙   Tell me then your dream.   20

Theron. I thought you said . . nay, I will swear you said . .
More than one heard it . . that you could not wish
The nearest to your heart more perfect joy
Than Theron's love.
    Zoe.   Did I?
    Theron.   The Gods in heaven
Are witnesses, no less than woodland Gods,
That you did say it. O how changed! no word,
No look, for Theron now!
    Zoe.   Girls often say
More than they mean: men always do.
    Theron.   By Pan!
Who punishes with restless nights the false,
Hurling the sleeper down the precipice   30
Into the roaring gulph, or letting loose
Hounds, wolves, and tigers after him, his legs
Meanwhile tied not quite close, but just apart,
In withy bands . . by him I swear, my tongue,
Zoe! can never utter half my love.
Retract not one fond word.
    Zoe.   I must retract
The whole of those.
    Theron.   And leave me most unblest!
    Zoe. I know not.
    Theron.   Heed not, rather say. Farewell.
    Zoe. Farewell. I will not call you back again.
Go, Theron! hatred soon will sear your wound.   40
    Theron. Falsehood I hate: I can not hate the false.
    Zoe. Never? Then scorn her.
    Theron.   I can scorn myself,
And will; for others are preferr'd to me;
The untried to the tried.
    Zoe.   You said farewell.
    Theron. Again I say it.
    Zoe.   Now I can believe
That you, repeating it, indeed are gone.
Yet seem you standing where you stood before.
Hath Pan done this? Pan, who doth such strange things.
    Theron. Laugh me to scorn: derision I deserve:
But let that smile . . O let it be less sweet!   50
Sorrowful let me part, but not insane.
    Zoe. I know some words that charm insanity
Before it can take hold.

THERON AND ZOE

Theron.   Speak them; for now
Are they most wanted.
   Zoe.   I did say, 'tis true,
If on this solid earth friend dear enough
Remain'd to me, that Theron is the youth
I would desire to bless her.
   Theron.   To avoid
My importunity; to hear no more
The broken words that spoilt our mutual song,
The sobs that choakt my flute, the humidity   60
(Not from the lip) that gurgled on the stops.
   Zoe. I would avoid them all; they troubled me.
   Theron. Now then, farewell.
   Zoe.   I will do all the harm
I can to any girl who hopes to love you;
Nor shall you have her.
   Theron.   Vain and idle threat!
   Zoe. So, Theron! you would love then once again?
   Theron. Never; were love as possible and easy . . .
   Zoe. As what?
   Theron.   As death.
   Zoe.   O Theron! once indeed
I said the words which then so flatter'd you,
And now so pain you. Long before my friends   70
Left me through envy of your fondness for me,
No, not the dearest of them could I bear
To see beloved by you. False words I spake,
Not knowing then how false they were.
   Theron.   Speak now
One that shall drown them all.
   Zoe.   My voice is gone.
Why did you kiss me, if you wisht to hear it?

DAMÆTAS AND IDA

[Published in 1846; reprinted with variants 1858, and with minor variants 1859.
1876.]

Damætas is a boy as rude
As ever broke maid's solitude.
He watcht the little Ida going
Where the wood-raspberries were growing,

Title. Damætas] *(rectius* Damœtas) Damœtus *1858.* Ida] Phillis *1858.*   3 He ..
Ida] One morning he saw Phillis *1858.*   4 wood-raspberries] wild-raspberries *1858.*

And, under a pretence of fear
Lest they might scratch her arms, drew near,
And, plucking up a stiff grey bent,
The fruit (scarce touching it,) he sent
Into both hands: the form they took
Of a boat's keel upon a brook;
So not a raspberry fell down
To splash her foot or stain her gown.
When it was over, for his pains
She let his lips do off the stains
That were upon two fingers; he
At first kist two, and then kist three,
And, to be certain every stain
Had vanisht, kist them o'er again.
At last the boy, quite shameless, said
"See! I have taken out the red!
Now where there 's redder richer fruit
Pray, my sweet Ida, let me do't."
"Audacious creature!" she cried out,
"What in the world are you about?"
He had not taken off the red
All over; on both cheeks 'twas spread;
And the two lips that should be white
With fear, if not with fear, with spite
At such ill usage, never show'd
More comely, or more deeply glow'd.
Damætas fancied he could move
The girl to listen to his love:
Not he indeed.

> *Damætas.*   For pity's sake!
> *Ida.*   Go; never more come nigh this brake.
> *Damætas.* Must I, why must I, press in vain?

    10

    20

    30

12 splash . . . stain] balk her aim or splash *1858.*   *For ll.* 15–16 *1858 substitutes:*
         And lookt down on his head while he
         First kist two fingers, then kist three.
20 See . . . have] I have here *1858.*   21 redder] riper *1858.*   22 my sweet Ida]
gentle Phillis *1858.*   25 off] out *1858.*   26 over; on both] over both her *1858.*
spread] spred *1858–1859.*   27 the two] both her *1858.*   31 Damætas]
Damœtus *1858.*   *For ll.* 33–42 *1858 substitutes six lines:*
         Not he.
                 She said, "For pity's sake,
       Go; never more come near this brake.
       The boldest thing I ever knew,
       Impudent boy! was done by you;
       And when you are a little older,
       By Dian! you may do a bolder."

DAMÆTAS AND IDA

Ida. Because I hate you.
   Damætas.   Think again!
Think better of it, cruel maid!
   Ida. Well then . . because I am afraid.
   Damætas. Look round us: nobody is near.
   Ida. All the more reason for my fear.   40
   Damætas. Hatred is overcome by you,
And Fear can be no match for two.

LYSANDER, ALCANOR, PHANÖE

[Published in 1846; reprinted 1847, 1859, 1876.]

   Lysander. Art thou grown hoarse by sitting in the sun
Of early spring, when winds come down adrift
To punish them they find asleep at noon?
   Alcanor. Hoarse I am not, but I am tired of song,
Therefore do I retire, where, without pipe,
The goat-foot God brought all the nymphs to sit
Half-way up Mænalos. If she I love
Will follow me, I swear to thee by him,
Bitter to those who slight him or forswear,
Thou shalt hear something sweet, do thou but stay.   10
   Lysander. Lysander well can stay, do thou but sing.
   Alcanor. But not unless a Nymph or Nymph-like maid
Will listen.
   Lysander. Here comes Phanöe. Thou art pale.
Sing: Phanöe! bid him sing.
   Phanöe.   By Artemis!
I bade him never more repeat my name,
And if he disobeys me . . .
   Lysander.   Hush! 'twere ill
To call down vengeance upon those who love:
And he hath sworn by Pan that he will sing
If thou wilt follow him up Mænalos.
   Phanöe. He may snatch off my slipper while I kneel   20
To Pan, upon the stone so worn aslant
That it is difficult to kneel upon
Without my leaving half a slipper loose.
Little cares he for Pan: he scarcely fears
That other, powerfuller and terribler,
To whom more crowns are offered than to Zeus,

Title 1859 has and Phanöe.

309

HELLENICS

Or any God beside, and oftener changed.
In spring we garland him with pointed flowers,
Anemone and crocus and jonquil,
And tender hyacinth in clustering curls;
Then with sweet-breathing mountain strawberry;
Then pear and apple blossom, promising
(If he is good) to bring the fruit full-ripe,
Hanging it round about his brow, his nose,
Down even to his lips. When autumn comes,
His russet vine-wreath crackles under grapes:
Some trim his neck with barley, wheat, and oat;
Some twine his naked waist with them: and last
His reverend head is seen and worshipt through
Stiff narrow olive-leaves, that last till spring.
Say, ought I not to fear so wild a boy,
Who fears not even *him!* but once has tried
By force to make me pat him, after prayers?
How fierce then lookt the God! and from above
How the club reddened, as athirst for blood!
Yet, fearing and suspecting the audacious,
Up Mænalos I must, for there my herd
Is browsing on the thorn and citisus
At random.
    Lysander. He hath not endured thy frown,
But hurries off.
    Phanöe.   And let him.
    Lysander.   Captious Pan
On one or other may look evil-eyed.
    Phanöe. I mind my Goddess, let him mind his God.

. . Away she went, and as she went she sang.
Brief cries were heard ere long, faint and more faint.
Pan! was it thou? was it thou, Artemis?
Frolicsome kids and hard goats glassy-eyed
Alone could tell the story, had they speech.
The maiden came not back: but, after rites
Due to the goat-foot God, the pious youth
Piped shrilly forth and shook off all his woe.

        40 till] til *1859.*   56 Frolicsome] Frolicksome *1859.*

310

30

40

50

60

HYPERBION

[Published in 1846; reprinted 1847, 1859, 1876.]

Hyperbion was among the chosen few
Of Phœbus; and men honoured him awhile,
Honouring in him the God. But others sang
As loudly; and the boys as loudly cheer'd.
Hyperbion (more than bard should be) was wroth,
And thus he spake to Phœbus: "Hearest thou,
O Phœbus! the rude rabble from the field,
Who swear that they have known thee ever since
Thou feddest for Admetus his white bull?"
"I hear them," said the God. "Seize thou the first,   10
And haul him up above the heads of men,
And thou shalt hear them shout for thee as pleas'd."
Headstrong and proud Hyperbion was: the crown
Of laurel on it badly cool'd his brow:
So, when he heard them singing at his gate,
While some with flints cut there the rival's name,
Rushing he seized the songster at their head:
The songster kickt and struggled hard: in vain.
Hyperbion claspt him round with arm robust,
And with the left a hempen rope uncoil'd,   20
Whereon already was a noose: it held
The calf until its mother's teat was drawn
At morn and eve; and both were now afield.
With all his strength he pull'd the wretch along,
And haul'd him up a pine-tree, where he died.
But one night, not long after, in his sleep
He saw the songster: then did he beseech
Apollo to enlighten him, if perchance
In what he did he had done aught amiss.
"Thou hast done well, Hyperbion!" said the God,   30
"As I did also to one Marsyas
Some years ere thou wert born: but better 'twere
If thou hadst understood my words aright,
For those around may harm thee, and assign
As reason, that thou wentest past the law.
My meaning was, that thou shouldst hold him up
In the high places of thy mind, and show
Thyself the greater by enduring him."
Downcast Hyperbion stood: but Phœbus said

3 Honouring] Honoring *1847, 1859.*   9 Admetus] Admetos *1859.*   22 its] the *1859.*

"Be of good cheer, Hyperbion! if the rope   40
Is not so frayed but it may hold thy calf,
The greatest harm is, that, by hauling him,
Thou hast chafed, sorely, sorely that old pine;
And pine-tree bark will never close again."

ALCIPHRON AND LEUCIPPE

[Published in 1846; reprinted 1859, 1876.]

An ancient chestnut's blossoms threw
Their heavy odour over two:
Leucippe, it is said, was one,
The other then was Alciphron.
  "Come, come! why should we stand beneath
This hollow tree's unwholesome breath,"
Said Alciphron, "here's not a blade
Of grass or moss, and scanty shade.
Come; it is just the hour to rove
In the lone dingle shepherds love,   10
There, straight and tall, the hazel twig
Divides the crooked rock-held fig,
O'er the blue pebbles where the rill
In winter runs, and may run still.
Come then, while fresh and calm the air,
And while the shepherds are not there."
  Leucippe. But I would rather go when they
Sit round about and sing and play.
Then why so hurry me? for you
Like play and song and shepherds too.   20
  Alciphron. I like the shepherds very well,
And song and play, as you can tell.
But there is play I sadly fear,
And song I would not have you hear.
  Leucippe. What can it be? what can it be?
  Alciphron. To you may none of them repeat
The play that you have played with me,
The song that made your bosom beat.
  Leucippe. Don't keep your arm about my waist.
  Alciphron. Might not you stumble?
  Leucippe.   Well then, do.   30
But why are we in all this haste?
  Alciphron. To sing.
  Leucippe.   Alas! and not play too?

14 still] stil *1859.*

312

IPHIGENEIA

[Published in 1846; reprinted 1847, 1859, 1876.]

Iphigeneia, when she heard her doom
At Aulis, and when all beside the king
Had gone away, took his right-hand, and said,
"O father! I am young and very happy.
I do not think the pious Calchas heard
Distinctly what the Goddess spake. Old age
Obscures the senses. If my nurse, who knew
My voice so well, sometimes misunderstood,
While I was resting on her knee both arms
And hitting it to make her mind my words,   10
And looking in her face, and she in mine,
Might not he also hear one word amiss,
Spoken from so far off, even from Olympus?"
The father placed his cheek upon her head,
And tears dropt down it, but the king of men
Replied not. Then the maiden spake once more.
"O father! sayst thou nothing? Hear'st thou not
Me, whom thou ever hast, until this hour,
Listen'd to fondly, and awaken'd me
To hear my voice amid the voice of birds,   20
When it was inarticulate as theirs,
And the down deadened it within the nest?"
He moved her gently from him, silent still,
And this, and this alone, brought tears from her,
Altho' she saw fate nearer: then with sighs,
"I thought to have laid down my hair before
Benignant Artemis, and not have dimm'd
Her polisht altar with my virgin blood;
I thought to have selected the white flowers
To please the Nymphs, and to have askt of each   30
By name, and with no sorrowful regret,
Whether, since both my parents will'd the change,
I might at Hymen's feet bend my clipt brow;
And (after these who mind us girls the most)
Adore our own Athena,* that she would
Regard me mildly with her azure eyes.
But father! to see you no more, and see
Your love, O father! go ere I am gone!"

* Pallas Athena was the patroness of Argos. [L.]

Title Iphigeneia and Agamemnon *1847, 1859.*   6 Old age] Old-age *1847, 1859.*
23 still] stil *1847, 1859.*

Gently he moved her off, and drew her back,
Bending his lofty head far over her's,   40
And the dark depths of nature heaved and burst.
He turn'd away; not far, but silent still.
She now first shudder'd; for in him, so nigh,
So long a silence seem'd the approach of death,
And like it. Once again she rais'd her voice.
"O father! if the ships are now detain'd,
And all your vows move not the Gods above,
When the knife strikes me there will be one prayer
The less to them: and purer can there be
Any, or more fervent than the daughter's prayer   50
For her dear father's safety and success?"
A groan that shook him shook not his resolve.
An aged man now enter'd, and without
One word, stept slowly on, and took the wrist
Of the pale maiden. She lookt up, and saw
The fillet of the priest and calm cold eyes.
Then turn'd she where her parent stood, and cried
"O father! grieve no more: the ships can sail."

42 still] stil *1847, 1859.*

PART II. FROM *HELLENICS*, 1847.

["The Hellenics of Walter Savage Landor. Enlarged and completed. London: Edward Moxon, Dover Street. MDCCCXLVII." had on pp. iii–iv the following address to the Pope:]

TO POPE PIUS IX

NEVER UNTIL NOW, MOST HOLY FATHER! DID I HOPE OR DESIRE TO OFFER MY HOMAGE TO ANY POTENTATE ON EARTH; AND NOW I OFFER IT ONLY TO THE HIGHEST OF THEM ALL.

THERE WAS A TIME WHEN THE CULTIVATORS OF LITERATURE WERE PERMITTED AND EXPECTED TO BRING THE FRUIT OF THEIR LABOUR TO THE VATICAN. NOT ONLY WAS INCENSE WELCOME THERE, BUT EVEN THE HUMBLEST PRODUCE OF THE POOREST SOIL.

VERBENAM [Verbenas], PUERI, PONITE THURAQUE [turaque].
[Horace, *Odes,* i. xix. 14.]

IF THOSE BETTER DAYS ARE RETURNING, WITHOUT WHAT WAS BAD OR EXCEPTIONABLE IN THEM, THE GLORY IS DUE ENTIRELY TO YOUR HOLINESS. YOU HAVE RESTORED TO ITALY HOPE AND HAPPINESS; TO THE REST OF THE WORLD HOPE ONLY. BUT A SINGLE WORD FROM YOUR PROPHETIC LIPS, A SINGLE MOTION OF YOUR EARTH-EMBRACING ARM, WILL OVERTURN THE FIRMEST SEATS OF INIQUITY AND OPPRESSION. THE WORD MUST BE SPOKEN; THE ARM MUST WAVE. WHAT DO WE SEE BEFORE US? IF WE TAKE THE BEST OF RULERS UNDER OUR SURVEY, WE FIND SELFISHNESS AND FRIVOLITY: IF WE EXTEND THE VIEW, INGRATITUDE, DISREGARD OF HONOUR, CONTEMPT OF HONESTY, BREACH

THE CHILDREN OF VENUS

OF PROMISES: ONE STEP YET BEYOND, AND THERE IS COLD-BLOODED IDIOCY, STABBING THE NOBLES AT HOME, SPURNING THE PEOPLE EVERYWHERE, AND VOIDING ITS CORROSIVE SLAVER IN THE FAIR FACE OF ITALY. IT IS BETTER TO LOOK NO FARTHER, ELSE OUR EYES MUST BE RIVETED ON FROZEN SEAS OF BLOOD SUPERFUSED WITH BLOOD FRESH FLOWING. THE SAME FEROCIOUS ANIMAL LEAVES THE IMPRESSION OF ITS BROAD AND HEAVY FOOT ON THE SNOW OF THE ARCTIC CIRCLE AND OF THE CAUCASUS. AND IS THIS INDEED ALL THAT EUROPE HAS BROUGHT FORTH, AFTER SUCH LONG AND PAINFUL THROES? HAS SHE ENDURED HER MARATS, HER ROBESPIERRES, HER BUONAPARTES, FOR THIS? GOD INFLICTED ON THE LATTER OF THESE WRETCHES HIS TWO GREATEST CURSES; UNCONTROLLED POWER AND PERVERTED INTELLECT; AND THEY WERE TWISTED TOGETHER TO MAKE A SCOURGE FOR A NATION WHICH REVELLED IN EVERY CRIME, BUT ABOVE ALL IN CRUELTY. IT WAS INSUFFICIENT. SHE IS NOW UNDERGOING FROM A WEAKER HAND A MORE IGNOMINIOUS PUNISHMENT, PURSUED BY THE DERISION OF EUROPE. TO SAVE HER HONOUR, SHE PRETENDED TO ADMIRE THE COURAGE THAT DECIMATED HER CHILDREN: TO SAVE HER HONOUR, SHE NOW PRETENDS TO ADMIRE THE WISDOM THAT IMPRISONS THEM. CUNNING IS NOT WISDOM; PREVARICATION IS NOT POLICY; AND (NOVEL AS THE NOTION IS, IT IS EQUALLY TRUE) ARMIES ARE NOT STRENGTH: ACRE AND WATERLOO SHOW IT, AND THE FLAMES OF THE KREMLIN AND THE SOLITUDES OF FONTAINEBLEAU. ONE HONEST MAN, ONE WISE MAN, ONE PEACEFUL MAN, COMMANDS A HUNDRED MILLIONS, WITHOUT A BATON AND WITHOUT A CHARGER. HE WANTS NO FORTRESS TO PROTECT HIM: HE STANDS HIGHER THAN ANY CITADEL CAN RAISE HIM, BRIGHTLY CONSPICUOUS TO THE MOST DISTANT NATIONS, GOD'S SERVANT BY ELECTION, GOD'S IMAGE BY BENEFICENCE.

WALTER SAVAGE LANDOR.

[After the address to the Pope there was a preface, without heading, as follows:]

IT is hardly to be expected that ladies and gentlemen will leave on a sudden their daily promenade, skirted by Turks and shepherds and knights and plumes and palfreys, of the finest Tunbridge manufacture, to look at these rude frescoes, delineated on an old wall high up, and sadly weak in coloring. As in duty bound, we can wait. The reader (if there should be one) will remember that Sculpture and Painting have never ceased to be occupied with the scenes and figures which we venture once more to introduce in poetry, it being our belief that what is becoming in two of the Fine Arts is not quite unbecoming in a third, the one which indeed gave birth to them.

THE CHILDREN OF VENUS

[Published in 1847; not reprinted in same form. For later version published in 1859, reprinted 1876, see notes at end of volume. Text 1847.]

Twain are the sons of Venus: one beholds
Our globe in gladness, while his brother's eye
Casts graver glances down, nor cares for woods
Or song, unworthy of the name of Love.

Title. The Boys of Venus, *1859.*

Nothing is sweet to him, as pure and cold
As rain and Eurus.
                What dissension thus
Severed the beauteous pair? Ambition did.
With heavy heart the elder bore that he
Whom often with an arrow in his hand
He saw, and whetstone under it, and knew   10
To spend the day entire in weaving flowers
Or drawing nets, as might be, over birds,
That he should have men's incense, he have shrines,
While only empty honour, silent prayer,
Was offered to himself.
                On this he goes
And makes Silenus arbiter. The eld
With gentle speech would fain assuage his wrath;
It rises but the higher: he bids him call
The Idalian to his presence, then decide.

With downcast eye, and drooping wing, and cheek   20
Suffused with shame, the little one advanced,
And "Brother! did you call me? Then at last
The poor Idalian is not quite despised?"
The kindly arbiter in vain attempts
To bring together two such potent hands.
"No" said the taller; "I am here for this,
This only, that he learn, and by defeat,
What is my power."
                Hereon Silenus, "Go!
Kiss first: then both (but with no enemy)
In power and honour safely may contend."   30
The younger leaps upon the elder's neck
And kisses it and kisses it again:
The austerer could not, tho' he would, resist
Those rapid lips; one kiss he did return,
Whether the influence of the God prevail'd,
Or whether 'tis impossible to stand
Repelling constantly a kindly heart.
But neither his proud words did he remitt
Nor resolution: he began to boast
How with his radiant fire he had reduced   40
The ancient Chaos; how from heaven he drove
The darkness that surrounded it, and drew
Into their places the reluctant stars,
And made some stand before him, others go

THE CHILDREN OF VENUS

Beyond illimitable space; then curb'd
The raging sea and chain'd with rocks around.
  "Is not all this enough for you?" exclamed
The brother; "must my little realm be stript
Of every glory? You will make me proud
In speech, refusing what is justly due.   50
Upon my birth the golden ether smiled.
What Chaos was I know not, I confess;
I would let every star fly where it list,
Nor try to turn it: her who rules them all
I drew behind the Latmian cliffs; she prayed,
She promist ever to perform my will
Would I but once be friendly. 'Twas her first,
'Twas her last vow . . and it was made to *me*.
Now you alike inhabit the same heaven,
And she must know you, yet none other Love   60
Acknowledges save him whom you despise.
To me what matter are the raging seas,
Curb'd or uncurb'd, in chains or out of chains?
I penetrate the uttermost retreat
Of Nereus; I command, and from the deep
Dolphins rise up and give their pliant backs
For harps to grate against and songmen ride;
And, when I will'd it, they have fondly wept
For human creatures human tears, and laid
Their weary lives down on the dry sea-sand.   70
Desert thou some-one, and he knows it not;
Let me desert him, let me but recede
One footstep, and funereal fire consumes
His inmost heart.
               "The latest guest above
With basket overturn'd and broken thread
Lay lithe as new-mown grass before the gate
Of Omphale: a fondled whelp tug'd off
The lion-skin, and lept athwart his breast.
Vast things and wonderful are those you boast.
I would say nothing of the higher Powers,   80
Lest it might chafe you. How the world turns round
I know not, or who tempers the extremes
Of heat and cold and regulates the tides.
I leave them all to you: give me instead
Dances and crowns and garlands; give the lyre,
And softer music of the river-side

317

Where the stream laps the sallow-leaves, and breaks
The quiet converse of the whispering reeds:
Give me, for I delight in them, the clefts
Of bank o'ergrown by moss'es soft deceit.
I wish but to be happy: others say
That I am powerful: whether so or not
Let facts bear witness: in the sun, the shade,
Beneath the setting and the rising stars
Let these speak out; I keep them not in mind."
  "Scarce less thy promises" the other cried.
He smiled and own'd it.
                "You will soon educe
Bolder assertion of important deeds
Who things terrestrial haughtily despise.
Decline your presence at the blissful couch,
And boast you never make those promises
Which make so many happy, but with eye
Averted from them gaze into the deep,
Yet tell me, tell me, solemn one, that swearest
By that dark river only, *who* compel'd
Pluto to burn amid the deepest shades,
Amid the windings of the Stygian stream
And panting Phlegethon? while barkt the dog
Three-throated, so that all his realm resounds.
And *who* (here lies the potency) *who* made
The griesly Pluto please the captive bride?
Mere sport! If graver, better, things you want,
This is the hand, and this the torch it held
(You might have heard each drop the Danäid
Let fall, Ixion's wheel you might have heard
Creak, as now first without his groans it roll'd)
When the fond husband claspt Eurydice,
And the fond wife the earliest slain at Troy."
  The arbiter embraced him: more composed
He turn'd toward the other and pronounced
This sentence.
             "O most worthy of thy sire
The Thunderer! to thy guidance I committ
The stars (if he approve of it) and storms
And seas, and rocks coercing their uproar,
If Amphitrite smile, if Neptune bend.
But, O thou smaller one of lighter wing,
Source of the genial laugh and dulcet smile,

90

100

110

120

THE CHILDREN OF VENUS

Who makest every sun shed softer rays,
And one sole night outvalue all that shine,
Who holdest back (what Jove could never do)   130
The flying Hours! thou askest nought beyond;
And this do I award thee. I bestow
On thee alone the gentle hand hand-linkt . .
Thy truest bond . . on thee the flowers, the lyre,
The river's whispers which the reeds increase,
The spring to weave thy trophies, the whole year
To warm and fill it with the balm of spring.
Only do thou" . . he whispered in the ear
Of Love, and blusht in whispering it . . "incline
Ianthe . . touch her gently . . just the point . .   140
Nor let that other know where thou hast aim'd."

PAN AND PITYS

[Published in 1847, not reprinted in same form. For later version published in 1859, reprinted 1876, see notes at end of volume. Text 1847.]

Cease to complain of what the Gods decree,
Whether by death or (harder!) by the hand
Of one prefer'd thy loves be torne away,
For even against the bourn of Arcady
Beats the sad Styx, heaving its wave of tears,
And nought on earth so high but Care flies higher.
   A maid was wooed by Boreas and by Pan,
Pitys her name, her haunt the wood and wild;
Boreas she fled from; with more placid eye
Lookt she on Pan; yet chided him, and said . .   10
"Ah why should men or clearer-sighted Gods
Propose to link our hands eternally?
That which o'er raging seas is wildly sought
Perishes and is trampled on in port;
And they where all things are immutable
Beside, even they, the very Gods, are borne
Unsteddily wherever love impels;
Even he who rules Olympus, he himself
Is lighter than the cloud beneath his feet.
Lovers are ever an uncertain race,   20
And they the most so who most loudly sing
Of truth and ardour, anguish and despair,
But thou above them all. Now tell me, Pan,
How thou deceivedst the chaste maid of night,

HELLENICS

Cynthia, thou keeper of the snow-white flock!
Thy reed had crackled with thy flames, and split
With torture after torture; thy lament
Had fill'd the hollow rocks; but when it came
To touch the sheep-fold, there it paus'd and cool'd.
Wonderest thou whence the story reacht my ear? 30
Why open those eyes wider? why assume
The ignorant, the innocent? prepared
For refutation, ready to conceal
The fountain of Selinos, waving here
On the low water its long even grass,
And there (thou better may'st remember this)
Paved with smooth stones, as temples are. The sheep
Who led the rest, struggled ere yet half-shorn,
And dragged thee slithering after it: thy knee
Bore long the leaves of ivy twined around 40
To hide the scar, and stil the scar is white.
Dost thou deny the giving half thy flock
To Cynthia? hiding tho' the better half,
Then all begrimed producing it, while stood
Well-washt and fair in puffy wooliness
The baser breed, and caught the unpracticed eye."
    Pan blusht, and thus retorted.
                                    "Who hath told
That idle fable of an age long past?
More just, perhaps more happy, hadst thou been,
Shunning the false and flighty. Heard I have 50
Boreas and his rude song, and seen the goats
Stamp on the rock and lick the affrighted eyes
Of their young kids; and thee too, then averse,
I also saw, O Pitys! Is thy heart,
To what was thy aversion, now inclined?
Believest thou my foe? the foe of all
I hold most dear. Had Cynthia been prefer'd
She would not thus have taunted me: unlike
Thee, Pitys, she looks down with gentle glance
On them who suffer; whether they abide 60
In the low cottage or the lofty tower
She tends them, and with silent step alike
And watchful eye their aking vigil soothes.
I sought not Cynthia; Cynthia lean'd to me.
Not pleased too easily, unlovely things

ll. 25 ff. Cynthia &c] see Virgil, *Georgics*, iii. 391–3. [W.]

PAN AND PITYS

She shuns, by lovely (and none else) detain'd.
Sweet, far above all birds, is philomel
To her; above all scenes the Padan glades
And their soft-whispering poplars; sweet to her
The yellow light of box-tree in full bloom   70
Nodding upon Cytoros. She delights
To wander thro' the twinkling olive-grove,
And where in clusters on Lycæan knolls
Redden the berries of the mountain-ash;
In glassy fountain, and grey temple-top,
And smooth sea-wave, when Hesperus hath left
The hall of Tethys, and when liquid sounds
(Uncertain whence) are wafted to the shore . .
Never in Boreas."
     "What a voice is thine!"
She said, and smiled. "More roughly not himself 80
Could sound with all his fury his own name.
But come, thou cunning creature! tell me how
Thou couldst inveigle Goddesses without
Thinning thy sheepfold."
     "What! again" cried he
"Such tart and cruel twitting? She received,
Not as belov'd, but loving me, my gift.
I gave her what she askt, and more had given,
But half the flock was all that she required;
Need therefor was it to divide in twain
The different breeds, that she might make her choice. 90
One, ever meager, with broad bony front,
Shone white enough, but harder than goat's hair
The wool about it; and loud bleatings fill'd
The plains it battened on . . for only plains
It trod; and smelt . . as all such coarse ones smell.
Avarice urged the Goddess: she sprang forth
And took, which many more have done, the worse.
"Why shake thy head? incredulous! Ah why,
When none believe the truth, should I confess?
Why, one who hates and scorns the lover, love? 100
Once thou reposedst on the words I spake,
And, when I ceast to speak, thou didst not cease
To ponder them, but with thy cool plump palm
Unconsciously didst stroke that lynx-skin down
Which Bacchus gave me, toucht with virgin shame
If any part slipt off and bared my skin.

I then could please thee, could discourse, could pause,
Could look away from that sweet face, could hide
All consciousness that any hand of mine
Had crept where lifted knee would soon unbend.　　　110
Ah then how pleasant was it to look up
(If thou didst too) from the green glebe supine,
And drink the breath of all sweet herbs, and watch
The last rays run along the level clouds,
Until they kindle into living forms
And sweep with golden net the western sky.
Meanwhile thou notedst the dense troop of crows
Returning on one track and at one hour
In the same darkened intervals of heaven.
Then mutual faith was manifest, but glad　　　120
Of fresh avowal; then securely lay
Pleasure, reposing on the crop she reapt.
　　"The oleaster of the cliff; the vine
Of leaf pellucid, clusterless, untamed;
The tufts of cytisus that half-conceal'd
The craggy cavern, narrow, black, profound;
The scantier broom below it, that betray'd
Those two white fawns to us . . what now are they?
How the pine's whispers, how the simpering brook's,
How the bright vapour trembling o'er the grass　　　130
Could I enjoy, unless my Pitys took
My hand and show'd me them; unless she blew
My pipe when it was hoarse; and, when my voice
Fail'd me, took up, and so inspired, my song."
　　Thus he, embracing with brown brawny arm
Her soft white neck, not far from his declined,
And with sharp finger parting her smooth hair.
He paus'd.
　　　　　　"Take now that pipe," said she "and since
Thou findest joyance in things past, run o'er
The race-course of our pleasures: first will I　　　140
The loves . . of Boreas I abhor . . relate.
He his high spirit, his uprooted oaks,
And heaven confused with hailstones, may sing on:
How into thine own realms his breath has blown
The wasting flames, until the woods bow'd low
Their heads with heavy groans, while he alert
Shook his broad pinions and scream'd loud with joy.
He may sing on, of shattered sails, of ships

PAN AND PITYS

Sunk in the depths of ocean, and the sign
Of that wide empire from Jove's brother torn;   150
And how beneath the rocks of Ismaros
Deluded he with cruel sport the dream
That brought the lost one back again, and heard
The Manes clap their hands at her return.
Always his pastime was it, not to shake
Light dreams away, but change them into forms
Horrific; churl, from peace and truth averse.
What in such rival ever couldst thou fear?"
   Boreas heard all she spoke, amid the brake
Conceal'd: rage seiz'd him: the whole mountain shook.   160
"Contemn'd!" said he, and as he said it, split
A rock, and from the summit with his foot
Spurn'd it on Pitys. Ever since, beneath
That rock sits Pan: her name he calls; he waits
Listening, to hear the rock repeat it; wipes
The frequent tear from his hoarse reed, and wears
Henceforth the pine, her pine, upon his brow.

153 lost one]=Eurydice, cf. Virgil, *Georgics*, iv. 486 ff. [W.]

CUPID AND PAN

[Published in 1847. For shorter version published in 1859, reprinted 1876, see notes at end of volume. Text 1847.]

Cupid saw Pan stretcht at full length asleep.
He snatcht the goatskin from the half-covered limbs,
And, now in *this* place now in *that* twitcht up
A stiff curv'd hair: meanwhile the slumberer
Blew from his ruddy breast all care about
His flock, all care about the snow, that hung
Only where creviced rocks rose bleak and high,
And felt . . what any cork-tree's bark may feel.
His hemlock pipe lay underneath his neck:
But even this the wicked boy stole out,   10
And unperceived . . save that he twinkled once
His hard sharp ear, and laid it down again.
"Jupiter! is there any God" said Love,
"Sluggish as this prick-ear one! verily
Not thy own wife could stir or waken him."
   Between his rosy lips he laid the pipe
And blew it shrilly: that loud sound did wake
The sleeper: up sprang then two ears at once

Above the grass; up sprang the wrathful God
And shook the ground beneath him with his leap.   20
But quite as quickly and much higher sprang
The audacious boy, deriding him outright.
"Down with those arrows, wicked imp! that bow,
Down with it; then what canst thou do?"

                                    "What then,
Pan, I can do, soon shalt thou see . . There! there!"
  He spake, and threw them at Pan's feet: the bow,
The golden bow, sprang up again, and flowers
Cradled the quiver as it struck the earth.
"'Twould shame me."

                         "In my conflicts shame is none,
Even for the vanquisht: check but wrath: come on: 30
Come, modest one! close with me, hand to hand."
  Pan rolled his yellow eyes, and suddenly
Snatcht (as a fowler with his net, who fears
To spoil the feathers of some rarer bird)
Love's slender arm, taunting and teasing him
Nearer and nearer. Then, if ne'er before,
The ruddy color left his face; 'tis said
He trembled too, like one whom sudden flakes
Of snow have fallen on, amidst a game
Of quoits or ball in a warm day of spring.   40
  "Go! go!" the Arcadian cried "and learn respect
To betters, at due distance, and hold back
Big words, that suit such littleness but ill.
Why, anyone (unless thou wert a God)
Would swear thou hast not yet seen thrice five years,
And yet thou urgest . . nay, thou challengest
Me, even me, quiet, and half-asleep.
Off! or beware the willow-twig, thy due."
  Now shame and anger seized upon the boy;
He raised his stature, and he aim'd a blow   50
Where the broad hairy breast stood quite exposed
Without the goatskin, swifter than the bird
Of Jove, or than the lightning he has borne.
Wary was the Arcadian, and he caught
The coming fist: it burnt as burns the fire
Upon the altar. The wise elder loost
His hold, and blew upon his open palm
From rounded cheeks a long thin breath, and then
Tried to encompass with both arms the neck

324

And waist of the boy God: with tremulous pulse   60
He fain would twist his hard long leg between
The smoother, and trip up, if trip he might,
The tenderer foot, and fit and fit again
The uncertain and insatiate grasp upon
A yielding marble, dazzling eye and brain.
He could not wish the battle at an end,
No, not to conquer; such was the delight;
But glory, ah deceitful glory, seized
(Or somewhat did) one born not to obey.
When Love, unequal to such strength, had nigh   70
Succumbed, he made one effort more, and caught
The horn above him: he from Arcady
Laught as he tost him up on high: nor then
Forgot the child his cunning. While the foe
Was crying "Yield thee," and was running o'er
The provinces of conquest, now with one
Now with the other hand, their pleasant change,
Losing and then recovering what they lost,
Love from his wing drew one short feather forth
And smote the eyes devouring him. Then rang   80
The rivers and deep lakes, and groves and vales
Throughout their windings. Ladon heard the roar
And broke into the marsh: Alphëus heard
Stymphalos, Mænalos (Pan's far-off home),
Cyllene, Pholöe, Parthenos, who stared
On Tegea's and Lycæosis affright.
The winged horse who, no long while before,
Was seen upon Parnassus, bold and proud,
Is said (it may be true, it may be false)
To have slunk down before that cry of Pan,   90
And to have run into a shady cave
With broken spirit, and there lain for years,
Nor once have shaken the Castilian rill
With neigh, or ruffling of that mighty mane.
"Hail, conqueror!" cried out Love: but Pan cried out
Sadder, "Ah never shall I see again
My woodland realm! ah never more behold
The melting snow borne down and rolled along
The whirling brook; nor river full and large,
Nor smooth and purple pebble in the ford,   100
Nor white round cloud that rolls o'er vernal sky,
Nor the mild fire that Hesper lights for us

To sing by, when the sun is gone to rest.
Woe! woe! the blind have but one place on earth,
And blind am I .. blind, wander where I may!
Spare me! now spare me, Cupid! 'Twas not I
Began the contest; 'tis not meet for me
First to ask peace; peace, peace is all I ask;
Victory well may grant this only boon."
Then held he out his hand; but knowing not   110
Whether he held it opposite his foe,
Huge tears ran down both cheeks. Love grew more mild
At seeing this, and said ..

                "Cheer up! behold
A remedy; upon one pact applied,
That thou remove not this light monument
Of my success, but leave it there for me."
   Amaranth was the flower he chose the first;
'Twas brittle and dropt broken; one white rose
(All roses then were white) he softly prest;
Narcissusses and violets took their turn,   120
And lofty open-hearted lilies their's,
And lesser ones with modest heads just rais'd
Above the turf, shaking alternate bells.
The slenderest of all myrtle twigs held these
Together, and across both eyes confined.
Smart was the pain they gave him, first applied:
He stampt, he groan'd, he bared his teeth, and heaved
To nostril the broad ridges of his lip.
After a while, however, he was heard
To sing again; and better rested he   130
Among the strawberries, whose fragrant leaf
Deceives with ruddy hue the searching sight
In its late season: he grew brave enough
To trill in easy song the pliant names
Of half the Dryads; proud enough to deck
His beauty out .. down went at last the band.
Renewed were then his sorrow and his shame.
He hied to Paphos: he must now implore
Again his proud subduer. At the gate
Stood Venus, and spake thus.

               "Why hast thou torn   140
Our gifts away? No gentle chastisement
Awaits thee now. The bands my son imposed,
He would in time, his own good time, remove.

CUPID AND PAN

O goat-foot! he who dares despise our gifts
Rues it at last. Soon, soon another* wreath
Shall bind thy brow, and no such flowers be there."

* After the death of Pitys he wore the pine. [L.]

DRYOPE

[Published in 1847. For later version, published in 1859, reprinted 1876, see note at end of volume. Text 1847.]

FAMOUS and over famous Œta reign'd
Dryops: him beauteous Polydora bare
To the river-god Sperchios: but above
Mother and sire, far brighter in renown,
Was Dryope their daughter, the beloved
Of him who guides thro' heaven his golden car.
Showering his light o'er all things, he endues
All things with colour, grace and song gives he,
But never now on any condescends
To lower his shining locks; his roseate lips   10
Breathe an ambrosial sigh on none but her.
He follows that shy Nymph thro' pathless ways,
Among the willows in their soft grey flowers,
In their peel'd boughs odorous, and amid
The baskets white and humid, incomplete:
He follows her along the river-side,
Soft to the foot and gladdened by the breeze;
He follows where the Nereids watch their fords
While listen the Napæan maids around.
Tending one day her father's sheep, she heard   20
A flute in the deep valley; then a pipe;
And soon from upright arms the tymbrel trill'd.
Dryads and Hamadryads then appear'd,
And one among them cried to her aloud
"Knowest thou not the day when all should sing
Pæan and *Io Pæan?* Shunnest thou
The lord of all, whom all the earth adores,
Giver of light and gladness, warmth and song?
And willest thou that Dryops stand above
Admetos? from thy sight thus banishing   30
And shutting from thy fold the son of Jove."
   She, proud and joyous at the gay reproof,
Stood silent. They began the dance and games.
And thus the day went on. When evening came

327

They sang the hymn to Delios. Nigh the seat
Of Dryope, among the tufts of grass,
A lyre shone out; whose can it be, they ask;
Each saw the next with her's upon her knee;
Whether Theano's or Autonöe's gift,
Dryope takes it gratefully, and trills   40
The glimmering strings: and now at one she looks,
Now at another, knowingly, and speaks
(As if it heard her) to it, now on lap
And now on bosom fondly laying it.
Behold! a snake, a snake, it glides away.
They shriek: and each one as she sate reclined
Throws her whole body back. Striving to rise,
Autonöe prest upon a fragile reed
Her flattened hand, nor felt it: when she saw
The blood, she suckt the starting globe, and sought   50
The place it sprang from. Hither, thither, run
The maidens. But the strings, and tortoise-shell
That held them at due distance, are instinct
With life, and rush on Dryope, too slow
To celebrate the rites the sires had taught
And Delios had ordain'd. One whom the flight
Left nearest, turn'd her head, stil flying on,
Fearful til pity overcame her fear,
And thus she cried aloud.
                     "Look back! look back!
See how that creature licks her lips, her eyes,   60
Her bosom! how it seizes! how it binds
In the thick grass her struggles! Where is now,
Where is Apollo proud of Python slain?
Whether she sinn'd thro' silliness or dread,
Poor inexperienced girl! are snakes to teach?
Are they fit bonds for love? can fear persuade?
Phœbus! come hither! aid us! Ah, what now
Would the beast do? how swells his horrid crest?"
Various and manifold the dragon brood.
Some urge their scales along the ground, and some   70
Their wings aloft, some yoked to fiery cars,
And some, tho' hard of body, melt in air.
    Callianira now was brave enough
To stop her flight: on the first hill she rais'd
Her eyes above the brambles, just above,
And caught and held Diaule at her side,

DRYOPE

Who, when she stopt her, trembled more and more.
But arguments are ready to allay
Her terror; all strong arguments, like these.
"Are there not many things that may deceive   80
The sight at first? might not a lizard seem
A dragon? and how pleasant in hot days
To hold a lizard to the breast, and tempt
Its harmless bitings with the finger's end!
Dragon or lizard, rare the species is.
What! are they over . . Dryope's alarms?
She treats it like a sister. Lo! her hand
Upon its neck! and, far as we are off,
Lo! how it shines! as bright as any star.
Vainly exhorts she, first Autonöe,   90
And then Diaule, to come on; alone
She ventures; vainly would they call her back.
   And now again the creature is transform'd.
Lizard nor serpent now, nor tortoise-shell
Chelys, is that which purple flutters round,
And which is whiter here and darker there,
Like violets drifted o'er with shifting hail.
Golden the hair that fluctuates upon neck
None of its own. A bland etherial glow
Ran over and ran thro' the calmer maid.   100
At last her fellow Nymphs came all around,
And Delios stood before them, manifest
No less to them than to his Dryope:
For with a radiant nod and arm outstretcht
He call'd them back; and they obey'd his call.
He lookt upon them, and with placid smile
Bespake them, drawing close his saffron vest.
Their eyes were lower'd before him as they stept
Into his presence; well they knew what fears
He shook throughout the Dryads, when he gave   110
His steeds and chariot to his reckless son,
When the woods crasht and perisht under him,
And when Eridanos, altho' his stream
Flows down from heaven, saw its last ripple sink.
Well they remembered how Diana fled
Among the woods and wilds, when mightier bow
Than hers was strung, and Python gaspt in death.
Potent of good they knew him, and of ill,
And closed the secret in their prudent hearts.

329

At first they would have pitied the hard fate   120
Of Dryope; but when she answered not
The words of pity, in her face they lookt
Stealthily.
        Soft the moisture of her brow,
Languid the luster of her eyes; a shame
Rosier and richer than before suffused
Her features, and her lips were tinged with flame
A God inspired, and worthy of that God.
    Each had her little question; but she stopt
As tho' she would reprove: at this they ply
Joke after joke, until they bring her home.   130
All they had known they would make others know,
But they had lookt too near and seen too well,
And had invoked the God with dance and hymn;
Beside, Diana would have sore avenged
Her righteous brother, who deals openly
With mortals, and few facts from them conceals.
    Dryope soon became Andræmon's wife,
And mother of Amphissos. Every spring
They chaunt her praises; her's, who trill'd so well
The plectron of Apollo; in the vale,   140
Of her own shady Œta do they sing.

    140 vale,] *mispr.* vale; *in 1847 is here corrected.* [W.]

CORESOS AND CALLIRHÖE

[Published in 1847. For a later version published in 1859, reprinted 1876, see notes at end of volume. Text 1847.]

THE girls of Calydon now celebrate
The feast of Bacchus. Two whirl round and round
A rope entwined with flowers, and make the rest
Run into and leap over it by turns.
A playful one and mischievous pusht on
Her who stood nearest, laughing as her foot
Tript and her hair was tangled in the flowers.
    Ah now, Callirhöe! burning shame flew up
Into thy face, nor could thy mother's prayer
Bring thee before the altar: now, 'tis said,   10
A tear roll'd down thy cheek, not quite exempt
From anger; but thy hand conceal'd thy face.
    Coresos, rising from his lofty seat,
Came forward, and stood ravisht with her charms:

CORESOS AND CALLIRHÖE

Coresos was it who then ruled the rites,
Beauteous, and skill'd to praise his God in song.
Unhappy youth! to see her in that hour!
In any other had he seen her first,
She might have loved him as he now loved her,
And he, had never he beheld her shame   20
And tears at falling, might have lived and played
On idle pipe the vacant cares of love.
   Neither the struggles of devoted goat
Nor the sweet wine they pour upon its horns
Engage his notice; not the God himself,
Giver of joy, gives any joy to him:
Nor after, when short laugh is faintly heard
Among the bushes, and the star of eve,
Eve's star and Love's, alone is overhead,
And shrubs are shaken which no breezes shake,   30
Gave he his eyes to sleep, his limbs to rest.
Where the long grasses hung with dews malign,
Beneath an ilex sat he quite alone
And meditated much, forgetting all
He fain would say to her; her face itself
Was shaken in his memory by his throbs:
Vainly would he recall it; up there comes
Another, less ingenuous, more in want
Of grace and beauty, not (alas!) of scorn.
   Many the days he wooed her, and the nights   40
Many he mourn'd that he had wooed in vain.
At last no longer could he see her near.
If barks the dog, she starts; if stranger lift
The door-latch, up she springs; the humid thread
She snatches from her mouth with trembling hand
And holds before her lips, and throws her hair
Back, which had fallen and hung loosely down
While close below the lintal slopes her ear.
If in the court she hears a louder step
She thinks him coming; come, if one less loud.   50
   The cane that long has quivered in the wind
Hardens; the maiden thus who long has fear'd:
Callirhöe would not trust her mother once,
No, nor herself; but now would gladly hear,
Alone or with her parent, him who sued;
For she had sharpen'd the bright point of speech
In readiness to pierce his open breast:

Nor slight is the offender's new offence
Thus to avoid it.
    As the coral bends
Beneath the Erythræan sea, but grows   60
Harder and harder when it feels the air,
So did this virgin, soft and flexible
In her first nature. Shyness, which confused
Her features lately, now quite disappear'd.
She minds not what men tattle, nor desires
Their ignorance of what she blusht to know;
She laughs if any whisper in her ear
That *he* is coming, laughs to see him stop
Suddenly, thus (a long way off) observ'd.
Afar she would not wish him, would not wish   70
His folly less, his madness less. She trod,
And knew she trod, upon a sacred flame,
Unscared, contending with the mighty Gods,
And rendering their best gifts of no avail.
 Ah! in what region grows a dittany
To heal the wound Love's poison'd barb hath left?
He who with quiet bosom can sit down
With wrongs like these cast into it, loves not;
Nor he who fiercely bursts the bond at once.
 Coresos siez'd her hand and threw it back   80
Disdainful, but sigh'd deeply, fixing fast
His looks upon her; then more calmly spake.
 "Callirhöe! I no more bemoan to thee
The love thou spurnest: pity ask I none
For such a vain, such an unworthy grief.
Be sure the tear thou now despisest, falls
The last that I shall shed or thou shalt see,
And therefor in the hour of death it falls.
For look around thee how the plague devours
Men's festered limbs! how fly the old to learn   90
The will and oracles of heaven, and how
From the hill-tops look out for their return
Those who have given them the last embrace.
The blameless fall; and shall the guilty stand?
 "Contemn'd I was, and I deserv'd contempt.
But never it repents me that in youth
Those arts I cherisht which, if age had come,
Had given grace and dignity to age.
Tis not for me: upon my brow too soon

CORESOS AND CALLIRHÖE

The crown thou placest; and the flowers that deck   100
An altar near at hand to thee are sweet.
Worthy I was, Callirhöe! then I sued;
Unworthy am I now, and now retire,
Broken in spirit, pierced with arrows, aim'd
Less by my lurking foes (for these are few)
Than by the heartless levity of friends.
Once (let me boast it) I might beat them all
Where agile strength the wrestler's olive gave,
Or where the Gods bestow'd the gift of song,
Or, boon to me more precious! in thy love.   110
Kings may hold prizes forth: the ores of earth,
The gems of ocean, may adorn small men
And make them marvels to more small below;
The Gods alone on mortal can confer
Genius and beauty, the pure wealth of heaven.
Ah! why do they to whom these gifts befall
Stand so apart? ah why shouldst thou condemn
To moulder each in barrenness away?
Beauty we worship in her high career,
But let her wane, and where the worshiper?   120
And Genius, mournful Genius, unapproacht,
Like Saturn from his lofty citadel,
Looks with an iron light down on a world
Torn from him."
           While he speaks, there now return
The elders, with their temples filleted,
For mildness, virtue, piety, revered,
Besought and prone with purer hands to touch
The altar, and the wrath of heaven avert.
   Callirhöe, whom the crowd call'd out by name,
Beheld them and turn'd pale, presaging ill: 130
Pale also turn'd Coresos, and endured
Yet worse his aching breast the ribald words
Flung by the people on the modest maid.
Forward he rusht to lead her from a throng
Madden'd with rage against her. In his flight
Palæmon stopt him.
           "Stay thy steps" cried he,
"And thou too, wretched maiden! hear the Gods,
Whose sentence on thy crime I now repeat.
Against thee shall the nation rise no more,
No more the dying virgin lift her eyes   140

Against thee, and no longer shall the torch
Where mothers crowd our funerals, bear thy name."
Coresos sprang to clasp the neck she turn'd,
And cried in loud devotion,
                      "Hail, O sire
Who fillest with thy deity the groves
Of thy Dodona, and whose look benign
Hath given to the air and earth below
Health and serenity! This maid henceforth
To me alone will be the source of pain.
More than Iacchus whom I serve, and more   150
Than happiest dream could promise, is thy gift."
   Troubled in mind, Palæmon shook his head
And thus continued.
                "Much art thou deceived
By such bright hopes, O gentle youth! Thyself
Shouldst see the future, favored by thy God;
But thou thyself dost hold before thine eyes
Love's dazzling saffron vesture, and believe
That what is coming can be only Love.
   "Step forward, ye young men! for Jupiter
Calls on ye all, and honors thus his son   160
Of Semele begotten. Lead ye forth,
Lead ye, a victim to appease his ire,
Callirhöe."
            That loud sound ran thro' her heart,
Ran thro' her limbs, and swept their strength away.
Down fell she. But strong arms had now seiz'd hers
And drag'd her to the temple.
                 Sense return'd
At the close tramp of those who hurried by,
(Some to see only, some with zeal to pile
The altar), at the smoke of frankincense,
At the cold sprinkling of the sacred lymph   170
Upon her temples, and at (suddenly
Dropt, and resounding on the floor) the sword.
   "Take it!" with tremulous voice Palæmon said.
"This is thy office; often on that head
Hast thou call'd down due vengeance from above:
Take, hold it, use it. Dost thou now retract?
'Tis not permitted. To no prayer of thine
Our Gods grant this, but are resolved to show

161 Semele] mother of Bacchus; *mispr.* Semale *is here corrected.* [W.]

334

CORESOS AND CALLIRHÖE

That wrong'd are they when men like thee are wrong'd.
If from the people one came forward, friend,   180
Relative, parent, willing to devote
His life instead of yon unhappy maid's,
Thro' that man's blood the city shall receive
Safety; for Jove thus reconciles his son."
    Upon the trembling victim gazed the youth,
And with back-hand swept off a tear.
                      "Thy sire"
Said he "is dead: and others are content
To have stood higher in thy grace than I.
Look! listen! what light footsteps glide away!
Now with firm breast, Callirhöe! and fixt eye   190
I dare to look on thee. In father's stead,
In lover's stead, I stand; and I perform
The sacred duty by the Gods imposed."
    Cries, clamours, groans, rise, spread. They see the limbs
Of young Coresos on the earth; and fear
Seizes them lest they tread that holy blood.
The temple moans aloud; the city swarms
With rumours, and the groves and fields around.
Now 'tis reported that the youth has fallen
By his own hand to save the virgin; now   200
That both were stricken by the fire of heaven.
With its own violence the crowd is swayed
Hither and thither, thickening; as the waves
Conglomerate under the propelling storm.

THE ALTAR OF MODESTY

[Published in 1847; not reprinted in the same form. For a longer version published
in 1859 see notes at end of volume. Text 1847.]

WHERE turns the traveler from Sparta's gate
And looks toward Elisis old citadel,
Where the first ford runs with white rill across,
Close by Eurotas was an altar rais'd
To Modesty. 'Twas hither Leda brought
Helen, whom Theseus lately bore away,
And thus reproved her, where none heard beside.
"O daughter! how couldst thou have left thy home,
Thy parents, thy twin-brothers, bright as stars?
With what persuasion could have toucht thy heart   10
That Theseus? Surely neither bland nor chaste,

Nor even young. Me one more great allured
Among the swans, in semblance of a swan;
Then did that cruel petulant deride,
And more derided he the more I blusht;
Whom when I chided, he assumed a tone
Of grief, and whined and muttered *Ah poor thing!*
Sad work with Leda! How ashamed was I!   20
Once I was passing by the wrestler's ring . .
Not very near . . he slanted out his lips
Into a beak-like form; another time
He made short twitters from a hollow reed;
Another, down his shoulders he drew wings
And shook (the wretch!) as any swan might shake.
Bad! but how bad grant Heaven thou hast not known!
Come; here the place is proper; tell me all."
Then Helen . . yet some sighs she first breath'd forth . .
" If the false guest who ran away with me
Was very bad, Pirithöus was worse;
For he had talkt and sung of me before,   30
And rais'd me over all our Spartan maids,
And, wild with rapture, shown me to his friend.
O! I will never dance again near him
To celebrate Diana's festival."
"Talk to me now of Theseus, and none else,"
Said Leda. She obeyed, and thus went on.
"Praising the joyous life in Cecrops-land,
And brides and maidens with gold grasshoppers
Among their hair embraided, he preferr'd
The simple hair of Helen over gold.   40
The men are brave at Athens, brave are they
But gentle too: Pallas, however stern,
On them looks never sternly; and each Grace
Chastens their little faults and smiles them down.
Then there are harps and dances that shake off
The olives their white blossom; then are there
Theatricals all autumn, taught by him
Who conquered India, and whose sole command
Was that all mortals upon earth be blest.
Theseus said *he* was wretched; and his voice   50
Proved it . . he pled for pardon; as 'twere he
Who did the harm; as 'twere a crime to grieve.
I was not very cruel, I confess;
Enough to seem a little so; enough

336

THE ALTAR OF MODESTY

To look unpitying of his sighs and prayers.
Then said I, 'Who would ever try the flame
Of love, when under friendship's cooler shade
He might repose, and there hear all commend
Himself, and one whose courage fixt his choice
To run with, ride, swim, wrestle, and converse.   60
There is Pirithöus now . . young, ardent, prompt
At anything with you: him you may make
Your very counterpart . . more apt than I
For arms, and more compliant to your will.
Such was that youth in beauty who was borne
From Ida by the tawny bird of Jove,
Such he who perisht by Apollo's quoit.
But never can you hope for praise with me,
Never to conquer or compose my fears.'
Then he. 'Not always, Helen, is the ear   70
Inclined to praise; not always is the breast
Vacant to friendship. Often have the maids
Of Sparta turn'd this friendship into blame.
Soon in Pandion's city shalt thou see
How warm the lover when so warm the friend.'
'But they do say, O Theseus, they do say,
That you once left behind you in that ile
Famed for its hundred cities, one you loved.'
And now, sweet mother, hear his own reply
In refutation of that ill report.   80
We know how cruel Minos is, we know
The law imposed on Athens he subdued.
Theseusis mother would have sent him here
To free him from that law; but uncompel'd
Sailed Theseus to Jove's birth-place; there he slew
The monster: Ariadne gave the thread
That guided him: he show'd no perfidy
To Ariadne, but his heart was doom'd
For Helen: yes, his last and only care
Should Helen be: by all the Gods above,   90
Ever propitious to him, she alone
The man, who won so many, should possess,
And marble house, and hills of honeycombs.
Ah mother! why say more? My cunning nurse,
Who knows the whole, hath surely told you all;
For when I lay disrobed along the couch,
One knee thrown over it, that creature stoopt

Peering (she trod on my loose hair) then spat,
And turn'd away, and claspt her hands and cried,
'Jupiter! thou hast saved thine own from shame!   100
A miracle! a miracle! beyond
All miracles! The madman! Hero he?
He kill the Minotaur! I well believe
He left the virgin upon Dia's shore;
What could he else? Degenerate age! to rear
No better man than Hercules and him!'"
 The scornful speech of that old crone, retold,
Gladdened the heart of Leda, and sweet tears
Fell from her eyes as the dense cloud dissolved.
"And now" said she "since all turns out less ill   110
Than might have happened, learn how better far,
While thou wert absent, fared a wiser maid.
The sacred torch in order due was borne
Before Ulysses and Penelope.
Icarius, tho' their love he had approved
And call'd his daughter's chosen from his home,
Tho' above all men prudent, and expert
In war by sea and land, and tho' his ile
Rose up securely from the rocks and waves,
Icarius felt how sad and sorrowful   120
Is the departure of a child we love.
While those of his own age were seated by,
The feast was well enough: 'twas not amiss
To link the present and the past with flowers
And cool the brow with ivy: then came sleep
With mild and genial influence over him.
But in the morning, when he sees the wreaths
Hang limber round the cups and from the doors,
And when he hears the neighing of the steeds
That shake them, and remarks the servants run   130
Hither and thither, grief (til then remote)
Strikes on his temples, and his ears sob loud,
And his knees, tottering under him, give way."
 "How piteous, poor Icarius!" Helen cried,
"How cruel was Ulysses!"
        "One alone
Is crueler," said Leda, "she who leaves
The fondest parent for a stranger's arms;
And but one parent wretcheder than he . .
The parent of that daughter." Then she askt

Why Helen fled: but Helen turn'd aside 140
The question, and "Heaven grant Penelope
May be a blessing to her father yet!"
At this ambiguous wish did Leda smile,
And with one finger pat that pretty face,
And draw the chin from forth the neck it prest.
Helen then, looking round her, gravely said,
"I will confess the whole, for I perceive
You have no mind to ask me such odd things
As that old woman did; she must be crazed.
Unless she took me for a lion's cub 150
Would she have whispered, 'didst thou bite the wretch?'
Then nods and winks, and winks and nods again,
Words without meaning, meaning without words.
Such manners, my sweet mother, may become
Poor sister Clytemnæstra, never me:
Never, when any hurt me, did I bite
Or scratch; I only trembled as, when all
The strings of harp or lyre are swept at once,
Water runs trembling to the vase's rim."
Leda had listened with her cheek prest down 160
Against the turf, dreading to lift her eyes,
And nipt unconsciously the tough grass-blades.
"He did not hurt thee then?" said she.
"Nor wish
To hurt me," said the maiden; "that he swore;
Nay, he protected me with arms and breast."
"Gods! Goddesses!" cried Leda, "what a tale,
O wretched one, is this! go on, go on,
Extinguish fear with anguish . . tell the whole.
Not even the modest are from blame exempt,
But thine, how great is thine! If harsh and stern 170
Thy sister Clytemnæstra would rebuke
The audacious boys, and swell against their games,
Thou wouldst hear all they said and turn again,
And ask them what they meant; when they had said,
Make them repeat it, and repeat the worst
Thyself, and toss it back to them, and laugh.
Something of sad there may be and severe
In modesty at times, but there is power
To quell it, and the brow whereon it hung
Shows that serenity which shines from heaven." 180
Urged to confess, the daughter thus went on:

"A grove there is, not very far away,
But hidden from us by the town and hill,
A gulley runs aside it, which the rains
May fill in winter, but in summer-time
Its course is dark with moss and crumbling mould.
The winds had thrown a rough old tree across
Whose bark and branches form'd an easy road.
He saw it, Theseus did, and lept (and made
Me leap too) from the car: he seated me 190
Upon the grass: afraid that I might fear,
He tried my bosom with such patient hand
And took such gentle care of me, lest damp
(The herbs were very damp there) or a stone
Or broken stick should hurt me" . .

       Leda's breath
Wafted more quickly now her daughter's hair
Across the shoulder. "Nemesis will come
Unless thou truly, fully, dost relate
This horrid story."

     "To repeat the whole
Is difficult . . the way, the wood . . beside 200
The seizure, the recovery . . these disturb
My memory; then my brothers, and their steeds,
Shaking the harness that creakt thick with brass.
Angry was Theseus . . gentle just before . .
Rein'd in the horses, bounded from the car,
And call'd down curses on his luckless head,
First to himself, then louder . . bade me go . .
Bade me stop where I was. Now other steeds
Advancing,

    "'Hush!' he whispered 'Not a word!'
The coursers of the Twins aside of his 210
Rear'd (pull'd up fiercely close to us) and chafed
The foaming bits. Javelins are level'd! 'Stop!
Stop, robber! we have arms, and thou hast none.'
Then lay they hands upon him, swift as stars
That swell and struggle with a running stream.
Their hands with open hand he turn'd aside,
And 'Boys! what would ye? Think ye me afraid
Of javelin? I respect your tender age,
Your parent's more advanced one I revere.
Take back your sister in her purity; 220
I know by signs and tokens, to my vows

Heaven is averse.' He paus'd, and they abstain'd.
Then, rolling here and there his restless eyes,
'And must the youthful Menelaüs wed
Affianced Helen? Beardless boys attract
Wan withering age: but firmer manhood best
Pleases the tenderer and more feeling maid;
Theseus might Helen. Why should fortune thwart?
Why should not Menelaüs take for bride
Tall Clytemnæstra? fair enough, and more   230
Befitting that wild Argos, that coarse man.'
Then said he, with wet cheek,
                  "'Prometheus! bear
The pouncing bird and bloody rock; endure,
Endure it all; well mayst thou: lightnings strike
Thy sleepless eyes, eternal beaks devour
Thy breast, thy liver, that but heave for them,
Yet thou hast never seen another man
Step to the chamber of thy soul's beloved.'"
   It shamed the maiden to relate the first,
The second part it pain'd her to relate,   240
But every word she told, and every sigh;
Which, lest the mother should remark, she prayed
To hear about Ulyssessis return.
Leda thus interwove it with advice.
"Whomever Love hath rightly joined, on those
Life showers down golden days, and every hour
Is bridal. Thou art young, and young the man
Who seeks thee in espousal. Think how far
Chaste love excels unchaster, and become
A new Penelope. Her father ill   250
Endured to lose her; it was grief to say
Farewell; and he had said it: first he turn'd
His face and bent it weeping to the wall,
Then rais'd it; for he heard the feet of steeds
Distinctly . . indistinctly where the road
Was paved no longer and was farther off.
His spirit then broke down; he rusht away,
Weaker with hurry, both in step and sight.
He speeded; he came up to them; for soon
Slackened his pace Ulysses, thus to hear   260
Better the voice of her he bore away.
Icarius, panting heavily, exclamed,
'Return her to me! I did give . . 'tis true . .

My treasure to thy prayers .. but then, O then
I was not childless; nor so deaf wert thou.
Many there are who may please *thee;* but one,
One only, is the comfort of my age;
Give, give her back .. or both return with me.'
Ulysses heard, and drew the reins in tight.
Gently the bride received her sire, and wept   270
Receiving him: her arm embraced his neck,
And tenderest kisses cool'd his throbbing breast.
The bridegroom then bespake him.

                      "'Sparta long
Detained me, long and willingly; but home
Now calls me back; I have a father there,
A land, a people; there too I have Gods
Protectors, whom it were a sin to leave.'
     "'If thou art pious,' cried the father, 'here
Display thy piety, and yield my child.'
     "'Be hers the choice' he answered.

                "At that word   280
Penelope cast on the ground her eyes;
Her right-hand held his garment; she bent low
To hide the anguish of her sobbing breast.
'Choose!' said the father. 'Think who bore thee! think
Of me thy father! think, and pity me!'
Tortured as was that bosom while he spoke,
Silent for ever as she would remain,
Yet when Ulysses added,

                  "'Speak, my own
Penelope!' she lowered her face, she prest
A closer arm around her father's neck,   290
But, covering with her veil her tearful eyes,
Inclined her own upon the lover's breast.
Happier and prouder was the sire that day;
He entered with firm step his house again,
And other fathers envied him; they rais'd
Amid the chaunting of our youths and maids
(Why wert thou absent, Helen?) rais'd of turf
An altar dedicate to Modesty."

ACON AND RHODOPE; OR, INCONSTANCY

[Published in 1847; not reprinted. A sequel to "The Hamadryad". See p. 283.]

THE Year's twelve daughters had in turn gone by,
Of measured pace tho' varying mien all twelve,
Some froward, some sedater, some adorn'd
For festival, some reckless of attire.
The snow had left the mountain-top; fresh flowers
Had withered in the meadow; fig and prune
Hung wrinkling; the last apple glow'd amid
Its freckled leaves; and weary oxen blinkt
Between the trodden corn and twisted vine,
Under whose bunches stood the empty crate,   10
To creak ere long beneath them carried home.
This was the season when twelve months before,
O gentle Hamadryad, true to love!
Thy mansion, thy dim mansion in the wood
Was blasted and laid desolate: but none
Dared violate its precincts, none dared pluck
The moss beneath it, which alone remain'd
Of what was thine.
     Old Thallinos sat mute
In solitary sadness. The strange tale
(Not until Rhaicos died, but then the whole)   20
Echion had related, whom no force
Could ever make look back upon the oaks.
The father said "Echion! thou must weigh,
Carefully, and with steddy hand, enough
(Although no longer comes the store as once!)
Of wax to burn all day and night upon
That hollow stone where milk and honey lie:
So may the Gods, so may the dead, be pleas'd!"
Thallinos bore it thither in the morn,
And lighted it and left it.
     First of those   30
Who visited upon this solemn day
The Hamadryad's oak, were Rhodope
And Acon; of one age, one hope, one trust.
Graceful was she as was the nymph whose fate
She sorrowed for: he slender, pale, and first
Lapt by the flame of love: his father's lands
Were fertile, herds lowed over them afar.
Now stood the two aside the hollow stone

343

And lookt with stedfast eyes toward the oak
Shivered and black and bare.
                              "May never we   40
Love as they loved!" said Acon. She at this
Smiled, for he said not what he meant to say,
And thought not of its bliss, but of its end.
He caught the flying smile, and blusht, and vow'd
Nor time nor other power, whereto the might
Of love hath yielded and may yield again,
Should alter his.
                  The father of the youth
Wanted not beauty for him, wanted not
Song, that could lift earth's weight from off his heart,
Discretion, that could guide him thro' the world,   50
Innocence, that could clear his way to heaven;
Silver and gold and land, not green before
The ancestral gate, but purple under skies
Bending far off, he wanted for his heir.
    Fathers have given life, but virgin heart
They never gave; and dare they then controll
Or check it harshly? dare they break a bond
Girt round it by the holiest Power on high?
    Acon was grieved, he said, grieved bitterly,
But Acon had complied . . 'twas dutiful!   60
    Crush thy own heart, Man! Man! but fear to wound
The gentler, that relies on thee alone,
By thee created, weak or strong by thee;
Touch it not but for worship; watch before
Its sanctuary; nor leave it till are closed
The temple-doors and the last lamp is spent.
    Rhodope, in her soul's waste solitude,
Sate mournful by the dull-resounding sea,
Often not hearing it, and many tears
Had the cold breezes hardened on her cheek.   70
Meanwhile he sauntered in the wood of oaks,
Nor shun'd to look upon the hollow stone
That held the milk and honey, nor to lay
His plighted hand where recently 'twas laid
Opposite hers, when finger playfully
Advanced and pusht back finger, on each side.
He did not think of this, as she would do
If she were there alone.
                         The day was hot;

344

ACON AND RHODOPE

The moss invited him; it cool'd his cheek,
It cool'd his hands; he thrust them into it   80
And sank to slumber. Never was there dream
Divine as his. He saw the Hamadryad.
She took him by the arm and led him on
Along a valley, where profusely grew
The smaller lilies with their pendent bells,
And, hiding under mint, chill drosera,
The violet shy of butting cyclamen,
The feathery fern, and, browser of moist banks,
Her offspring round her, the soft strawberry;
The quivering spray of ruddy tamarisk,   90
The oleander's light-hair'd progeny
Breathing bright freshness in each other's face,
And graceful rose, bending her brow, with cup
Of fragrance and of beauty, boon for Gods.
The fragrance fill'd his breast with such delight
His senses were bewildered, and he thought
He saw again the face he most had loved.
He stopt: the Hamadryad at his side
Now stood between; then drew him farther off:
He went, compliant as before: but soon   100
Verdure had ceast: altho' the ground was smooth,
Nothing was there delightful. At this change
He would have spoken, but his guide represt
All questioning, and said,
                              "Weak youth! what brought
Thy footstep to this wood, my native haunt,
My life-long residence? this bank, where first
I sate with him . . the faithful (now I know,
Too late!) the faithful Rhaicos. Haste thee home;
Be happy, if thou canst; but come no more
Where those whom death alone could sever, died."   110
   He started up: the moss whereon he slept
Was dried and withered: deadlier paleness spred
Over his cheek; he sickened: and the sire
Had land enough; it held his only son.

345

HELLENICS

THE ESPOUSALS OF POLYXENA

[Published in 1847. For a later version published in 1859 see notes at end of volume. Text 1847.]

"In Troy, O virgin, shall thy blood remain,
And last beyond Achilles thy espoused."
So sang the Fates together; and their song
Now from Apollo's mouth Polyxena,
Led by her mother to the shrine, received.
The mother chided with long speech her dread,
Opening before her many happy days;
But none of them saw she: grave Hecuba
Wondered that one so pious could despair.
"How, when thus deigns Apollo to confirm 10
His oracle with omens! What large light
Smiles over heaven! and sweeter breathes the air
Since thy return, sweet as it was before.
Lo! the flowers rise thro' the first dust of spring
As if no enemy had trodden them,
And often by one bramble are two graves
United o'er the slayer and the slain:
Such and so many are the signs of peace."
"I see, I feel it," sighed Polyxena.
"Even that dust which now the tepid breeze 20
Blows over us, once lived with Trojan blood,
And that blood's moisture fed these very flowers.
O sun! thou shinedst with no other light
When the Achaian keels first scraped our shores,
With light no other when Achilles shook
Our walls with war-cry, car, and clattering arms,
Alas! and with no other when our Gods
Departed, and left Hector maim'd and dead."
Saddened at this, the mother then exclamed
"Why have I broken silence? On this day 30
I had ceast weeping for my children slain,
For now Pelidesis fierce valour comes
To save us, not to crush us; and dost thou,
Impious! hold back? nor see our Gods return'd?
Ruling o'er kings, with ancient wealth elate,
And hastening to show Asia, won at last,
United to Mycenai, and restore
Helen, in vain by adverse Mars opposed,
Atrides would far rather him for son

Than all those glories, all that wealth and power.　　　40
Iphigeneia did not thus refuse
When he was drawn reluctantly to arms,
Intact his shining shield: the goddess-born,
The born to procreate a race of gods
Thou wavest from thee. She pour'd forth her blood
That Troy might fall not, that thy hand might save.
But thou hast gathered up the random words
My poor Cassandra utters: thou hast fears,
And fearest not Achilles!"
　　　　　　　　Then submiss
Replied the daughter.
　　　　　　　　"If the Gods command　　　50
My marriage, as indeed they do command,
Or even my slavery, to them I bow;
There is no hardship, there is no disgrace;
But, mother, let me weep; my parent's will,
Since they do not relent, I must obey.
I must be given up to him whose car
Drag'd Hector, drag'd stil breathing, thro' the sands
We tread on, where we promise faith and love,
And praise the Gods for this. Pity my grief;
It never can diminish. Can the Gods　　　60
Themselves, who see and bid and do such things,
Show me one joy my broken heart may hold?
O tombs! O thou before me, which the last
Of friendship twined with brittle cypress-leaves,
Wither'd and shed, and prest the turf close round!
And all ye others, numberless, that draw
The short thin grass about more recent bones!
Ye are the boundaries of weal and woe.
But we have promist if Apollo wills . .
Ensue but peace from it! . . Enough! my troth　　　70
Is plighted . . Mother! mother! I comply."
　　Then Hecuba, and gaspt with grateful tears.
"My last-born child! my life's last, only, hope!
What joy, how intermitted, do thy words
Restore! Believe me, my beloved one,
Not what thou fanciest is thy valiant spouse.
The fates and fortunes of an aged king,
The roof that Gods have dwelt beneath, now touch
His generous bosom, deeplier stil thy youth
And beauty: these perhaps, and these alone,　　　80

347

Have made him ask what else he might have seiz'd.
Beside he fear'd (he could not fear that thou
Wouldst be, as was Briseis, unavenged)
He fear'd lest thou by lot shouldst be transfer'd
To that proud tyrant as his lawful prize;
For sure enough his prescient mind foresaw
The fall of Ilion and . . forgive me, Heaven!
For uttering it . . Palladium he derides,
And dreads not any God since Hector slain."

Beneath the hill where stand the towers of Troy 90
The open plain buzzed all the way with crowds,
From the warm channel of the stony brook
Quite to the brakes of Ida; tired of fight,
Yet resolute, if need, to fight again;
But hoping now, from every omen, peace.
Mixt with the Dardans in Apollo's fane
The Achaian chieftains divers thoughts revolved.
One blamed Æacides, Atrides one,
Many the downfall of the town delaid,
Many saw treachery, hid from the unwise, 100
And some smelt treasure stealthily received
And knew whose tent 'twas under.

To that fane
Went Priam and the consort of his realm.
There followed these, but followed slow, thro' grief
At many losses in each house, his friends
And kindred, and that progeny erewhile
So numerous and so prodigal of life:
His veil'd stepdaughters closed the stately train,
Led veil'd not long ago for no such hour:
Alone, at home, to while that hour away, 110
Andromache, oft chided by her child,
Sate, and turn'd slow the spindle, sorrowing.
Meantime how many hearts are throbbing quick
To see so many famous men so nigh,
And know those arms and faces, ill discern'd
Amid the whirl of war. Onward they press
And onward; then halt suddenly; some fear
Lurks with them stil; they call it pious awe,
And, better to dissemble, crouch before
The feet and altar of their placid God. 120
Polyxena, for whom they all make way,
Grasps, without knowing it, the hand she dreads.

THE ESPOUSALS OF POLYXENA

Beauteous, more beauteous even than she . . surpast
By Helen only, in that snow-white brow
And eyes before whose light Apollo's fell,
Rushes with shrill loud shout thro' friend and foe,
Cassandra.
        Silent, trembling, stood they all,
As if some God had entered; she alone
Could speak; and thus (words not her own) she spake.
"Hopest thou, sister! sister! happy days   130
Awaiting thee? Look thou at Troy, behold
The work of Neptune and Apollo, Troy,
Ramparts and towers that Pallas dwells within.
I see them totter under arms and flames,
And Simöis and Xanthus swift with blood.
Behold! the ruin comes when war hath ceast,
And Gods and sons of Gods walk slow with wounds.
O flower! which yonder fierce Thessalian hand
Is plucking, on what altar art thou laid?
Why blaze so the Sigæan shores, the torch   140
Unkindled yet; those rocks of Tenedos,
Why throw they back again that trailing light?
Fly! let us fly! Citheron, and the towers
Chaonian, the Ceraunian rocks, the strand
Of Achelöus (hear!) reverberate
The clamour, the loud plaint of Ilion.
Behold the monster scale the walls, and champ
The marble manger! hear his voice! his voice
Is human! Why delay? What idle words!
Rise, O my parents! O my kindred, rise!   150
Turn from the realms of Thrace your sight away!
Whither, O Polydoros, callest thou?
What does that shady cornel show and hide?
Why, as they drop and bound and roll along,
Tinkle the loose stones from that recent tomb?
Ah me, who can not drown such sights in tears
Nor scatter them in madness! Sweet espoused
Sister! who sittest with thine arms unbound
That thy pure bosom may receive the sword,
To me hold forward, while thou canst, those arms,   160
And give undying love one long embrace.
Save, save her, Pyrrhos! By thy father's shade!
Guiltless is she! Spare! Dying I implore,
And will implore it, in, and after, death."

Uttering these words, her handmaids closed around
And took her to the cool and quiet gloom
Of her own chamber. In the fane meanwhile
A buz is heard. An arrow slid unseen
Amid the tumult, and so far transfixt
The sinew of Achilles in the heel　　　　　　　　　170
That the brass barb clankt on the marble floor.
The chiefs around him saw him bend and glare
Terrific; then they saw the shaft, and then
A globe of blood. They seize their spears; they tear
Vervain and olive (now no sign of peace)
From every helm, and throw and stamp them down.
Nor would they now hear Priam, scattering dust
On his thin hair, nor would they mind the spouse,
Sinking as if in death: no, nor did he,
Her wooer, aid, or ask for aid himself.　　　　　　180
He saw his hour draw nigh, and brought to mind
Predictions, but coerced the rising wrath
Of those around, and gave these last commands.
"Peace! 'tis my will. Let never mortal dare
Avenge Achilles: from this blood hath sprung
One worthy to avenge it, one alone.
Alcimos and Automedon! return
And keep my Myrmidons within the camp,
Lest they should lose obedience and due awe
Of those whose orders bear no dreadful mark.　　190
Diomed! Ajax! leave me; leave a frame
Unequal to the weakest thing alive.
No; leave me not: bear me away: let none
Who hate or fear me, see me and rejoice.
Ah! must the flocks and herds of humbled Troy
Tread on my bones and pasture on my tomb?
Cease, whosoe'er thou art, cease thou whose tears
Drop hot upon my shoulder! Fain my eyes
Would look on thee, but they are turn'd to iron,
And may not know again thy friendly face.　　　200
Fate calls for me. Take from my neck your arms;
They weary me; they weigh me down; worn out,
With heavy languor's deadly bale consumed.
I grieve not that Larissa holds the bones
Of my forefathers in their quiet graves;
I grieve not for my mother in the halls
Of Tethys, from the power of Death exempt;

I grieve that Ilion should be thus avenged
Without her thousands fallen round me slain.
  "Dark art thou, standing o'er my head, O Death!   210
Most bitter is this wound; it smites my heart.
Open the turf afresh, remove the stone
And the black fragments of the boughs above;
The urn that holds Patroclos, now shall hold
Achilles: then push from the shore my barks,
And, if your great Atrides grant you leave,
Bring back from Pthia (now at play perhaps
With some new armour, and in hopes to share
His father's glory, not to hold his place)
My own brave boy, predestined to bring down   220
That ruin which the Pelian shaft prepared.
  "Hear ye my voice? or fall my words in vain
Attempts to reach you? Troubled so my mind,
I do not know what wishes I exprest
Or what I left unuttered. Far from you
Be such oblivion . . of a dying friend!
And now that Orcos hurries me away,
My shade may all the greater shades receive
And all the lesser fear!
                "Farewell, farewell,
My far-off Pyrrhos! Ah! what care shall guide   230
Thy youth? in thee what Chiron shall rejoice?
No hand of father to applaud thy lyre,
Thy javelin, or thy chariot, known and hail'd
By all beholders in the foremost dust."

SILENUS

[Published in "Hellenics", 1847; not reprinted.]

SILENUS, when he led the Satyrs home,
Young Satyrs, tender-hooft and ruddy-horn'd,
With Bacchus equal-aged, sat down sometimes
Where softer herbs invited, then releast
From fawn-skin pouch a well-compacted pipe,
And sprinkled song with wisdom.
                    Some admired
The graceful order of unequal reeds;
Others cared little for the melody
Or what the melody's deep bosom bore,
And thought Silenus might have made them shine.   10

They whisper'd this: Silenus overheard,
And mildly said "'Twere easy: thus I did
When I was youthful: older, I perceive
No pleasure in the buzzes of the flies,
Which like what *you* like, O my little ones!"
　Some fancied he reproved them, and stood still,
Until they saw how grave the Satyr boys
Were looking; then one twicht an upright ear
And one a tail recurv'd, or stroked it down.
Audacious innocence! A bolder cried　　　　　　20
"Sound us a song of war;" a timider,
"Tell us a story that will last til night."
　Silenus smiled on both, and thus replied.
"Chromis hath sung fierce battles, swords of flame,
Etherial arrows wing'd with ostrich-plumes,
Chariots of chrysolite and ruby reins,
And horses champing pearls and quaffing blood.
Mnasylos tells wide stories: day is short,
Night shorter; they thro months and years extend.
When suns are warm, my children, let your hearts　　30
Beat, but not beat for battles; when o'ercast,
Mnasylos and his tepid fogs avoid.
　"I hear young voices near us; they are sweet;
Go where they call you; I am fain to rest;
Leave me, and ask for no more song to-day."

ll. 1–6 repeat, at first with minor and then with larger variants, the brief prelude to "Gebir", 1798 (see vol. i.). Rejected in "Gebir", 1803, but in a Latin form retained in "Gebirus", 1803, this prelude was suggested by Virgil's sixth Eclogue. In a footnote to "Gebirus" the adaptation of a Virgilian setting was acknowledged. After *l.* 6 of the 1847 poem, save the names of Chromis (*l.* 24) and Mnasylos (*l.* 28), Landor borrows little from Virgil, while Silenus becomes far less discursive than he was in the eclogue that often bears his name. [W.]

PART III. FROM *HELLENICS*, 1859, *HEROIC IDYLS*, 1863, and *LANDOR: A BIOGRAPHY*, 1869.

"The Hellenics of Walter Savage Landor; comprising Heroic Idyls, &c. new edition, enlarged, Edinburgh: James Nichol, 104 High Street. London: R. Griffin and Co M.DCCC.LIX" had on p. iii a Dedication to General Sir W. Napier, for which see notes at end of volume, and on p. v the following:

PREFACE

Prefixing a preface is like keeping an invited friend at the hall-door, instead of conducting him at once into the house.

Little in these pages will gratify the generality of readers. Poetry, in our day, is oftener prismatic than diaphanous: this is not so: they who look into it may see through. If there be anywhere a few small air-bubbles, it yet leaves to the clear vision a wide expanse of varied scenery.

[Some of the poems in the volume, recast from earlier versions, are given elsewhere in the present edition. The following were first printed in 1859.]

[PROEM TO HELLENICS]

[Published in 1859; reprinted 1876.]

COME back, ye wandering Muses, come back home,
Ye seem to have forgotten where it lies:
Come, let us walk upon the silent sands
Of Simois, where deep footmarks show long strides;
Thence we may mount perhaps to higher ground,
Where Aphroditè from Athenè won
The golden apple, and from Herè too,
And happy Ares shouted far below.
 Or would ye rather choose the grassy vale
Where flows Anapos thro anemones,   10
Hyacynths, and narcissuses, that bend
To show their rival beauty in the stream?
 Bring with you each her lyre, and each in turn
Temper a graver with a lighter song.

MELITON AND LILY

[Published in 1859; reprinted 1876.]

There was a time when Flowers could speak more plain
Than Poets now do; and for once again
A Flower shall answer what a Poet said ..
Meliton *he* was, Lily was the maid.
Sit on this garden-bench and hear a song,
Maybe not tiresome, certainly not long.

HELLENICS

Lily! why dost thou shower on me the gold
Off thy white bosom, dazzling to behold?
Must I confess to thee, another Flower
I love stil better at this very hour,
And she shall (if not over) place thee nigh　　　　　10
A bosom pure as thine, where never sigh
(I hope) shall shake thee, Lily! now goodbye,
Forgetting not, nor ready to disown
Thy friend of other days, thy Meliton.
Before thee, at an early season, burst
A Rose, and whispered low . . *You loved me first.*

LILY.

You are inconstant, now I know,
I often heard it long ago
But never thought to tell you so.　　　　　20
I need no blush; but every day
She blushes; yes, and well she may.
Pure let her be! well! who should care?
Is she, pray tell me, quite as fair?
You do not answer what I ask.

MELITON.

I dare not; it's too hard a task.

LACON AND DORA

[Published in 1859; reprinted 1876.]

Dora (wakening him). Feedest thou upon poppies? drowsy drone!
Lacon. Haply my breathing was a little hard,
Hard it is always when I think of thee.
Dora. Do idle shepherds snort like porpuses?
I know what such hard breathing means with men;
We never practise it.
Lacon.　　　　　Us men ye make
Practise it often.
Dora.　　　　　Why not keep awake?
Lacon. Too long awake ye keep us.
Dora.　　　　　　　　　When you dance;
But dance makes me sleep sounder.

Title. Acon (not Lacon). Landor's *MS.* note.

LACON AND DORA

Lacon.   You mistake
My meaning?
    Dora.   Is there any?
    Lacon.   Day and night   10
Of all hard breathing ye enforce the worst . .
Unheeded sighs.
    Dora.   Bad! but the worst are those
That burst from nostril; hast thou none beside?
    Lacon. I could breathe softer in a patient ear:
Sit by my side and hear the difference.
    Dora. Quiet now! wilt not let me seat myself?
    Lacon. I would but help thee: soon we both will rise
Together. They who sigh but once have learnt
Imperfect love: beginning, middle, end,
There are in all things; we have barely come   20
Halfway.
    Dora.   O impudence! is that halfway?
Then when, I wonder, shall we reach the end?

ACON AND KEPOS

[Published in 1859; reprinted 1876.]

ACON.

Kepos! what brings thee from the market-place?

KEPOS.

What drove me from it, rather ask.

ACON.

          Well, what?

KEPOS.

There was a scramble round about my stall,
And two unlucky boys were fighting hard
Which of them should sweep off the fruit; at last
They overturn'd the board: 'twas time to run.

ACON.

And were the people then indifferent?

KEPOS.

At first they were not; presently they laught
To see a split pomegranate's slippery fruit

Drop from the fingers of the foremost two,
With nothing left between them but hard rind
And deeply-dyed and ever-during stain.

10

ACON.

Children of Hellas! learn your lesson here,
Nor touch pomegranate in the market-place.

LEONTION, ON TERNISSA'S DEATH
(EPICUROS ALSO DEPARTED)

[Published in 1859; reprinted 1876.]

BEHOLD, behold me, whether thou
Art dwelling with the Shades
    below
  Or with the Gods above:
With thee were even the Gods
    more blest . .
I wish I could but share thy rest
  As once I shared thy love.

'Twas in this garden where I lean
Against thy tombstone, once the
    scene
  Of more than mortal bliss,
That loiter'd our Ternissa; sure 10
She left me that her love was pure;
  It gave not kiss for kiss.

Faint was the blush that over-
    spred
Thro' loosen'd hair her dying head;
  One name she utter'd, one
She sigh'd and wept at; so wilt
    thou,

If any sorrows reach thee now . .
  'Twas not *Leontion*.

Wert thou on earth thou wouldst
    not chide
The gush of tears I could not hide
  Who ne'er hid aught from
    thee. 21
Willing thou wentest on the way
She went . . and am I doom'd to
    stay?
  No; we soon meet, all three.

The flowers she cherisht I will
    tend,
Nor gather, but above them bend
  And think they breathe her
    breath.
Ah, happy flowers! ye little know
Your youthful nurse lies close
    below,
  Close as in life in death. 30

Title. See "Imaginary conversation": Epicurus, Leontion, and Ternissa, 1829.
The poem which follows may also be supposed to have been written by Leontion. [W.]
10 our] *so in corrigenda 1859. once in text.*

[Published in 1846.]

CLXIV.

TERNISSA! you are fled!
  I say not to the dead,
But to the happy ones who rest below:

LEONTION, ON TERNISSA'S DEATH

For, surely, surely, where
Your voice and graces are,
Nothing of death can any feel or know.
  Girls who delight to dwell
  Where grows most asphodel,
Gather to their calm breasts each word you speak:
    The mild Persephone   10
    Places you on her knee,
And your cool palm smoothes down stern Pluto's cheek.

HYMN AND OFFERING OF TERPANDER TO JUNO

[Published in 1859; reprinted 1876.]

I TOUCH the soil of Samos, where the queen
Of heaven is worshipt, and her priests ordain'd
Accept with gracious hands the gift of poor
And rich alike, and even frame the prayers
Of such as can not make them as beseems.
What priests upon the earth so bountiful?
What land so lovely? not even Rhodes, where Spring
Serenely smiles at Winter's languid wrath,
And where Apollo by the will of Zeus
Reigns the sole God.
                    Do thou with face benign   10
O Herè! take this votive vest today,
Brought by no hand impure, and well besprent
With lustral water, which the grateful fumes
Of incense rest on, and will rest on long,
Until they reach thee at thy dome above.
Do thou, O Herè, lay before the throne
Of Zeus all my petitions, all my prayers;
For well thou knowest 'twere audacious deed
In me without thy intercession, queen,
To plead before him for offence of mine,   20
Or favor at the Almighty Thunderer's hands.
  Stand afar off, ye unbelieving men,
While I with reverence lay before the feet
Of Herè this my offering, from a woof
Which maids of Sidon labored to intwine
With gold and purple. Stand afar, profane,

Title. Terpander's Hymn to Herè. *Landor MS.* Terpander of Lesbos (*fl.* 700 B.C.),
the father of Greek music. [W.]

357

Who doubt if they who on Olympus dwell,
Wear such thin raiment when they take delight
And clap their hands to see a Cloud and Wind
(Eurus or Boreas or Apeliotes)   30
Run races on the summit in the snow.
    I, happy in thy worship and thy care,
Seek not to vary this my happiness,
Nor would partake nor would impose a yoke.
I know that Love and Hymen when they meet
Are apt to quarrel; Hymen presses hard,
But Love with lighter wing eludes the grasp.
I shudder when I see a saffron robe
And torch before it. Herè! I am weak;
Direct my steps, direct them to thy fane   40
As now, and back again as now, alone.

       30 Apeliotes] *sc.* Ἀπηλιώτης = east wind. [W.]

SOPHRON'S HYMN TO BAKKOS

[Published in 1859; reprinted 1876.]

STAND afar off, irreverent and profane,
While I ascend the temple of a God
Miraculously born; a woman's child,
The nurseling of no woman, but enwrapt
In the soft swatheing of a father's thigh.
    Hail, earthborn son of Semele and Zeus!
Earthborn yet more, and in more lands, adored
Than Zeus himself. Grant me the power to sing
Thy praise, thy glorious conquests to rehearse
Beyond the Ganges and Gangetic iles   10
Numberless, where fierce tigers didst thou quell,
Stripping their skins from off them ere half-dead,
And whirling round thy neck their tawny legs,
And round thy shoulders to thy loins the length
Of their rich spoils: then first did Greece behold
Fangs such as never since hath Calydon
Yielded, when Meleager was avenged.
    Better than victories are benefits;
And these are thine too; greater none the Gods
Bestow on mortal. By thy hand the chain   20

   Title. Sophron of Syracuse (*fl. c. 480 B.C.*). Theocritus modelled two idylls on his
poems. [W.]   17 Meleager] *mispr.* Melcager, *here corrected.*

SOPHRON'S HYMN TO BAKKOS

Is loosened on the captive, and holds down
The neck of kings, who toss and toss in vain
And change the pillow, right and left, and start,
Dreaming they hear the heavy scepter drop.
　　Who praises now Lykourgos? who but shrinks
At that accursed name? 'twas he that spurn'd
Thy precious gift, nor spared the graceful curl
Of lucid tendril, nor pubescent down,
Nor fragrant bloom that waits the later spring.
　　We hear what nectar is, we hear whose hand　　　　30
Presents it in her golden cup to Zeus,
Tasting it at his nod and smile; then he
Drinks from the margin which her lips had toucht;
The nectar is not nectar until then:
Thou knowest, Dionysos, thou alone,
Whether it came from his own native Crete,
Or from his daughter's Cypros; both produce
Beverage which Hebe need not blush to bear.
　　Is there in city, hamlet, woodland, croft,
A festival without thy genial gifts,　　　　　　　　40
Thy presence, tho' unseen? Is there a birth
Of infant but thou gladdenest more the sire,
And the sire's friends, who sing thy praise aloud?
　　Thou knowest I was ever temperate
And worshipt thee in purity; thou knowest
I loved the Nymphs because they fondled thee
And carried thee an infant in their arms.
Modest as these am I; therefor unblamed
I may invoke thee in the midst of them.
One there is, Dionysos, at whose song　　　　　　　50
Sorrow hath often fled from me; do thou
Incline thine ear, and haply she may sing,
Altho' her songs were never framed for thee.
　　Hail, Dionysos, once again, and bless
This hospitable city; bless the sires
Of her brave sons, and them! long may they raise
The ancestral cup, and pass it friend to friend!

25 Lykourgos] king of the Edonians, expelled Dionysos and was punished by the god. See Apollodorus, iii. 5. 1. [W.]　　　39 in] *so in corrigenda 1859*, a *in text.*

HELLENICS

BLESSING ON PYTHAGORAS

BY AN ANCIENT PYTHAGOREAN.

[Published in 1859; not reprinted.]

BLESSED be he who taught us to abstain
From flesh of animal, and bean as bad,
But stated days appointed wherein fish,
Marine or fluvial, scaly or smooth-skin'd,
And pullet eggs, and certain mild legumes
Which rise not up rebellious like the bean,
Were unprohibited. Be blessed he
Who fearless walked upon his golden thigh
Over the sea from Egypt's holy land
Until at length he reacht our Italy,
Pythagoras.
                    We stil keep his commands,
Save only those which rigidly forbid
Bloodshed, of beast not only, but of man:
This the most righteous pray the Gods to grant.
    I do confess, and would repent, my sins,
But harder is repentance than confession,
For bovine I have eaten, nor abstain'd
From porcine, and would rather shed such blood
Than blood of fellow man.
                    "Thou art perverse,"
The righteous say, and deem this abstinence
Capricious.
        *"Why not slay him if thou slay
Creatures more innocent?"*
                    Such argument
Baffles reply; therefor I, hastening home,
Lay napkin upon knee and carve my beef.

THE FAMINE IN ETRURIA*

[Published in 1859; reprinted 1876.]

BEYOND the confines of a race cognate,
Pelasgic, and their hunger well appeas'd,
Had travel'd the Etrurians: age alone
Would have protected them throughout all lands
When it was widely known they sought the God
At Delphi; now they stood beneath his fane.
But some of them had rashly pluckt the boughs
Of bay in passing; when a voice was heard
In modulated tones; and these the words.
Impious the man who snaps the budding bay,   10
Or bruizes it, thus hastening its decay:
This may be pardon'd in the goats and swine;
Brutes know not what is awful and divine.
   Obedient were they all.
                When they approacht
The temple, one alone received a branch,
And he was bidden to come forth and speak.
Then came he forth and, kneeling, thus spake he.
   "The springs are sunk into the earth again,
Thou seest, Apollo, who seest all below,
And, where the fountains bubbled up, the bats   20
Widen their wings and crouch, nor seek for flies,
For even the flies around are dead with drought,
And the thin knats, now thinner, cease to whirr.
   Not only the light wanderers of the air,
The very serpents, mother Earth's first-born,
And living in all lands, live not with us.
Python, the glory of thy silver bow,
Would not have rais'd his threatening head, but croucht
At his full length, and panted, not defied.
   Piteous it is, if we can pity now   30
Aught but ourselves, to see the oxe's ribs

---

* Dionysius of Halicarnassus records this famine and its consequences, adding the appeal to the oracle, which oracle demanded, in addition to arrears, a tenth of the males. After this their calamity, the Etrurians, who were the Japanese of Europe three thousand years ago, in civility and industry, lost the dominion of Italy, stil observing the oracle, and devoting a tenth of their possessions and of their children to their Gods' vicegerent and subordinates. [L.]   According to Herodotus it was because of a famine lasting eighteen years that one half of the Lydians left their own country and, after many wanderings, settled in Etruria. Dionysius of Halicarnassus rejected the legend that Etruscans were descended from Lydian colonists. [W.]

White under him who drove them to the field,
And drying as they drop his bitter tears.
Where now the poppy-crown? where harvest-home?"
Fain would I rest upon a thought so sweet,
If sweet be any thought of happiness
Departed, and hope with it.
                    Worse remains.
A mother had no heart to kill her babe,
But offered it to one who had: he said
A plumper turnip was too high a price;   40
And she turn'd back in anger and in scorn . .
But soon (even scorn and anger sank) return'd,
For she had one babe left, and one might live.
    The God was deaf to every prayer; at length
They sought his oracle with better hopes;
Then said he from his inner shrine,
                    " 'Tis here.
Here only should ye seek me, willful men!
Depart; and sacrifice to me the tenth
Of all that earth may bear to you henceforth.
After due reverence to the priest ordain'd   50
To take it; he will lustrate you and bless
Your children."
               Joyous they return'd, such joy
As could find entrance in such shrunk abodes.
They brought the priest his tenth: he scowl'd on them.
    "Bring the tenth child," cried he "The God we serve
Delights in song, and song our God must have."
"Few are now left us" said the weeping sires,
And hunger leaves not even voice behind,
Nor are all fit for it."
               "Begone, perverse!"
Cried he . . "but ere ye go I promise ye   60
We of our temple can bring voices out,
And they shall warble in our sacred choir:
The virgins we will shut from eyes profane."
Sorrowing the Etrurians led their children forth
Devoted to the God of light and song.

---

52 such] *so in corrigenda 1859.* if *in text.*   53 As could find] *so in corrigenda 1859.* Ever found *in text.*   shrunk] *so in corrigenda 1859.* lank *in text.*

FROM *HEROIC IDYLS*, 1863, and *LANDOR: A BIOGRAPHY*, 1869.

"Heroic Idyls, with additional poems. By Walter Savage Landor London: T. Cautley Newby, publisher. 30, Welbeck Street, Cavendish Square 1863" had after title the following dedication and preface. See notes at end of volume.

To Edward Twisleton.

Dedications are often superfluous, and sometimes worse. Forgive my first fault of the kind. Vanity is almost as common to the old as to the young, and I feel it creeping on me when I remember your expression of regret that you had not known me earlier in life than last spring. All my old friends are dead, let their place continue to be supplied by Edward Twisleton.

Florence, August 25th, 1863.

Preface.

He who is within two paces of the ninetieth year may sit down and make no excuses; he must be unpopular, he never tried to be much otherwise, he never contended with a contemporary, but walked alone on the far eastern uplands, meditating and remembering.

To the Idyls a few slight matters have been appended, as tassels are to a purse. The Greek proper names have Greek terminations, not Latin, or French, or English.

[Some of the poems in the volume, recast from earlier versions or not included in this section, are given elsewhere in the present edition. The following were first printed in 1863:]

NIOBE

[Published in 1863; reprinted 1876.]

Amid nine daughters slain by Artemis
Stood Niobe: she rais'd her head above
Those beauteous forms which had brought down the scath
Whence all nine fell, rais'd it, and stood erect,
And thus bespake the Goddess enthroned on high.
"Thou heardest, Artemis, my daily prayer
That thou wouldst guide these children in the pass
Of virtue, through the tangling wilds of youth,
And thou didst ever guide them: was it just
To smite them for a beauty such as thine?   10
Deserv'd they death because thy grace appear'd
In every modest motion? 'twas thy gift,
The richest gift that youth from heaven receives.

1 nine daughters] Homer and Hesiod say there were only six; Sappho that there were nine. In the Uffizi gallery, Florence, statues of Niobe and fourteen children are arranged in a group; but one of the fourteen is duplicated and two others belong, it is thought, to another group. [W.]   5 enthroned] throned *Landor's MS. emendation.*   7 pass] path *in two MSS.*

True, I did boldly say they might compare
Even with thyself in virgin purity:
May not a mother in her pride repeat
What every mortal said?

                          One prayer remains
For me to offer yet.
                  Thy quiver holds
More than nine arrows: bend thy bow: aim here,
I see, I see it glimmering through a cloud.
Artemis thou at length art merciful.   20
My children will not hear the fatal twang."

Between *ll.* 20–1 one MS. has:

                     Blessed, blessed, blessed
      Be that pale glimmer of the silver bow!
      And that one arrow which atones for all.

PAN

[Published in 1863; reprinted 1876.]

PAN led me to a wood the other day,
Then, bending both hoofs under him, where moss
Was softest and where highest was the tuft,
Said he, "sit thou aside me; there is room
Just for us two; the tinklers are below
To catch the little birds and butterflies,
Nor see us nor would heed us if they saw.
I minded thee in Sicily with one
I dearly love; I heard thee tell my loss
Of Pitys; and he swore that none but thou   10
Could thus contend with him, or ever should.
Though others had loud lyres and struck them well,
Few could bring any harmony from reeds
By me held high, and higher since thou hast breath'd
Thy gentle breath o'er Pitys and her Pan."

5 tinklers]= rhymsters. The word was used by Aaron Hill in *Advice to Poets*, 1731.
[W.]   8 one] *sc.* Theocritus. [W.]

A FRIEND TO THEOCRITOS IN EGYPT

[Published in 1863; reprinted 1876.]

DOST thou not often gasp with longdrawn sighs,
Theocritos, recalling Sicily?
Glorious is Nile, but rather give me back
Our little rills, which fain would run away

A FRIEND TO THEOCRITOS IN EGYPT

And hide themselves from persecuting suns
In summer, under oleander boughs,
And catch its roses as they flaunt above.
Here are no birds that sing, no sweeter flower
Than tiny fragile weak-eyed resida,
Which faints upon the bosom it would cool.   10
Altho' the royal lotos sits aloof
On his rich carpet, spred from wave to wave,
I throw myself more gladly where the pine
Protects me, loftier than the palace-roof,
Or where the linden and acacia meet
Across my path, in fragrance to contend.
Bring back the hour, Theocritos, when we
Shall sit together on a thymy knoll,
With few about us, and with none too nigh,
And when the song of shepherds and their glee   20
We may repeat, perchance and gaily mock,
Until one bolder than the rest springs up
And slaps us on the shoulder for our pains.
Take thou meanwhile these two papyrus-leaves,
Recording, one the loves and one the woes
Of Pan and Pitys, heretofore unsung.
Aside our rivers and within our groves
The pastoral pipe hath dropt its mellow lay,
And shepherds in their contests only try
Who best can puzzle.   Come, Theocritos,   30
Come, let us lend a shoulder to the wheel
And help to lift it from this depth of sand.

EUCRATES TO THE GOD SLEEP

[Two versions A, B published in 1863; B reprinted 1876. Text A. 1863.]

No God to mortals oftener descends
Than thou, O sleep! yet thee the sad alone
Invoke, and gratefully thy gifts receive.
Some thou invitest to explore the sands
Left by Pactolos, some to climb up higher,
Where points Ambition to the pomp of War;
Others thou watchest while they tighten robes

Title. An old Poet to Sleep. B. 1863. [In Lucian there is mention of one Eucrates at whose table philosophers came to blows. Another Eucrates is named by Pausanias as the father of Procles of Carthage. W.]   2 sleep] Sleep *B.*   3 gifts] gift *B.*

Which Law throws round them loose, and they meanwhile
Wink at the judge, and he the wink returns.
Apart sit fewer, whom thou lovest more   10
And leadest where unruffled rivers flow,
Or azure lakes neath azure skies expand.
These have no wider wishes, and no fears,
Unless a fear by motion to molest
The silent, solitary, stately swan,
Disdaining the garrulity of groves
Nor seeking shelter there from sun or storm.
    Me also hast thou led among such scenes,
Gentlest of Gods! and Age appear'd far off
While thou wert hovering round about the couch   20
Until he stoopt and said, close over it,
"Sleep often plays with me, as once he used,
"Refreshing in his way the vernal flowers,
"Flowers that had droopt and but for him had died.
"He now departs from thee, but leaves behind
"His own twin-brother, beauteous as himself,*
"Who soon shall take my place . . men call him Death.
"Thou hearest me, nor tremblest, as most do,
"In sooth why shouldst thou? what man hast thou wrong'd
"By deed or word? few dare ask this within."   30
    There was a pause; then suddenly said Sleep
"He whom I warn'd approacheth: so farewell."

* There is an ancient statue of a Genius representing *Death* in the form of a beautiful youth. Dr. Young has introduced the God, in full feather, to the *world*, leading him to a seat of eyelashes not damp under him. [L. See Young's "Night Thoughts ", i. 1–6. The statue referred to is in the Uffizi Gallery, Florence. Pausanias says that there were statues of Sleep and Death at Sparta. W.]

9 at the] at a *B.*   14 by motion], in turning, *B.*   20 wert . . . about] wast standing close above *B.*   21 Until . . . it] And whispered'st, in whisper not un-heard *B.*   *ll.* 22–4 *om. B.*   25 He . . . departs] I now depart *B.*   leaves] leave *B.* 26 His . . . beauteous . . . himself] My . . . friendly . . . myself *B.*   28 hearest] *so in B and a manuscript. mispr.* heavest *in A.*   tremblest] *so in B and a manuscript. mispr.* troublest *in A.*   31 Sleep] *so in B and a manuscript.* ? *mispr.* Age *in A.* 32 warn'd] named *B.*

THE MARRIAGE OF HELENA AND MENELAOS

[Published in Forster's "Landor: a Biography" 1869.]

MOUNTED upon a tall Thessalian steed
Between two purely white rode Menelaos,
The sons of Leda were his company.
On drove they swiftly to where stood, above

THE MARRIAGE OF HELENA AND MENELAOS

Eurotas, a large mansion, large but low;
There they dismounted, two of them well known,
The third was never seen that way before.
Under the shelter of the house's roof
Sate with an idle spindle in the hand
Two seeming equal-aged, and yet was one   10
A mother, one her daughter; both sprang up.
"O Polydeukes!" the fond mother cried
(He had embraced her first), "O Kastor! come
Both of you to my bosom; long, how long
Have ye been absent!
                Helena! no word
Of welcome to your brethren?"
                     From the neck
Of Kastor, whereto she had clung, she turn'd
Her eyes a moment on the stranger's face,
Whispering in Kastor's ear, "Whom bring ye back?
Mild as he looks he makes me half-afraid."   20
But Kastor, without answering, ran where stood
His mother and their guest; to her he said,
"Here, my sweet mother, we have brought to thee
The son of Atreus, brother of that king
Who rules the widest and the richest realm
In all this land. Our guest is Menelaos."
Extending her right arm and open hand,
"Enter," said she, "a humble domicile,
Which Gods have enter'd and vouchsafed to bless."
Whereto with due obeisance he replied,   30
"O Leda, where thou art the Gods indeed
May well have enter'd, and have left behind
Their blessing, and to such I bend my brow;
Thy sons announced the welcome thou hast given."
  "And not one word to *me*!" said Helena,
With a low sigh, which Kastor caught and broke,
Thus chiding her: "Come thou too, unabasht,
Bid my friend welcome; speak it."
                  "I must not
Until our mother tells me," said the maid.
"Then I *do* tell thee," Leda said; whereon   40
Helena rais'd her head, but timidly,
And bade him welcome: gazing on his face
More confidently now by slow degrees
She question'd him about the world abroad,

And whether there were rivers bright and cool
As her Eurotas, on whose stream were swans,
"Until rude children mockt their hoarser tones,
And pelted them with egg-shells if they hissed.
My gentle mother could but ill endure
To see them angry, stretching out their necks   50
Ruffled, as they are never till provok'd;
For she loved swans, the tamest one the most,
So tame that he would let her hold his beak
Between her lips and stroke his plumage down:
This fondler was her favourite long before
I saw the light, when she was of my age.
Ah! we have no such now, I wish we had.
There still are birds of red and azure wing,
Beautiful to behold; and here are heard
Among the willows some who sing all night,   60
Unsociable and shy, and shun the feast
Of other birds upon the sunny field.
Are any such elsewhere? these you shall hear
When sleep hath carried off the weariness
Which that proud prancing creature must have caused."
   Night came, but slumber came not quite so soon
To four faint eyes: the lark was up in air
When Helena arose; the mother first
Had left her chamber, and the board was spread
With fruits and viands ready for the guest.   70
Presently he and his two friends sate down;
But Helena was paddling listlessly
In the fresh river, with unbraided hair
And vesture cast aside; some irksomeness
She felt which water could not all remove.
The cool and spacious hall she enter'd soon,
Where Menelaos and her brethren sate;
The guest was seated at her mother's right,
And she was bidden to the left, close by.
Often did she look forward, to drive off   80
The flies that buzz'd about the stranger's head . .
Flies never were so troublesome before.
Complacently saw Leda the device,
But Menelaos saw the care alone
Of a young maiden hospitably kind.
The brothers were impatient of delay
Until they both could urge their parent on

THE MARRIAGE OF HELENA AND MENELAOS

To give their sister to a man so brave:
Such too was Leda's wish when she had learnt
How throughout Argos honour'd and beloved   90
Was Menelaos: she warn'd Helena
More earnestly than ever, more profuse
Of sage advice and proverbs from the depth
Of ancient lore, how youth runs fast away,
And beauty faster; sixteen years had flown
Unwaringly, and had she never thought
To wed?

       "O mother! I am but a child,"
Cried she; "do any marry at sixteen?"
The mother shook her head and thus pursued: 100
"Remember how few moons have risen since
A wild Cecropian carried thee from home,
And well bethink thee that another time
Thy brothers may be absent, in the chase
Or far in foreign lands, as now of late."
  Helena made excuses, and the more
She made the more she wished them overcome;
But if her mother and her father Zeus
So will'd it, 'tis her duty she must yield.
She ran across the court wherein three steeds
Were standing loose; there Polydeukes trimm'd   110
His courser's mane, there Kastor drew his palm
Down the pink nostril of his dapple-gray,
And just beyond them the Thessalian steed
Stampt at neglect, for Menelaos lay
Sleepless past sunrise, which was not his wont.
Incontinent the brothers rais'd their heads
And shouted,

       "Here, thou sluggard! here before
Our busy sister come to pat the necks
Or throw arm round them."

       Scarcely were these words
Spoken ere Menelaos was at hand.   120
Helena, who had watcht him thus advance,
Drew back as one surprised, and seem'd intent
To turn away, but Polydeukes sprang
And caught her arm and drew her, struggling ill,
To where his brother with their comrade stood.
At first she would have turn'd her face aside,
But could not: Menelaos gently toucht

Her shrinking arm; little it shrank, nor long.
Then he entreated her to hear the words
Of true and ardent love, for such was his
He swore; she shook her head, with brow abased.
"What ardent love can mean I never heard;
My brothers, if they knew it, never told me,"
Said she, and lookt amazed into his face.
"Simplicity and innocence!" exclaim'd
The wondering Argive. "What a prudent wife
Will *she* be, when I win her, as I hope,
Diffident as she is nor prone to trust;
Yet hope I, daughter though she be of Zeus,
And I but younger brother of a king."
    Day after day he grew in confidence,
And gave her all he gain'd in it, and more.
Hymen was soon invok'd, nor was averse;
Eros had long been ready, the light-wing'd,
And laught at his slow step who marcht behind.
Chaunted were hymns to either Deity
By boys and maidens, tho' they understood
No word they sang: serious was Hymen's face
When Eros laught up into it and twitcht
The saffron robe, and heeded no reproof.
'Tis said they sometimes since have disagreed
More seriously: but let not me report
The dissidence and discord of the Gods.

130

140

150

NOTES

SECTION II. DRAMAS AND DRAMATIC SCENES

P. 1. GIOVANNA OF NAPLES. Part II of the trilogy opens shortly after the murder, on September 18, 1345, of Andrea. The barbarous punishment of Filippa and others falsely accused of complicity in the crime is related by several speakers in Act I, though not yet known to Giovanna. Filippa died under torture in August, 1346; her grand-daughter Sancia, wrongly called Sancia Terlizzi, was burnt in the following December. The Queen dowager Sancia, mentioned as still living, had died in July, 1345. In Act III Giovanna is shown as appearing in person before Rienzi. He was Tribune from May to December, 1347, when he fled from Rome; but most writers state that Giovanna sent deputies to plead her cause. In the last scene of Act V Giovanna and Luigi of Taranto meet as cousins. They were married August 22, 1347, so the middle play must be supposed to end shortly before that date; unless one or two scenes were disarranged, if none were discarded, by Forster.

P. 44. FRA RUPERT. Part III of the trilogy opens thirty-four years after the close of Part II. During the interval Luigi of Taranto, Gio-vanna's second husband, had died in 1362. Two years later she married James of Majorca, who died 1375. In 1376 she gave her hand to Duke Otho of Brunswick. In April, 1380, having incurred the enmity of Pope Urban VI she was pronounced by him excommunicate and no longer a queen. In Act I of *Fra Rupert* Urban informs her nephew and adopted son, Charles of Durazzo, that if he agrees to certain conditions he shall take her kingdom; and history records that, conditions being agreed to, Charles was crowned at Rome as King of Naples on June 1, 1381. Except for the share assigned to Fra Rupert in the intrigues that put Charles on a throne the play proceeds without marked divergence from history till the scene where Otho, in a desperate attempt to rescue Giovanna from captivity, is wounded and dies in her arms. History says that he was taken prisoner, was released after Giovanna's death, and died later.

In Act V, Scene V, people in Naples learn that the dethroned queen is dead. Historians have given conflicting accounts of the event, but it is almost certain that she was murdered May 22, 1382. In the last scene of Landor's drama Fra Rupert on the day of her funeral stabs himself to escape the just penalty of his misdeeds. Why he should be a dominant figure in the play is hard to explain. The villainous monk, properly called Robert di Mileto, disappears from history long before the period covered in this concluding part of the trilogy.

P. 101. THE SIEGE OF ANCONA, *ll.* 37–8. As printed in 1846 and 1876 *edd.* Stamura's responses to street cries seemed to be the initial and only words of two curtailed verses. In the present edition these responses are properly placed not as beginning but as ending the same lines, and following in each case the street cry which had reached Stamura's ear. This was certainly Landor's intention, and no more than a slight trans-position was required to avert the misunderstanding likely to be caused by the text as first published.

NOTES

P. 132. GUZMAN AND HIS SON. Lopez de Vega (*ob.* 1636) wrote a drama on the same incident, but Landor may have found it either in Mariana or in Richard Ford's *Handbook of Spain*, 1845. Don Alonzo de Guzman, ancestor of the Dukes of Medina-Sidonia, offered to hold Tarifa for a year. Aided by the Infante Juan, King Sancho's traitor brother, the Moors attacked the stronghold. Guzman's son had been page to Juan, who threatened to kill the lad unless the place was surrendered. Guzman preferred "death without a son to death with dishonour". According to Ford, the boy was nine years old at the time, but Landor (l. 30) gives sixteen as his age.

P. 134. THE CORONATION. Ferdinand II, king of the Two Sicilies, who became infamous as "King Bomba", succeeded his father in 1830. The title may have been added by Forster in ignorance of the fact that rulers of this line were not crowned. There would, however, be a special service at the Cathedral and a state procession.

P. 138. FIVE SCENES. *Scene IV* was published in *The Keepsake for 1851* with title and footnote as follows:

BEATRICE CENCI AND POPE CLEMENT VIII *

By WALTER SAVAGE LANDOR

* The true history of Cenci, by Adionello, is greatly more pathetic than Shelley's noble tragedy. Throughout my dramatic scene the horrible is kept in deep obscurity: the merit, if there is any in it, is this. [L.] [Footnote not reprinted. The book cited is *Beatrice Cenci, Storia del secolo XVI*, by Agostino Ademollo (not Adionello).—W.]

The *Scene* is dated at end *February 24th* [1850].

Writing to Leigh Hunt Landor said: "My preface will show you that I intended no rivalry or competition with Shelley. . . . My admiration of him is equal to yours. I had not read *Cenci* since its first publication; on reading it again, it struck me as impossible that a criminal and hypocrite could boast of his cruelty. Scene 3 is beyond all credibility."

See *Beatrice Cenci*, by Corrado Ricci, Milan, 1923, for the best account yet given of her life and death. [W.]

P. 161. DEATH OF BLAKE. Both in this scene and in an imaginary conversation, "Admiral Blake and Humphrey Blake", Landor may have relied on Hepworth Dixon's *Robert Blake, Admiral*; a work pronounced by competent critics to be untrustworthy. Admiral Robert Blake, returning to England after having defeated the Spanish fleet, died on board his ship, the *George*, at the entrance to Plymouth Sound, August 17, 1657.

P. 164. ANTONY AND OCTAVIUS. In reply to Forster's objection that Cleopatra and Cæsarion were made too young in the *Scenes* Landor wrote, December, 1855:

"I don't think the point so certain as you appear to think it is. There were differences between Cleopatra and her brother at the time when Julius Cæsar went into Egypt; and he settled them on his arrival. She was carried up into his bedroom on a man's shoulders in a coverlet. She and her brother were minors, under tutelage. Eastern kings are not minors after twelve. At twelve girls are marriageable. I doubt if Cleopatra was much above *thirteen* when Cæsarion was born; certainly not *fourteen*. Now, it is easy to know at what time Antony came into Egypt, and when he died."

DRAMAS AND DRAMATIC SCENES

P. 202. SCENE. JAMES I OF SCOTS, &c. Both *edd.* have "James II" in the title, while Forster in *Landor: a Biography* named "the fine old Scottish king, the second James" as the murdered sovereign. This error, corrected in the present volume, cannot have been due to Landor's ignorance since both in the *Scene* and in a shorter poem, to be included in Section VI, there is evidence that the history of the life and death of James I was well known to him.

P. 204. DIANA DE POICTIERS. To the MS. from which the present version is printed Landor appended the following note:

"Francis seduced Diana, for which her father the Count de St. Vallier reproached him in open court. St. Vallier was accused as an accomplice in the conspiracy of Constable de Bourbon. The young Caillette was educated with Diana. She married De Brézé, Grand Seneschal of Normandy. She kissed Caillette before the king and his court, holding in her hand the pardon he had obtained for her father.

"Francis and Henry IV have always been the favorites of the French. They were a couple of brave scoundrels at the best; each of them would have been gibeted had he been a private man.

"Generally the cleverest man was appointed to the dignity of fool *a latere* and in this capacity he had more opportunities of suggesting good advice than chancellor or archbishop." [L. *not in 1876.*]

This account of the chief persons in the piece does not agree with that given by the best authorities, who do not accept the story that Diana was seduced by Francis I, though Bayle believed it, and find no evidence that Caillette shared with Triboulet and Brusquet the dignity of Court Jester. [W.]

P. 211. THE SHADES OF AGAMEMNON AND IPHIGENEIA. In his *Pericles and Aspasia*, 1836, Landor gives this dialogue as the composition of Aspasia, sent by her to Cleone with a letter in which she says: "I imagine then Agamemnon to descend from his horrible death, and to meet instantly his daughter. By the nature of things, by the suddenness of the event, Iphigeneia can have heard nothing of her mother's double crime, adultery and murder."

P. 223. MENELAUS AND HELEN AT TROY. See the description in Pausanias (v. 18. 1) of the chest of Cypselus, where Menelaus sword in hand is advancing to slay Helen, the scene clearly laid at the taking of Ilium. See also Bayle (*s.v.* Helen): "Menelaus behaved himself like a good natured man; he reconciled himself to his wife without much difficulty and took her very lovingly home again."

P. 229. ACHILLES AND HELENA ON IDA. A prose version of this dialogue, differing greatly from the metrical text of 1858 and slightly, except for the change to blank verse, from that of 1859, was published in *Imaginary Conversations of Greeks and Romans*, 1853, and reprinted 1876. The 1859 metrical text, reprinted 1876, is given below:

ACHILLES AND HELENA ON IDA.

Helena. Where am I? O ye blessed ones above,
Desert me not! ye Twain who brought me hither!
Was it a dream?
　　　　　Stranger! thou seemest thoughtful;

373

Couldst thou not answer me? why silent? speak,
I do implore thee.
  Achilles.   Neither they nor feet
Of mules have borne thee where thou standest, Helena!
Whether 'twas in the hour of early sleep
Or whether 'twas in morning's, know I not,
But Aphrodite, listening to my prayer,
And Thetis with her, gentle as herself,   10
Have wafted thee into these solitudes,
And to me also pointed out the way,
That I the pride of Sparta might behold
And the Earth's marvel. How my heart expands,
But agonizes too, at thee, the cause
To Hellas of innumerable woes.
  Helena. Stranger! thy voice, thy stature, and thy mien
Approve thee one whom Goddesses and Gods
Might well conduct and glory in; but who,
If earthly, art thou?
  Achilles.   Son of Peleus am I.   20
Tremble not, turn not pale, bend not thy knee.
  Helena. Spare me, thou Goddess-born! thou cherisht son
Of silver-footed Thetis! Sure, Chryseis
And she who rais'd within thy generous breast
More pity than disdain for cruel wrong,
Briseis, now might soften it: lead not
Me too into captivity. Ah! woes
I have brought down on Hellas; on myself
Have fallen woes, and will for ever fall.
  Achilles. Daughter of Zeus! what words are thine! they raise 30
No pity in my breast, none needest thou
Within my reach to give, but bitter wrath
Thou raisest at indignity and wrong.
Chryseis, daughter of that aged priest
Who in this land performs due sacrifice
To his Apollo, was another's lot.
Insolent and unworthy, he hath brought
More sorrows on our people even than thou,
And dogs and vultures prey upon the brave
Who fell without a wound.
      Mine is indeed   40
Briseis, chaste and beautiful Briseis,
He contumatious, proud at once and base
Would tear her from me.
     Gods above! what land
Behold ye where the wolf hath dared to seize
Kid which a lion hath taken.
     Never fear
Mortal shall lead thee into servitude;
What impious wretch would dare it? hath not Zeus
Thundered above these mountains? Doth he,

48 Doth he] Doth Zeus *1853. The 1859 text has* Doth not he. *The negative perverts the meaning of the question; but the error, now corrected, was repeated without comment in 1876.*

Wide-seeing, see all earth but Ida? watch
Over all creatures but his progeny?   50
Capaneus and Typhœus less offended
Than would the wretch whose grasp should violate
The golden hair of Helena.
                          Tremblest thou,
Irresolute, distrustful?
    Helena.   I must tremble,
And more and more.
    Achilles.   Then take my hand.
    Helena.   And may I?
May I? and hold it? I am comforted,
    Achilles. The scene around us, calm and silent, ought
To comfort thee: turnest thou to survey it?
Perhaps it is unknown to thee.
    Helena.   'Tis so.
Since my arrival I have never gone   60
Beyond the city-walls.
    Achilles.   Gaze freely then,
Perplext no longer. Pleasant are these downs,
Pleasant the level eminence, by broom
Surrounded, and with myrtle underneath
And crispleaved beech and broad dark pine above.
Rare place for boars: why are my dogs at home,
And where for sylvan sport my leisure hours.
    Helena. But those are gloomy places, not so this.
Frightful are boars and wolves and such like things.
But here how pretty is the slender grass   70
Bent by the glossy insects as they climb
Or light upon it, or upon the tall
Sisterhoods of grey lavender! their names
I recollect now I have found them here
Within this very hour and seen them close.
The dark-eyed cistus and gay citisus
Are here too.
    Achilles.   Wonderful! how couldst thou learn
To name so many plants?
    Helena.   I could name ten.
Look! see the little troops of serpolet
Running in wild disorder here and there.   80
Thou knowest these perhaps and many more.
    Achilles. Keiron taught *me*, while walking at his side
And he was culling herbs to cure the hurt
His brother Centaurs might in play recieve.
Wonderous his knowledge; I was proud to learn.
Sometimes he seated me and made me sing:
Sometimes he took the lyre and sang himself.
At intervals I catch the fleeting words
He sang to me.
    Helena.   He sang of war, no doubt.
Repeat his words, if thou art loth to sing.   90

          51 Typhoeus] *rectius* Tyhhöeus *1853.*

Achilles. Look at those yellow poppies! were the words
They are come out to catch whate'er the sun
Will throw into their cups; their faces show
Their joyance. Son of Peleus! they begin
Their nodding dance, and wait but for the lyre.
Helena. Childish! for one with such a spear against
His shoulder; even its shadow terrible,
It seems to make a chasm across the plain.
Achilles. To talk or think as children think and talk
Is not at all times such a proof of folly;   100
There may be hours when it shall push aside
Griefs, where the strength of graver wisdom fails.
Helena. But Keiron, when he sang to thee of flowers
Show'd little.
Achilles.   To his lyre he sang the loves
Of Hyacinthos and Narcissos, brought
Back by the Hours on their unwearied feet,
Regular in their courses as the stars.
Many of the trees and bright-eyed flowers once lived
And moved, and even spoke, as we are speaking.
Memories they yet may have, tho they have cares   110
No longer.
Helena.   They then have no memories,
They see their beauty only.
Achilles.   Helena!
Thou turnest pale and droopest.
Helena.   Gum or blossom
Or this high place, or something else unseen,
Hath made me dizzy: can it be the wind?
Achilles. Air there is none.
Helena.   I wish there were a little.
Achilles. Be seated now.
Helena.   The feeble are obedient.
Achilles. 'Twas on this very ground where we repose
They who conducted me by certain signs
Told me the prize of beauty was awarded.   120
One of them smiled; the other, whom in duty
I love the most, lookt anxious and let fall
Some tears.
Helena.   Yet she was not one of the vanquisht.
Achilles. Goddesses then contended. Helena
Was absent, and too young.
Helena.   Alas! how fatal
Was the decision of the arbiter.
Could not thy sire the venerable Peleus,
And could not Pyrrhos, child so beautiful
And helpless, have detain'd thee from this war?
Achilles. No reverence and no friendship for the race   130
Of Atreus brought me against Troy; I hate,
Detest and execrate alike both brothers;
Another is more odious to me stil,
I will forbear to name him. The brave man

Holding the hearth as sacred as the temple,
Violates never hospitality.
He carries not away the gold he finds
Within the house, folds not up purple linen
Workt for solemnities, conveying it
Stealthily from the cedar chest to stow   140
In the dark ship, together with a wife
Confided to him by her absent lord.
I will not say to love thee was a crime;
Priam or Nestor might, even at their years,
But to avow and act on the avowal
Is what the Gods, if righteous, will chastise.
    Helena. But Aphrodite urged me, day and night,
Telling me that to make her break her vow
To Paris was inexpiable sin.
So she told Paris at the selfsame hours,   150
And quite as often, he repeated it
Every morning, showing how his dreams
Tallied with mine exactly. So, at last . .
    Achilles. The last is not yet come. By all the Gods
If I should ever meet him, face to face
I with this spear transfix him.
    Helena.   Pray, do not,
For Aphrodite never could forgive thee.
    Achilles. I am not sure of that; she soon forgets.
Variable as Iris, she one day
Favors, the next forsakes.
    Helena.   She may forsake   160
Me then!
    Achilles. But other Deities
Watch over and protect thee. Thy brave brothers
Are with them at this very hour, and they
Are never absent from their festivals.
    Helena. Oh! were they living! that thou couldst have seen them!
    Achilles. Companions of my father on the Phasis
They were his guests before they went, all three,
To hunt the boar of Calydon; that day
Brought many sorrows upon brave men's hearts,
A woman was the cause.
    Helena.   Horrible creature!   170
The boar, I mean . . Didst thou not see the Twins?
    Achilles. I saw them not; desirous as I was
That I might learn from them and practice with them
Whatever is most laudable and manly.
My father, fearing my impetuosity
(Old men will call it so) and inexperience
Sent me away. Soothsayers had foretold
Some mischief to me from an arrow-wound:
Among the brakes an arrow may fly wide
Glancing from trees.
    Helena.   Hadst thou but seen the Twins!   180
Tho 'twere but once. The Sun will never shine

With his bright eyes upon such youths again.
Ah my brave brothers! how they tended me!
How loved me! often wishing me to mount
Each his horse first: they made me poise and hurl
Their javelins: they would teach me archery . .
But they could only teach me to swim with them:
It gratified me rather to be prais'd
For anything than swimming.

                             Happy hours!
Soon over! does then happiness depart   190
Sooner than beauty? Surely it might stay
That little while.

                  Dear Kastor! Polydeukes
Stil dearer! often shall I think of you
As you were, and as I was, on the bank
Of the Eurotas.

       Achilles.   Is there not at home
One once as dear?

      Helena.   Ah poor Hermione!
A babe was she who could not play with me,
Yet 'twas my pride and pleasure to survey
Her roseate fingers on my unrobed breast:
And I could almost envy then the goat   200
That stampt and feebly cried to give her milk.
My brothers teazed her for it, wicked pair!
Terrible, and almost as beautiful
As thou art. Be not wroth; blush not for me.

    Achilles. Helena, Helena of Menelaos!
My mother is reported to have left
About me only one part vulnerable;
I have at last found where it is. Farewell!

    Helena. O leave me not! I do beseech, I implore,
Leave me not thus alone! these solitudes   210
Are terrible: wild beasts must roam among them;
There certainly are Fauns and Satyrs, there
Cybele, who bears towers upon her head,
Abhorring Aphrodite, persecuting
All those *she* favors; and her priests so cruel
That they are cruel even to themselves.
She sees grim lions yoked before her car
And hears their dismal roar, and sits serene.

    Achilles. They who have brought thee hither in a cloud
Will reconduct thee in a cloud, unseen   220
And safely to the city: be thou sure.
Daughter of Leda and of Zeus, farewell!
Not even this arm could save thee if our host
Saw thee descending, trust the Gods who can,
The Gods who sent me hither to announce
That Helena should close her eyes in Greece.

P. 246. ÆSCHYLOS AND SOPHOCLES. No date can be assigned for this
meeting of the two dramatists. Æschylus is believed to have written

DRAMAS AND DRAMATIC SCENES

Prometheus before going a third time to Sicily, where he died 456 B. C.
But *Antigone* and other plays by Sophocles to which the elder writer
is made to refer are unlikely to have been written then, and were certainly
not acted till long afterwards.

P. 247. MARCUS AURELIUS AND LUCIAN. Major variants between texts
1859, 1863 are given below, minor variants were noted on pp. 247–50.

Between ll. 20–1 1863 has forty-six lines, here numbered 1–46:

Aurelius. Gratitude to the Gods, to men, good will—
Is the religion I would cultivate,
Leaving as many gods upon the ground
As, season after season, may spring up
And stifle one another.
    Lucian.   Well, no harm!
Aurelius. Let each man weed his croft, not turn his kine
Into his neighbour's. What, if some prefer
The lofty holyhock, another bend
Over the bed where hang the modest bells
Of early cluster-lily.
           When we fight   10
The Parthian, 'tis not that we hate his God,
The glorious Sun, for he is our God too.
When Alexander saw the Ganges roll
Before him, did he persecute a race
Devote to Budda? did that race cut throats
To make men run the readier at their side?
All things deteriorate, religions most.
    Lucian. I set a drunken man upon his legs
And show him his own door, but enter not,
Therefore he curses me, and calls me lost,   20
And spits at me, and bids me go to hell.
    Aurelius. Altho' we now are talking in our Greek,
We both know Latin.
    Lucian.   Well, what then?
    Aurelius.   I hate
Quotations, and hate worse to intermix
Two languages: this we may do in talk,
But not in writing; you Greeks never did.
    Lucian. 'Twere folly; for what leg gets faster on
By straddling round the shoulders of another?
    Aurelius. Little of Roman poetry I hold
In memory, yet one sentence comes to hand   30
From the most amiable and least prolix.
    Lucian. What then could he have said upon religion?
    Aurelius. Somewhat, if indirect, yet applicable.
All have not the same faces, yet they all
Bear sisterly resemblance.
    Lucian.   *His* nymphs might,
Our last was born in the decrepitude
Of her poor mother, and now leans on crutch,

33 Somewhat . . . yet] *so in corrigenda 1863;* Nothing indeed, but somewhat *text 1863,*
1876.   *ll.* 34–5 *cf.* Ovid, *Met.* ii. 10–11. [W.]

379

NOTES

Which she can swing about her if provoked.
Her dogmatists would narrow our Elysion,
And would extend the realm of Tartaros   40
And dam up Phlegethon to overflowing.
   Aurelius. Lucian! I think as thou dost, but abstain
From words that irritate where all should soothe.
I seldom laugh, and never in men's faces.
   Lucian. The peace proclaimers bellow the most loud;
My voice by nature is too weak to curse.   46

ll. 39–41 added in corrigenda 1863.   *46 curse.] In 1863, 1876 six lines that follow
(= ll. 21–6 1859 are wrongly printed as spoken by Lucian. This error was noted in corrigenda 1863, but left uncorrected in 1876.*

*For ll. 33–44 in 1859, 1863 substitutes twenty-three lines, here numbered
1–23.*

And spared the Druids, proud unruly race,
Nor with their bloody rites would interfere.
Ambition was his fault, but clemency
Could over-rule ambition . . .
   Lucian.   When the world
Lay at his feet and he too, was a God.
   Aurelius. Ambition is at best but selfishness,
And stoops to scramble as the needy do.
   Lucian. O Marcus, Marcus! art not thou ambitious?
Who holding in one hand the peopled globe,
Yet wouldst thou more?
   Aurelius.   Lucian! Not I indeed.   10
   Lucian. Thou wouldst have much beyond this visible
Diurnal sphere, wouldst catch Fame, flying Fame.
   Aurelius. Quiet be mine! and let Fame follow me.
Say on.
   Lucian. Well then thou art an innovator,
Thou art a revolutionist.
   Aurelius.   How so?
   Lucian. Ay, greatest of all revolutionists,
The battle-field, O Marcus, thou hast turn'd
Into the corn-field. What would Julius say,
If Julius were not now among the Gods?
   Aurelius. He did some evil, he removed much more.   20
He would not irritate weak intellects,
Nurst in religion, learnt by heart and rear'd
Upon a mother's knee, thence justly dear.   23

*15 Before Thou 1863 text has Lucian! which is deleted in corrigenda 1863 but retained
in 1876 text.*

For ll. 50–67 in 1859, 1863 substitutes fourteen lines, here numbered 1–14.

   Aurelius. The mildest and most genial is our own.
   Lucian. Five carts conveying hither Gods from Veii,
Broke down and left their fragments in the road,
Yet plenty stil remain to pick and choose,
And all are not fastidious; stern would look
Old Cato at some tasters of our fasti

DRAMAS AND DRAMATIC SCENES

And pelt them with what turnips were unsound,
Or but half rotten in his frugal farm:
His addled eggs he kept for favorite slaves,
Severe he would be where one calls a God   10
To help him in his vengeance on a neighbour,
Who puts his left leg where he should the right,
And will not draw it back, but walk strait on.
His God was Terminus, his fane, the field.   14

ll. 11-13 with minor variants = ll. 81-3 of 1859 text.

P. 251. HOMER, LAERTES, AGATHA. The 1859 version has for title
Homer and Laertes * with footnote as follows:

* Poets are not bound to chronology. About Homer and Laertes as
little is known as about Polyphemos and Calypso. To the glory of God,
let us believe that He created a Homer one and indivisible: we know he
created a Shakespeare. After this he rested from his Labour a hundred
years: then he called to Him the nearest of the Angels, made a model,
breathed his own spirit into it, and called it Milton. [L.]

Variants in 1863 from the 1859 version of the dialogue are as follows:

ll. 1-2 not in 1859.   *For ll. 3-12 1859 has four lines as follows:*

> Laertes. Gods help thee! and restore to thee thy sight!
>   My good old guest, I am more old than thou,
>   Yet have outlived by many years my son
>   Odysseus and the chaste Penelope.

l. 24 Homer's speech ends in 1859 at it was.   *ll. 24-44 yet . . him not in 1859.*
For ll. 45-57 1859 has three lines:

> Laertes.   First let us taste
> My old sound wine, and break my bread less old,
> But old enough for teeth like thine and mine.

58 hearty] such good *1859.*   59 hearty . . . beside] such a friend as thou *1859.*
For ll. 60-3 1859 has:

> Far hast thou wandered since we met, and told
> Strange stories. Wert thou not afraid some God
> Or Goddess should have siez'd [*sic*] upon thy ear
> For talking what thou toldest of their pranks.

l. 65 and . . . morose] none painful, none profane *1859.*   68 never . . . me] did not
treat me quite *1859.*   69 harried] treated *1859.*   70 hymn: the] chaunt for *1859.*
ll. 71-3 not in *1859.*   75 songster's] poet's *1859.*   79 'twas upon] but one year,
1859.   80 I will] will I *1859.*   85 The gifts] The gift *1859.*   87 [*Agatha . . .*
wine]] (*Girl enters*) *1859.*   88 seat] sit *1859.*   there] down *1859.*   him sing]
a song *1859.*   89 what] which *1859.*   might] may *1859.*   90 that cup] the
flask *1859.*   91 assuaged] allaid *1859.*   92 songmen] poets *1859.*   *In 1859
portions of ll. 94-119 of 1863 text, with variants noted below, are printed among* ADDITIONS.
97 solacer of] remedy for *1859.*   98 unload the] uplifts it *1859.*   *For ll.* 100-14
1859 has thirteen lines:

> And, Agatha, do thou bring speedily
> The two large ewers, and fill brimfull the bath
> Capacious; that of brass; Penelope's
> Own bath, wherein she laught to see her boy
> Paddle, like cygnet with its broad black oars,
> Nor shunn'd the chilly water he threw up
> Against her face . . he who grew soon so sage!
> Then do thou, maiden, from hot cauldron pour

NOTES

Enough to make it soothing to the feet;
After, bring store of rushes, and long leaves
Of cane sweet-smelling, from the inland bank
Of that famed river far across the sea
Opposite, to our eyes invisible.

117 through all] throughout *1859*.   118 Aye . . . look] Aye, aye, and *1859*.   **118**
After before *1859 has two lines:*

May thou rest well, old wanderer! Even the Gods
Repose, the Sun himself sinks down to rest.

In 1859 the dialogue ends here.

P. 267. HIPPOMENES AND ATALANTA. *Corrigenda*, 1863, has "*For* Hippomenes *read* Hippomanes". This direction was followed by Forster in 1876 but should have been ignored. See Ovid, *Met.* x. 560, Theocritus, iii. 40, and Sir James Frazer's notes on Apollod. i. viii.

P. 277. A MODERN GREEK IDYL. Landor found the "story" in *Household Words*, February 25, 1854, where it was quoted from *Chants Populaires de la Grèce moderne*, par C. Fauriel, Paris, 1824–5.

SECTION III.   HELLENICS

P. 283. THE HAMADRYAD. When this Idyl was published in 1842 at the end of Landor's essay on Theocritus, he introduced it with the following remarks, not reprinted either by himself or by Forster:

"In the poem we subjoin we claim no merit of imitation. The subject was taken from a short note of the scholiast on Pindar; and our readers may wonder and regret that it attracted no earlier and abler pen. Our hope is that it will be found of that order of simplicity which is simple in the manner of Theocritus."

The scholiast's note here referred to is in *Pindar's Epinician Odes*, ed. J. W. Donaldson, 1841, p. 386. Writing to Forster, who sent him the book, Landor said: "I took the idea [of *The Hamadryad*] from your Pindar. I had forgotten the story." He might have read it in the scholiast's note on Apollonius (Argon. ii. 479), in Bayle, *s.v. Hamadryades*; in *The Spectator*, 3 September, 1714; or in Leigh Hunt's *Indicator*, 13 September, 1820. The scholiast's version is also quoted in Chalmer's *English Poets*, in a note on Fawkes's translation of the *Argonautics*.

For Landor's sequel to *The Hamadryad*, see *Acon and Rhodope*, p. 343.

P. 290. THE PRAYER OF THE BEES FOR ALCIPHRON. Certainly not the Alciphron who wooed Leucippe (see p. 312); but it is doubtful to whom the bees were grateful. In the *Epistles* of another Alciphron, a contemporary of Lucian, there is mention of bees and their vocation; and Bishop Berkeley, in *Alciphron, the minute Philosopher* (1792), had something to say about Mandeville's *Fable of the Bees*. It is possible, however, that in the poem now dealt with, Alciphron is no other than Landor himself.

P. 292. THRASYMEDES AND EUNÖE. The story of Thrasybulus, or Thrasymedes, and the daughter of Pisistratos, Tyrant of Athens, was told by Plutarch (*Apoth.*) and by Polyænus (*Strat.*). It was referred to by Dante (*Purgat.* xv. 88 *ff.*) and in *The Spectator* (November 4, 1712). Landor may have found it in St. John's *Manners and Customs of Ancient Greece*, i. 417.

382

HELLENICS

P. 294. ICARIOS AND ERIGONÈ. Landor may have found this legend in Plutarch, *Paral.* 9, or in Apollodorus, iii. xiv. 7; unless he first met with it in St. John's *Ancient Greece*, ii. 354.

P. 297. DRIMACOS. An account of the slave revolt led by Drimacos is given in St. John's *Ancient Greece*, iii. 13, on the authority of Athenæus, v. 265.

P. 301. ENALLOS AND CYMODAMEIA. St. John in *Ancient Greece* relates this story with a reference to Athenæus, xi. It is also mentioned twice by Plutarch (*de solert. animal.* 36; *Sept. Sap.* 20); but in substituting Lemnos for Lesbos (1. 19) Landor may have followed Bayle, *s.v.* Lemnos.

P. 313. IPHIGENEIA. Writing from Bath in March 1845, to Theodosia Garrow (afterwards Mrs. T. A. Trollope), Landor said: "I am busied in collecting my verses etc., for a new and complete edition. Many I had given away without keeping a copy; and among these is the one I shall now transcribe."

Then follows in the same script an early, if not the earliest, version of *Iphigeneia and Agamemnon at Aulis. ll.* 23–5 and 37–42 of the 1846 text (see above, pp. 313–14) are not in the MS. Other variants are:

8 misunderstood] misunderstood me *1845.*   9 arms] hands *1845.*   10 hitting] striking *1845.*   19 awaken'd me] awakened oft *1845.*   33 brow] head *1845.*   36 Regard] Survey *1845.*

Thanks are due to Dr. Ashley-Montagu for a copy of Landor's letter and the 1845 version of *Iphigeneia.*

P. 315. THE CHILDREN OF VENUS. First written in Latin and so published with title *Veneris Pueri* in 1820. The English version on p. 315 was recast and so published with altered title in 1859. The 1859 text is given below:

THE BOYS OF VENUS.

TWAIN are the boys of Venus: one surveys
Benignly this our globe; the other flies
Cities and groves, nor listens to their songs
Nor bears their converse; hardly is he known
By name among them; cold as Eurus, pure
As gusty rain.
        What discord tore apart
The brothers? what beside ambition could?
The elder was aggriev'd to see the sparks
Shoot from the younger's whetstone as he turn'd
His arrow-barbs, nor pleas'd that he should waste   10
Day after day in wreathing flowers for crowns,
Or netting meshes to entrap the birds;
And, while rose incense to that idle child,
To him were only empty honors paid.
Bitterly to Silenus he complain'd,
Entreating him to arbitrate his wrongs
But hearing no remonstrance, mild as were
The wise God's words; they only fann'd his ire.
"Call that Idalian" cried he "then decide."
He did so.
       "Brother! was it me you call'd?"   20

Said the sweet child, whose wings were hanging down
Heavily from both shoulders, and his face
Suffused with shame.
      "Will you not even own
Your little brother from Idalia? come,
Let us be friends." Then, turning to the judge,
"Did he not send for me?"
       To this appeal
Before Silenus could reply, before
He could, as now he tried, unite their hands,
"Yes," interrupted the ferocious one,
"I did, that you may now learn who I am."   30
Silenus smiled, and beckoning, fondly said
 "Hither now! kiss each other; I may then
Say which is best: each shall have due reward,
And friend from friend."
      At this the lesser lept
And threw his arms about his brother's neck
Turn'd scornfully away, yet many a kiss
He gave it; one, one only, was return'd;
For even the brother could not now resist,
Whether such godlike influence must prevail
Or whether of repulsing it ashamed;   40
Stil neither would he his intent forego
Nor moderate his claim, nor cease to boast
How Chaos he subdued with radiant fire,
How from the sky its darkness he dispel'd,
And how the struggling planets he coerced,
Telling them to what distance they might go,
And chain'd the raging Ocean down with rocks.
 "Is not all this enough for you?" replied
The gentler, "envy you my narrow realm?
Denying me my right you raise my plumes,   50
You make me boast that on my birth there broke
Throughout the heavens above and earth below
A golden light. I do not recollect
What Chaos was, it was before my time;
Where flew the stars about I neither know
Nor care; but her who governs them I drew
Behind the Latmian cliffs, entreating me,
And promising me everything, to grant
Her first and last desire: tho you reside
In heaven with her, and tho she knows your fame,   60
She knows no love but what is scorn'd by you.
What are sea-shores to me? I penetrate
The inmost halls of Nereus; I command . .
Up spring the dolphins, and their purple backs
I smoothe for timorous harper to bestride:
At losing him, on the dry sands they pine.
Desert you anyone, he heeds it not,
But let me leave him and funereal flames
Burst from his bosom. Your last guest from earth,

When I was angry with him, threw aside 70
The spindle, broke the thread, and lay before
The gate as any worthless herb might lie,
And gamesome whelps lept over that broad breast.
About the Gods above I would not say
A word to vex you: whether rolls the orb
We stand upon I know not, or who trims
The fires ethereal, or who rules the tides.
If these I yield to you, to me concede
Free laughter and sly kiss; fresh flowers give me,
And songs the lyre delights in, give the lull 80
Of reeds among the willows upon banks
Where hollow moss invites and then betrays.
Let me be happy: some have call'd me strong;
Whether I am so, let recorded facts
Declare, in every land perform'd by me
Under the rising and the setting sun,
Too numerous for a memory weak as mine."
  "Scarce more so than your promises" exclaim'd
The taunter.
          Smiling, blushing too, the child
Acknowledged his forgetfulness . . at times . . 90
But added,
          "Do not make me boast again.
If you pretend contempt for earthly cares
And stand apart from nuptial scenes, and make
No promises that leave so many blest,
But turn aside your face and gaze upon
The dismal depths, and Styx alone adjure,
Pray tell me who made Pluto, by the pool
Of that same Styx and panting Phlegethon
Pant also, while the dog with his three throats
Growl'd and roar'd out? who taught the unwilling bride 100
To bear him? it was I, it was my sport.
In his dominions better deeds were mine.
Following this torch and guided by this hand
You might have heard amid the silent shades
The water, drop by drop, fall from the urn
Of the condemn'd; the wheel you might have heard
Creak, with no human groans from it; thro me
Laodameia met again the youth
She died for, and Eurydice met her's."
  The generous Judge embraced the generous God, 110
Then tranquilly bespake the other thus.
  "O worthy child of thy grave sire! to thee
I give the stars in keeping, with his leave,
And storms and seas and rocks that hold them in
With Neptune's, asking Amphitrite's too.
Thou, lesser of the winged ones! the source
Of genial smiles, who makest every sun
Roll brighter, and ten thousand fall far short
Of one such night as thou alone canst give;

Who holdest back the willing Hours at play,   120
And makest them run weariless aside
Thy quickest car! be thou with this content.
To thee do I assign thy modest claim.
Write it in thy own words . . The linkèd hands,
And every flower that Spring most gladly wears,
And every song the quivering lyre of youth
Delights in; and the whispers of the reeds
Under the willows; and the mossy tuft
Dimpling but to betray: should anywhere
Be sweeter whispers, be they also thine   130
Do thou but " . . then he blusht and lowered his head
Against the boy's . . "touch gently with thy dart,
So that no mortal see . . Ianthe's breast."

P. 319. PAN AND PITYS. First written in Latin and so published in
1815. The myth of the nymph beloved by Pan is told at length in Bayle's
Dictionary, *s.v.* Boreas. See also Lucian, *Dial. Deor.* xii. 4.

The English version on p. 319 was recast and so published in 1859,
reprinted 1876. The 1859 text is given below:

PAN AND PITYS.

CEASE to complain of what the Fates decree,
Whether shall Death have carried off or (worse)
Another, thy heart's treasure: bitter Styx
Hath overflowed the dales of Arcady,
And Cares have risen to the realms above.
By Pan and Boreas was a Dryad wooed,
Pitys her name, her haunt the grove and wild:
Boreas she fled from, upon Pan she gazed
With a sly fondness, yet accusing him
Of fickle mind; and this was her reproof.   10
  "Ah why do men, or Gods who ought to see
More clearly, think that bonds will bind for ever!
Often have stormy seas borne safely home
A ship to perish in its port at last;
Even they themselves, in other things unchanged,
Are mutable in love; even he who rules
Olympus hath been lighter than his clouds.
Alas! uncertain is the lover race,
All of it; worst are they who sing the best,
And thou, Pan, worse than all.
                             By what deceit   20
Beguiledst thou the Goddess of the night?
O wary shepherd of the snow-white flock!
Ay, thy reeds crackled with thy scorching flames
And burst with sobs and groans . . the snow-white flock
Was safe, the love-sick swain kept sharp look there.
Wonderest thou such report should reach my ear?
And widenest thou thine eyes, half-ready now

20 worse] *so in corrigenda, not in text, 1859.*   25 sharp] *so in corrigenda 1859,*
a sharp *in text.*

386

To swear it all away, and to conceal
The fountain of Selinos. So! thou knowest
Nothing about that shallow brook, those herbs   30
It waves in running, nothing of the stones
Smooth as the pavement of a temple-floor,
And how the headstrong leader of the flock
Broke loose from thy left-hand, and in pursuit
How falledst thou, and how thy knee was bound
With ivy lest white hairs betray the gash.
Denyest thou that by thy own accord
Cynthia should share thy flock and take her choice?
Denyest thou damping and sprinkling o'er
With dust, and shutting up within a cave   40
Far out of sight, the better breed? the worse
Displayed upon the bank below, well washt,
Their puffy fleeches glittering in the sun.
Shame! to defraud with gifts, and such as these!"
    Pan, blushing thro both ears as ne'er before,
Cried "Who drag'd back these fables from the past?
Juster and happier hadst thou been to scorn
The false and fugitive. With hoarse uproar
I heard thy Boreas bray his song uncouth,
And oldest goats ran from it in affright.   50
Thee too, beloved Pitys, then I saw
Averse: couldst ever thou believe his speech,
His, the most bitter foe to me and mine.
From Cynthia never fell such hard rebuke.
Different from thee, she pities them who mourn;
Whether beneath straw roof or lofty tower,
She sits by the bedside and silently
Watches, and soothes the wakeful til they sleep.
I wooed not Cynthia; me she wooed: not all
Please her; she hates the rude, she cheers the gay,   60
She shrouds her face when Boreas ventures near.
Above all other birds the nightingale
She loves; she loves the poplar of the Po
Trembling and whispering; she descends among
The boxtrees on Cytoros; night by night
You find her at the olive: it is she
Who makes the berries of the mountain-ash
Bright at her touch: the glassy founts, the fanes
Hoary with age, the sea when Hesper comes
To Tethys, and when liquid voices rise   70
Above the shore . . but Boreas . . no, not she."
Then Pitys, with a smile.
                              "Ha! what a voice!
My lover Boreas could not roar his name
More harshly. Come now, cunning lightfoot! say
How was it thou couldst take the Goddess in,
And with a charge so moderate on thy fold?"
    "Again, O Pitys, wouldst thou torture me?
Gifts not as lover but as loved I gave;

C C 2

I gave her what she askt: had she askt more
I would have given it; 'twas but half the flock: 80
Therefor 'twas separated in two parts;
The fatter one, of bolder brow, shone out
In whiteness, but its wool was like goat-hair,
And loud its bleating for more plenteous grass;
Strong too its smell: my Goddess heeded not
The smell or bleat, but took the weightier fleece.
Why shakest thou thy head, incredulous?
Why should I urge the truth on unbelief?
Or why so fondly sue to scorn and hate?
Pitys! a time there was when I was heard   90
With one long smile, and when the softest hand
Stroked down unconsciously the lynx-skin gift
Of Bacchus on my lap, and blushes rose
If somewhat, by some chance, it was removed.
In silence or in speech I then could please,
I then at times could turn my face aside,
Forgetting that my awkward hand was placed
Just where thy knees were bending for a seat:
Then could I at another hour look up
At the sun's parting ray, and draw the breath   100
Of fresher herbs, while clouds took living forms
Throwing their meshes o'er the azure deep,
And while thy gaze was on the flight of crows
Hoarse overhead, winging their beaten way
At regular and wonted intervals.
Then, never doubting my sworn love, anew
Thou badest me swear it: pleasure lay secure
On its full golden sheaf.

                Now, alas, now
What comfort brings me on the barren shore
Pale oleaster, or gay citisus   110
That hides the cavern, or pellucid vein
Of wandering vine, or broom that once betray'd
The weak twin fawns! how could I join the glee
Of babbling brook, or bear the lull of grove,
Or mind the dazzling vapor from the grass,
Unless my Pitys told me, and took up
The faltering reed or interrupted song?"
Thus he, enclosing with his arm hirsute
Her neck, and stroking slow her auburn hair.
  "Up with the pipe" said she "O Pan! and since   120
It seems so pleasant to recall old times,
Run over those we both enjoy'd alike,
And I will sing of Boreas, whom I hate.
He boasts of oaks uprooted by his blast,
Of heaven itself his hailstones have disturb'd,
Of thy peculiar heritage afire,
And how thy loftiest woods bow'd down beneath
His furious pennons black with bale and dread.
He boasts of ships submerged, and waves up-piled

High as Olympus, and the trident torn 130
From Jove's own brother: worst of all, he boasts
How often he deluded with his voice,
Under the rocks of Ismaros, that true
And hapless lover when his eyes sought sleep,
And made his wandering mind believe the sound
Rose from the Manes at his wife recall'd.
His pleasure is to drive from lids fresh-closed
Fond dreams away, and draw false forms about,
And where he finds one terror to bring more.
Can such a lover ever be beloved?" 140
　　Boreas heard all: he stood upon the cliff
Before, now crept he into the near brake;
Rage seiz'd him; swinging a huge rock around
And, shaking with one stamp the mountain-head,
Hurld it . . and cried
　　　　　　　" Is Boreas so contemn'd? "
It smote the Dryad, sprinkling with her blood
The tree they sat beneath: there faithful Pan
Mused often, often call'd aloud the name
Of Pitys, and wiped off tear after tear
From the hoarse pipe, then threw it wildly by, 150
And never from that day wore other wreath
Than off the pine-tree darkened with her gore.

P. 323. Cupid and Pan. First written in Latin and so published in
1820.
　　The English version on p. 323 was recast and so published in 1859.
The 1859 text is given below:

CUPID AND PAN.

Cupid one day caught Pan asleep, outstretcht:
He snatcht the goatskin hung about his loins,
And now and then pluckt at a cross-graind hair
Bent inward: yet the God, immovable,
Blew heavy slumbers from his ruddy breast,
Feeling as any corktree's bark might feel.
Behind his neck was laid his favorite pipe,
But this with furtive touch the boy withdrew,
Not quite insensibly, for one sharp ear
Quivered a little.
　　　　　　　Cupid now waxt wroth, 10
Exclaiming, "Zeus above! was ever God
So dull as this? even thy own wife would fail
To rouse him."
　　　　　　Then he clapt the sevenfold reeds
To his own rosy lip and blew them shrill.
Both ears were now rais'd up, and up sprang he,
The God of Arcady, and shook the ground;
But high above it sprang the lighter God,
Laughing his threats to scorn.
　　　　　　　　　" Down with that bow,

389

NOTES

Wicked young wretch! down with those arrows!" cried
The indignant eld, "then see what thou canst do."   20
"What I can do, Pan, thou shalt also see."
Thus spake he; and the bow lept from the sod
With golden ring, and the young herbs embraced
The quiver.
    "What! contend with thee! 'twere shame . .
"Scoff on," said Cupid; "when thy wrath subsides,
Even to be vanquisht will excite no blush.
Come, shamefaced! strike away; thy foe awaits."
The blusterer roll'd his yellow eyes, then caught
(As 'twere a bird he caught at, a rare bird
Whose pretty plumage he would grieve to hurt)   30
At the slim boy who taunted him too long.
'Tis said the color now first left the face
Of the cow'd child; as when amid a game
Of quoit or hoop suddenly falls the snow,
And that he trembled, fain almost to fly.
 "Go, child!" said the grave Arcad: "learn to fear
Thy elders; and from far: check yet awhile
Ferocious beauty. Thou, who challengest
The peaceful, hast seen scarcely thrice-five years.
Off! or beware a touch of willow-twig."   40
 Cupid, ashamed and angered, springing up,
Struck where the goatskin covered ill the breast;
Swift as an eagle or the bolt he bears
The Arcad, quick of sight, perceived the aim
And caught the hand, which burnt like purest fire
Upon the altar: Pan drew back his own
Extended palm, and blew from rounder cheek
A long cold whiff, and then again advanced,
Trembling to interwine his hairy shank
With that soft thigh and trip him up, nor ceast   50
To press the yielding marble from above.
He grew less anxious to conclude the fight
Or win it; but false glory urged him on.
Cupid, now faint and desperate, siez'd one horn;
Pan swung him up aloft; but artifice
Fail'd not the boy; nay, where the Arcad cried
Conquered at last, and ran both hands about
The dainty limbs, pluckt out from the left wing
Its stiffest feather, and smote both his eyes.
Then loud the rivers and the lakes afar   60
Resounded, and the vallies and the groves;
Then Ladon with a start and shudder broke
That marsh which had for ages crost his course;
Alpheios and Spercheios heard the shout
Of Mænalos; Cyllenè, Pholoë,
Parthenos, Tegea, and Lycaios, calld
Responsively, nor knew they yet the cause.
'Tis said the winged steed sprang from the highths
Of his Parnassus and ran down amid

390

The murky marshes, his proud spirit gone,   70
And there abided he, nor once drave back
Castalia's ripples with his neigh and mane.
  "Hail, conqueror!" Cupid cried.
                      In lower tone
The Arcad,
         "Never shall my eyes behold
My woodland realms! never the ice afloat
Under the Zephyrs, and whirld round and round,
Or the foam sparkling dasht upon the ford;
Never the pebbles black and white below,
Smoothen'd and rounded by assiduous plash,
Nor silvery cloud expanded overhead,   80
Nor Hesper, come to listen to my song.
Ah! for the blind there is one spot alone
Upon the earth, and there alone stand I.
I did not challenge; should I sue? suffice
Thy victory!"
        He held forth his hand, nor knew
Whether he held it strait before the boy,
While from both cheeks fell tears: compassionate
Was Cupid.
     "Soon" said he "a remedy
Shall be provided."
         Soon were gathered flowers,
Nor long ere platted.
         "I bestow them all"   90
Said he "on one condition: that thou wear
These, and these only, til I take them off."
The first was amaranth; too brittle that,
It broke ere well applied; then roses white,
White were all roses in these early days,
Narcissus, violet, open-hearted lily,
And smaller ones, no higher than the grass,
Slender and drooping they, yet fresh and fair;
A spray of myrtle held together these.
But when they toucht his eye he stampt and yell'd   100
And laid wide-open his sharp teeth until
The quivering nostril felt the upper lip.
  Soon slept he better mid the strawberries,
And more and more he thought of Hamadryads,
Recalling all their names, and linking them
In easy verse, and fancying it was time
To take a little care of form and face:
The goatskin for the fawnskin he exchanged
And stroked complacently the smoother pelt,
And trim'd and drew the ivy round his waist . .   110
It must not be too full . . too scant were worse . .
Lastly he doft the bandage from the brow.
Then was renew'd the series of his woes,
And forced was he to implore again the help

Of his proud conqueror, at the Paphian fane.
There found he Venus in the porch itself.
"So 'twas thy pleasure" said she "to remove
The flowers we gave thee. No slight chastisement
For this! It was thy duty and thy vow
To wear them til the hands that laid them on   120
Releast thee from them.
                    "Goat-foot! he who scorns
Our gifts, scorns never with impunity:
Round that horn'd brow, to ake again ere long,
A wreath less soft and fragrant shalt thou wear."

P. 327. DRYOPE. First written in Latin and so published in *Idyllia*,
1815, with *Argumentum* as follows:

Dryope ab Apolline amata est: festo ejus die, lyræ similitudinem sibi deus induit,
quæ cum in sinam locaret ea, serpens fit: fugiunt comites; Apollo suam interim
formam recuperat, Nymphâ potitur.

Antoninus Liberalis, 32, is given as the authority for this myth. Ovid,
Met. ix. 325, describes the transformation of Dryope, after her marriage
to Andræmon, into a lotus.
The English version of Landor's poem on p. 327 was recast and so
published in 1859. The 1859 text is given below:

DRYOPE.

ŒTA was glorious; proud of ancestry
There Dryops reign'd: Spercheios was his sire,
His mother Polydora; but above
All ancestry went forth his daughter's fame,
Dryope, loved by him whose radiant car
Surmounts the heavens. With light he irrigates
The earth beneath, to all things gives their hue,
Motion, and graceful form, and harmony:
But now the tresses of his golden hair
Wills he to fall and his warm breath to breathe   10
On Dryope alone; her he pursues
Among the willow of pubescent flower
And fragrant bark stript off the tender twigs,
Moist, split, and ready for the basket-braid.
He followed her along the river-bank,
Along the shallow where the Nereids meet
The Dryads.
                She was tending once her flock
In a deep valley, when there suddenly
Burst forth the sound of horn and pipe, and clash
Of cymbal rattling from uplifted palms;   20
Dryad and Hamadryad, wild with joy,
Ran on before, ran on behind; one stopt
And cried to her, ere past ..
                        "Art thou alone
Forgetful of the day, our festival?
Is Dryops greater than Admetos, king
But shepherd too: Apollo watcht his flock,

Apollo scared the stealing wolves away,
And even Apollo now is scared from thine!
Thus daughters place their seat above their sire's."
  Dryope laught, no little proud, at taunt   30
Like this.
        And now the revels were begun,
And circling dance succeeded; and the day
Closed with the chorus of the pæan hymn.
Weary with dancing Dryope reclined
On the soft herbage: lo! before her feet
Shone forth a lyre amidst it; whose that lyre
Each askt, and none replied, for surely each
Had hers: was it Autonöe's? was it like
Theano's? Whose-soever it might be
She took it, and with twinkling finger ran   40
Over the chords: and now at one she glanced
Now at another, with a nod that said
She knew their mischief, and to punish them
She thrust it in her bosom. Ha! behold!
A snake glides out. All shriek aloud, all throw
Their bodies back and spring up all at once.
Autonoë dasht upon her fragil reed
Her tender hand in rising, but scarce felt
The wound until she saw one ruddy globe
Enlarging, then she shuddered, then she suckt   50
The whole away, and but two rims appear'd.
Faster the others ran, they knew not where,
Thro' every field about: the choral shell
Around whose loosen'd strings the snake had coil'd
Was now all snake. He rusht on Dryope,
So slow in due performance of the rites,
Rites which the fathers for their God ordain'd.
Then spake Autonöe to the only Nymph
Remaining nigh, stil fleeing both away,
Both looking back; for pity rose o'er fear.   60
"See! see! the wicked serpent! how he licks
Her eyes and bosom! how he bends her down
When she would rise and run away! where now
Can be Apollo, proud of Python slain?
Scorn'd by one inexperienced, feard by one
Silly, he seems to think that Fear can win
Where Love was driven off.
               Help, Phœbus, help!
How swells the creature's neck! how fierce his crest!
A cloud hides all below. The dragon race
Is various: now they shake their scales on earth,   70
Now shine their feathers in the sky; now flame
In cars athwart; now their hard bodies melt
In the thin air nor leave a trace behind."
  Deep in a woody dell beneath a cliff,

38 Autonöe's] The name is spelt thus in 1847 *ed.* and in the Latin version of the poem.
The 1859 text has Antonöe in *ll.* 38, 47, 58.

393

Scarce daring yet to lift her eyes above
The lowest bush, Callianeira held
Diaula, dubious to run on or stay,
And argued with her thus.

                 "Since now the grass
In the warm spring lies closer and grows higher,
And many things may at first sight decieve,   80
Might it not be a lizard she caught up
Into her bosom? What is pleasanter
Than in hot days to hold a lizard there
Panting, and gently with a finger's tip
Provoke its harmless bite? The species seems
Rare, it is true. Behold how sisterly
Dryope treats it."

               "Lizard! no indeed!"
Replied the maiden with wide-open eyes,
"No lizard can be seen a whole field off,
Nor so spring up as that bold animal."   90
Neither Diaula nor her arguer dared
Procede: Callianeira went alone
Toward Dryope midway.

             Again, whate'er
It was erewhile, the form is changed; no more
A serpent, nor indeed a lizard now,
Nor chelys, is that orb by purple veil'd
One moment and then alter'd into white;
As violets under hailstones when the wind
Blows hurriedly and fitfully above.
Then partly mused and partly uttered some.   100
"That hair is surely hers: another Nymph
Not of our company, and practised more
In quelling serpents, may have intervened,
Or witch in gleeful mischief played her pranks.
What hand is under her? what hair like hers
Is waving over?"

            Delius now appear'd
Himself among them, and with radiant nod
And arm outstretch recall'd the fugitives,
Drawing his purple vest more closely round.
They came with downcast eyes, remembering well   110
Their terror when he lent his lofty car
To that ambitious son, and how the lakes
Shrank under him, and how the rivers paus'd
In silence, and how Po himself, although
From heaven descended, was enwrapt in flames;
Remembering too the clangor of his bow
Bent against Python, when Diana's self
Trembled at her deliverer: well they knew
The power, for good or evil, of the God,
And kept the fearful secret in their breasts.   120
  Soon they recovered; soon they pitied her
The victim of such cruelty: the words

Of pity Dryope well understood,
Replying not. They lookt into her eyes
A little languid; on her neck they lookt
A little moist; they own'd her pouting lip
Was worthy of the God.
              Each slily askt
Some little question; she could only blush.
Slowly, nor staying to reprove, she went
Amid their giggles to her father's house.   130
They, growing bolder, might mayhap have told
The tale to others, but had gazed too near
For bashful Nymphs; beside, Diana's wrath
They dreaded if her brother they betraid.
    Dryope, now Andræmon's happy spouse
And mother of Amphissos, every spring
Is celebrated thro' the groves and vales
Of Œta, where the pæan had been sung.

P. 330. CORESOS AND CALLIRHÖE. First written in Latin in 1809 and
so published in 1815. Founded on a story in Pausanias, vii. 21. 1, which
was quoted in Sir George Wheeler's *Journey into Greece*, iv. 292. The
Rev. William Thompson (*ob. c.* 1766) wrote a poem on the same topic;
but Landor may never have seen either this or another, by the same hand,
"On a Present of Three Roses from Ianthe."
    The English version on p. 330 was recast and so published in 1859.
The 1859 text is given below:

CORESUS AND CALLIHROË.

WITH song and dance the maids of Calydon
Had met to celebrate the yearly rites
Of Bacchus. Where two taller whirl around
The rope, and call another to run in,
A wanton one pusht forward her who stood
Aside her; when she stumbled they all laught
To see her upright heels and scattered hair.
'Twas then, Callirhoë, that thy mother fail'd
Even with prayer to bring thee back again
Before the altar: it is said a tear   10
Roll'd down thy cheek from shame, and not without
A blush of anger . . who on earth can vouch
For this? since both thy hands hid both thy cheeks.
    Rising from his high seat the youthful priest
Came forward, pitying her: of graceful mien
Coresus was, and worthy of his God.
Ah poor Coresus! luckless was the hour
Of his first meeting her; there might have been
Hour more propitious; she perhaps had loved
Distractedly the youth she now abhor'd;   20
He too, unless her blushes and her tears
Had penetrated deep his generous heart,
Might have loved on and sung his woes away.
Now neither butting goat nor honeyed must

Pourd by the straining boys between his horns
Regarded he; no, nor with wonted cheer
Appeard to him the God of gamesome glee.
Not even when Hesper call'd his winking train
Around him, and when shook the lower shrubs
More than the breeze had shaken them erewhile,   30
Would he decline his aking eyes to sleep;
But out of the inclosure, where the grass
Was rank with fallen leaves and heavy dew,
Lonely he stood beneath an ilex shade,
And meditated long and soon forgot
The words he had to say: he could recall
(He thought) her features, but before him rose
A face less beautiful, not less severe.
Many the days he sought the maid in vain,
Many the nights he stood before the house;   40
She waits not even to be seen; no foot
Passes her door, and the dog barks, but strait
Up springs she from her chair; she surely hears
And knows his tread; what other can it be?
When she would break a thread off with her teeth
She stops, and holds it in a trembling hand
Suspended, just above the humid lip
White now with fear; and often her loose locks
She dashes back to place a surer ear
Against the hinge: is any footfall heard   50
Passing the portico, he steps that way;
If soft the sound, he stands there, none but he:
If none, he certainly is close behind.
    The reed grows harder from perpetual winds,
From fears perpetual harder grows the maid.
At first Callirhoë scarcely would confess
To her own mother, scarcely to herself;
Now she is ready, now she is resolved
With savage speech his fondness to repay,
Words she would gather for his punishment,   60
And is more angry when she finds not one;
An aggravation of his past offence.
    Flexible is the coral branch beneath
The Erythræan sea; to air exposed
It stiffens, no strong hand can bend it back:
Such was her nature: she had laid aside
Her former manners; its ingenuous shame
Quitted that cheek it lately discomposed;
Crouds she avoided not, nor greatly cared
If others knew what she but yesterday   70
Was vext at knowing: she rejoiced to hear
A name she loath'd so late. Vainglory caught
And made a plaything of an empty heart.
When she hears footsteps from behind, she checks
Her own, to let him either stop or pass;
She would not wish his love nor him away,

Conscious that she is walking over fire
Unwounded, on a level with the Gods,
And rendering null the noblest gifts they gave.
    Where grows a dittany that heals the smart   80
Love's broken arrow leaves within the breast?
He loves not who such anguish can endure,
He who can burst asunder such a bond
Loves not.
             Hard-breathing from his inmost soul
Coresus siez'd her hand, then threw it back
And pour'd forth with stern look these bitter words.
"No longer ask I pity on my grief,
Callirhoë! tis unworthy of us both,
But there is one who knows it, one above,
And will avenge it. Thou hast seen the last   90
Of all the tears these eyes will ever shed;
This grieves me, and this only . . Pestilence
Now stalks in darkness on from street to street,
And slow steps follow: wasted, worn away,
The aged are gone forth to learn the will
Of those we worship; and their late return,
Lookt for since dawn from all the higher roofs,
In vain is lookt for. Thro the city lie
Children whom dying parents would embrace,
Innocent children! they have not been spared,   100
And shall the guilty before heaven escape?
    I was contemn'd, and I deserv'd contempt,
I loved imprudently; yet throughout life
Those arts I cherisht which lead youth aright,
And strengthen manhood and adorn old-age.
Old-age! for me there will be none: my brow
Hath worn its crown . . for what? that festal songs
May rise around the altar, sung by thee.
Worthy I was to woo, and woo I did;
I am unworthy now, and now abstain,   110
Subjected to the levity of all,
Even my own friends: and yet might I have stood
Above those equal-aged, whether the prize
Were olive, given by heroes, whether bay
Which only Gods, and they on few, bestow,
Or whether, O Callirhoë! in thy love.
    Let kings throw largesses around, let earth
And ocean be explored that vulgar eyes
May gaze at vulgar heads rais'd somewhat higher,
The Gods alone give genius, they alone   120
Give beauty . . why so seldom to unite!
She shines her hour, and then the worshiper
Rises and goes. Genius stands cold, apart,
Like Saturn in the skies; his aspect seems,
To mortal men below, oblique, malign . . ."
    While he was speaking and about to pause,

85 Coresus] *so in corrigenda 1859; mispr.* Catillus *in text here corrected.*

Downcast, with silent and slow step approacht
They who went forth to touch with purest hands
The altar, and appease the offended Powers.
The virgin saw them coming; soon she heard   130
A croud's tumultuous outcries and turned pale;
But paler was Coresus who presaged
The impending evil; paler when he heard
Curses and (painfuller) immodest speech.
He hastened to withdraw her; but aloud
Palæmon cried,
           "Stay here! stay here thou too
O wretched girl! and take the words I bring,
The God's own words: no longer shall the throng
Around thee rise infuriate, nor shall maids
And matrons turn on thee their dying look   140
Or call the torch funereal by thy name."
   Impatient and exultant sprang the youth;
Wildly he threw his arms around her neck,
Then, falling on his knees,
           "Hail thou" he cried,
"Who fillest with thy deity the grove
Of high Dodona, and with brow serene
Hast clear'd the troubled sky!
           She lives! she lives!
The source of sorrow to none else than me:
Neither my dreams nor Bacchus promist this."
Palæmon, after solemn silence, spake: 150
   "Alas! how sadly do young hopes decieve!
The sight of future things was granted thee
In vain: Love lowers his saffron veil, runs off,
And thro the dimness thou seest only Love.
   Forward, ye youths! since Jupiter ordains,
And since the son of Semele hath deign'd
To honor and avenge his chosen priest,
Lead the peace-offering, the pure victim, forth . .
Lead forth Callirhoë."
           Thro the maiden's veins
The blood crept cold: she staggered, fell . . upheav'd   160
And drag'd away by some strong arm, she reacht
The temple: consciousness (not soon) return'd
Thro the loud tramplings, on the marble floor,
Of those who carried incense fresh-alight,
And the salt sprinklings from the frigid font.
   "Take" said Palæmon, trembling as he spake,
"Take thou this sword, Coresus! 'tis thy part.
Often hast thou the avenging Gods invoked,
And wouldst thou cast aside the vows they grant?
Impious! impossible! no grace is this   170
To thee, but sign to all that in his priest
Wrong'd and offended is the God he serves,
Warning to all that vows be wisely vow'd.
But if among this concourse there stand one

Who pities so the victim, that for hers
He yields his life, then shall the pestilence,
Under Jove's saving son, our Bacchus, cease."
    With his veind hand a tear the youth swept off:
Less mournfully than scornfully said he,
    "Listen! how swift, how still, their steps retreat!   180
Now then, Callirhoë! now my breast is firm;
None stand before me: in a father's place
And in a lover's I will here discharge
No empty duty."
                        Cries and groans are heard,
And seen upon the pavement where he stood
His writhing limbs.
                        With sudden terror flies
The croud bewildered, dreading lest a blood
So sacred should run on and reach their feet.
The temple and the grove around it moan,
And other murmurs, other cries, than rose   190
So lately, fill the city and the plain.
    First flies the rumor that the priest had fallen
By his own hand; it gathered force, and soon
That both were smitten by the wrathful Gods.
From its own weight is that vast multitude
Pusht onward, driven back, conglomerated,
Broken, disperst, like waves on stormy seas.

P. 335. The Altar of Modesty. To the Latin version, *Pudoris Ara*,
published in *Simonidea*, 1806, a reference to Pausanias (iii. 20. 10 *seq.*)
was prefixed. In *Idyllia*, 1820, the abduction of Helen by Theseus was
said to have occurred on Diana's feast day, Plutarch being given as the
authority. Bayle, *s.v.* Penelope, after quoting Pausanias remarks: "here
are some lively stories of the character of an honest woman."
    The English version of Landor's poem on p. 335 was recast and so pub-
lished in 1859. The 1859 text is given below:

THE ALTAR OF MODESTY.

Soon as the stranger turns his step away
From Lacedæmon, and pursues the road
Toward the towers of Elis, where a ford
Whitens with rippling wave the river-bank,
Sacred to Modesty an altar stood.
Hither the gentle Leda brought her child,
Her Helena, whom Theseus had borne off,
And thus reproved her, by none other heard.
"How couldst thou, Helena, leave house and home
And parent, and twin brothers, bright as stars?   10
With what discourse could Theseus tempt thee hence?
He is not tender, is not bland, nor chaste,
Nor even young.
                    I too was once beguiled
By a white stately swan I loved to feed,
Who drove the rest away that followed him;
And wicked Theseus, then a boy, laught loud

Seeing my downcast eyes; and, when I turn'd
To chide him, *Ah poor Leda!* whined the rogue.
Once as I watcht him wrestling in the ring,
Me, tho' I stood far distant, he espied   20
And waddled nearer, and whined childishly
Poor Leda! what a pity! naughty swan!
And shaped his lips as deftly as he could
Into a beak; then from a reed within
Whistled low querulous notes, as swan may do,
Lastly, to crown his impudence, drew wings
Over his shoulders, shaking them outspred.
 Where am I rambling? What has this to do
With such a folly as was his and thine?
Tell me . . now we are seated . . all that past."   30
 Then Helena . . but first sigh'd more than once.
"Blamable was our guest, but worse his friend
Pirithöos, who extol'd me far above
All other Spartan maids, and earnestly
Pointed me out to him. No, never more
In presence of Pirithöos will I dance,
Afraid to celebrate Diana's games."
 "I want to hear of Theseus, not of him"
Said Leda. She obeyed.
       "He prais'd the land
Of Cecrops, its convivial hours, its girls   40
Waving a golden tettinx in their hair,
Yet Helena's prefer'd he unadorn'd.
Brave, said he, were his countrimen, and mild
And facil were their Gods; not Pallas' self
Beheld them ever with unkindly glance,
Standing among the Graces, and but shook
Her head at any little fault of theirs.
Harp, song, and dance, beneath the olive-trees,
He promist me, on turf where tymbrels shed
Showers of white blossoms on the sandal'd feet: 50
And then in autumn O what rites and games!
Such as when Bakkos, India's kings subdued
And India's tigers crouching under him,
Pronounced this one command, *Be happy all!*
Yet Theseus was himself most miserable;
He said it, and, as if it were a crime
To suffer, humbly prayed me to forgive.
I was not merciless; it was enough
To seem so in the midst of tears and sighs.
 'Who would,' said I, 'prefer the cares of love   60
That could beneath the shade of friendship rest
And hear the praises of himself and friend;
Thine is Pirithöos, flourishing in youth
And ready to learn anything from thee,
And any danger at thy side incur,
Nearer to thee in years, and beautiful
As was the royal youth an eagle bore

400

From Ida, beautiful as he who fell
Beneath Apollo's quoit; but never hope
With me such praises; never hope to calm   70
(Whatever thou persuadest me) my fears.'
Then he. 'Not always is the ear content
With praises, nor with friendship is the breast:
Of this the girls of Sparta seem aware,
And often chide me for it. When we reach
Pandion's city thou shalt prove thro life
Fond is the lover as is firm the friend.'
    I answered, 'There are others thou hast left,
Perfidious Theseus, in that ile afar
Where tower a hundred cities.'
                    Mother dear,   80
Now listen what he own'd and what denied.
We know how cruel Minos was, what law
When he had conquered Athens he imposed;
Which to avoid, the father sent his son
Hither; strong, ardent, uncontrolable,
Away he burst to lands where Zeus was born,
And there he slew the Minotaur: the thread
That guided him throughout that labyrinth's
Intricate turns was Ariadne's gift.
Nor was he faithless to her, but he loved   90
Me better, and he swore by every God
Of late propitious to him, he who left
Wealth, kingdom, beauty, should be mine alone;
Mine marble palaces, Hymettos mine,
And that sweet honey from those thymy knolls
Where only bees have anything to do.
    Now, mother! should I, can I, tell you more?
My poor old prying nurse, who really knows
Many things, but imagines she knows more,
Thinking I must be weary and might want   100
To rest my ankles higher than the floor,
Lifted up one above the couches edge;
Then down she stoopt that she might better peer.
Well I remember it, because she trod
On my loose hair; then doubling under her
Both knees, she looked quite close, sagaciously,
Then, rising up, she spat behind her back,
And then ran out, lifting in wonderment
Her head aloft and spreading out both arms,
Exclaimed, *Zeus! Zeus! be prais'd! he hath preserved*   110
His child: then muttered she with scornful voice,
A hero! of mad heroes most insane!
He indeed! he slay Minotaurs! I now
Believe he left the virgin on the shore
Of Dia; what could he do else? O age
Degenerate! which for prowess can but boast
Such men as Theseus and Alcides are.
Ah! in my day . . but all such days are past."

NOTES

These words repeated by the unwary maid
Sooth'd Leda's breast; and softly fell her tears,   120
Softly too fell her daughter's at the sight.
"Mother, I think I did not love him much,
I am quite sure I do not love him now,
And why I went with him I can not guess.
Do not be angry; he will be ashamed
To come again, ashamed as much as I.
If I had not return'd you might have been
A little sorry, certainly I should,
But here you see me fresh and fond as ever."
After a while said Leda, "Thou hast told   130
The happier part, and now relate the rest,
Nor canst thou do it in a fitter place;
For here Odysseus * (unlike thy return)
Beneath love's chaster torches carried home
Penelope. Her sire Icarios,
Altho he had approved the worthy choice,
Altho he had invited to his house
The future son, and altho far beyond
All others, brave, and wary, and expert
In household thrift was Laertiades,   140
And safe, with rocks around, his iland stood,
Felt now the grief a parent ever feels
To lose a child.
              The nuptial festival
Proroged his sorrows with his guests about,
For Bakkos wound with ivy and with flowers
Together Age and Youth upon that day.
All was well then, and jocund dreams enwrapt
The soundly sleeping sire: but when arose
Morn, and he saw the coronels collapst
Droop down the chamber door, and heard the neigh   150
Of steeds, and saw the broken cates removed
From the piled table, then, ah then indeed
Sorrow, awhile remoter, prest again
Upon his temples, his ears sob'd, his knees
Gave way."
          Then shuddered Helena, and said,
"How cruel was Odysseus thus to pain
Poor old Icarios."
              "Crueller," replied
Leda, "is she who seeks a home unknown
Leaving a parent ignorant of her flight."
    Strong as may grief be, curiosity   160
Creeps over and beyond it.
                Leda, calm'd,
Could now resume her questioning; she askt
What caus'd her error: Helena would turn

* Odysseus here recovers his proper name instead of *Ulysses*, he being neither Roman nor English. But it is only where those of his country are supposed to be speaking: in us it would be affectation: with us he is naturalized. [L.]

402

The question, and entreated to know more
About Penelope, and what result.
"Grant, O ye Gods! she may be safe at home!"
Leda could now but smile, with gentle palm
Patted her cheek, and from her bosom drew
With finger slipping back the chin that dropt
Into it, obstinate to keep its place.   170
Then Helena, first looking round about,
Pursued her narrative.
                              " I will relate
The whole; for now I see you will not ask
Such idle questions as the nurse, insane,
Else how could she deem me so tiger-like
As bite? She gave me signs by nod and wink,
Finding her words convey no sense at all:
Hardly such rudeness can the crone object
To sister Clytemnestra: well you know,
Sweet mother, that your Helena was taught   180
Far different manners, nor would, even tho hurt,
Use tooth or nail, but tremble as the strings
Of a lyre tremble if swept all at once."
Leda, to hide her blushes, prest her face
On the fresh herbage, fearing to look up,
And twicht unconsciously the brittle grass.
"He did not hurt thee, then?"
                              "Quite the reverse;
He swore he would not, and he kept his word:
Instead of hurting, he protected me
Completely."
                "O ye Gods above!" exclaimed   190
The mother in alarm.
                      "Ah what a tale!
Yet, yet, go on with it; lay bare the whole
And end with it my pangs of grief and fear.
Thou hast been shown by me that even the shy
Have err'd from steddiness; how far hast thou!
If more austere thy sister than befits,
If at the wanton boys she stamps her foot,
Thou art too ready to incline an ear
To their excuses. I have seen thee stand,
Trip on, turn back, and ask what *can* they mean,   200
And wait, nor over-readily dismiss
The laughing urchins with responsive laugh.
   Nature may throw a gloom o'er Modesty
But she serenes the brow with purer light,
Light pure as on Olympos Gods enjoy."
   She paus'd, and sigh'd.
                          Commanded to confess,
The daughter said, "A grove there is not far
Beyond the city, but from thence unseen,
Because the city and the little hill

Conceal it; there in winter runs a brook,   210
But at this season its steep crumbling banks
Are join'd together by a fallen oak
The winds have thrown there: boughs and bark afford
An easy passage over.
              Theseus lept
From the low car that bore us: when we reacht
The farther side, percieving my alarm
He laid me on the grass, with gentlest hand
Pressing my bosom to allay my fear,
And often was it careful to provide
That neither stick, nor stone beneath, nor bent   220
Should harm me; for the bent in woods is stiff."
  While she all this was saying, Leda's breath
Blew hard and thick upon her braided hair.
"Nemesis will o'ertake thee," she sigh'd out,
"Unless thou tell it all from first to last."
Now somewhat less dissembling, thus adjured,
Helena spake again.
             "To bring back all
Into my mind, so hurried by the road,
The rapine, the recovery, and the spears
Of my two brothers thrust against the reins,   230
Is hard.
          The lover, lately so submiss,
Grew furious and sprang down: first to himself
He muttered, then to me; he bade me go,
He bade me stay. We hear the tramp of steeds.
Away, cried he, and threw me on the car.
But my two brothers had come up: the bits
Drawn tightly in, the javelins vibrated.
Stay, robber! they exclame, their angry eyes
Glaring like stars that struggle with a stream.
What! arm'd against the unarm'd! cried he in scorn,   240
Turning aside the points with open hand,
*Off, boys! what would ye? think ye that I dread
Your javelins? no; your youth, your parentage,
Awes me; take homeward, take with you unharm'd
Your virgin sister; for the Powers above
Have by sure omen disapproved my deed.*
Thus he; and they abstain'd: then, to himself,
*Patiently bear thy vultur, patiently
Look down from thy chain'd neck and watch uptorne
Thy growing liver by insatiate beak;*   250
*Rest, O Prometheus, on the piercing flints,
Endure the lightning on unclosing eyes,
Never hast thou endured love torne away
Upon the threshold from thine open arms."*
  The maiden blusht as she began the tale
And sorrowed as she closed it: half afraid
Her mother might observe her, she besought
The sequel of Penelope: aware

HELLENICS

Of her devices, Leda sweetly gazed
And thus began to moralize her tale.   260
   "On those united by an equal love
Smiles every morning, every evening brings
Fresh hymenæals: youthful maid should find
A youthful husband; such be thine, my child,
And ever mindful how chaste love excells
Unchaste, be thou Penelope, be thine
Odysseus.
              I related how it grieved
Icarios to have bid his child farewell.
At first he turn'd away his tearful eyes,
And rested on the lintel of the door   270
His troubled brow; but soon he heard the tramp
Of the car-horses and the rolling wheels
That grated near, then where the stones no more
Paved the highway and sounds came indistinct,
Brought to him only by the fitful breeze,
Rushing out wildly thro the city gate,
Broken in spirit, weak in sight, he saw
Odysseus, who had slackened now the reins
To hear more leisurely the low discourse
Of his beloved.
            Thro deep husky groans,   280
In broken voice, *Restore my child!* he cried,
True, I did yield her to thee; not so deaf
Wast thou that day, no, nor that day was I
Childless as now thou makest me: restore
My only daughter, my heart's sole delight,
My age's sole support. Thee many a maid
May please as well as she. O give her back
In pity, or come with me both again.
   Odysseus heard and checkt and loost the reins.
The gentle daughter threw her left arm round   290
The old man's neck, and sooth'd his wrinkled cheek
With her warm tears: the youth had paus'd, then spake.
Me Sparta might detain, me might the home
Of our Penelope, but home have I,
Home, people, aged sire, and household gods,
Neglected never with impunity.
   Pious! if thou art pious, said the sire,
Restore her: she is willing, as thou seest.
   Let her then choose, said he of Ithaca.
Penelope cast down her pallid brow   300
While her right hand held tight the hero's vest,
And sobs shook heavily her struggling heart.
   Choose, choose Icarios cried; *remember her*
Who bore thee; pity me.
              Fierce tortures wrung
Nor broke her silence.
           Speak, Penelope!
Said softly her Odysseus. Round the neck

Paternal stil her arm was left, her face
Turn'd to the other side, her veil drawn close,
Heavy with tears, until with groan and gasp
The weak neck fell upon the neck less weak.　　　　310
Sorrowful, and yet proud at heart, return'd
Icarios home: the elders his compeers
Came forth and envied him and soon consoled:
Hence was devoted (why wert thou away?)
That low turf altar rais'd to Modesty."

P. 346. THE ESPOUSALS OF POLYXENA. First written in Latin and
published with title *Sponsalia Polyxenæ* in 1819, reprinted 1847 with
"Argument" as follows:

Conveniunt Græci Trojanique: irrumpit Cassandra: mortem et Achillis et Polyxenæ
prædicat. Ea dum abducitur, Achilles vulneratur; suos alloquitur, flet absentem
filium.

Bayle, *s.v.* Achilles, quotes Pausanias, i. 22 and x. 25, adding: "Others
say that Paris killed him treacherously in a temple where Achilles was
gone to treat about his marriage with Polyxena, daughter of Priam."
The English version of Landor's poem on p. 346 was recast and so published in 1859. The 1859 text is given below:

THE ESPOUSALS OF POLYXENA.

"THY blood, O pious maiden! shall remain
In thy own city; and thou shalt survive
Its foe who now espouses thee."
　　　　　　　　　　　The song
Of the three Sisters in three voices sang
These words, so comforting a mother's heart
To her Polyxena; and from the shrine
Of Thymbra, from Apollo's mouth the same
When she had led her thither.
　　　　　　　　　　　"Future days
Of peace and happiness," said she "expand
Before thee, and thou seest them not, O child!　　　　10
Pious, yet even by that God's voice unmoved.
Behold! how bright the sky! how sweet the air
Breathes round about us! sweet when we came forth,
But how much balmier now! the flowers arise
Under the spring's first dust, as if no foot
Of foe had trampled them, and sip the dew
Joyous as if they felt thy wedding-day.
Continuous heaps extend along the plain,
Heaps where one briar binds more than one below,
Foes lately, now united evermore."　　　　20
"I see the flowers, I see the sepultures"
Polyxena said sighing, "and I feel
The breeze, no balmier than it breath'd before:
That tepid moisture which the plants inhale
Was theirs; and ah! those flowers were Trojan blood.
Not other now shines forth thy light, O sun,
Than when the Achaian anchors graspt our strand

HELLENICS

Amid the clamor of the host, amid
Cars rattling on the stony beach, and shields
Struck in defiance. Ah! nor otherwise   30
When every God left Hector."
                      Here she wept,
Here wept the mother too.
                  "But why thus break
Silence, if only to make way for grief?
I had ceast almost so deeply to bemoan
My children when Achilles was defence,
Not terror, to us all. Canst thou refuse
To see the Gods now with him, friends to Troy?
King above kings, rich with ancestral stores,
And now about to bring all Asia bound
Into Mycenai, and, despite of Mars,   40
Polyxena, thee now doth he prefer
To all these glories: ere they yet were won,
Iphigeneia never had declined
His proffer'd hand while yet his shield was white,
Nor had the Nereid, she from whom he sprang,
Brought the Vulcanian armure he now bears.
Him born of Gods and worthy to beget
Their semblances, rejectest thou? She shed
Her blood upon the altar that thy hand
Might rescue Troy. Thou fearest the wild wail   50
Of our Cassandra; if there must be fear,
Is not Achilles what thou mightest dread?"
  Briefly the yielding daughter thus replied,
"Whether the Gods command me, as they do,
To wed, or whether to be bound a slave,
I follow the behest: where no disgrace
No hardship is . . but let me weep awhile.
I will, O mother! yes, I will obey
A parent . . for this also they command,
Hoping they may recall or may remitt   60
This one decree. Must I be given up
To him behind whose wheels my brother's corse
Was drag'd along, drag'd while his breast yet heaved
And plowed and fill'd the furrow with his blood.
Oh! on this very ground our feet now press
Plighted are nuptial vows! are Gods invoked!
Thanksgivings offered them! Oh! pardon grief
That nothing can abate: what can the Gods
Do now to lighten it?
                Ye moundering heaps
Which friendly hands heapt up and covered o'er   70
With turf, not solid yet; where cypresses,
Green lately, drop their hard and withered leaves;
And ye that cover corses numberless
In happier union, ye but separate
The resting soul from soul that knows not rest.
I gave my promise; thus Apollo will'd;

Let then his oracles, by me observ'd,
Bring (to me never!) to my country peace."
Hecuba gaspt for breath, tears gushing down,
"O my last child! my only hope in life!   80
Cried she, "unmerited unhoped-for weal
Restorest thou: not what thy terror feigns
Wilt thou soon find him: his stern heart relents
At Priam's sad reverses; he beholds
A house the Gods have visited and deign'd
To share its hospitality; he looks
With pity and with fondness on thy youth
And beauty; else he never would hold out
His hand in amity, nor blandly take
What he could tear away: beside, he fears   90
That thou, beyond the reach of his revenge
(Unlike Brisëis whom his sword reclaim'd)
Shouldst be by equal lot another's prey.
For long ago he saw our certain fate,
Deriding the Palladion, nor afraid
Of any Gods, when Gods saw Hector fall."
Another, not a happier, morn arose.
    Under the walls of Dardanos a plain
Lies open: it was covered now with crowds
Even to the root of Ida, past the banks   100
Of those two stony rivers, since alike
Rendered immortal by immortal song.
Unwearied, tho grown hoary under arms,
And from the omen fondly hoping peace,
Commingled with the Trojans, in the fane
Of their Apollo, the Achaians held
Stern silence, or in whispers a discourse
That varied. Some regretted the delay
Of the doom'd city; some dared blame the king,
And some Peleides; others muttered words   110
On treachery, then on bribes, and knew the tent
That covered them stow'd carefully from sight.
    Hither came Priam; slower came behind
His aged consort, and her sons, now few;
Prodigal had the rest been of their blood.
The wives of the survivors hither came,
All deeply veil'd and all with brow abased.
Hither they once had come led joyfully
Mid hymenæal song, by hands now cold:
Alone at home remain'd, and tried to wear   120
Away with restless spindle the sad hour,
Andromache, oft chided by her child.
    In every street of the wide city, throngs
Rusht forth impatiently to see the shields
So long opposed to them, and helmets caught
Before by glimpses only thro the dust.
    Close to the altar of the placid God
Polyxena held tightly by the arm

Achilles, and scarce knew it; beautiful
Above her sister, beautiful almost   130
As Helena herself; so white that brow,
So pure the luster of those gentle eyes.
   Cassandra suddenly with horrid scream
Rushes beyond the congregated host . .
All tremble, all are stricken mute, as when
Enters some Deity. She speaks, alone,
And not her words speaks she, but words compell'd.
"Sister, believest thou the Destinies
Are friendly to thee? Sister! turn thine eyes
Back from this temple, turn them on the walls   140
Poseidon aided by Apollo rais'd.
In vain hath Pallas dwelt within . . I see
Prodigies, I see arms and flames o'er-ride
The ancient towers; Xanthos and Simoeis
I see run swifter now with streams of blood
And heroes rising heavily from wounds,
And ruin following when the battles cease.
O flower! upon what altar art thou laid,
Cull'd by Thessalian hand! why, ere the torch
Be lighted, flames so the Sigæan shore   150
And Tenedos the level ray prolongs?
Fly! let us fly! Citheron calls aloud;
Sound the Chaonian towers, resound the horns
Of Achelöos, and, high up above,
The thunder-rent Keraunian rocks reply.
Hearest thou not the marble manger crack
Under the monster's jaw? it scales our walls
And human voices issue from its bulk?
Why then delay? why idle words? Arise
My parents! . . turn, ah! turn away the sight   160
From those Bistonian, those betraying realms.
Why, Polydoros, callest thou? why waves
A barren cornel o'er a recent tomb
While the loose pebbles tinkle down the base?
Me neither tears nor madness are vouchsafed;
Do thou, devoted sister! now thy chains
Are taken off that thy pure blood may flow
More readily, step back one little step
From where thou sittest on the fagot; come
And give me, all I hope, one last embrace.   170
   Oh spare her thou! And thee too I implore,
Pyrrhos! Oh, by the manes of thy sire!
Haste forward. She deserves it not, no crime
Is hers. This only my last breath implores."
   Uttering such words her maidens drew her home.
Another noise was heard within the fane.
Silent and dark an arrow from across
Amid the tumult struck the heroe's heel,
And, passing thro and thro, the brazen point
Rang on the marble floor. The chiefs around   180

Wonder to see the weapon and small bead
Of blood: they sieze their spears, and tear away
The olive and verbena from their crests
And stamp them underfoot: not Priam's voice
Was heard, who gathering dust with desperate grasp
Strew'd with it his grey hairs; nor was the bride
Heeded, tho sinking as if into death.
Achilles neither helpt her nor required
Help for himself; aware the day was come,
Foretold him: he with failing voice represt   190
The wrath of his compeers, yet strong enough
Thus to command.
             "Lay ye your arms aside;
Let none avenge Achilles but his son.
Alkimos and Automedon! detain
Within our tent the Myrmidons: my voice
They might no longer mind who see me now,
Fallen ignobly . . Ajax! Diomed!
Leave here a corse not worth a beast alive,
Or hide it where no Trojan may rejoice.
Ah! must his herds then graze upon my grave!   200
   Let not thy tears drop over me, whoe'er
Thou art upon my left! my eyes of iron
See none, see nothing . . take those friendly arms
From off my shoulder . . they now weary me
And weary you with their too vain support.
Not that Larissa in a quiet tomb
Holds my brave ancestors grieve I, O Death,
Not that my mother will lament my loss,
Lone in the bower of Tethys, for a while;
I grieve that Troy should ever thus exult   210
Without more slaughter of her faithless race.
Open the turf, remove the blackened boughs,
And let the urn of Menætiades
Take my bones too.
              Launch from this hateful strand
The bark that bore us hither.
                    With the leave
Of your Atreides . . send for . . now at play
In Ptheiai, and expecting the return
Of playmate . . my own Pyrrhos, my brave boy . .
To bring destruction with the Pelian spear.
   Hear ye my voice? or with its pants and gasps   220
Expires it, and decieves me?
                    I forget . .
Such is the mist of mind that hangs on me . .
What are the orders I have given, and what
My wishes yet unspoken: be not ye
Forgetful of me as I am of these;
Sure, although Orcos drags my wounded limbs
Beneath, the Shades shall know and fear me there.

   213 Menætiades] *rectius* Menœtiades= Patroclus. [W.]

HELLENICS

Pyrrhos! my child, my far-off child, farewell!
Whose care shall train thy youth? What Keiron stoop
To teach thee wisdom? what parental hands   230
Be loud in the applauses thou shalt win
For lyre, for javelin, for Thessalian car
Seen above others in the foremost dust."

P. 364. A FRIEND TO THEOCRITOS. See Landor's essay on Theocritos
(*Last Fruit*, p. 218), "Among his friends in Egypt was Aratus ... Philetus
the Coan was another ... Aratus was more particularly his friend."